THIS SEAT *of* MARS

THIS
SEAT *of* MARS
WAR AND THE BRITISH ISLES,
1485–1746

CHARLES CARLTON

YALE UNIVERSITY PRESS
NEW HAVEN AND LONDON

For information about this and other Yale University Press publications, please contact:

U.S. Office: sales.press@yale.edu   www.yalebooks.com
Europe Office: sales@yaleup.co.uk   www.yalebooks.co.uk

Set in Adobe Caslon by IDSUK (DataConnection) Ltd
Printed in Great Britain by TJ International Ltd, Padstow, Cornwall

Library of Congress Cataloging-in-Publication Data

Carlton, Charles, 1941-
  This seat of Mars : war and the British Isles, 1485-1746/Charles Carlton.
  p. cm.
  ISBN 978-0-300-13913-6 (cl: alk. paper)
  1. Great British—History, Military—1485-1603. 2. Great Britain—History, Military—1603-1714. 3. Great Britain—History, Military—18th century. I. Title.
DA66. C37 2011
355.020941'0903—dc22
                                                        2011013533
A catalogue record for this book is available from the British Library.

10 9 8 7 6 5 4 3 2 1

MIX
Paper from
responsible sources
FSC
www.fsc.org   FSC® C013056

To Wolfson College, University of Cambridge

CONTENTS

ILLUSTRATIONS

Plates

Maps

Tables

ACKNOWLEDGEMENTS

Trip no further, pretty sweeting;
Journeys end in lovers meeting
Every wise man's son doth know.
Twelfth Night, II, iii, 24–26

THIS, THE FIRST THING MOST READERS READ AND THE LAST MOST authors draft, is always a pleasure to write, not just because it marks my journey's end, but because it is an opportunity to thank all those who have made my adventure so enjoyable. It is the friendship and kindness of people, some strangers, others lifelong comrades, that make writing books both possible and pleasant.

My journey began in Australia where a visiting fellowship at the Australian Defence Force Academy enabled me to start the basic research. John Reeve was the perfect host, while Peter Dennis, John Coates, Robin Prior and Jeff Grey were especially generous with their time and insights. Early in this project I was able to develop ideas at seminars at the Australian Defence Force Academy, Flinders University, the University of South Australia, Newcastle University, Monash University, the University of Tasmania and the Pacific Coast Conference on British Studies. Closer to home I have been able to run ideas past members of the Triangle Institute for Security Studies, particularly Dick Kohn, Alex Roland, Caroline Pumphrey, Joe Caddell and Joe Hobbs. At North Carolina State University and Duke University my students let me test ideas on them in lectures. The staffs of the Cambridge University Library and North Carolina State University Library were unfailing in their outstanding help. For over a quarter of a century, Wolfson College, Cambridge, has provided a fertile and congenial base for summers' research in England, a debt that I have tried to recognize in the dedication.

I am grateful to David Trim for reading Chapter 4, saving me from grievous errors and greatly improving my arguments. Joe Slavin did the same for the first four chapters, Ian Gentles read Chapters 7 and 8, Bill Speck Chapters 10 and 12, and John Reeve Chapter 11. Thanks to John Wall and Robert Bearman I was able to discover that the Bard had not served in the militia. Simon Harris, historian and anaesthetist, answered questions about Admiral Sir Cloudesley Shovell and the effects of wounds. Peter Paret and N. A. M. Rodger responded warmly to emails from a complete stranger with the generosity that is the hallmark of the true scholar. Padraig Lenihan provided useful figures on Irish casualties. Tom Hester furnished valuable insights into John Donne. Over the decades I have benefited immeasurably from the friendship and wisdom of Wallace MacCaffrey, the sage of Cambridge University Library's tea room. As always John Morrill was a source of information, strength and encouragement. With him, and Mark Kishlansky and Jonathan Scott, I have enjoyed stimulating discussions about Charles I. With his incomparable knowledge of the British Army, Tony Clayton saved me from many errors. Paul Seaver, Thomas Cogswell, Edith Sylla, John Riddle and Gene Rasor kindly answered email queries. Sarah Hartnell read a final draft. I am grateful to Joanna Bourke for sharing the ordeal of 9/11 with me and my wife. It was a time that reminded us that the evils about which historians write can be all too real. I am grateful to my friend and physician Douglas Hammer both for his care and for many stimulating discussions about writing history. Since retiring in 2006, I have served as a volunteer guide at Fort Macon, North Carolina, where I have enjoyed many enlightening conversations, particularly with Paul Branch and John Rhodes, about the American Civil War, which have illuminated my understanding of the British Civil Wars. Heather McCallum of Yale University Press in London has been both a dear friend and valued editor, who has done much to quell an author's insecurity, while helping me produce (I believe) a far better book. While being finely tooth combed is not the most pleasant of experiences, I am most grateful to Rachael Lonsdale, Tami Halliday and Richard Mason of Yale University Press, and to the outside readers, Peter Gaunt, Mark Stoyle and Mark Fissel, all distinguished historians, for going through drafts of the manuscript so thoroughly. My thanks to Richard Slatta for helping sort out word processing problems. Last—and far from least—my greatest debt is due to my wife Caroline, who has cheerfully read my drafts, accompanied me across many a rainy battlefield, and generally put up with me.

The year starts on 1 January, with the date usually eleven days behind that on the continent. I try to give an individual's rank at the time he is mentioned. Similarly, where possible I have provided mid-twentieth-century regimental names, and not the current ones that are the product of so many—far too many—amalgamations. I have tended to combine reference notes when it is possible to see from the context to what they refer. There is no accepted nomenclature for England, Scotland, Ireland and Wales. Some have suggested the 'Atlantic Archipelago', which has the virtue of including the Channel Islands and the Isle of Man, but is awkward. Others talk of 'The Three Kingdoms', which excludes Wales and thus offends my Cymmrodorion heritage. To constantly add 'and Ireland' to Britain gets a little tedious. To make things even more confusing, when does Britain include Scotland? Before James VI and I's accession in 1603? Before the 1707 Act of Union? What about Henry V's army at Agincourt? Was it an English, an Anglo-Welsh, a British, or even a British and Irish army? Fortunately, Captains Fluellen, MacMorris and Jamy had better things to argue about. Thus I have decided to use 'Britain' and 'British' to include all three kingdoms and Wales. The *New Oxford English Dictionary* defines the 'British Isles' as including 'Great Britain and Ireland with all their offshore islands'. For much of the previous three, even four, centuries people happily talked about the British Army and Navy, the British Constitution and the British Empire. Even today Scots, Welsh and Irish scholars read papers at the North American Conference of *British* Studies and make splendid contributions to *H-Albion*.

Beaufort, North Carolina;
St David's Day, 2010.

INTRODUCTION:
THIS SEAT OF MARS

This royal throne of kings, this scepter'd isle
This earth of majesty, this seat of Mars.
Richard II, II, i, 42–43

L ONG AGO—FAR LONGER THAN I CARE TO REMEMBER—I FIRST
visited Culloden Moor in Scotland. There were four of us, part-time
soldiers in Britain's Territorial Army from different infantry regiments,
halfway through a selection course for the Special Air Service. We were
young, we were incredibly fit, confident in having passed the first half of
the selection, apprehensive about the second, a gruelling trial in the Cape
Wrath area right at the north-west tip of Scotland. We knew little about
what had happened at Culloden, although we knew that what the young
men had endured there over two centuries ago was far worse than
anything we would encounter. As the Land Rover drove across the dark
wet battlefield (which then was far more forested and dismal than it is
today), all of us felt a sense of unease—even shame. If any of our regiments had fought at Culloden, they would not have proudly borne the
battle honour on their colours, for it is a victory that the British Army
does not commemorate: it is one it would prefer to forget. We felt as if the
ghosts of the dead Highlanders resented the presence of the uniformed
military heirs of those who slew them so callously on 16 April 1746. And
thus we climbed back into the Land Rover and drove away.

While there are many reports of supernatural sightings connected
with battlefields (including seven at Culloden alone), it would, of
course, be absurd to suggest that ghosts really exist, haunting sites
where men have been slaughtered long ago.[1] Yet there is something
special about battlefields. They are places where human beings legitimately
kill each other.

Killing

Killing is crucial in three ways. First, it is the central act of war, giving war its uniquely horrible character. Second, killing makes war effective, in the sense that taking lives, for better or worse, decides things: cultures and societies that cannot effectively fight and kill tend not to survive. Third, killing has become a central focus of the study of war, fundamentally changing military history. Thus this book will examine a culture and society, early modern England, and then Britain, that was extremely good at fighting and killing, and in doing so flourished mightily.

Killing is fundamental to war. Leo Tolstoy, the novelist who served in the Russian Army, declared that 'the reality of war' was 'the centrality of killing'. Just before the Third Battle of Murfreesboro (1864), the confederate general Nathan Bedford Forrest observed that 'war means fighting and fighting means killing'. Professor Paul Fussell, who fought as an American infantryman in the Second World War, described war as 'a culture dominated by fear, blood and sadism, by irrational action and preposterous (and often ironic) results'. The seventeenth-century poet Samuel Butler put it more pithily: 'War is a cessation of humanity.' That gentle poet and pastor, George Herbert, agreed that 'War is death's feast.'[2] Few animals kill members of their own species: none but man does so in large numbers.

> Which is the basest creature, Man or Beast?
> Birds feed on Birds, Beasts on other prey
> But savage man alone does man betray.

Thus observed John Wilmot, earl of Rochester, in 1705. A generation earlier Edward Hyde, earl of Clarendon, wrote that 'War is a license to kill . . . it distinguishes not of age or of sex or of dignity but exposes all things and passions, sacred and profane to the same contempt and confusion.'[3] Jonathan Swift once defined a soldier as 'a Yahoo hired to kill in cold blood as many of his own species, who have never offended him, as he possibly can'.[4]

If licensed killing is so terrible, so inhumane, so uncivilized, why then has war, to use Gwynne Dyer's phrase, always been 'a central institution in human civilization'?[5] The answer is that war is decisive, and thus, either through man's nature or through evolution, rewards those who are good at it.

States or societies go to war usually because they believe that it will produce advantageous decisions. Theodore Roosevelt, one of war's bulliest proponents, called it 'the supreme arbitrament'. John Fletcher, the dramatist and Shakespeare's contemporary, agreed that war was the 'grand decider'.[6] Societies spend huge resources in men, material and money on wars, not only because they perceive there to be great advantages in winning, but because the costs of losing are so horrendous. The vanquished may be killed, their property destroyed, their children abused, their women raped or consigned to concubinage.

But individual men (for war has for long been an overwhelmingly male activity, particularly when it depended on physical strength) fight for complicated, often irrational reasons. Today many would agree with S. L. A. Marshall, the great American military historian, that 'The starting point of the understanding of war is the understanding of human nature.'[7] But what is our nature as humans? Are we, as the Elizabethan portrait painter Sir William Segar observed in 1602, all 'in some sort disposed to make war'? Was Sigmund Freud right when after the First World War he told Albert Einstein that 'man has in him an active instinct for hatred and destruction'? That instinct, Freud continued, came from man's libido, his sexual drive being too often expressed in violence that enhanced his sense of self-worth as a man.[8] The links between male sexuality and violence are nigh universal, having been charted in some 112 different societies. These links have remained fairly constant over time. Just as US Marine Corps recruiters used to promise 'to build men', so Captain Abraham Stanton avowed that as a result of the British Civil Wars, 'Myriads of men now bear arms that bore nothing but only shapes of men before.'[9] Three decades earlier Edward Hyde called Lord Somerset, the duke whom Charles I made a general notwithstanding his complete lack of military experience, 'a virgin soldier'.[10] Freud was, of course, influenced by Charles Darwin, who has added immeasurably to our understanding of human beings and thus of war. The men best fitted for violence were best fitted to survive and hand on their genes: females were, all too often, the victors' spoils. In other words, evolution rewards aggression.

Herein lies a paradox, for evolution may both destroy and develop societies and civilizations. War, that most unsociable of society's acts, requires strong social bonds and organization to be successful. Young men must be willing to die. Society must approve the killing of its enemies, and must agree that doing so is a legitimate way of solving its problems.[11] War—like pornography—both attracts and repels. Many men—more than we would care to admit—actually enjoy war. It would have been 'a pleasant sight, if a man's skin had not been in hazard,' thought John Taylor about the fighting in Calais in 1513. Thus Robert E. Lee, the leading confederate general in the American Civil War, rightly observed that 'It is well that war is so terrible—otherwise we would grow too fond of it.'[12]

We are also ambivalent towards those who fight our wars. We are fond of those violent men, who armed with the tools of war protect us, and at the same time we are afraid that they may turn upon us. Dr Johnson reflected this paradox. While thinking less of himself for not having been a soldier, he defined 'Redcoat' and 'Tar' as terms of contempt. Ambivalence can turn to loathing. In 1700 the newspaper the *London Spy* declared that only two things like a soldier, 'whores and lice'. Perhaps Thomas Becon, the seventeenth-century Puritan, was unconsciously reflecting Freud's link between violence and sexuality when he railed against soldiers, 'What whoredom is committed among them! What maid escape unflowered? What wife departeth unpolluted?'[13] In peacetime soldiers are, as William Cecil (Lord Burghley), Elizabeth I's adviser, told his son, 'like chimneys in summer'. In peace it's mostly a case of 'Tommy, go away!' But as Rudyard Kipling went on to observe, 'It's "thank you Mr. Atkins", when the bands begin to play.'[14] Over two centuries earlier, Francis Quarles, the seventeenth-century poet, agreed that attitudes towards soldiers changed between war and peace:[15]

God and the soldiers we like adore
When on the brink of ruin—not before:
The danger past, both are alike requited,
God is forgotten, and the soldier slighted.

Recently, military historians have come to focus on the centrality of killing and fighting. Michael Howard, who won the Military Cross as an infantry captain in the Second World War before becoming the Chicele Professor of the History of War at Oxford, insists that 'at the centre of the History of war ... is *fighting*'.[16] In the Second World War S. L. A. Marshall borrowed the techniques of time and motion studies from industry to discover what soldiers actually did in combat. Other historians such as Sir John Keegan applied his methods to see what really happened in past battles.[17] War is studied in its widest context. While accepting that war has changed, the new military historians have emphasized continuity, particularly of the experience of combat. 'The essential soldier remains the same,' argues General Sir John Hackett. Buffy Sainte-Marie, the Canadian folk singer, described 'The Universal Soldier':[18]

He's four foot two, and he's six foot four
He fights with muscles and with spears.
He's all of thirty one and he's only seventeen
Been a soldier for a thousand years.

Much in battle has remained the same. Fear felt no different at Bosworth Field (1485) than it did at Culloden (1746): the pain from wounds was just as agonizing, the anguish of mourning no less intense. Thus this book will use examples from recent times, when records are more comprehensive, to illuminate the experience of early modern Britain when such records are less copious. Take, for example, Edmund Ludlow's symptoms after the Battle of Edgehill (1642), his first taste of combat. He reported that he could not open his mouth to eat, explaining that having been without food for so long he must have forgotten to do so. But such a rationalization is incomprehensible. Humans cannot forget how to eat. His experience only makes sense in the light of reports of similar symptoms from both Normandy and Burma in 1944 of post-combat lockjaw— the result of clenching one's teeth so hard to counter the terror of battle that it was several hours before the victims could open their mouths again.[19] So by focusing on the actualities of war, on killing, by examining continuity as well as change, and by using a wide range of sources, the new military historians have transformed the discipline.

And about time too! For a century, at least, British academic historians have had harsh things to say about military history. They deemed it 'an arcane and disagreeable speciality, like the history of pornography, not to be encouraged in a decent university'.[20] For Marxist academics war is incidental—the inevitable, preordained product of economic forces. War does not fit into the Whig view of a restrained, rational, civilized flow of British history: it has no place in the liberal story of peaceful constitutional progress.[21] In America most male academics, at least of my generation, remember the Vietnam War as an experience that their graduate deferments enabled them both to avoid and despise. The military, unlike academia, is an authoritarian, hierarchical organization: its values are alien; its function—killing—is repulsive. Such academic attitudes surprised Professor Lawrence Stone, that great cultural and social historian (who served on an aircraft carrier in the Royal Navy during the Second World War); he sardonically observed that it was 'extraordinary' that 'war ... should have been so neglected for so long by those who regard themselves as in the forefront of the historical profession'. Sergeant—later Professor and Sir—Geoffrey Elton agreed.[22]

Of course, the frightfulness of war has discouraged the teaching of its history—a conundrum not shared with, say, Holocaust Studies. But just as teaching about Auschwitz does not justify gas chambers, so the teaching of war does not condone killing. R. H. Tawney, another great British historian, who as a young sergeant saw more than his fair share of killing at the Somme in 1916, called 'the institution of war the most neglected factor in social development'.[23] To be sure, military history has been used, if not abused, particularly by the military, to learn lessons from past wars in order to win future ones: all too often it has been turned into what General J. F. G. Fuller, another giant of the discipline, has called 'a bloody romance'. But as Karl von Clausewitz, the nineteenth-century Prussian who founded the modern study of war, warned, 'It is to no purpose, it is even against one's own interests to turn away from the consideration of the real nature of the affair, because the horror of its elements excites repugnance.'[24] One of war's victims, Captain Charles Sorley, who was killed at the Battle of Loos in 1915, wanted us to confront that repugnance:[25]

When you see millions of the mouthless dead
Across your dreams in pale battalions go,
Say not soft things . . .

Outline: Macro and Micro

In this book I will try not to say soft things, but rather examine the hard reality of how war—which Tolstoy called 'the vilest thing in life'—affected the history of early modern Britain.[26] It did so at two levels that—to borrow a concept from economics—may best be described as the macro and micro. Since the two were intimately linked, instead of dealing with them separately in two parts where they may become truncated, in this book I will try, as far as possible, to merge them with interleaving chapters.

The first impact of war, the macro, is essentially chronological, affecting the state, international relations, the economy, society and institutional development. It reflects the policies of those in power—first the king, and then parliament—being in essence a story.

The opening narrative in Chapter 1 starts on 22 August 1485 with Henry VII's (r. 1485–1509) victory at the Battle of Bosworth Field, which ended the Wars of the Roses and established the stable Tudor dynasty that united England and Wales. His son, Henry VIII (r. 1509–47), tried to recapture the glories of the Hundred Years War by invading France. Chapter 3 deals with the reign of his daughter, Elizabeth (r. 1558–1603), which in many ways set the pattern for future military developments: intervening on the continent to help protect allies; conquering Ireland; initiating imperial ambitions outside Europe; and establishing the founda-tions of naval hegemony. In essence English military efforts were basically inwardly directed, a characteristic that continued until the Glorious Revolution of 1688. Chapter 5 deals with James I (r. 1603–25), who was loath to fight, and with his son Charles I (r. 1625–49), who got involved in a series of botched military expeditions in the late 1620s. Chapters 7 and 8 describe the British Civil Wars (1642–51) and the Commonwealth (1649–60), a defining moment when violence was as internalized as it was widespread and intense. These wars were both a conflict within England, Scotland, Ireland and Wales, and a contest between the three nations and principality, from which England emerged the undisputed leader. After the execution of Charles I in 1649, Oliver Cromwell used the new British republic's unprecedented military prowess to shift the focus of violence abroad, fighting in the Caribbean and on the continent. Chapter 10 deals with the generation after the restoration of the monarchy in 1660, when Charles II continued the policy of external warfare. He founded a standing army and professionalized the Royal Navy. Chapter 12 shows how the Glorious Revolution of 1688 enabled a number of themes to coalesce, permitting the English to suppress Ireland and conquer most of Scotland, and establish a secure tax base that let them borrow to expand the armed forces rapidly; those who paid the most taxes controlled parliament. The king lost power to a prime minister as the executive shifted from the crown to the House of Commons. With its victories in the Nine Years War (1688–97) and the War of the Spanish Succession (1701–14), Britain became the preeminent world and imperial power that she was to remain for over two centuries. By the Battle of Culloden in 1746 there was no doubt that this process was well and truly completed.

While the macro impact of war changed over time, the micro effect, that on the individual soldier and sailor, tended to be cyclical and constant, and will be treated as such in the thematic chapters. Admittedly the stages of the cycle were not clear-cut: for instance, untrained troops could be thrown into battle, veterans might be subjected to retraining. Neither were the influences on each force distinct. Honour could prompt a man to join in the first place, as well as keep him from running while campaigning or in combat.

The micro cycle of war began, as Chapter 2 reveals, with recruitment and training. Military manuals elucidated the theories and practicalities of combat, which during fighting good leadership made possible. Chapter 4 asks the age-old question 'Why did men fight?' Not why did they join to fight, but why they entered into combat and stayed there overcoming their fears. Chapter 6 shows that much of a soldier's or a sailor's time was not spent battling, but in garrison duty or campaigning, in port or cruising, in 'low-intensity warfare'. Admittedly the latter could be most stressful, for, although exposure to danger was small, it lasted a long time. In contrast, battles and sieges (the subjects of Chapter 9) are examples of high-intensity combat, being usually short, and certainly sharp, bloody and decisive. While Karl von Clausewitz noted 'Battles decide all,' sieges could be equally bloody and decisive: drawn out, they could be costly in men and materiel.[27] Naval warfare, the subject of Chapter 11, was different from that on land, mainly because the sea was already such a dangerous place, with storms, shipwrecks and diseases, that fighting there only marginally increased one's chances of dying. The price paid by the millions caught up in the micro cycle of war is the theme of Chapter 13. For some it was the supreme one: for many more it was paid in wounds, both mental and physical, with imprisonment, loneliness, the loss of limbs or friends, and even rejection by the civilians for whom they had been fighting. War deprived many women of the opportunity of marriage— thought to be the proper and natural state for females. Women and children had to come to terms with the death of husbands, sons and fathers. Sometimes society tried to help with pensions or veterans' hospitals, such as Chelsea or Greenwich in London. More often the victims of war were left to their own devices, charity, or friends and family.

The Conclusion provides a very rough estimate of how many people in the British Isles died directly or indirectly as a result of war, and shows that there were three periods of intense hostilities: the last third of Elizabeth I's reign, the British Civil Wars, and the world wars that followed the Glorious Revolution. These were periods of state formation. The chapter also argues that between 1485 and 1746 there was hardly a person in the British Isles unaffected by war. It was an ordeal that all remembered and few wanted to repeat. None who survived combat ever forgot the experience. They wished their children, their posterity—us—to know what they had endured. In 1760, at the age of 83, an anonymous dragoon, the eleven-year veteran of the War of the Spanish Succession, and prisoner of war for two years, told his son why he had spent the past year composing his autobiography: 'I have writ it that your children's children may see a little of a great deal what their grandfather had gone through.'[28]

CHAPTER I

EARLY TUDOR WARFARE, 1485–1558

And let their heirs—God, if thy will be so,
Enrich the time to come with smooth-fac'd peace.
Richard III, IV, iv, 49–50

THE FIRST ARMY TO REACH THE FIELD OF BATTLE IN LEICESTERSHIRE, on 22 August 1485, was Richard III's.[1] The king arrayed his forces, nine to ten thousand strong, placing himself in the centre with John Howard, duke of Norfolk's division, to the west, and that of Henry Percy, earl of Northumberland, to the east. About a mile to his south east were the five thousand men, commanded by Thomas Stanley, earl of Derby, whose commitment to Richard's cause was doubtful. Henry Tudor approached from the west with an army five thousand strong. His military record was undistinguished: in 1483 he had tried to land at Poole Harbour, but the local militia drove him back. Two years later, on 7 August 1485, he landed at Milford Haven with two thousand troops, the sweepings of France's jails: a more evil coterie, Philippe de Commynes, a contemporary historian noted, one could not find. For the first ten days after landing in Wales few flocked to join Henry's standard. Eventually recruits trickled in, although his army was considerably out-numbered and out-positioned when it met Richard III's at Bosworth Field.

The battle began early on the morning of 22 August when Norfolk's division charged Henry Tudor's forces.[2] Hand to hand, the fighting was brutal:[3]

At once arrows flew forth on both sides, men swinging with their axes, brandishing their swords, and struggling with each other. Like butchers killing cattle in a slaughterhouse, they massacred each other fearlessly.

In such bloody combat the duke of Norfolk was slain, and his division began to panic. So Richard ordered his reserves under Northumberland

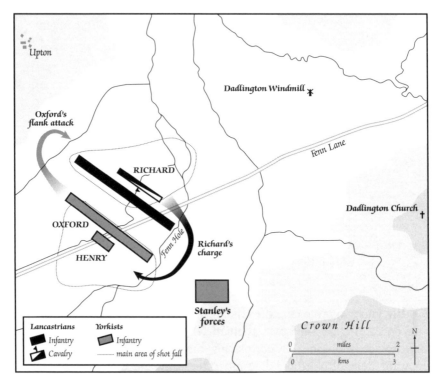

1. Battle of Bosworth Field (22 August 1485).

to plug the gap. Northumberland refused, saying that he best wait until he knew what Stanley would do. Richard had no doubt as to the answer. The king ordered the immediate execution of Stanley's son (a command that was not obeyed), and personally led eighty of his most faithful followers in a sudden left hook around Norfolk's men to assault Henry Tudor, whose standard he had spotted about a thousand yards away. Why Richard did so we cannot tell. He may have wanted to relieve Norfolk's broken division, to prevent Stanley from intervening, to crush Northumberland's mutiny in the bud, or even out of an hot-tempered wish to punish those he regarded as traitors. It was a reasonable gamble: the rebellion would have collapsed had Richard slain Henry Tudor.

He nearly did. With his battleax Richard killed William Brandon, Henry's personal standard-bearer. While dispatching Sir John Keyne, a knight renowned for his strength and courage, Richard himself was dismounted. But instead of cravenly begging (as Shakespeare would have us believe) for 'A horse! A horse! My kingdom for a horse!' Richard continued to fight on foot. 'Alone,' wrote Polydore Vergil, a contemporary historian, until 'he was killed fighting manfully in the thickest press of his enemies'.[4] The king's crown, having fallen off his helmet, was handed to Henry Tudor, who by right of conquest became Henry VII.

In several ways Bosworth Field marks an excellent turning point from medieval to early modern England—and thus a good starting point for this book. Looking back, the battle signalled the end of a military and political system that has been described as feudalism, in which land holding was organized to provide for war, and where war—with religion—became the predominant ethos. It also marked the end of the Wars of the Roses, a generation of violence, where the warlike elements intrinsic to medieval society culminated. Finally, the battle completed the building of the English nation. Looking forward, it heralded the start of 157 years of 'smooth-fac'd peace', the next major battle on English soil being Edgehill in 1642.[5] Bosworth Field did not produce immediate stability. Henry VII had to suppress several rebellions to keep his crown on his head, while his successors, Henry VIII (r. 1509–47), Edward VI (r. 1547–53), Mary I (r. 1553–58), and Elizabeth I (r. 1558–1603), all had to deal with similar challenges to their authority. But Henry VII's reign produced enough stability to allow his son, Henry VIII, to embark on two initiatives: the Reformation of the Church, which influenced British history for centuries to come, and wars with France that were an attempt to return to the glorious days of the Hundred Years War.

The Medieval Background

Had a soldier who had fought at the Battle of Hastings in 1066 been able to experience to Bosworth Field over four hundred years later, he would have noticed little difference. To be sure the firing of cannon and harquebuses (an early form of musket) would have surprised him, but they were only used in the opening stages of the battle. He might have noted how armour had changed from chain mail to solid body-hugging pieces, but would have been familiar with the infantry melees in which archers provided covering fire. In many ways this is ironic, for the two great military changes of the previous four centuries—the dominance of the heavily armoured knight, and then their destruction by longbowmen—played little part at Bosworth Field.

Militarily, the most important result of the Norman Conquest of 1066 was the growth of feudalism, still a useful, albeit controversial, term. William I (r. 1066–85) divided the land of England amongst his followers and the church, who were known as tenants in chief, keeping about a quarter for himself. When called upon, each tenant in chief had to supply a set number of fully armed knights, usually for forty days a year. They

could subdivide their lands to other knights who would serve them whenever the king mobilized his forces. At the bottom of the pyramid were the
peasants, Anglo-Saxons who in return for their own strips of land agreed
to work a knight's land for so many days a year, and whenever mobilized
to serve as his infantry.

For at least two centuries feudalism worked reasonably well. It was the
dominant social, judicial, economic and military system not just in
England but in western Europe. War, and the warrior ethic, were as deeply
ingrained in feudal life as the Church and religion.[6] Perhaps the most
popular medieval Englishmen were Thomas à Becket, the Archbishop
of Canterbury who was murdered in 1170 defending the rights of
the Church, and Richard the Lion Heart, who spent all but a year of his
ten-year reign (1189–99) overseas, fighting in a crusade to recover the
Holy Land. God and war were the most important themes in medieval
literature. War was glorious: every knight was brave, or if not (like the
coward who befouled his saddle in the twelfth-century poem *Chanson
de Guillaume*) he became a figure of ridicule.[7] War was the sport of the
Middle Ages—preferably for real in combat, or else in imitation through
jousting and the tournament. Indeed, so ubiquitous was war and so
powerful and prestigious was the warrior class that Sir Michael Howard
argues that the real question 'is not why there were so many wars, but
why there was ever any peace'.[8] Between 1066 and 1485 in England there
were only two periods of peace longer than thirty years. 'War was a way
of life,' concluded Garrett Mattingly, 'an ingrained habit of late feudal
society.'[9]

At first, for those at the top of feudal society it was a fairly safe habit.
'We are going to have some fun,' declared Baron Bertrand Du Bon, a
French knight as he charged into an affray, pretty confident that he would
emerge unharmed. Girded by armour he was secure from poorly armed
spear-men, and if dismounted and captured could expect quarter from his
fellows. Only four knights were killed and four hundred captured at the
Battle of Lincoln in 1141: in contrast two centuries later at Crécy fifteen
hundred heavy cavalry were slain.

The longbow produced this change, which was as much a social as it
was a military revolution. Six-foot long, made from the heart of ash or
yew, the longbow was a formidable weapon that fired a thirty-inch-long
arrow tipped with an iron head, which could be needle sharp, or barbed,
making it hard to pull out. An archer could fire ten, perhaps twelve, times
a minute, producing a hail of arrows. During the sixty seconds or so it took
the first wave of ten thousand French cavalry to charge at Agincourt in
1415, the English and Welsh archers could have fired fifty thousand
arrows, an average of five per target. Jean Froissart, the contemporary

French historian, recalled that the arrows flew 'so wholly and so thick that it seemed like snow'.[10]

Unlike snow, arrows did terrible damage: at sixty yards they penetrated armour or three inches of oak; at a hundred yards they decimated the enemy; and at three hundred yards they killed many and wounded even more. Until the introduction of the bolt-action magazine rifle in the late nineteenth century, the longbow was the most effective weapon an infantryman could carry. Unlike the rifle, and its predecessor, the musket, the longbow took years of training to master. Only the strongest could pull an eighty- to a hundred-pound bow.

The heavy cavalry responded to archers by becoming even heavier, wearing up to eighty pounds of armour. This decreased a knight's manoeuvrability in combat, required a stronger, and thus stouter and slower horse, and meant that a dismounted rider would, if stunned, wounded or exhausted, find it hard to regain his feet, becoming highly vulnerable to archers, who could dispatch him with their daggers. Ultimately, a horse could never carry enough armour to protect itself and its rider from arrows.

Longbowmen had other advantages over heavy cavalry, who were usually proud and independent nobles or gentry, lacking discipline, too arrogant to obey uncongenial orders, and loath to cooperate as units. According to the feudal contract they were only expected to serve for forty days a year. Mercenary longbowmen had no such restrictions. Most of them were single, so if killed they left no widows and orphans. They were well trained, dedicated volunteers, who, unlike feudal peasants, were eager for a fight—so long as it ended in pay and plunder. So successful were they that by the end of the fourteenth century there was hardly a household in England and Wales that was not graced by at least one piece of precious continental loot.[11]

The longbowmen achieved their finest hours during the Hundred Years War. It began in 1337 when Edward III claimed the French throne. He won a resounding victory at Crécy in 1346, as did his son Edward, the Black Prince, at Poitiers ten years later. Even more complete was Henry V's victory at Agincourt. Yet within a generation England had lost all of its French territories (apart from Calais), thanks to Henry V's premature death in 1422, Joan of Arc's charismatic appeal to French nationalism, and the French use of primitive cannon, which negated the lethal impact of the longbow. So by the time of Bosworth Field the two dominant weapons of medieval warfare, the heavy cavalry and longbow, had long passed their prime. Yet the latter still had many proponents. For Roger Ascham (Elizabeth I's childhood tutor), the longbow was a nostalgic symbol of the good old days when the English routinely thrashed the French. In 1549 Bishop Hugh Latimer preached that the longbow was 'a gift of God that he hath given us to excel all other nations'. He reminisced how his father had diligently taught him as a boy how to shoot with the weapon. Nowadays young men no longer bothered, bemoaned the bishop, preferring instead 'whoring within towns'.[12] The military attractions of the longbow continued for centuries. Charles I thought it should be used in the English Civil War; Ben Franklin urged its adoption during the American Revolution.[13]

In one sense it was strange that Henry Tudor's army fought and won at Bosworth Field under the flag of the Ddraig goch—the Red Dragon of Wales—and not the red and white cross of St George. The battle marked the conclusion of a process of English nation building. Nation building is a complex business, very different from state formation. The former is a bottom-up process relying on consensus; the latter, a top-down method dependent on coercion, is thus more difficult to achieve. With two disastrous world wars, a fascist dictatorship and countless prime ministers, modern Italy proves this point. Twenty-two years before its unification by force of arms in 1871, Prince Metternich contemptuously observed, 'Italy is a geographical expression.' Afterwards its prime minister Massimo D'Azeglio supposedly remarked, 'We have made Italy. Now we must make Italians.'[14]

In contrast, the English were made long before the making of England. The first English historian, the Venerable Bede, wrote *The Ecclesiastical History of the English People* in 731. Historians have debated when England became a nation. With a common language, a common ruler, a common Church, and shared legal systems, argued James Campbell, 'Late Anglo-Saxon England was a national state.' Marc Bloch, the French medievalist, agreed that England 'was a truly unified state much earlier than any continental kingdom'.[15] The Norman Conquest of 1066 slowed this process of nation building. Indeed, the violent imposition of an alien elite with their centralized form of government and land holding was more akin to top-down state formation. But after Henry I's victory at Tinchebray in 1106, in which the Anglo-Saxons, namely, the English, helped William I's fourth son, Henry I, conquer Normandy, the process of nation building continued. It was consolidated by events such as the sealing of Magna Carta in 1215; Simon de Montfort's parliament of 1265; the growth of the monarchy; the development of common law and a common Church; a standardized language (as evidenced by Geoffrey Chaucer); and the emergence of a distinct sense of national identity, particularly during the Hundred Years War.[16]

The Search for Stability

After the Battle of Bosworth Field few in England suspected that the vicious Wars of the Roses had come to an end, and that there would be no more successful rebellions against the crown until the middle of the seventeenth century. Nine months after Bosworth a rebellion broke out in Worcester, led by Francis, Lord Lovell, and Humphrey and Thomas Stafford. Although according to G. R. Elton 'the rising itself was utterly insignificant', it did show how readily the insignificant were willing to rise.[17] The following year Lambert Simnel reminded Henry VII of the fragility of his position. Probably a joiner from Oxford, Simnel masqueraded as Edward V, the prince whom many believed Richard III had murdered in the Tower. Simnel was persuasive enough to convince Margaret of Burgundy and a group of Irish nobles led by Gerald of Kildare (who admittedly needed little convincing) to have him crowned Edward V in Dublin in May 1487. The following month Simnel landed in Furness, Cumbria, with two thousand German and Irish mercenaries, picking up strength as they marched south. They numbered eight thousand when they met the king's forces, twice as strong, at Stoke in Derbyshire on 16 June 1487. Initially, it seemed that Henry Tudor might be defeated, but his centre under John de Vere, earl of Oxford, not only managed to hang on, but to counter-attack. Withering arrow fire broke the rebels, and in the ensuing rout half of the enemy were killed, many hacked to pieces in a bottle-neck that became known as the Red Gutter. Lambert Simnel was taken prisoner and, as if to say that his rebellion was a trifle, Henry gave him a job as turnspit in the royal kitchens.[18]

Two years later, in the summer of 1489, a revolt broke out in the north of England in protest against a 10 per cent tax rise. The king sent the earl of Northumberland to placate the rebels, but in June a mob murdered him at Cock Lodge, Yorkshire. By the time the king and his army reached York the rebellion had collapsed, the assassination of Northumberland, a leading nobleman, having alienated the aristocracy and gentry. Realizing that further resistance was futile, many rebels surrendered to the king, with nooses about their necks: while admitting they deserved to be hanged, they begged for mercy. Henry pardoned fifteen hundred of them.[19]

Undeterred by the possibility of having to work as a skivvy in the royal kitchen, Perkin Warbeck, an impostor from Tournai in the Low Countries, followed Simnel's example by going to Ireland, where he convinced many—who were all too willing to be persuaded—that he was the rightful king of England, being Richard IV, Edward IV's younger son who had supposedly been murdered in the Tower. Warbeck landed near Deal on the Kent coast in July 1495 with six hundred mercenaries. They were a sorry lot, whom Thomas Gainsford, the Tudor soldier and historian, described as 'bankrupts, sanctuary men, thieves, vagabonds, and divers servants of dishonest rebellion'.[20] They were certainly not fighters. With the help of the local militia the mayor of Sandwich repulsed them, killing and executing a third. So Warbeck sailed to Scotland to seek James IV's help. A year later, with fifteen hundred freebooters, James crossed the border into England. After the Scots had plundered enthusiastically, an advancing English army forced them to retreat with equal zeal.

The following year Henry had to confront a serious rebellion based in Cornwall. Prompted by tax increases to pay for the Scots War, and instigated by a blacksmith, Michael Joseph, this started as a popular rising. Fifteen thousand rebels led by James Touchet, baron Audley, marched on London. Henry personally led twenty-five thousand men out of the city, and on 17 June 1497 surrounded the rebel camp at Blackheath. In the ensuing rout perhaps as many as two thousand rebels lost their lives, while the leaders were executed as traitors.[21] None of this deterred Warbeck, who after failing to raise soldiers in Ireland landed in the West Country, where eight thousand rallied to his standard. Their attempt to capture Exeter failed. Four hundred were killed, Warbeck was taken prisoner. After twice trying to escape from the Tower he was hanged.

In view of the terrible price paid for failure, and the slim chances of success, one wonders why there were so many rebellions. Often they started as popular movements, but as the Cornish Rebellion, begun by a blacksmith and taken over by a baron, showed, the gentry played a significant part in these uprisings. Many of them believed that if Henry Tudor's rebellion of 1485 could succeed, so might theirs. After all, the king was weak militarily: he only had five hundred permanent troops, the Yeomen of the Guard, his personal bodyguard, plus another thousand stuck in garrisons, and thus had to raise volunteers to deal with emergencies. Since rebellions broke out at the peripheries, such as Cornwall and in the North, far from London and the king's authority, they had time to develop before being confronted by royal forces.

Wales was the exception to this rule. After 1485 no rebellion has ever broken out in the principality, which firmly identified itself with the Tudor dynasty.[22] Just as Bosworth Field completed the building of an English nation, so it produced an Anglo-Welsh one, a remarkable achievement considering that the long and bitter rebellion led by Owain Glyndwr had ended but eighty-two years earlier. Before Bosworth Field hundreds of Welshmen joined the colours to fight under the banner of the Red Dragon. Afterwards the principality's elite became Anglicized: many Welshmen flocked to London to further their careers, or went to Jesus College, Oxford, to improve their education, or joined the Yeomen of the Guard to protect their new Welsh king.[23]

Even though for fourteen years of his twenty-four-year reign Henry Tudor was threatened by some rebellion or conspiracy, he still had time for other military matters.[24] In June 1492 he sent fifteen hundred men under

Robert, first baron Willoughby, to Cherbourg to stop the marriage of Anne, duchess of Burgundy, to Charles VII. The French easily repulsed the English, and their king wed the duchess. The following October Henry dispatched a huge force of fourteen thousand on two hundred ships to Calais to work with the emperor Maximilian I for the return of lost French territories. When Maximilian signed a peace with the French, England was left in the lurch. Henry's efforts to build up the Royal Navy were a little more effective. Although he inherited eight naval ships, and left his son seven, these were larger and more seaworthy, such as the *Regent*, a six-hundred-ton vessel, the first English ship with cannon behind gun ports on the lower deck. These guns had been cast at the forge that the king established on the Kent/Sussex border, and were tested on his range at Mile End, east of London.

When Henry died in 1509 he had achieved the goals he had set for himself at Bosworth Field. He died as king in his own bed, the first monarch not to be deposed since 1422, and the first to pass his kingdom to an adult male heir since 1413. By defeating rebellions, incorporating the Welsh, building up trade, and strengthening the crown's income, he restored stability and gave his successor the opportunity to do grand things. And what that successor yearned to do—more than anything else—was to wage glorious war.

'To exceed the glorious deeds of his ancestors'

Today Henry VIII is best remembered as the larger than life figure of gross proportions and even grosser appetites who brawled, belched and bawded his way through six wives, countless banquets and one reformation. Instantly recognizable, the subject of many films and television series, Henry's waxen image, flanked by those of his six wives, dominates Madam Tussaud's in London, while his portrait is one of the best-selling postcards at London's National Portrait Gallery.[25] He also fascinated his contemporaries. 'The King of England, this Henry, clearly lies,' fulminated Martin Luther, 'and with his lies acts more the part of a comic jester than a king.' The French ambassador called him 'a sly old fox'.[26]

Henry never intended to be the much married man, who broke with Rome, established the Church of England, founded the roots of English hegemony and, some would argue, produced a Tudor revolution in government. Instead, he wanted to be remembered as a warrior. 'Our king is not after gold, or gems, or precious metals, but virtue, glory, immortality,' boasted William Blount, Lord Mountjoy, the distinguished scholar, to Erasmus in 1509. 'His ambition,' King Henry asserted, 'was not merely to equal, but to exceed the glorious deeds of his ancestors.'[27]

A craving for honour was at the root of the king's personality.[28] Honour is hard to define, and has changed over time. Mainly a male concept, it has a lot to do with a man's self worth as a man. To use John Skelton's phrase, Henry wanted to be 'Mars's lusty knight'.[29] In addition to being a contemporary playwright and poet, Skelton was also known for his wicked wit, which would support the suspicion that the king's public passion for honour and glory could have been a compensation for private doubts about his manhood. When the imperial ambassador hinted in the late 1520s that Henry might not be physically capable of satisfying Anne Boleyn, a woman sixteen years his junior, the King furiously retorted, 'Am I not a man like other men? Am I not? Am I not?'[30] The size of the codpiece on Henry's suite of armour (see ill.2), suggests that Henry did protest too much.

As a young man Henry trained for war, hurling javelins, shooting arrows in the butts, wrestling in the ring and taking part in tournaments. He read all the books on chivalry, such as Sir Thomas Malory's *Morte D'Arthur*, romances about the Trojan Wars and tales of Charlemagne and Roland, that poured off the recently invented printing presses. He took special delight in showing visitors to Winchester the round table around which Arthur and his knights had supposedly sat. He encouraged John Bourchier, Lord Berners, to translate Jean Froissart's *Chronicles* of the Hundred Years War, because of 'the great pleasure that my countrymen of England take in reading the worthy and knightly deeds of their valiant ancestors'.[31] Henry, like many a king, was haunted by the achievements of his forebears, once admitting that he wanted to reconquer France in order to eclipse his father's great victory at Bosworth Field.

In 1511, two years after ascending the throne, Henry sent fifteen hundred archers to Cadiz in southern Spain to help Ferdinand II of Aragon fight the Moors of North Africa. On arrival the English troops were informed they were no longer needed, and should go home. So they 'fell to drinking of hot wines,' wrote Edward Hall, the contemporary historian, 'some ran to the stews, some broke hedges, and spoiled orchards, and vineyards, and did many other outrageous deeds.'[32] The five thousand men whom Thomas Grey, the marquess of Dorset, led to Aquitaine the following summer were no better. Their mission was to support Ferdinand's invasion of Guienne, but instead Dorset decided to attack Navarre. With nothing to do, the English troopers enthusiastically sampled the local wines, their diet consisting mainly of fruit and garlic. Not surprisingly, dysentery broke out, killing eight hundred. The rest mutinied, and returned home in disgrace.

Henry was so angry with their performance that he decided to lead the next expedition in person. Most of the twenty-four thousand invasion force were longbowmen, the small cavalry, artillery and engineering contingents being mercenaries. After landing at Calais, on 30 June 1513, the king immediately rode to St Nicholas' Cathedral to dedicate himself to the service of God by claiming that he was fighting a Holy War. He certainly did not fight an uncomfortable one. For three weeks Henry and his retinue, 855 strong, feasted and amused themselves. Eventually on 21 July they set out on campaign, with patrols scouting the countryside— 'spoiling and burning all the way,' a soldier recalled—to make sure the enemy could not approach the king.[33] Even if they had, a formidable bodyguard plus a sixty-pound suit of armour protected the royal personage, who spent every night in a warm feather bed, usually inside a portable wooden shed, complete with its own thunderbox.

For most soldiers life was not so comfortable. 'I assure you never was an army so falsely victualled,' Sir Edward Howard complained in 1513 about the meager rations.[34] In the first eleven days the king's army marched but forty miles. On 16 August they came across a strong French cavalry patrol, which, after a brief skirmish, bolted, leaving behind six standards, a duke, a marquess and a vice admiral. Henry turned this incident, which was promptly dubbed the 'Battle of the Spurs', into a second Agincourt. The following day in a letter to Margaret of Savoy, the Regent of the Netherlands, he described the altercation with all the dramatic detail one might expect from a participant. Significantly, Henry failed to mention that he had been a mile away from the action. Henry was, however, present at the Siege of Thérouanne, which fell on 24 August. A month later he captured Tournai, where he spent three weeks celebrating, before returning home to London.

War with France inevitably meant war with Scotland, for as a young member of parliament, Thomas Cromwell, observed in 1523, 'who that intendeth France to win, with Scotland let him begin.'[35] The origins of Anglo-Scots hostilities go back centuries. It has been estimated that between 1286 and 1568 the English invaded Scotland on twenty-two occasions, and reivers in pursuit of plunder raided across the border innumerable times.[36] Henry's attack on France in 1513 gave James IV of Scotland the opportunity to invade England. On 9 September his forty-thousand-strong army—the largest Scotland had ever assembled— took up position at Flodden, in Northumberland, on a five-hundred-foot ridge south-east of Coldstream. With more men and heavier artillery James should have won. Having run out of food, the English, about twenty-six thousand strong under the septuagenarian Thomas Howard, earl of Surrey, were obliged to fight. Although outflanked, the earl of Home's division broke the English right. But instead of pursuing the routed enemy, the Scots plundered English corpses, exposing themselves to a charge by Thomas, Lord Dacre's cavalry. Savage hand-to-hand fighting ensued. The battle turned into a bloodbath. While Scots praised their monarch's bravery, claiming that James had personally killed five Englishmen, they damned his leadership. 'He is courageous, even more than a king should be,' wrote one contemporary, ruefully adding that 'He is not a good captain, because he begins to fight before he has given his orders.'[37] Estimates of the Scots dead range from five to ten thousand (as compared to one thousand to fifteen hundred English). They included James IV, twelve Scots earls, thirteen barons, three bishops and a brace of abbots. Of the seventy recruits from the town of Selkirk, only one returned home alive.[38]

For the next two decades Henry VIII's reign was relatively peaceful. In 1523 he sent an expeditionary force under Charles Brandon, duke of Suffolk, to France: it got within sixty miles of Paris, but the French refused to fight, and, running out of supplies, the English had to retreat home. The king became increasingly preoccupied with his marital problems; his desire to 'divorce' his first wife Catherine and marry his mistress Anne Boleyn led to the break with Rome in 1534. The Reformation dramatically changed the nature of warfare, giving it a religious context that made fighting far more bitter and bloody.

This became immediately apparent. In 1536, two years after parliament ended papal authority in England, the Pilgrimage of Grace broke out in the North. Its causes were complicated and various. Some of the rebels were protesting enclosures of land, which turned tenants off their fields so landlords could use them to graze sheep. Other rebels, notably the powerful Percy family, objected to the growing centralized authority of the crown. For many, perhaps most rebels, religion, especially the closing of the monasteries, which had played an unusually useful charitable role in the North, was the key issue. The rebellion started in Lincolnshire in October. Within five days ten thousand men marched on Lincoln. Three days later they dispersed home peacefully. The Lincolnshire rising prompted a larger and more serious one in Yorkshire. Led by Robert Aske, the pilgrims occupied York, where they reinstated expelled monks and nuns to their houses. On 27 October, with thirty or forty thousand pilgrims in attendance, Aske negotiated a pardon with the king's emissary, the duke of Norfolk. Early the next year the king used an outbreak of rebellion in Cumberland and Westmorland, led by Sir Francis Bigod, as an excuse to cancel his pardon, sending troops under Norfolk back north to execute at least a hundred and fifty of the rebels.[39]

The growing power of the central government in London, which had helped provoke the Pilgrimage of Grace, was applied to Ireland by Thomas Cromwell, the king's great minister, when he replaced the crown's rather loose medieval lordship with a stronger kingship. Those Irish who resisted were deemed traitors. After the English massacred the fifty-man garrison of Maynooth Castle, who had surrendered in March 1534 on the promise of quarter, the phrase 'the pardon of Maynooth' became a euphemism for the cold-blooded murder of prisoners of war. Such gallows humour would not have amused Thomas Fitzgerald, earl of Kildare. Even though he and his five uncles had surrendered on the guarantee of mercy, Henry VIII had them hung, drawn and quartered at Tyburn in 1537.[40]

For half a dozen years after the Pilgrimage, England remained at peace. Having given time for the Reformation to take hold, and freed from the restraining hand of Thomas Cromwell (whom Henry had callously executed in 1540), the king turned his thoughts again to war. It was as if he were in a midlife crisis striving to regain the virility of youth.[41] While he provoked hostilities with Scotland, the king also sought war with France, thus reviving the 'Auld Alliance' between Edinburgh and Paris. A rash of border raids broke out in the summer of 1542. That October the duke of Norfolk led an expeditionary force into Scotland, but was readily repulsed. The following month a Scots army of as many as eighteen thousand men under Robert, Lord Maxwell, crossed the border, where on 24 November they came across an English force of three thousand led by Sir Thomas Wharton. What should have been a Scots triumph turned into a tragedy: at Solway Moss, only seven English and twenty Scots lost their lives in battle, but several hundred more Scots drowned while trying to escape, and twelve hundred became prisoners of war.

Securing his northern frontier enabled Henry to continue his preparations for the invasion of France. In mid-June 1544 an advance party under the duke of Norfolk sailed for Calais, where for a month they devoted themselves to rest and recreation. 'Numbers of shameless prostitutes came at every tide from England,' fulminated Elis Gruffudd, a disgusted Welsh captain, continuing 'there was great rejoicing to sin without fear of retribution.'[42] The English soldiers also plundered without fear of punishment, taking 'poor man's hens, chickens, pigs and other provision, and pay nothing for it except,' declared *A Discourse of the Commonweal* (1549), 'to ravish his wife or daughter'.[43] The arrival of the king on 14 July put some backbone into his forty-four thousand soldiers. On 19 July they started to besiege Boulogne, a small port twenty miles south-west of Calais, where the king directed the fire of his cannon, and urged his men into battle (see ill.3). Henry had a grand old time. His men were less enthusiastic. Captain Gruffudd noted he 'never saw Welshmen and Englishmen so bad hearted and so unadventurous'. Another observer recalled that during the siege 'there was some shooting with the guns and no great hurt on either party'.[44] Nonetheless on 18 September Boulogne surrendered, and the king entered the town in great triumph. Twelve days later he was back home, much happier, and far poorer. His men were less happy and even poorer. Captain Gruffudd reported that 'soldiers coming from Calais and Boulogne were dying along the road from Dover to London and along the roads from London to every quarter of the kingdom.'[45]

The Founder of the Royal Navy

To send expeditions to France Henry used the first-rate naval force that he created. Several historians have credited him with founding the Royal Navy—an honour he supposedly shares with Alfred the Great. But the navy Alfred helped found consisted basically of floating castles. Broad in the beam, they were unable to sail much into wind, but waddled lubberly downwind. In battle they almost drifted into each other: sailors fought hand to hand, trying to defeat the enemy by boarding. Height was so vital that at the expense of sea-worthiness ships had high castles at either end from which archers could fire down upon the enemy (hence the word 'forecastle').

During the late fourteenth and early fifteenth centuries shipbuilders developed what Geoffrey Parker, a leading military historian, has called 'one of the greatest technological achievements of medieval Europe'.[46] They constructed long, relatively narrow vessels with three masts that could sail faster (since speed is proportionate to length), and point further into wind, their deep hulls being able to grip the water. Such ships could carry enough stores and cargoes for long voyages. After the invention of hinged gunports, they mounted heavy cannon on their lower decks, lowering their centre of gravity and thus making them more seaworthy. In the 1540s William Levett, rector of Buxted, Sussex, developed a process of casting iron cannon from high-phosphorous ore in vertical moulds barrel up, which allowed impurities to rise to the top, thus strengthening the end of the cannon where the initial explosion took place. At a third of the cost of the old bronze weapons, iron cannon could be fired much faster with a higher muzzle velocity, which enhanced the impact of their rounds. Since cutting a hole in the bow or stern of a vessel dangerously weakened her hull, cannon ports were built into the side. Attempts to widen the ports so cannon could be slewed for and aft were of limited use, so over the next four centuries ships fought broadside to each other.[47]

These new ships were so expensive that only wealthy states could afford them.[48] Having inherited seven ships from his father, Henry built eighteen more in the first six years of his reign, including the *Great Harry*, a monstrous vessel of over a thousand tons, with 43 heavy and 141 light guns. After peaking at twenty-five ships in 1520, the size of the Royal

Navy fell to eleven in 1540, and then increased to thirty-two in 1545, reaching thirty-seven five years later. These were modern vessels, averaging 459 tons.[49] Equally important, they were supported by a sophisticated series of bases at Portsmouth, Deptford and Woolwich, which were administered by the Office of Ordnance, founded in 1544, and the Navy Board, established two years later.

While these administrative changes were most important, giving the Royal Navy a permanent bureaucratic foundation, they must be seen in context. Compared to the French or Spanish, the English navy was small. It lacked a blue-water capability since its primary mission was coastal defence and supporting amphibious operations: the first time an English ship sailed south of the equator was in 1555.[50] The navy carried troops to France, and supported English invasions of Scotland. But it was not strong enough to be relied upon to defend England from invasion. To complement the navy's coastal defence role Henry spent £375,500 building twenty-four forts stretching from Calais to Berwick, from the Thames around the south coast to Milford Haven, which were 'larger in scale than anything attempted until the twentieth century'.[51]

Without doubt the greatest ship Henry built was the *Mary Rose* (see ill.4). Unlike previous fighting ships, *Mary Rose* had a high length to width ratio, its length giving it a much faster maximum theoretical sailing speed. Its heavy iron cannon were located low down, lowering the *Mary Rose's* centre of gravity, enabling her to sail faster in a beam or head wind. This advantage was lost when refits of 1529 and 1536 added an additional upper deck, making her top heavy. Ropes between the cannon and the side of the hull absorbed the recoil when the guns were fired through raised ports, which were supposed to be lowered in heavy seas to keep water out. Open gunports, plus the new higher centre of gravity, proved the *Mary Rose's* undoing. On 19 July 1545 the French attacked Portsmouth, and the *Mary Rose* was ordered to make sail to repulse them. As she was making a sudden turn, the top-heavy ship heeled over, and was hit by a sudden gust. It was enough to allow water to flood into the gun ports, whose lids were lashed open in anticipation of action. Discipline broke down. Captain Sir George Carew shouted he had lost control of his crew.[52] As the ship rolled, chaos turned into panic, and more water flooded aboard. Guns, cannon balls and stores fell free, worsening the list. Within moments, in front of a horrified crowd that included the king, she capsized, taking as many as seven hundred men to the bottom of the Solent. (There she remained until 11 October 1982, when she was raised to be exhibited in Portsmouth Dockyard as one of the most important ships in the Royal Navy's history.)[53]

Henry's wars and massive military expenditures left one lasting legacy— a financial one—that showed the king up as 'a rank amateur with money to burn'.[54] It could be argued that Henry's continental wars may have delayed English colonization of America and conquest of Ireland by half a century. Without doubt they cost a great deal in men and money. The king made extensive use of expensive foreign mercenaries—six thousand in 1513 and again in 1522, and ten thousand in 1544. Between 1510 and 1523 Henry summoned seven parliaments, all to vote taxes for war.[55] The last request, misleadingly known as the 'Amicable Grant', engendered a taxpayer revolt that forced the king to back down. During the French and Scots wars of the 1540s, three-quarters of the aristocracy—virtually all the able-bodied—saw service.[56] During the last five years of his life, Henry spent roughly £2 million on war. He raised this gigantic sum by debasing the coinage (which helped produce massive inflation), by selling a third of the land he had confiscated from the monasteries during the Reformation, and by resorting to forced loans and gifts: he 'borrowed' church plate, which he promptly melted down for silver coins. 'God help us,' exclaimed Sir Thomas Wriothesley, the councillor responsible for raising all this money, 'it maketh me weary of my life.'[57]

Edward VI and Mary Tudor

When Henry died in 1547 his two immediate successors, Edward VI and Mary I, were weak monarchs: the first because he was a minor, in whose name regents ruled, the second because she was a women and Catholic, who made a disastrous marriage to King Philip II of Spain.[58] If their predecessors, Henry VII and Henry VIII, and their successor, Elizabeth I, were great Tudors, they were the little ones.

Although there was no doubt that the young Edward VI was interested in military matters (his diary being full of reports of battles and plans for fortifications), the responsibility for facing the immediate military challenges to his regime fell to the regent, Edward Seymour, Lord Protector Somerset.[59]

The first challenge, war with Scotland, came as a result of Henry VIII's overplaying the hand he won at Solway Moss. In what became known as 'The War of the Rough Wooing' the king had forced through a marriage treaty between the six-months-old Mary, Queen of Scots, and his three-year-old son, which would turn Scotland into an English puppet. Naturally the Scots resisted. A series of border incursions followed, and the English were defeated at the Battle of Ancrum in 1545. But that did not end hostilities. On 1 September 1547 Lord Protector Somerset led a well-trained English army, between fifteen to nineteen thousand strong, into Scotland. Ten days later at Pinkie, just outside Edinburgh, the English encountered a larger Scottish army of about twenty-two thousand men with plenty of cannon. The Scots descended from a good defensive position near Inveresk, coming into range of the cannon aboard the English fleet off the coast. After an hour or so of bombardment and several cavalry charges, the Scots broke. A contemporary illustration (see ill.5) shows a classic 'panic fear' in which men at the sides and back of the infantry formations started to run, precipitating a rout of the rest. For six hours the English chased the Scots until nightfall. Perhaps as many as six thousand were killed. Some drowned in marshes, others simply ran themselves to death, more were slaughtered like cattle. The bloodbath at Pinkie did not end the misery. When the English again invaded Scotland in 1548, Captain John Brande reported, 'The country is so wasted that there is nothing to destroy.'[60]

The two rebellions that Edward VI's regime had to face a couple of years later were serious threats.

As its name suggests, the Prayer Book Rebellion that broke out in Devon and Cornwall in the summer of 1549 was a protest against the adoption of a Protestant form of worship and the confiscation of church property. The rebels' slogan 'Kill all the gentlemen' suggests that it was also a social movement. Anyway its leadership was poor and, after the rebels failed to capture Exeter, a royal army under John Russell, earl of Bedford, crushed them, killing four thousand in hot and cold blood.[61]

The outbreak of the Prayer Book Rebellion was followed by another rising, known after its leader Robert Kett. While Kett's Rebellion was centred in East Anglia, it was part of a wider series of disturbances that affected much of south-east England and the Thames Valley. It began as a protest against enclosures, and within a week fifteen thousand rebels assembled at Mousehold Heath, outside Norwich. At the end of July they took the city. A month later John Dudley, earl of Warwick, led fourteen thousand troops (including a thousand foreign mercenaries) to Norwich, where they routed the rebels, killing three thousand in the process.[62]

Such monstrous retribution did not deter Wyatt's Rebellion. Led by Sir Thomas Wyatt, the insurrection broke out in Kent in January 1554 to protest Queen Mary's forthcoming marriage to Philip II of Spain, a fellow Catholic, and to replace the queen with her sister, the solidly Protestant Princess Elizabeth. After seizing Rochester, Wyatt's forces marched on the capital, but, unable to cross London Bridge, they moved west, crossing the Thames at Kingston, to enter the city with three thousand men. Wyatt's demands were so excessive that he lost public support. The rebellion fell apart and Wyatt and a hundred of his followers were executed.

For every one of the nearly ten thousand people who died as a result of Tudor rebellions, they were a profound calamity. In comparison the last rebellion of Mary's reign, that of Thomas Stafford in April 1557, was a farce that ended in tragedy. Claiming to be the duke of Buckingham, Stafford landed from French ships at Scarborough, and with thirty men took over the castle declaring that he intended rescuing England from 'the naughty nation of the Spaniard' and from her 'unrightful and unworthy queen'.[63] The rebellion was easily crushed, Stafford and twenty-six of his fellow traitors suffered the ultimate fate, but it scared the Privy Council enough to agree with Mary's proposal that England declare war on France to support her husband, Philip II of Spain. A small force left Calais to campaign in northern France, where it engaged in some petty skirmishing, before returning to England. Sensing that Calais was vulnerable, the duke of Guise led his army of twenty thousand foot, four thousand horse and thirty cannon across the frozen marshes that surrounded the enclave. On New Year's Day his forces appeared before the walls. Twelve days later the governor, Thomas Wentworth, surrendered Calais.[64]

It was a humiliating defeat in which eight hundred English died. Henry Machyn, the London undertaker, confided in his diary that the news was 'the heaviest tidings to London and to England that ever was heard of'. 'The loss of Calais,' lamented George Ferrers, the poet, 'was such a buffet to England as had not happened in more than a hundred years.' Mary was so upset that just before she passed away early on the morning of 17 November 1558 she told an attendant, 'Open my heart . . . when I am dead and you shall find Calais written there.'[65]

Early Tudor warfare was a little bit like the *Mary Rose*: whenever a wind blew up, particularly a French one, it tended to capsize. To be sure Henry VII's victory at Bosworth Field was a profound turning point between medieval and early modern England. It engendered an era of relative peace and stability. Henry used his victory to bring about political and financial reforms, which did much to strengthen his regime while diverting as few of his resources as possible to war. Yet for a long time after Bosworth Field many failed to recognize the growing strength of the Tudor regime. Economic rebellions such as Kett's, religious ones, such as the Prayer Book, xenophobic ones such as Wyatt's, even plain wacky ones such as Stafford's all showed how many underestimated the growing military power of the Tudor state. The same could be said about the Scots who were decimated at Flodden, Solway and Pinkie. But England's victories north of the border capsized: three years after Pinkie every single English soldier had been driven out of Scotland.

Henry VIII was the exception. Whereas his father Henry Tudor wanted peace to consolidate his power, and his children Edward VI and Mary were too weak to wage war effectively on their own, Henry VIII knew few limits. His two great actions, the French wars and the break with Rome, were essentially proactive. He need not have embarked upon either. His wars had a profound effect less in terms of what they achieved than in what they prevented from happening. Had he not spent so much time and treasure in vainglorious attempts to reconquer France, while having to protect his Scottish border, had he not sold off many of the church lands confiscated during the Reformation, Henry would never have needed to call parliaments to raise money to fight future wars, and the crown could well have followed the French or Spanish model by becoming absolutist. Thus Henry's wars may have changed England's constitutional history. Admittedly this is mere speculation; what is undeniable is that for over a century and a half after the Reformation, England's wars were basically religious ones. Ironically, as we will see in the next chapter, religion played little part in persuading men to join the armed forces.

CHAPTER 2

GIVE ME SPIRIT:
JOINING AND TRAINING

Falstaff: Will you tell me, Master Shallow, how to choose a man? Care I for the limb, the thewes, the stature, bulk, and big assemblance of a man! Give me spirit, Master Shallow.

Henry IV, Part II, III, ii, 124–25

B ETWEEN THE BATTLES OF BOSWORTH FIELD AND CULLODEN, WAR affected millions of inhabitants of the British Isles. For many it was the most important experience of their lives—for too many it was the last. For instance, of the period's seventy leading literary figures, twenty-one (or 30 per cent), saw combat, which profoundly affected many of them.[1] For instance, fighting as a young man in the French Wars of Religion made Sir Walter Raleigh more sceptical, perhaps an atheist. Edmund Spenser's experiences during the Irish Wars permeate his poetry. John Donne's combat during the 1596 Cadiz and 1597 Azores expeditions was so traumatic that Thomas Hester, a leading authority on the poet, has called it 'Donne's Vietnam'. The theme of war, argued Hester, imbues his poems and sermons as he tried to make sense of his ordeal.[2] Other combatants tried to come to terms with their military experiences by keeping diaries or writing memoirs, of which, according to a cursory survey, 236 have survived in print. The vast majority come from the long seventeenth century (1603–1714), which is not surprising since these years covered the British Civil Wars, the Nine Years War and the War of the Spanish Succession. Twenty-three deal with the Tudor period (1485–1603), and nine with the relatively peaceful years from 1714 to 1746. The overwhelming majority of these diaries or memoirs, 186, describe land warfare. Only six of them were by other ranks, and only two by women, one of whom was a 'she-soldier', who fought disguised as a man.

Joining

Many wondered what sort of men could possibly want to go for a soldier. The answers were far from complimentary. Most Englishmen, wrote Geoffrey Gates, the veteran of Elizabeth I's wars, despised the profession of arms as 'a vile and damnable occupation'.[3] James Boswell even denied that sleeping with a grenadier's wife had been adultery, since 'a soldier's wife is no wife'. (Dr Johnson must have been unaware of his biographer's opinion when he observed that 'every man thinks meanly of himself for not having been a soldier'.)[4] 'Tosspots and Ruffians ... Rogues and vagabonds' were your typical recruits, thought Barnaby Rich. Half a century later Thomas Barnes agreed they were 'corrupt men, to whom it is a sport to destroy houses, to rob Churches, to ravish virgins, to ruinate cities'. They had 'a whore in one hand and a pair of dice in the other'.[5] Over half a century later in Sir Aston Cokayne's play *Trappolin*, the protagonist asks Captain Mattemores, 'What is a soldier?' He replies, 'A soldier, Trappolin, is he that does venture his life a hundred times a day. Would—in his country's and prince's cause—stand cannon shot and wood of steel pikes. Would, when his body's full of wounds, all night lie in the field.'

'Venture my life, so many times a day,' Trappolin interjects. 'There is more safety and gain in turning a thief.' No wonder when Matthew Bishop told his mother that he was enlisting in the army to fight in the War of the Spanish Succession (1701–14), she railed, 'Have you a mind to break your friends' hearts? Pray, do not think of such a thing for it will be your utter ruin.'[6]

Men joined the armed forces for a number of reasons. Some were pulled by the attractions of service, others were pushed by problems in civilian life. Many had several reasons. All of them had little idea of the reality of what they faced. 'War is delightful to those who have had no experience of it,' noted Desiderius Erasmus, while George Gascoigne, that seasoned soldier (and poet), agreed, writing 'how sweet war is to such as know it not' (see ill.7). Gascoigne went on to argue that men joined the armed forces for three main considerations: first, to win honour, fame and glory; second, in the hope of money and plunder; and third, to escape poverty, crime, or family problems.[7] The trouble was that these motivations could be contradictory. The desire for honour and glory could appeal to the best; the craving for money and plunder to the worst. General George Monck recognized this contradiction:[8]

There are two things that cause men to be desirous of this profession: the first is Emulation of Honour, the next is that they have by license to do evil, as the aims of the first are Virtuous, so will they do good service:

the others by strict Discipline may be brought to do good Service. But
if that Discipline be neglected then they prove the scum of an Army.

Some men joined the army for the basest of reasons. Even though he was
writing a *Defence of the Militarie Profession* (1579), Geoffrey Gates confessed
that such men went to war 'more to spoil than serve', and to wallow in
'swearing, drunkenness, shameless fornication'.[9] Others enlisted from a sense
of adventure. 'My shoes were made of running leather,' the Elizabeth veteran
and dramatist Thomas Churchyard explained his thirty-year military career,
'and born I was about this world to roam to see the wars.' One of *The Four
Prentices of London* in Thomas Heywood's play (1615) confessed that he had
as much capacity to resist the recruiting drum as he had not to eat when he
was hungry.[10] Sir James Turner (see ill.13), the Scottish mercenary, felt much
the same way while a student at the University of Glasgow. 'But before I
attended to the eighteenth year of my age, a restless desire entered my mind,
to be, if not an author, a least a spectator of these wars.' Peter Carew, the third
son of a Devonshire gentleman, became a mercenary soldier in 1526 because
he was bored at school, refusing 'to smell a book'. Weary of studies, the
eighteen-year-old undergraduate Anthony Cooper recalled:[11]

> When first to Oxford, fully intent
> To study learned science there I went,
> Instead of logic, physic, school converse,
> I did attend the armed troop of Mars.
> Instead of books, I sword, horse, pistols bought.

Cooper served for eighteen years, being thrice wounded, thrice taken
prisoner, and thrice besieged. Two years at Balliol College were enough for
Richard Atkyns. No longer able to 'read a Greek or Latin book with
pleasure', the Oxford undergraduate joined the king's forces at the start of
the Civil War, eventually becoming a captain.[12]

Others sat down and made a careful intellectual decision about joining,
particularly during the Civil Wars. In April 1642 John Hutchinson read
all of the pamphlets that came pouring off the presses before concluding
he should enlist with the parliamentary forces. Another parliamentary
captain turned to prayer. 'When I put my hand to the Lord's Work in
1642,' recalled John Hodgson, 'I did it not rashly, but had many an hour
and night to seek God to know my way.' Sir William Campion, a cavalier
from Sussex, found the decision to fight equally difficult. Echoing the
words of the marriage service, he wrote: 'I did not rashly or unadvisedly
put myself upon this service, for it was daily in my prayers for two or three
months together to God to direct me in the right way, and besides I had

conference with diverse able and honest men for advice, who confirmed me in my judgment.'[13] On 4 December 1691 Colonel William Maxwell explained why he was going to war: 'the power of France is that which chiefly stands in opposition to the advancing of Christ's kingdom. . . . I'll therefore go with cheerfulness to jeopardize my life for His interest.'[14] On the outbreak of the War of the Spanish Succession, John Blackadder (see ill.21) wrote in his diary, 'The important crisis of my life is approaching near, and I am again to mingle in the troubles, dangers and toils of a new war. This morning I took a solitary walk and went up to the crag at Craigforth, and there renewed my covenant with Christ.'[15]

Most recruits experienced some degree of compulsion, be it economic, social, or outright coercion.

Poverty was a powerful recruiting tool. In his play, *The Funeral, Or Grief-A-La-Mode* (1701), Richard Steele, who had served as an officer in the Life Guards, described a conversation between Ensign Campley and Private Matchlock.[16] On being asked why on earth he had enlisted, Matchlock replies, 'I was whipped from constable to constable.'

'But what pretense had they for using you so ill,' asked his officer, 'You did not pilfer?'

'I was found guilty of being poor.'

Whenever labourers' wages fell below soldiers' pay, noted Daniel Defoe, 'thousands of men will run into the army'.[17] For the starving, soldiering was the job of last resort. 'Hungry dogs must follow such as give them bread,' noted the Elizabethan Captain Roger Williams. According to the duke of Marlborough, a 'hard winter' raised 'more men in a day than in a week' during the spring.[18] Thus colonels sent officers back to Britain to raise men in the winter, for spring training and summer fighting. A few enjoyed their furloughs at the expense of their duty. In 1746 Lieutenant Colonel Windus of the 93rd Regiment (Argyle and Sutherland Highlanders) complained that some of his junior officers 'are apt to become a little Giddy & mind their Country Diversions more than Recruiting'.[19]

For officers the hope of finding or regaining their fortunes, rather than escaping penury, was a common reason to enlist. After Star Chamber fined Sir John Smythe two hundred pounds and imprisoned him in the Fleet in 1590 for brawling at court, 'finding I was brought into further displeasure with Her Majesty,' he recalled, 'I determined with her license to go beyond the seas. . . . That I might recover Her Majesty's good opinion and favour.' After failing as a lawyer and courtier, and having spent time in Bedford jail as a debtor, in 1572 George Gascoigne volunteered for Dutch service, hoping that it might 'make him rich again'.[20] Having spent his wife's ten-thousand-pound dowry in gambling and debauchery, George Goring joined the British troops fighting for the Dutch, and even managed to persuade his father-in-law to buy him a colonelcy. Patrick Gordon explained why he left Scotland in 1651 to become a mercenary, 'my patrimony being small, as being the younger son of a younger brother of a younger house'. In 1707 John, first baron Cutts's obituary told a similar story. 'He was a Cambridgeshire gentleman of a pretty good fortune, which was unhappily squandered ... which put him in a kind of necessity of undertaking a military life.'[21] During his service as a chaplain to the Royal Scots, Samuel Noyes, who was present at Blenheim, wrote frequently to John Sharp, Archbishop of York, in the hope that his descriptions of Marlborough's campaigns would win him preferment. It worked. Noyes was appointed a prebend of Winchester Cathedral.[22]

Women, family trouble, a boring job, or a cruel master could make men enlist. The very popular tune 'Over the Hills and Far Away' (1706) gave vent to all these motivations:[23]

Our prentice Tom may now refuse
To wipe his scoundrel Master's Shoes,
For now he's free to sing and play
Over the hills and far away.

We all shall lead more happy lives
By getting rid of Brats and Wives
That scold and brawl both night and day—
Over the hills and far away.

The seventeen-year-old Sydenham Poyntz volunteered for the Thirty Years War (1618–48) to escape 'a costly wife' and an apprenticeship, which 'I deemed little better than a dog's life'. Captain George Carleton was persuaded to seek his fortune in Scotland as a soldier by 'A most indiscreet marriage ... though to a very good woman'.[24] The proverbial wicked step-mother forced the twelve-year-old Samuel Gledhill to join the Royal Navy in 1698. John Bernardi joined the army to escape a tyrannical father, vowing never to return home until the old man was dead. Born into a Denbighshire county family, Samuel Bagshawe disliked his guardian, an uncle, so much that in 1731, aged eighteen, he ran away to enlist as a private. It has been suggested that Ben Jonson, the playwright, enrolled in an English regiment in Dutch employ in 1591 because he was angry with his father for dying before he was born, and hated his stepfather, a bricklayer to whom he had been forceably apprenticed. Later he boasted of killing an enemy in single combat, perhaps to assuage his resentment or else assert his manhood.

Jonson could well have been a naturally violent man, for he murdered a fellow actor in a brawl, but got off by pleading benefit of clergy.[25]

Crime forced men into the ranks. George Monck did so in 1627 to escape punishment after beating up the undersheriff of Devon who was trying to arrest his father. Convicted criminals might enlist to avoid jail or the gallows. This practice was especially prevalent during the War of the Spanish Succession. In 1708, for instance, justices of the peace drafted 1,493 criminals to 57 infantry battalions, an average of 26 per unit of roughly six hundred men: one hapless battalion got 125 convicts.[26]

Many men were conscripted into the armed forces. Before the Civil Wars the normal practice was for the Privy Council to set each county a quota of draftees, which the lord lieutenants would subdivide for each village constable. In towns the city authorities were responsible for levying men: many wanted to avoid serving. At St Paul's Cross, the most important venue for sermons in London, Roger Hacket preached against draft dodging: 'When Saul called upon the people,' declared his *Sermon needful for these times* (1591), 'they hired not others but came in person.'[27] The same year the city authorities sealed off the churches during Sunday Communion so recruiting officers could have their pick. Within four years the quality of London's recruits was so bad that the Privy Council reprimanded the Lord Mayor for using the draft 'to rid the city of rogues and loose people'.[28]

When the levy was new, with small quotas of one or two conscripts per village, the constable would select undesirables, the rowdy, the work-shy, or—if he had nubile daughters—lotharios. According to Captain Barnaby Rich, the Elizabethan soldier and author, he would choose 'Any idle fellow, some drunkard or seditious quarrelers, some privy picker, or such as has some skill at stealing a goose'. The authorities sometimes endorsed this practice. One Lord Lieutenant ordered that 'idle persons who will not labour' be drafted for the 1544 Boulogne expedition.[29]

If such draftees never returned it was a case of good riddance to bad rubbish. So after the failure of the Mansfeld expedition in 1625 there were few recriminations. Sent to the Rhine delta in winter without adequate food, clothing and shelter, only six hundred of the original twelve thousand made it home.[30] Greatly expanded draft calls for the expeditions to Cadiz in 1626, to the Isle of Rhé in 1627 and La Rochelle in 1628 meant that sober, well-connected young men began to be called up and killed, so alienating public opinion.

During the Civil Wars of the 1640s the crown tended to use a commission of array to raise men, whereas Parliament relied on the militia. As fighting widened, both sides resorted to outright conscription. A commission of array was basically a commission from the king to a powerful local figure to form a regiment, who would bill the crown for the costs. Coercion was often used in this process. Landlords forced their tenants to enlist, usually in their own regiments. Sir Bevil Grenville threatened to 'thrust them out of house and home' if his tenants did not join his battalion. In 1642 Colonel Sir Thomas Tildsley summoned his tenants to a rendezvous at Warrington, and force-marched them to Edgehill, from which battle 'most of them never returned again'.[31] To avoid such a fate some mutilated themselves. A Boston man cut off his big toe.[32]

Using the militia to raise men was more effective, if only because by volunteering for part-time service during the peace, in war they became full-time soldiers less reluctantly. Henry Foster joined the London trained bands with his fellow apprentices, most likely motivated by that peer-group pressure that is so strong among adolescent males. By the time war broke out in 1642, he had just finished his apprenticeship and was promoted sergeant in Denzil Holles's Regiment. On 19 August the regiment marched off to fight in high spirits. Three days later, after having got rid of their colonel, whom Foster called 'a Goddamn blade and doubtless hatched in hell', they had a grand time drinking, plundering, and chopping up altar rails for firewood.[33]

Once inducted, and if they were lucky, conscripts were issued basic outfits, and were then marched under the command of sergeants to rendezvous points, where they joined their units. A ballad described those marched to Portsmouth in 1625:[34]

> With an old Motley Coat and a Malmsey nose
> With an old Jerkin that's out at the elbows
> And with an old pair of boots drawn on without hose
> Stuffed with rags instead of toes.

It's not surprising that when two hundred draftees from Hampshire reached Portsmouth, Sergeant Major Sir George Blundell rejected three-quarters of them as unfit for service.[35]

Old sweats who had volunteered for the army had little time for draftees. Corporal Matthew Bishop called them 'stubborn and sulky, and ready to comply with anything that is villainous'. Other veterans found instructing draftees, reluctant to the point of stupidity, extremely frustrating. 'I am teaching cart horses,' fulminated Edward, Viscount Conway, about the recruits he was trying to train in Newcastle in 1640.[36] Many deserted. In about 1689 a Jacobite officer lamented that on the way to their units most of his Irish draftees had ran back to 'their former security, slavery and beggary in the mountains'.[37] Captain Robert Barret, who was involved in drafting men for Elizabeth's wars, described them as 'scum of their county'. Yet, like Wellington's 'scum of the earth', they could fight. Indeed, it was reasonably easy to desert on one's way to join a unit, and those who did so were rarely executed, the death penalty being mostly reserved for those who ran in the face of the enemy. So by not going absent without leave, conscripts had implicitly consented to being soldiers, and more readily adapted to the hardships of military life. Captains John Smythe and Roger Williams both agreed that they 'had rather have three hundred soldiers rogues than five hundred volunteering soldiers', because 'the rogues can abide more hunger, cold, travail, and better shift for themselves.'[38]

After the Civil War, recruiting became the responsibility of individual regiments of roughly a thousand men, being organized by the colonel and conducted by recruiting sergeants. Admittedly, a few men were shanghaied into service. In 1692 Richard Welsh, a tavern handyman, got drunk, was loaded on to a troop ship, and woke up to find himself en route to serve in Holland. 'I raved, tore my hair, and cursed my drunken folly,' he wrote to his wife, Christian. 'I am now a private sentinel of foot, where I fear I must pass the remainder of my wretched life.'[39] Most men volunteered after being subjected to high-pressure salesmanship from recruiting sergeants who promised them a life of ease, adventure, happiness and glory if they would only take the 'king's shilling'—the first use of the phrase was in 1707. John Scot described how six years earlier Captain John Campbell inveigled him into joining the Royal Scots Fusiliers:[40]

And with a very good will he proferred the lads
A pint of Scots ale and a gill
And some bits of silver he slipped to them
And then drew them in with his purse.

In addition to wine, songs were used to recruit soldiers. One, sung to the tune now used for 'Waltzing Matilda', described how[41]

A Gay Grenadier come marching down through Rochester
Bound for the Wars in the Low Countries
And he sang as he rode through the crowded streets of
Rochester.
Who'll be a soldier with Marlboro and me?

In his play *The Recruiting Officer* (1706), George Farquhar (who had been one) has Sergeant Kite tell the young men gathered in Shrewsbury's main square (see ill.20):

If any gentlemen, soldiers or others have a mind to serve Her Majesty, and pull down the French King, if any prentices have severe masters, any children undutiful parents, if any servants have too little wages, or any husband too much wife, let them repair to the noble Sergeant Kite, at the Sign of the Raven in the good town of Shrewsbury, and they shall receive present relief and entertainment.

This pitch persuaded five men to enlist, although Kite's officer discharged one for being literate. 'I will have no body in my company that can write,' declared Captain Plume, explaining that 'A fellow who can write can draw petitions.' Such a man might, for instance, petition against the fraudulent way he was recruited. So, Plume concluded, 'Those that know the least make the best soldiers.'[42]

Many found such practices repugnant. A 'very barbarous' mob attacked Captain Gabriel Crespigny as he was recruiting in Wigan about the same time as *The Recruiting Officer* was first performed, and broke a rib and bruised him so badly that he had to go to Bath for medical treatment. 'This vexing trade of recruiting vexes my mind,' wrote Lieutenant Blackadder the previous year, 'Sobriety itself is here a bar to success. I can see the greatest rakes are the best recruiters. I cannot ramble and rove, and drink and cannot tell stories or insinuate, if my life were lying at stake.'[43]

Training

In war a soldier's life is always at stake, and one of the best ways to reduce the odds of being killed is effective training. As General George S. Patton observed, 'A pint of sweat will save a gallon of blood.'[44] In addition to preserving one's life, killing the enemy and thus winning the war, training had other purposes: it taught men how to overcome scruples about killing; it turned civilians into soldiers; and it taught them how to use their weapons both as individuals and as members of a group.

Unlike today, early modern training paid little attention to overcoming the Sixth Commandment, 'Thou shalt not kill'—which is surprising since the Bible was the greatest intellectual influence on peoples' lives. Training then lacked what now would be called 'battle proofing'. Recruits did not, for instance, charge screaming to stick bayonets in the guts of straw-filled dummies.[45] Only in the Civil Wars were serious attempts made to justify killing, and then because the victims were fellow countrymen. Charles I personally told his men that the enemy were in fact 'Brownists, Anabaptists and atheists', while a best-selling parliamentary pamphlet called them 'Papists and Atheists . . . inhuman, barbarous and cruel . . . the enemies of God'.[46] The Reverend Robert Ram's *Soldier's Catechism* (which went to seven editions between 1644 and 1645) maintained there was no contradiction between being a Christian and a soldier, and that killing was acceptable when sanctioned by the authorities.[47]

Killing a foreigner was far easier than killing a fellow countryman (who spoke one's own language), particularly if you could denigrate him into something alien, even subhuman. In 1596 William Lambarde called the French 'garish and light in apparel', the Dutch 'daily drunken', the Scots 'cowardly, sudden and ready to stab', and the Spanish 'insolent, fleshly and blasphemous'.[48] The Irish were even worse: papist subhumans they might, like modern 'gooks', be 'wasted' without compunction, and without using the word 'killing'. With the development of the standing army of professionals after 1660, soldiers no longer needed to be told that the enemy were evil people. Killing them, whoever they might be, was their trade.

There is a world of difference between a soldier's trade and most others. In war, quality and training will out. Or, as Barnaby Rich put it in 1587, a 'few men well practiced more availeth than great numbers unperfect'. On the other hand, the consequences of being untrained can in truth be fatal. As Thomas Audley, Henry VIII's provost martial, observed, 'it is a grievous pain to set a battle with untrained men.' Donald McBane was a raw recruit in 1687 when the Clan MacDonald ambushed his unit, and he bolted in abject fear. McBane never forgot the experience. As an old man of sixty-seven he justified writing *The Expert Swordsman's Companion* (1727) by telling the reader, 'Here's what to serve you to save your life.'[49] His rules would have outraged the marquess of Queensberry. 'Give a back cut to his throat,' McBane advised, 'only three or four inches at most will enter, and that will be sufficient.' He urged his readers actually to stab the enemy in the back, because 'all is fair play when swords are presented.'[50]

War is no place for the untutored: in battle the wages of ignorance are death; soldiers who study war no more get killed. Donald Lupton, a veteran of the Thirty Years War, wrote *A Warre-like Treatise of the Pike* in 1642 to warn civilians of the harsh realities of his profession. 'Soldiers are not for sport and jest, but for earnest. Neither is war to be accounted a May-game, or a Morris dance, but as a Plague and Scourge.'[51] In his dedicatory verse to Richard Elton's *Compleat Body of the Art Militarie* (1650), Captain Sam Jervis reiterated this point:

Till now we did but butcher victories
And were but sloven Death's men. What our eyes
Were wanting to our hands, we fell upon
A Miscellaneous Execution.
We that grieved the slain, that they must die
Without method and disorderly,

But now we have obtained the handsome skill,
By order, method, and by rule to kill.

Training makes soldiers of civilians, teaching obedience, and the penal-
ties for disobedience. In 1590 Captain Roger Williams pointed out that 'It
is an error to think that a soldier is suddenly made.' Colonel William
Barriffe noted that 'No man is born a soldier.' Lord Richard Ranelagh
observed in 1685 that 'a soldier is a trade and must (as all trades are), be
learned.' Training develops routine skills that are quite literally vital in the
chaos of combat, as well as a sense of unit cohesion that stops men from
running away in fear. Barriffe believed that training can steel a man for
combat, because as he wrote in his best-selling *Military Discipline* (1635),
no one 'can attain to any excellency in the Art Military without practice,
but by practice is gained knowledge; knowledge begets courage and
confidence'. In doing so he was echoing a commonplace first stipulated by
Vegetius Renatus in 378CE, and repeated by commentators such as Edward
Cooke (1626), John Raynford (1642), Colonel Richard Elton (1650), and
Thomas Venn in 1672. Today the motto of the British Army's parachute-
training school, 'knowledge dispels fear', makes exactly the same point.[52]
    Training teaches men to fire their weapons as a group in combat. For a
medieval archer, weapons training was more a matter of developing the
physical strength to pull a longbow. Muskets, which replaced muscle
power with chemical power, produced by gunpowder, could only be used
by following a number of complicated steps. In theory, there could be as
many as forty-four orders for reloading a musket, although in practice
these could be broken down into six stages. Muskets were very loud, and
recoiled viciously, bruising shoulders. Improperly used, they might explode.
So troops had to be taught not to be afraid of their weapon. They must
learn to trust it, to see it, wrote George Monck, as 'the security of our own
soldiers, the terror of the enemy, and the assured ordinary means of
Victory'.[53] They must be taught to clean and care for their weapon, not
just because it was the most costly piece of equipment most of them
would ever use, but to lessen the already high chances of a misfire: carbon
build-up in the barrel could cause a musket to burst, killing the firer and
comrades about him.
    Soldiers did not fire their weapons as individuals but as part of a group,
and had to be drilled into doing so. The origins of drill have been traced
back to Eannatum, king of Lagash, Sumeria, in about 214 BCE. Ever since
the Egyptians four millennia ago, soldiers have always stepped out left
foot first. The founder of modern drill, Maurice of Nassau, Captain
General of Holland (1567–1625), studied classical texts and, in an early
example of a 'time and motion' study, broke down firing weapons and

manoeuvring on the battlefield into basic steps, giving each a separate command. In 1607 Jacob de Gheyn published a manual with four pages of text and 119 illustrations of Maurice's drill movements, making them readily understandable to junior officers and drill sergeants. Many others such as Henry Hexham followed suite with his *Principles of the Art Militarie* (1637) (see ill.12). With so many commands, the number of men a colonel could control declined, and the size of an infantry battalion fell by about half to 440 men.[54]

Maurice's most important contribution to tactics was insisting that soldiers fired not as individuals, but together as part of a group in volleys. After the Civil Wars, firing patterns became more complicated with rolling volleys, when ranks or platoons fired in succession, laying down a continuous barrage that was far more devastating than a single-unison volley followed by a long pause for reloading. Drill enabled ranks to turn to face flank and rear attacks. Most important, it kept men together affixed in a unit, preventing them from running away. As Captain William Clark cryptically noted in 1650, the purpose of drill was 'Confusion Methodized and ordered upon the field of battle.' As James Achesone warned all young soldiers, 'Confusion is the mother of mischief.'[55]

Modern soldiers are trained in a structured process. After recruitment they go to basic training or boot camp, where civilians are broken down to be reassembled as soldiers.[56] Specialists, such as gunners or engineers, are sent to their own branches for further training, while officers are educated at military academies. Basic training is often traumatic and invariably boring. Henry Reed remembered its tedium during the Second World War:[57]

To-day we have naming of parts. Yesterday
We had daily cleaning, and tomorrow morning
We shall have what to do after firing. But to-day,
Today we have naming of parts.

There is no question that early-modern soldiers spent considerable time training, marching and wheeling in drill, constantly exercising their weapons, since without such practice they would have been unable to perform the complicated manoeuvres necessary to fight and stay on the field of battle. Surprisingly little evidence, however, has survived on how they were trained. Military memoirs, for instance, spent little time on training, and far more on actual fighting. Then soldiers learned their trade in two ways—through a practical apprenticeship, and by reading theoretical manuals. Although a huge number of such manuals has survived, they were probably the less important means by which civilians were turned into soldiers.

Recruits were straightaway sent to their regiments where, if they were
lucky, they would be trained before fighting started: or else they had to
learn on the job, relying on veterans to teach them what war was really
like. Before the very successful 1596 Cadiz expedition, the earl of Essex
reported to Sir Robert Cecil that 'I do mingle the old soldiers and the new
that one may help discipline the other.' Early in the Civil Wars Sir
William Brereton begged for 'some old soldiers for sergeants', since they
'would do wonderous well' in training and steadying his regiment.[58]
The militia were the exception, because in peacetime they had muster
masters, experienced sergeants whom the Lord Lieutenant employed to
train his county's units. Training could be perfunctory, especially when the
prospect of actually fighting seemed remote. In 1700 John Dryden wrote:[59]

The country rings around with loud alarms,
And raw in fields the rude militia swarms;
Mouths without hands: maintained at vast expense,
In peace a charge; in war a weak defence;
Stout once a month they march, a blustering band,
And ever, but in times of need, at hand.
Of seeming arms to make a short essay,
Then hasten to be drunk, the business of the day.

The tradition of having a drink or two after training was common. In 1688
Thomas Bellingham exercised his Preston troop of cavalry, after which 'I
treated them.'[60]

In early modern Britain military education was conducted primarily
through printed manuals. Often they were read out aloud to soldiers, who
(I suspect) welcomed them with the same enthusiasm as did Henry Reed.
A few manuals, such as Henry Hexham's *The Principles of the Art Militarie*,
were suitable for non-commissioned officers and other ranks, with their
forty-eight pictures showing how to fire and reload a musket (see ill.12).
Most, however, were aimed at teaching officers their profession. A few
stated the obvious. Thomas Audley's *A Treatise on the Art of War* advised
holding the high ground, 'because a man going downward is of more force
than he that goeth upward'.[61] Some manuals became over-complicated
with commands such as 'Bringer up stand, the rest pass through to your
left, and place yourself behind your bringer up.' That useful and ubiquitous
command, 'As you were,' was first found in Thomas Fisher's *The Warlike
Directions or the Souldier's Practice* (1634), and has survived until today.

Between 1489 and 1643, 165 military handbooks were printed in
English (many in multiple editions), and 450 on the continent. After the
outbreak of the Civil Wars sales of military manuals took off. To prepare

himself for command in March 1642, Colonel Edward Harley spent one pound, eleven shillings on six manuals. Such works were well used, being carried in battle. Sir John Gell's copy of Thomas Styward's *The Pathwaie to martial discipline* is much worn, being stained with human blood, presumably from the wounds Gell suffered at the Battle of Hopton Heath (1643).[62]

After the Civil Wars, with the growth of a standing army, military manuals were no longer written by individuals for sale for profit, but were replaced by standardized bureaucratically generated handbooks, which all troops were required to follow. The first of them appeared in 1675, with further editions in 1680, 1685 and 1686.[63]

In much the same way, uniforms reflected the growing uniformity of the standing army. While the famous British red coat may be traced back to the Battle of Clontibret in 1595, it did not become ubiquitous until the New Model Army fifty years later.[64] Just as livery was worn by personal servants, so uniforms indicated that the professional members of a standing army were servants of the state. After the Civil Wars, uniforms became more elaborate, as individual regiments personalized them by adding special features such as coloured facings. Elaborations such as the introduction of high boots, as opposed to shoes, and pipe-clayed belts, meant that soldiers had more to clean—spit and polish being a way in which they were (and are) trained to obey orders without thinking. Moreover, a standing army of long-serving professionals had plenty of time to fill. So it occupied its hours with cleaning, inspections and drill.

Just as the military turned civilians into soldiers, so wherever possible it borrowed peacetime systems to use in war. A common example was sport. General Bernard Montgomery talked about 'knocking the enemy for six' at El Alamein in 1942, and General Norman Schwarzkopf described his flanking movement in the First Gulf War (1990–91) as a 'Hail Mary' play—to the delight of cricket and American football fans respectively. In early modern Britain, jousting mimicked war, preparing courtiers for the battlefield: it was a highly orchestrated event in Henry VIII's reign, became more stylized in Elizabeth I's, and faded away during Charles I's.[65] Hunting was both far more popular and important in training men for combat. 'Hunting is a military exercise,' observed Lodowick Lloyd, one of Elizabeth's sergeants-at-arms, 'the like stratagems are often invented and executed in war against soldiers as the hunter doth against diverse kinds of beasts.'[66] Hunting taught men how to ride, gave them courage to jump fences, and the excitement of chasing a broken foe. It did not, however, teach them when and where to stop—which may explain why Charles I's high-born cavalry kept on charging, whereas Cromwell's more plebeian Ironsides regrouped, to return to the field to win the day.

Another way in which an army employed civilian norms was to mesh concepts such as the Great Chain of Being with its own ideas about obedience and hierarchy. The view that everything had its place, and should be in its place, accorded with the military chain of command. Children were brought up by their parents and social superiors so that obedience became an automatic habit. Before the Civil Wwar there could hardly be a recruit who had not heard the official sermon 'Against Disobedience and Willful Rebellion' at least a dozen times. Thus, even before he joined the armed forces a recruit had been thoroughly indoctrinated to do what his superiors told him.[67] Codes, in which superiors acted as gentlemen, and inferiors deferred to them, carried over from peace to war. The high levels of violence frequently used within the family and workplace, as well as state-imposed floggings and public executions, facilitated the often more brutal physical punishments of the military. Forty of the sixty-one offences in the 1627 Articles of War prescribed capital punishment.[68] The connection between military and civilian punishments is supported by the fact that in Britain public hanging and army floggings were both abolished in the same year, 1868.

Men preferred to fight within the frameworks they had known in peace, alongside comrades and under leaders they recognized from home. When possible, regiments tended to be recruited locally. 'I have seen,' preached Bishop James Pilkington in 1562, that when a 'gentleman hath gone to the wars, his tenants would strive who would go with him first'. 'If your Highness will be pleased to command me to the Turk or Jew or Gentile, I will go on my bare feet to serve you,' protested Thomas Dabridgecourt to Prince Rupert in 1644 on learning he was to be posted from Bristol to Ludlow, 'but from the Welsh, good Lord, deliver me . . .'[69] Welsh troops in particular preferred to be led by their own gentry, if only because they spoke the same language. When well led, those troops on the fringes of society—the Welsh, the Cornish, Scots Highlanders, the deprived, the rejected, the unemployed, the evicted, those scorned by the establishment—often made the best soldiers, perhaps because they felt a need to prove themselves.[70]

Retention

Once soldiers had been trained, and their officers educated, they had to be kept with the army as it campaigned, skirmished, and fought battles and sieges. Of course, for the few who actually enjoyed fighting, retaining such happy warriors was no problem. But most troops were kept in the armed forces through such 'enticements' as pay, food, clothing, leadership and honour. Because these influences worked at all stages of the military cycle, in examining them in this, as well as other chapters, some duplication is inevitable. For example, food and drink played an important part in keeping soldiers with the colours from recruitment to discharge, if only because they could not perform their strenuous duties without them. 'And God he knows the English soldier's gut must have his fill of victuals once a day,' noted George Gascoigne.[71]

Pay was probably the most important factor in retaining men. Take Captain Samuel Birch's company, which was mustered 'after much money spent and pains taken' in Manchester on 15 May 1648. It was a fairly typical territorial unit of 137 men, who over the next ten months took part in one major battle, two sieges and an ambush, in which they panicked. Of the thirty-eight members of this company who deserted, fourteen did so immediately before and after major combat, compared to the twenty-four who left after being paid.[72]

Punishment kept soldiers from running away, maintained discipline and taught lessons. Soldiers who were forced to watch a flogging or hanging learned what happened to those who broke the rules. Sometimes, as with running the gauntlet, in which the malefactor was forced to run through a line of comrades, who beat him along the way, his crime, usually stealing, was less against superiors but more against his comrades. Even moderate punishments could be effective. Robert Monro, a volunteer in a French Guard's regiment, recalled what happened when he was late on parade in 1626:[73]

> I was made to stand from eleven before noon to eight of the clock in the night Sentry armed with a Corselet, Head-piece, Bracelets, being iron to the teeth, in a hot summers day, till I was weary of my life, which ever after made me the more strict in punishing those under my command.

Monro learned his lesson well. He became a successful and brave commander in both the Thirty Years War and the British Civil Wars, who in old age wrote his memoirs. In them he asked himself what really made men fight when they were actually in combat. The answers will be found in Chapter 4.

CHAPTER 3

THIS HAPPY BREED OF MEN: ELIZABETHAN WARFARE, 1558–1603

This happy breed of men, this little world,
This precious stone set in the silver sea,
Which serves it in the office of a wall,
Or as a moat defensive to a house,
Against the envy of less happier lands.
Richard III, I, i, 47–51

HISTORY DOES NOT RECORD WHETHER DURING THE FIRST PERFORM-
ANCE of *Richard III*, probably in late 1591, any in the audience gave
a hollow laugh as John of Gaunt boasted that 'this happy breed of men'
was safe from 'the envy of less happier lands'. The plain fact of the matter
was that during the last third of Queen Elizabeth's reign 'this precious
stone' was plagued with war. Although the reign began fairly peacefully, by
its last two decades England increasingly became involved in wars, on land
and at sea, both abroad and in Ireland. In many ways the Armada of 1588
was a turning point. A great victory, it gave Englishmen both a degree of
self-confidence and the recognition that they must fight a long, all-out
war against Catholicism. War cost much money and many lives. Military
service became the norm: about half of all adult males served in the armed
forces in one capacity or another.[1] England developed a highly effective
military culture, which was reflected in numerous military manuals, many
stage plays, and in tensions between soldiers and civilians.

Confrontation Postponed

Initially, the memory of the huge financial burden of Henry VIII's military
escapades dampened any enthusiasm for war on the part of the queen and
her advisers. Sir William Cecil, Baron Burghley, Elizabeth's pre-eminent

counsellor, often complained of 'the uncertainty of the charge of war', the actual cost of operations being frequently thrice the amount that soldiers or sailors anticipated.[2] Mercenaries were both expensive and unreliable. As Machiavelli warned, 'How dangerous and pernicious it is of a Prince and his realm to be open to the trust of the service of strangers.'[3] So Elizabeth tried to postpone confrontation. She gave Philip II of Spain (her late sister's widower) the impression that she was in fact a Catholic who wanted to declare her faith and even marry him, but could not do so until she was safely ensconced on the throne. Of course, this was all absurd, but it worked well enough to delay the Armada for a dozen years, during which time England grew stronger militarily.

When Elizabeth came to the throne, England could deal with weak enemies in Scotland but not powerful ones on the continent. In February 1560, two years into the queen's reign, an English army of two thousand men under the duke of Norfolk crossed the border, and after winning a skirmish besieged the French garrison at Leith. After three weeks they tried to take the castle in one last desperate assault. It failed. The scaling ladders were six feet too short. But the French had to surrender in June, having received no supplies from home.[4] It was the last major Anglo-Scottish combat for seventy-nine years. Elizabeth used bribes to buy peace. 'Money,' declared Sir Francis Walsingham, her spymaster, 'can do anything with that nation.'[5] More important, Scotland became Protestant. The Anglo-Scots wars of the 1540s and 1550s severely weakened the Catholic Church north of the border: buildings and monasteries were destroyed, priests killed. So when John Knox returned from the Protestant reformer John Calvin's Geneva in 1559, Scotland was ripe for reformation and the spread of Presbyterianism.

While the Reformation brought peace with Scotland, it prompted wars elsewhere. In 1562, two years after the final expulsion of the French from Scotland, Elizabeth intervened in France to help the Huguenots, fellow Protestants, in rebellion against their Catholic king. She dispatched between five hundred and nine hundred English, Scots and Welsh volunteers to Normandy: for volunteers, their performance was mediocre, and they were readily defeated. Only 25 out of 120 men in Captain Henry Killigrew's company survived: those who did not die in combat or from disease were captured and executed or sent to the galleys. The debacle deterred Elizabeth from intervening on the continent for two decades.[6]

During this period the crown used the militia to deal with threats to internal security. The idea that all able-bodied men between sixteen and sixty were obliged to turn out to defend the realm went back to the Anglo-Saxon fyrd. In an early example of what today is called 'cost shifting', in the 1558 Horse and Armour Act Queen Mary's government transferred the financial burden of running the militia from the crown to its members by ordering that soldiers buy their own weapons. For instance, militiamen worth from £5 to £10 a year had to purchase an armoured jerkin, a steel helmet, and a halberd or longbow. At the other end of the scale, those worth over £1,000 a year had to provide sixteen horses, eighty suits of light armour, forty pikes, thirty longbows, twenty halberds, twenty harquebuses, and fifty helmets.[7] In theory, service was compulsory for all adult males (except the clergy) from sixteen to sixty, who were required to turn up for a number of drills each year.[8] To be sure, after training, the part-time soldiers might repair to a local tavern, where the entertainment must have helped foster a sense of a county community similar to that which their betters developed during the quarterly court sessions. Encouraged by a generous allowance of 8d. to 12d. a day, plus the prospect of liquid refreshments, most men were happy to train to defend their homes and families, especially when they believed that the threat was real. Within days seven hundred of Cambridgeshire's trained bands responded to the government's orders to mobilize to deal with a threatened invasion in 1599, 'as though the enemy were at our doors'. Not everyone was as willing to leap into the breach. In 1595 William Pace explained why he could not attend the muster of Kent's cavalry contingent: 'I am fallen into an infirmity called the piles, where I am scarce able to go much less sit upon a horse.'[9]

Even the least skilled militiaman had little difficulty in dealing with untrained and poorly armed rioters, who engendered an intense degree of fear and loathing.[10] Far from conceding that rioters might have reasonable grievances, authors such as Edmund Spenser, Philip Sidney and William Shakespeare portrayed them as dangerous buffoons and pernicious simpletons with unconscionable demands. Shakespeare asserted that they wanted to buy seven halfpenny loaves for a penny.[11]

Much more dangerous than peasant revolts was the aristocratic rebellion that took place in 1569. Centred on Durham and South Yorkshire, begun by the duke of Norfolk (who had ambitions of marrying Mary, Queen of Scots), and led by the Catholic earls of Northumberland and Westmorland, the Northern Rebellion was an attempt to stop the growing centralizing power of the crown. It was also a reflection of a distinct military culture produced by centuries of border warfare, which the North's bellicose ballads reflected.[12] The rebellion failed. The militia crushed it in six weeks. Although the rebellion was relatively bloodless, less than a dozen men losing their lives in combat, the queen ordered seven hundred rebels hanged, although 450 actually suffered the ultimate punishment.[13]

The Northern Rebellion was the last of a series of Tudor rebellions.[14] The state was growing too strong, and the aristocracy was becoming too weak, to risk such desperate ventures. In the first half of her reign Elizabeth did much to bring about this change. To be sure, it took time to shape her regime. As it continued the queen ennobled fewer peers, and learned to control both parliament and the powerful men who believed that the Great Chain of Being—that divinely ordained hierarchy of class and gender—meant that they should direct a woman ruler.[15] Elizabeth returned England to the Protestant faith, and became head of a Church that tried to follow the *via media*, the middle way that did not seek a window into any man's soul.

The Armada

Such policies stood Elizabeth in good stead in the last third of her reign when England faced its greatest military challenge. The Armada was the key event in a general European war that England fought for two decades, at sea, on the continent and in Ireland.[16]

The story of the Spanish attempt to invade England is so well known that it needs no long description, of how in April 1587 Sir Francis Drake 'singed the king of Spain's beard' by attacking the fleet he was assembling in Cadiz. Drake burned thirty ships, and destroyed vital naval supplies including wood being seasoned for making barrels. Next he blockaded Lisbon for a month, capturing Spanish merchant vessels worth £114,000. 'It may seem strange or rather miraculous that so great an exploit should be performed with so small loss,' Captain Thomas Fenner wrote to Sir Francis Walsingham. His explanation was simple: 'our good God hath and daily doth make his infinite power manifest to all papists.'[17] Religion was central to Elizabethan warfare.

Drake's successes were not enough to stop the Armada from sailing in May 1588. It was commanded (most reluctantly) by the duke of Medina-Sidonia, a grandee who admitted 'I have never seen war nor engaged in it.' He was particularly loathe to serve aboard ship since he suffered sorely from seasickness. On 19 July his fleet of 130 ships weighing 58,000 tons, carrying 30,000 men and 2,431 cannon, arrived off The Lizard. They confronted about two hundred English vessels, crewed by sixteen thousand men. Although smaller, the English ships were faster, could sail closer to the wind, were better led and manned, and had twice as many long cannon, with three times the firepower. These advantages became apparent as the Spanish fleet sailed in a crescent formation up the Channel, being unceasingly harassed for nine days. On 27 July it finally reached Calais, close to the rendezvous to pick up the duke of Parma's army from the Spanish Netherlands, and transport it to conquer England. But

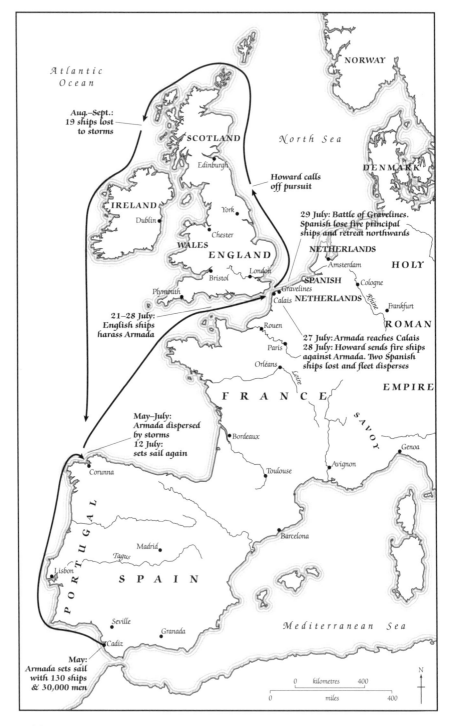

2. The Spanish Armada, May–September 1588.

Parma's army was not there. Worse still, the following night the English launched several fireships, panicking the Spanish. Some of their vessels caught fire, others cut their anchor lines and drifted aground on a lee shore or into each other. The next day off Gravelines the English followed up their attack by bombarding the enemy with their long-range guns.

Battles are won less by killing the other side and more by destroying their will and ability to fight. In this the English succeeded. Morale broken, the Spanish were unable to face the long tack against the prevailing winds south and west back down the Channel, running a gauntlet of English cannon fire. (They did not know the English were almost out of ammunition.) So Medina-Sidonia ordered his fleet to sail north around Scotland and Ireland. Bad weather, including the remnants of an early hurricane, bad food turned putrid in barrels made from unseasoned wood, inaccurate charts, poor seamanship and plain bad luck meant that a third of Philip's ships and two-thirds of his men never made it home. Ironically, at the time many English sailors did not realize that they had won a major victory. On 8 August 1588 Henry White, captain of the fireship *Talbot*, which had helped win the decisive battle off Dunkirk but ten days before, complained that 'our parsimony at home hath bereaved us of the famousest victory that ever our navy might have had at sea.'[18]

The Armada was not just a naval campaign. The build-up of land forces to resist a Spanish invasion has been described as 'an administrative feat of massive scope'.[19] A survey taken in November and December 1587 showed 130,000 men in the militia, of whom 44,000 were members of the trained bands, some of whom were extremely competent, being drilled and led by experienced captains and sergeants just home from the continental wars. By May 1588 the London bands were drilling weekly. To give warning of the enemy's approach, beacons were built, manned twenty-four hours a day by four men, paid 8d. a shift. Once the beacons were lit, 72,000 men could be mobilized on the south coast, with another 46,000 protecting London. In August the queen inspected her troops at Tilbury, where according to Thomas Deloney's ballad, 'The Queene's Visiting of the Campe at Tilbury' (1588), she told them:[20]

My loving friends and countrymen
I hope this day the worst is seen,
That in our wars you shall sustain
But if our enemies do assail you,
Never let your stomachs fail you

For the many Englishmen caught up in the Armada the experience must have been very profound and frightening. Some shared the intimacy of beacon watching, hoping for the best, but ready to light their warning fires in case of the worst. Deloney, a London silkweaver, played on their fears in his 'New Ballet [Ballad] on the strange whippes which the Spanyards had prepared to whippe English men' (1588). The political philosopher Thomas Hobbes recalled that his mother was so frightened that she prematurely gave birth to twins, of whom he was one. All were terrified about what might happen if the Spanish invaded. Stories of the sack of Antwerp in 1576, in which the Spanish—led by the aptly named Colonel Charles Fuckers—raped, tortured and murdered as many as seventeen thousand civilians, were grist for playwrights and pamphleteers such as George Gascoigne and Shakespeare. The former remembered seeing civilians at Antwerp drowned, burned, or with guts hanging out as if they had been used for an anatomy lesson.[21] Few Englishmen, women and children doubted they faced similar fates had the Armada landed. A defence in depth and scorched-earth tactics would not have repulsed the Spanish, whose infantry was regarded as Europe's finest. Certainly Philip II's men would have taken the south-east and London, and perhaps captured or killed the queen. But rather than meekly accepting a Catholic occupation the English—like the Dutch—would surely have waged a long and brutal war against Spain.[22]

Few Englishmen doubted that their 'scepter'd isle' had escaped a terrible fate. Once again Thomas Deloney voiced the public's feelings. As his 'A Joyful new Ballad' put it:[23]

Our pleasant country,
so fruitful and so fair,
They do intend, by deadly war;
to make both poor and bare;
Our towns and cities
to rack and sack likewise,
To kill and murder man and wife,
as malice doth arise
And to deflower
our virgins in our sight.

Officially, the queen gave the Almighty credit for the defeat of the Armada, striking a medal proclaiming 'Afflavit Deus et dissipati sunt— God blew and they were scattered.'[24]

The credit was not entirely His. The roots of the English victory went back a century or more. Elizabeth had built on naval foundations laid by her father. As we saw in the previous chapter, Henry VIII took advantage of the late medieval revolution in shipbuilding, producing new deep-hulled vessels, with three masts, and iron cannon firing through gun ports on the sides. But compared to the *Dreadnought*, which was launched in 1577, Henry's first battleship, *Henry Grace à Dieu*, and the even larger *Mary Rose*, were lumbering leviathans. Geoffrey Parker has written of a 'Dreadnought Revolution' in naval architecture that was as significant as the one that took place in the early twentieth century. Developed by Sir John Hawkins, the architect of the Elizabethan navy, the *Dreadnought* displaced seven hundred tons; it carried cannon weighing thirty-one tons, which amounted to 4.5 per cent of its total weight, packing a far heavier punch than Henry VIII's vessels, which had a 3.69 per cent ratio. This proportion continued to grow: averaging 6 per cent in the Armada, it reached 7.33 per cent by the queen's death.[25] Shipwrights, such as Matthew Baker at Chatham, used geometric models to build longer—and thus faster—vessels with length/beam ratios of five to one. Sir Francis Drake called Baker's most famous creation, the *Revenge*, the 'ideal ship of war'.[26] Such vessels were remarkably seaworthy. They could sail across oceans, even around the world. During Elizabeth's reign no major Royal Naval vessel was lost at sea.[27]

First-rate ships required many first-rate men to man and maintain them. Sailing vessels needed large crews, not just to cover attrition due to disease and accidents, but simultaneously to ply the guns, trim sails and board the enemy. In 1562 parliament mandated the eating of fish on Wednesdays, in addition to Fridays, to encourage the growth of the fishing industry, a crucial reservoir of trained manpower. At the start of Elizabeth's reign Lord Admiral Edward Fiennes de Clinton, earl of Lincoln, and Lord Treasurer William Paulet, marquess of Winchester, developed the system of permanent warrant officers, such as boatswains, attached to each ship, to maintain her when laid up, and as a cadre upon mobilization.[28] Sea fighting was a complicated task that demanded high levels of managerial and specialty skills. For instance, in 1588 the *Crescent* had twenty-nine officers, warrant and petty officers to command thirty-eight seamen, and three boys (as compared to an infantry company with two officers, two sergeants, and four corporals for a hundred and fifty men).[29] Since the sea was such a dangerous place, it demanded competence on the part of sailors, unlike life on land where status and birth were far more important. Sometimes the two collided. At the start of Sir Francis Drake's voyage around the world in 1577–80, Thomas Doughty thought that his high birth and excellent court connections entitled him to be the squadron's commander, and so he staged a mutiny. Drake court-martialled and executed him, telling his men: 'I must have the gentleman to haul and draw with the mariner and the mariner with the gentleman.'[30]

More often than not, gentlemen and mariners (who became known as tarpaulins) worked together—if only because the prospect of drowning encouraged cooperation—a stimulus that soldiers lacked. During the Armada, Lord Henry Seymour explained why a secretary was writing on his behalf: 'I have strained my hand with hauling of a rope.' To be sure, most naval captains had claims to gentility. Men such as John Hawkins or Francis Drake used naval careers not to join the gentry but to enhance their status within it. The sea could, as Drake put it, become 'The path to fame, the proof of zeal, and the way to purchase gold.'[31] Aristocrats who became captains were experienced sailors. Robert Dudley, the son of the queen's favourite, the earl of Leicester, studied seamanship and navigation from the age of seventeen, being the first Englishman to plot a grand-circle course, a very complicated mathematical feat. During Elizabeth's reign it first became acceptable for a gentleman's younger son to seek his fortune at sea.[32]

There were plenty of fortunes to be found there. Because wooden ships were relatively hard to sink and easy to capture, and were expensive prizes with lucrative cargoes, immense riches were to be made in privateering—a legalized form of piracy. Drake's voyage around the world produced a 4,700 per cent return, which did much to parry claims from the likes of Thomas Doughty that birth, not merit, made natural leaders. At sea, more than on land, in war, rather than in peace, necessity favoured not just the brave but the competent.

War at Sea after the Armada

The defeat of the Armada did not end hostilities: Spain's war machine was not broken. Indeed, during the next decade it was able to launch two more Armadas that, luckily for the English, storms turned back. Spanish raids on Cornish villages, such as Mousehole, Godolphin Cross and Newlands, were mere pinpricks. At Cawsand's Bay one man with a musket apparently drove the raiders away.[33]

Most Englishmen remained convinced that it would take more than a light carbine to thwart King Philip, who Sir William Cecil noted in 1590 wanted 'to be lord and commander of all Christendom, jointly with the Pope and with no other associate'.[34] To frustrate Philip's knavish tricks, England relied on sea power in three ways. First, the Royal Navy blockaded the Channel to prevent the Spanish from reinforcing their troops in the Netherlands and obtaining military supplies from the Baltic. In this the navy was remarkably successful. Less effective was the second English objective, seizing the Spanish treasure fleets from the Americas by capturing their ships at sea or in port. The third method, blockading the

Spanish coast, was beyond the Royal Navy's grasp since it could not remain at sea for months, especially during the winter, lacking sufficient supply vessels to support it. So the English had to resort to privateers. One consistent theme ran through all these strategies. As Robert Devereux, second earl of Essex, put it, England's objective in fighting Philip II was to 'cut his sinews and make war with him with his money'.[35]

Such was the guiding principle behind the expedition that Sir Francis Drake, as admiral, and John Norris, as general, led against Portugal in 1589. It was a large venture of eighty-three ships, sixteen thousand sailors and four thousand soldiers. Many of the latter were of poor quality. 'The justices,' complained Colonel Anthony Wingfield, 'have sent out the scum of the county.'[36] At first, the commanders disobeyed orders and attacked Corunna, where they believed a Spanish silver galley was moored. It was in fact in Santander, although in Corunna they did destroy three Spanish warships.[37] Two weeks later Drake and Norris sailed for their original target, Lisbon, where they were equally ineffective. The Portuguese had been forewarned, and the English split their forces, failing to coordinate between the army and navy, the latter being intent on plunder. After an equally inept attempt to capture the Azores, Drake and Norris sailed for England, leaving over half their men behind dead, deserted, or prisoners. On returning to London, five hundred unpaid survivors looted St Bartholomew's Fair, prompting the city authorities to call out a thousand troops from the trained bands. All in all it had been a 'miserable action', thought William Fenner, one of the lucky ones to make it home. William Monson, another survivor, agreed, noting that Drake 'was much blamed by the common consent of all men'.[38] The queen concurred, hauling Drake and Norris before the privy council. Drake languished in disgrace at his Devon home until 1595, when once more he was allowed to attack the Spanish Main. He died at sea the following year.

In 1596 the English attacked Cadiz in what David Loades has called 'one of the most efficient acts of war carried out by any Tudor government' (see ill.8).[39] For one thing the expedition's commanders—Essex, Lord Charles Howard, Lord Thomas Howard and Sir Walter Raleigh—worked well together, coordinating the efforts of seventeen Royal Navy ships, thirty Dutch vessels and seventy-three armed merchantmen. They held the town of Cadiz for two weeks, destroying twenty-four large ships, burning 1,300 buildings and inflicting £5.5 million pounds in damage. The English took booty worth £170,000 (most of which they surreptitiously appropriated, the bishop of Faro's library ending up in the Bodleian, Oxford), but failed to capture the Spanish treasure fleet. Elizabeth was outraged at the loss of so much plunder, as well as by the fact that the commanders knighted sixty men without her permission.

Philip II was so angry that he dispatched another Armada of a hundred ships, which a winter gale shattered in the Bay of Biscay, sinking a quarter of the Spanish vessels.[40]

Afterwards the Anglo-Spanish naval war became basically a privateering conflict. Some Englishmen, such as Sir John Hippisley, used privateering as a way to get out of debt, others to make their fortunes. The capture of the *Sao Phelipe* in 1587 brought (after heavy looting) cargo worth a tenth of England's annual imports, while that of the *Madre de Dios* five years later, valued at half a million pounds, was worth 50 per cent of yearly imports. Between the Armada of 1588 and peace with Spain in 1603, privateering profits comprised 10–15 per cent of imports, while earning the queen an average of £40,000 a year, two-thirds of the cost of her navy. In sum, privateering helped build up the English merchant marine, decimated that of Spain for three hundred years, and depopulated the Caribbean.[41]

War on the Continent

Far less profitable were the campaigns the English fought on the continent. After the Dutch became mostly Protestant in the 1560s, the Spanish tried to root out this new heresy by using the Inquisition, which with grievances about taxation provoked a revolt in 1568 that changed the nature of European warfare. Religion became the chief cause and motivation of struggles that grew increasingly brutal. Thomas Nun, a chaplain who took part in the 1596 Cadiz expedition, saw the conflict in ideological terms as an anti-papist, anti-Spanish crusade. Thomas Churchyard, the veteran Elizabethan captain, who had witnessed its horrors first-hand on the continent, called war 'a second hell'. George Gascoigne (see ill.7), an eyewitness of the terrible Spanish sack of Antwerp in 1576, agreed that 'war is ever the scourge of God.'[42]

Acting on the principle that the enemy of my enemy is my friend, in 1572 the English first sent troops to help the Dutch, their fellow Protestants.[43] All the officers, and many of the other ranks, were veterans. Landing at Flushing they fought ably, killing a hundred and fifty Spaniards for a loss of fifty men. The fifteen hundred reinforcements under Sir Humphrey Gilbert did not do as well, being ambushed near Sluys and routed at South Beveland. So cowardly was the English contingent that one observer prayed, 'God send them old beer that they may be more stabler and not to shit in their breeches and run away as often as they have done.'[44]

Alcohol alone could not stiffen the backs of the badly paid, wretchedly fed, woefully led and poorly supplied reinforcements. 'I fear I must trouble my Lord Leicester and Pembroke and yourself,' Captain Roger Williams, one of their captains, wrote to Sir Francis Walsingham in July 1582, 'for dinner and supper. Therefore your honours may do well to speak to her majesty to give me some.' Vittles were not forthcoming. 'You would not believe the poverty we are in,' Williams wrote a week later, adding in December, 'I never saw the like misery amongst soldiers.' No wonder some English troops vented their frustrations on their allies. 'When drunk they can scarcely stand,' wrote George Gascoigne of the Dutch, adding that in their country 'whoredom is accounted Jollytie'.[45]

On 20 August 1585 Elizabeth signed the Treaty of Nonsuch with the Dutch Estates General, promising to send to the Netherlands 7,400 troops under Robert Dudley, first earl of Leicester, in return for the towns of Brill, Ostend and Flushing. The expedition cost nearly half of the queen's annual income. The cold, wet climate of the Low Countries wreaked an even heavier charge on the recruits. 'Of the band that came over in August and September more than half are wasted, dead or gone, and many of the rest sick and feeble, fitter to be at home,' wrote Thomas Digges, master-muster general to the English forces.[46] Leicester admitted in July that his men were so hungry that five hundred men had deserted in the last two days: he had hanged two hundred for trying to board ship for England.[47] The sick furloughed home fared badly. Packed two to three hundred on the cold floors of parish churches, one observer described them as 'miserable and pitiful ghosts, or rather shadows of men'.[48]

After this inauspicious start, the English contribution to the Dutch war effort became more effective. Their numbers averaged six thousand men a year; supplies and pay improved; the quality of recruits got better. By the end of Elizabeth's reign, small but first-rate forces under captains such as Sir Francis Vere became increasingly integrated into the Dutch Army, where they learned the latest military tactics.[49] In all, Elizabeth's intervention ensured Dutch independence.

To help the Protestant Henri IV of France, who was also fighting Philip II, Elizabeth sent an expeditionary force to Brittany in 1589 and another to Normandy two years later. After destroying a Spanish army of three thousand men in Brittany, Elizabeth sent four thousand men (again, mostly conscripts) to Rouen under Essex and Sir Roger Williams. The siege began in September 1591. The fighting was callous. 'The continual burnings of the houses are great and pitiful to behold,' recalled Sir Thomas Coningsby.[50] The fires got out of control, exploding an ammunition dump, destroying two churches and two hundred houses. Within a month the siege had halved the number of fit English troops. Compared to the help the English gave Protestants in the Low Countries, the assistance rendered to them in France was of little value, especially after Henri IV converted to Rome in 1593.

The Conquest of Ireland

Henry VIII's break with Rome in 1533, and the subsequent Reformation, fundamentally changed the nature of Anglo-Irish relations until—some might say—even today. Ireland remained a Catholic country, which over the next half century thanks to the Counter-Reformation, became even more attached to Rome, as the English grew increasingly Protestant. Sectarian and ethnic differences made war between England and Ireland even more brutal. 'Withdraw the sword,' warned John Hooker, who fought against the Irish, 'and as the dog to his vomit, and the sow to her dirt and puddle, they will return to their old and former insolency, rebellion and disobedience.'[51]

The English viewed Ireland much as modern Americans were to deem Cuba—as an alien threat a few miles from their shores. In 1561 Sir Christopher Hatton called Ireland 'a postern gate through which those bent on the destruction of this country might enter'. More pithily the Jesuit Father Wolf told Philip II of Spain, 'he that England would win, let him in Ireland begin'. Tudor Englishmen were convinced that the loss of Ireland would have a domino effect that Sir William Fitzwilliam, the Lord Deputy, explained, 'would no doubt shake this whole state'.[52] Because Catholicism helped the Irish develop a rudimentary sense of nationalism, conflict there gradually became less a revolt or even a rebellion, and more a struggle for independence, even a war of national liberation. 'The rebels stand not as heretofore upon terms of oppression and country grievance,' recognized the Queen's Council in Dublin in 1597, 'but for the restoring of the Romanist religion, and to cast off England's laws and government.'[53]

During Elizabeth's reign, war in Ireland was an almost continuous dirge of raids, ambushes and atrocities. Four main campaigns, however, stand out.

In the first, the rebellion of Shane O'Neill (1560–67), two contestants for the earldom of Tyrone fought each other. Shane waged a long and bitter war, mainly in Ulster against the English, as well as against rival Irish chiefs, before being murdered by Scottish settlers, based in Country Antrim, with whom he had sought sanctuary.

The second campaign, the First Desmond Rebellion in Munster (1569–73), began when Sir Henry Sidney, the English Lord Deputy of Ireland, arrested Gerald Fitzgerald, fourteenth earl of Desmond, for exploiting Munster, and had him imprisoned in the Tower of London. Understandably, this provoked a revolt led by James Fitzmaurice Fitzgerald which the English brutally suppressed. The rebellion ended when the queen released Desmond from the Tower.

The third campaign, the Second Desmond Rebellion (1579–83), started when James Fitzmaurice Fitzgerald landed in Ireland with a thousand troops raised by the Pope. After they surrendered the next year at Smerwick, Earl Grey de Wilton's troops slew them in cold blood. Gerald Fitzgerald, the earl of Desmond escaped, and after leading a guerrilla campaign for three years, was murdered by the Clan Moriarty for an English reward of £1,000. His head was sent to the queen, and his body displayed in triumph on the walls of Cork Castle.

The last campaign, the Tyrone Rebellion (1594–1603), was the most significant, largely because it was fought in the context of the wider naval and continental conflict against Spain.[54] By 1594 Hugh O'Neill, second earl of Tyrone, had raised six thousand well-trained troops, for whom the thousand or so men the English had at Dublin were no match. Tyrone used his men to fight a guerrilla war. Exasperated, the English sent fifteen hundred men under Sir Henry Bagenal to relieve Blackwater Fort. Tyrone ambushed them at Yellow Ford, killing their commander and most of his troops. It was the worst defeat the English ever suffered in Ireland.

To ensure it was not repeated, the queen sent her favourite, Essex, to wage what one member of the privy council warned would be 'the longest, most chargeable, and most dangerous war'.[55] He landed in Dublin in April 1599 with the largest and best equipped army yet dispatched across the Irish Sea. Essex was a proven commander. 'By your own experience in the service of the Low Countries, Portugal and France,' grovelled Matthew Sutcliffe in the dedication to *The Practice, Proceedings, and Lawes of Armes* (1593), 'you both understand the practice of arms and the wants of soldiers.' Essex was so confident that he boasted, 'An army well chosen of 3,000 is able for numbers to undertake any action or fight with any army in the world.'[56] But instead of obeying Elizabeth's orders to invade Ulster, the bedrock of Tyrone's support, he marched around Munster before negotiating with the rebel earl. Stung by harsh reprimands from the queen, in September Essex absented his post without leave and rushed back to the court to throw himself on the queen's mercy. (It was not forthcoming, and seventeen months later Essex was executed for leading an abortive rebellion.)

The earl's folly proved a blessing in disguise because it led to the appointment of Charles Blount, Lord Mountjoy. Born in 1563, he had seen considerable action in the Low Countries and Brittany before succeeding Essex as commander of English forces in Ireland. Even though Essex opposed the appointment, telling the Privy Council that Mountjoy was 'too much drowned in book learning', he proved a highly practical general.[57] Before his appointment, a contemporary complained that English captains had loafed 'in great towns, feasting, banqueting and carousing with their dames'.[58] Now Mountjoy had them campaign throughout the winter, clearing vegetation from the edges of roads to thwart ambushes. He established a series of garrisons and waged several simultaneous offensives, provisioning his forces from ships, as he cut Ulster, the rebel heartland, in half. Because his soldiers were not crammed in barracks where germs easily spread, but were out in the fresh—albeit cold and wet—air, disease rates fell. To deny the enemy supplies he used a scorched-earth policy. Captain William Mostyn observed that Mountjoy beat the Irish 'by the cruelty of famine'.[59] Tyrone countered by improving the training and weapons of his troops, and sought help from Spain. But the landing of four thousand Spanish soldiers in Kinsale in September 1601 could not save Tyrone. After the Spanish capitulated the following January, the English murdered twelve hundred wounded prisoners (most of whom were Irish), and then they pursued eight hundred enemy survivors for two miles after which, one participant wrote home, the chase 'was left off, our men being tired with killing'. By the morrow the English had recovered their energies, hanging all the prisoners they could find. Three months later Tyrone surrendered.[60] He died an exile in Rome in 1619, still plotting to return to Ireland.

For many Englishmen service in Ireland was a fate worse than death. As a contemporary proverb maintained, 'better to be hanged at home than die like dogs in Ireland'.[61] Recruits were cruelly neglected. 'Many of his soldiers die wretchedly and woefully at Dublin, some whose feet and legs rotted off for want of shoes,' a government report noted of Sir Thomas North's company, adding 'yet were their names retained for the muster-roll.'[62] Of four thousand men sent to garrison Derry in 1566, only fifteen hundred were fit for duty after seven months: the town, a captain observed, was more 'a grave than a garrison'. The majority died from dysentery, a disease that did not ravage the native Irish, perhaps as Fynes Moryson, Mountjoy's secretary, suggested, because they drank locally distilled whiskey.[63]

As the Irish wars escalated, more and more conscripts were called up. On arriving at embarkation ports, they might mutiny rather than board ship. There were four mutinies at Chester, two in Bristol and London, and one each in Towcester and Ipswich. In the capital provost marshals were authorized 'to execute summary justice'.[64] In Bristol the mayor tried the ringleaders of one group, and sentenced them to be hanged before pardoning them on the gallows. Instead of thanking him for his efforts, the following year the Privy Council reprimanded the mayor for providing rations for those about to be shipped to Ireland: the food would be wasted: seasick conscripts would only puke it up. 'There was never beheld such strange creatures,' reported Bristol's authorities two years later, 'most of them either lame, diseased boys, or common rogues. Few of them have any clothes: small weak starved bodies, taken up in farms, market place and highways, to supply the place of better men kept at home.'[65]

At least the English saw these pathetic pressed men as men, unlike the Irish whom they thought of as subhumans (in much the same way as Germans in the Second World War thought of Jews as *Untermenschen* who could be exterminated without compunction). As Edmund Tremayne told the queen in his 'Notes on Ireland' (1571), the Irish were 'neither Papists or Protestants but rather such as have neither fear nor love of God in their hearts': thus there was no point in trying to win either their hearts or minds, or even treating them as fellow Christians.[66] Even their allies agreed: a Spanish Catholic officer who fought at Kinsale contended that the Irish were so base that he doubted whether Christ's death on the Cross was enough to redeem them. The English view that the Irish were not really human came down from the very top. Sometimes orders to kill were clouded by euphemisms. Captain George Flower was instructed to take a company to Bantry and to 'use all hostile prosecution upon the persons of the people as in such case of rebellion is accustomed'.[67] According to Edmund Spenser, his mentor, Lord Arthur Grey, the Lord Deputy of Ireland, regarded 'the life of Her Majesties [Irish] subjects no more than dogs'.[68] He boasted of having executed fifteen hundred leading Irishmen, not counting 'those of meaner sort'.[69] The English thought Irish women behaved like whores. They went about bareheaded—as did prostitutes back home. Fynes Moryson reported seeing Irish women urinate in mixed company, and then 'Wash their hands in cow dung.' Worse, the sluts would grind corn stark naked, pushing into the bread sacks any flour that had stuck 'upon their bellies, thighs or more unseemly parts'.[70] The English even accused the Irish of cannibalism. It was said that old women would light fires to attract cold starving orphans so they could eat them. Surgeon William Farmer described how Sir Arthur Chichester, whilst campaigning during the Tyrone Rebellion, came across five orphans who were devouring their mother, whom they had just roasted. After they explained that the English had stolen all their food, Chichester gave them vittles as well as money.[71]

Such generosity was rare: over the centuries far too many atrocities have blighted Anglo-Irish relations. In their attempt to conquer Ireland the Normans committed butcheries. For instance, in 1170 they executed seventy prisoners of war, throwing their bodies off a cliff, and fifteen years later sent the heads of a hundred rebels killed in Meath as booty to Dublin.[72] Through their casual cruelty the outrages of early modern Anglo-Irish wars remind one of the worst excesses of the Russian Front or the Pacific Campaign in the 1940s.[73] Some atrocities were committed in hot blood, making them more understandable, perhaps even excusable. In May 1567 at the Battle of Farsetmore, Donegal, an observer recalled that both sides 'proceeded to strike, mangle, slaughter and cut down one another'.[74] After the garrison of Dunboyne Castle surrendered in 1602, they were all hanged: eighty of them—men, women and boys—jam-packed from a fifteen-foot wooden beam, there being no convenient trees nearby.[75] Most cold-blooded atrocities were committed during what we would today call 'search and destroy' missions. Essex sent a patrol to punish Con Mackmilog who had killed thirty-five English settlers; the body of one he had boiled and fed to his dogs. The English repaid in like kind, by roasting Mackmilog to use him as dog food.[76] In 1597 Sir William Russell led a force through Glann-malhur, 'killing all that came in their way', and personally rewarded a sergeant who brought him an Irishman's head.[77] Three years later, Sergeant Major George Flower reported that near Cork his column 'got the heads of thirty seven notorious rebels beside others of less note'.[78] 'We have killed, burned, and spoiled all along the Lough,' Sir Arthur Chichester gloated to Mountjoy in May 1601, 'we have killed about a hundred people of all sorts, besides such as were burnt, how many I know not. We spare none of what quality or sex soever, and it has bred much terror in the people.'[79] Rather than rustle cattle, Captain Anthony Hungerford and Lieutenant Parker of the Leinster garrisons 'preferred to have some killing' and 'slew many churls, women and children'.

There was a rational justification for what was in effect English state-sponsored terrorism. Thomas Churchyard defended Sir Humphrey Gilbert's practice of forcing those who came to his tent to surrender to walk though a gauntlet of the heads of dead rebels by observing 'there was much blood saved through the terror.'[80]

Most atrocities, however, were the product of the nature of the war. As we have seen, the English dehumanized the enemy, making them easier to kill. The war, a vicious guerrilla struggle fought among wasteland and bogs, often in terrible rainy and chilly weather, made soldiers angry, ready to vent their spleen on the enemy or even on innocent civilians. Most English soldiers were draftees, ill-fed and equipped, often sick, usually cold and wet. They hated being in Ireland, and thus hated its inhabitants. Moreover, they did not see the Irish as real soldiers who fought fair. 'The Wars here is most painful,' remonstrated Captain John Zouch. 'We shall never fight with them unless they have a will to fight with us.'[81] Sir John Harrington, the political theorist, agreed, complaining that the Irish led the English in 'a Morris dance, by their tripping after their bagpipes, than any soldier-like exercise'. For much of the queen's reign Ireland was under martial law, so there were no legal limits on soldiers' behaviour.[82] Certainly officers did little to curb abuses. Anyway, asserted English commanders, the Irish were just as bad. In 1585 in County Antrim the Irish killed a thousand Scots soldiers and as many of their women and children as they could, so they were only getting their just deserts. As a final solution to the Irish problem Captain Barnaby Rich advocated castrating all the males, while Edmund Spenser, normally the kindest of men, preferred starving them to death. As he avowed in *The Faerie Queene*, Ireland could be civilized only through violence. Both Rich and Sir John Davies the Attorney General for Ireland, agreed that Ireland was 'A barbarous country [that] must first be broken by war before it will be capable of good government.'[83]

The Costs of War

Military statistics are notoriously hard to estimate. For instance, after the First Gulf War of 1992 the Pentagon, having used aerial photographs, electronic intercepts, computers, grave registration teams, newspaper and combat reports, had to admit that its estimate of enemy casualties was plus or minus 50 per cent. Estimates for early modern war are even more problematic. They can be given in vague terms such as 'few', 'many', or 'several thousand'. Or else an attempt can be made to use surviving evidence and the work of other analysts to come to a logical conclusion, while admitting to the weakness of the process. Because this is the way military intelligence officers work, it may be used by military historians.[84]

Estimates of the number of English and Welsh men who saw foreign service during the last third of Elizabeth's reign vary, being based on incomplete records.[85] We know from pretty good sources that between 1594 and 1602, 42,558 soldiers left English ports for Ireland—half of them from Chester. This figure does not include the large number of those who deserted before they arrived at the ports, nor those volunteers who made their own way to Ireland, but it does count veterans returning for additional tours of duty. Estimates of the total number of English and Welsh who actually served in Ireland range from thirty thousand to thirty-seven thousand. Because the total number of English troops in Ireland peaked at twenty thousand in 1593–1603, the top end of the range seems more likely and has thus been used.[86]

The most recent assessment of those who saw service on the continent is by David Trim, who estimates that between 1585 and 1603 the crown recruited 80,525 men for service there. If we reduce this figure by 10 per cent to take into account fictional soldiers listed on the roster for profit, known as 'dead pays', we get 72,472. In addition, according to Dr Trim, 48,066 men served mostly for the Dutch while a few fought for the Huguenots, neither of whom permitted 'dead pays'. In 1586, 68 per cent of the infantry in the Dutch Army were British.[87]

At sea perhaps forty thousand sailed in the Royal Navy, including 15,925 who took part in the Armada.[88] On average a hundred and fifty privateering ships with, say, an average crew of fifty left British ports each year between 1585 and 1603, giving a total of 135,000 men. Of course, the majority of these were veterans, many of them from the Royal Navy, discharged after the Armada of 1588, but assuming that a quarter were not, then it would mean that 33,750 served solely as privateers. This gives us a total of 73,750 with service at sea.[89]

The figures for land service in England are even more problematic. During the Armada campaign 90,000 served in the trained bands, 200,000 in the militia and another 16,000 in private feudal levies giving a total of 306,000. Duplications for domestic service are impossible to obtain. Many of those who served in the militia also served in other capacities at different times. A few of the trained bands actually fought overseas. On the other hand, since the figures for domestic service are for 1588, they do not take into account men who served and left before that date, or joined afterwards. Thus it would not be unreasonable to assume—for want of better data—that these figures balanced each other out, and that 306,000 men saw domestic service. Totals for military service in the last third of Elizabeth's reign are given in Table 1 below.

What do these rough estimates mean in terms of the proportion of men who served in the armed forces? At the end of Elizabeth's reign England had a population of 3.9 million, of whom about 975,000 were males aged

Table 1 Military service, c.1586–c.1603

Foreign	Numbers	Death rate	Deaths
Irish Service	37,000	50%	18,500
Continent, royal	72,472	37.5%	27,177
Dutch/Huguenot	48,066	37.5%	18,025
Royal Navy	40,000	33.3%	13,333
Privateers	33,750	33.3%	11,250
Total	231,288		88,285
Domestic			
Trained bands	90,000	3%	2,700
Militia	200,000	2%	4,000
Feudal levies	16,000	2%	360
Total	306,000		7,060
Total foreign and domestic	537,288		95,345

18–39. Of this military pool 23.7 per cent saw foreign service and 31.9 per cent domestic service, making a total of 55.6 per cent with some military service. While these figures are advanced with a fair degree of trepidation, I can take comfort in the fact that they support Shakespeare's contention that military service was one of the 'seven ages of man'. It was not, to be sure, as universal as 'mewling infancy', 'creeping schoolward', or old age 'sans everything', but some sort of military service was a stage through which over half of the Bard's compatriots passed.[90]

Whatever the real figures may be for the late sixteenth century—and we will never know for sure—one thing is certain. A huge number of people, English, Welsh, Scots and Irish, men, women and children, took part and suffered in the wars of the last third of Elizabeth's reign. How many of them died? Again there are only hints. During the Cadiz expedition of 1596, disease killed 114 of *Dreadnought*'s three hundred crew, leaving but eighteen fit enough to dock the ship when it returned to Plymouth.[91] In 1574 John Lingham listed the names of seventy-four English officers killed fighting in the Low Countries. Of a sample of 475 captains who served in Ireland, 65 (13.7 per cent) died in combat and 50 (10.5 per cent) were severely wounded; no figures have survived for those who perished of disease. Fifty-five English captains died serving the Dutch. Hiram Morgan suggests that at least fifty thousand, and perhaps as many as a hundred thousand, perished in Elizabeth's Irish Wars—most of them Irish.[92] Among soldiers death from disease was ubiquitous, running as high as 50 per cent a year. Edmund Spenser, the poet who fought in Ireland as a young man, noted in 1580 that of every thousand 'lusty able men' who came to Ireland, half were dead from disease or poor food within six months.[93] Sir John Smythe alleged that only one in forty of Essex's sick troops evacuated to England survived, so bad was their medical care. Fifteen thousand set out in the 'counter armada' of 1589; six thousand returned. The three thousand men whom Sir John Norris took to Brittany in 1591 required eight thousand replacements over the next three years, while the four thousand troops who landed in Normandy with the earl of Essex in 1591 needed ten thousand replacements over two years.[94] After seven months only six hundred of the eleven hundred men sent to Derry in 1566 were still alive, and a quarter of the four hundred sick were not expected to survive. In three months campaigning in Ireland, Essex lost between 12,175 and 17,300 men.[95]

We can make better sense of these episodic figures by estimating death rates and applying them to the totals given in Table 1 above. The results are summarized in the centre and right-hand columns.

Ireland was an especially lethal place in which to serve, so a 50 per cent death rate seems reasonable to apply to the thirty-seven thousand men who soldiered there. When Lord Mountjoy estimated in 1601 that three-quarters of the Irish who left to fight as mercenaries would never return home, he was including those who died or settled overseas.[96] If we assume that half of these Irish mercenaries died, we get a 37.5 per cent death rate. Applied to the 72,472 men who served on the continent in the queen's service and the 48,066 who fought there as Dutch or Huguenot mercenaries, this gives us 27,177 and 18,025 dead respectively—a total of 45,202 who perished on the continent. This death rate of 37.5 per cent seems reasonable, since Professor Rodger posits that a third of those who served at sea died.[97] So when this proportion is applied to Royal Navy sailors and privateers, we get 13,333 and 11,250 dead respectively, a total of 24,583 who perished at sea. Home service on land was far safer, with perhaps a 2 per cent rate for the militia and 3 per cent for the trained bands (who tended to serve longer), and for feudal levies. Table 1 suggests that in late Elizabethan England, 95,345 died directly or indirectly as a result of military service. This is 10.2 per cent of the military pool, or 2.44 per cent of the total population. In contrast 2.59 per cent of the total population died as a result of the First World War and 0.94 per cent as a result of the Second.[98]

Because governments are more concerned about their money than about young men's lives, better data exist on the financial costs of Elizabeth's wars. Between 1588 and 1605 England spent roughly £4,500,000 on defence, about £300,000 a year. About £1,700,000 went on the navy. Before 1580 naval expenditures averaged about £17,000 a year. In 1588, the year of the Armada, they reached £150,057, dropping to £31,050 in 1591, before peaking at £157,602 in 1598. The conquest of Ireland was even more expensive. According to the accounts of Sir Julius Caesar, James I's Under-Treasurer of the Exchequer, £1,845,696 was spent there from October 1595 to March 1603, which would agree with a recent estimate of £1,924,000 from 1594 to 1603.[99] This would make the estimate of Lord Treasurer Lionel Cranfield, earl of Middlesex, that over three million pounds were spent conquering Ireland too high. War on the continent, which required sophisticated equipment, was even more expensive. In 1588 Thomas Digges, Muster Master General of English forces in the Low Countries, reported that the annual cost of an infantry company was £1,686 10s. 3d.; of a cavalry troop, £3,700; and of an artillery train, £68,396 18s.[100] No wonder the queen complained that the war in the Netherlands was 'a sieve that spends as it receives'.[101] Corruption added to Her Majesty's costs. Half of the two thousand men on the rolls of the Connaught garrison in 1597 were dead pays.[102] But this was small change compared to the peculations of some of the queen's ministers. Three out of her seven Treasurers at War were infamously corrupt. One, Sir George Carey, embezzled £150,000 in eight years, in addition to the 40,000 ducats he supposedly looted during the 1596 Cadiz expedition.[103] According to Fynes Moryson, Mountjoy's secretary (and thus a highly reliable source), the queen 'was incredibly abused' by the mendacity of the generals who fought for her in Ireland.[104]

A Military Culture

Considering the time and effort, the blood and money that England spent on war in the last third of Elizabeth's reign, it is not surprising that, as J. S. Nolan has put it, 'The Militarization of the Elizabethan State' took place.[105] The change was so profound that some have—incorrectly—called it 'a military revolution'.[106] Nowhere was the growth of a military culture more obvious than on the stage, particularly when compared to painting or woodcuts, where, unlike on the continent, military themes were rare.[107] There were sixteen battle scenes in the thirteen extant plays the Queen's Men put on during the 1580s and 1590s. Shakespeare's *Henry V*, perhaps the greatest war play ever, was written and performed during the spring of 1599, when Essex was preparing to invade Ireland.[108] Shakespeare, Middleton, Marlowe, Jonson, Beaumont and Fletcher all knew that war—like patriotism—sold tickets. Christopher Marlowe is said to have used *Instructions for the Warres* by Raimond Fourquevaux, the French soldier and diplomat, in writing *Tamburlaine*. In his play, *The Famous Chronicle of Edward the First* (1593), George Peale has the Queen Mother boast:[109]

What warlike nation, trained in feats of arms
What barbarous people, stubborn and untam'd . . .
Erst have not quak'd and trembled at the name
Of Britain?

Stage effects—the louder the better—could bring down the house, both figuratively and literally. Crowds flocked to the theatre to see and hear them. Plays became so violent, noisy and dangerous that a 1574 proclamation condemned the 'sundry slaughter and mayhemmings of the Queen's subjects' caused 'by engines, weapons, and powder in plays'.[110] Such concerns about the audience's safety were not groundless. During a 1594 performance at the Rose Theatre (probably of Marlowe's *Tamburlaine*), an actor fired a musket that he believed was unloaded, and accidently killed a child and pregnant woman in the audience.[111] In 1613, during a performance of Shakespeare's *Henry VIII*, pyrotechnics set fire to the thatch roof, burning the Globe down to the ground in two hours.

No playwright portrayed war better than Shakespeare. So good was he that Duff Cooper, biographer and Conservative politician, argued (without a shred of evidence and with more than a scintilla of snobbery) that the Bard must have fought with Leicester on the continent as a sergeant, the provincial lad from Stratford-upon-Avon not being well-born enough to be an officer! Shakespeare must have talked to soldiers, and read their memoirs. For instance, he lifted the plot for *Twelfth Night* from Barnaby Rich's *Riche: His Farewell to Militarie Profession* (1581).[112]

War made good comedy. From Shakespeare's Falstaff to television's *Dad's Army*, England's civilian soldiers have been portrayed, at best, as figures of fun or, at worst, to quote Barnaby Rich, 'Drunkards and such other ill disposed persons'.[113] The recruiting scenes in both parts of *Henry IV* are hilarious, although one suspects that Thomas Mulsho, a gentleman from Northamptonshire, would not have enjoyed them. In the summer of 1597 (at about the same time as Shakespeare was writing the play), Mulsho complained to a friend how hard it was to fulfil his quota, twenty of his draft from Finedon having run away before the recruiting officer could interview them. 'I am at my wit's end,' Mulsho concluded.[114]

An indication of the impact of Shakespeare's portrayal of war was that years after his death in 1616, soldiers on active duty repeated the rhythms and themes of his plays. In the dedicatory verses to *The Master Gunner* (1625) Captain John Smith wrote 'All the world is but a martial stage', while in the text Robert Norton observed that England was 'strongly situated by nature, entrenched with a broad dike'. Fourteen years later, as he crossed the River Tweed at the start of the First Bishops' War, Sir John Suckling, the poet, recalled *Henry IV, Part I*, written 'by My Friend Mr. William Shakespeare'. The outbreak of the Civil War reminded Robert, the third earl of Essex, of Hotspur's soliloquy on the dangers of rebellion. (The Bard's eloquence was not enough, however, to stop the earl from accepting command of the rebel army.) 'We are both on a stage,' Sir Ralph Hopton, the royalist general, wrote to his friend Sir William Waller, the parliamentary commander, after the Civil War broke out, 'and must act out the parts which are assigned to us in this tragedy.'[115]

The popularity of war on the stage was matched by that of military manuals, sixty-six of which were published in Elizabeth's reign.[116] Obviously the main purpose of such manuals was to train troops, a subject discussed in Chapter 2. But they also shed light on the military culture. No self-help manuals, not even those on religion, sold better than those on war. For instance, Matthew Sutcliffe's *The Practice, Proceedings and Lawes of Armes* (1593), it was claimed, sold 1,200 copies in eight days.[117] Such sales reflected a growth in the general market for books caused by the expansion of the universities and inns of court, as well as the doubling of the literacy rate for the yeomanry. Yet readers purchased military manuals for the same reason that people today read military history and novels, or watch war

films or the History Channel. As Edmund Plumme wrote in his introduction to Robert Ward's *Animadversions of Warre* (1639), 'Here may you fight
by Book, and never bleed.' Such works naturally appealed to young male
readers. 'I ever from my tender years have delighted to hear histories read
that did treat of actions and deeds of arms,' recalled Sir John Smythe,
adding that as an undergraduate at Oxford, 'I gave myself up to the reading
of many other histories and books treating of matters of war.'[118]

The healthy market for military books then—as now—attracted
professional authors. For professional soldiers writing frequently posed
a challenge. Confessing that he was an 'unlettered man', Geoffrey Gates
had a ghostwriter pen *The Defence of the Militarie Profession* in 1579.[119]
All too often, hacks copied from each other, or slavishly repeated the
mantras of classical writers. There was 'not a more distasteful sound', wrote
Francis Markham (who claimed thirty years' military experience), than
listening to so-called 'book soldiers', who asserted they were experts on
war, even though they had never heard a shot fired in anger.[120] In *The
Fruits of Long Experience* (1604) Barnaby Rich likened them to 'women's
tailors', who 'can devise every day a new fashion'. Shakespeare dismissed
pundits who wrote 'bookish theoric' as producing 'mere prattle without
practice', and scorned those authors (such as himself) who had[121]

> Never set a squadron in the field
> Nor the division of a battle knows
> More than a spinster.

The venom of such attacks on book soldiers may well have been the
product of the paradoxes inherent in writing about war. If an amateur
wrote about war without first-hand knowledge, or slavishly followed
classical precedents, and got it wrong, then men could lose their lives.
Because war is so loathsome and may attract 'the scum of the earth', some
assumed that military authors were just as bad. In *The Solace for the Souldier
and Sailour* (1591) Simon Harward, a military chaplain with combat
experience, wrote that soldiers lived a 'most wicked and dissolute life'. The
same year Sir William Garrard's *The Arte of Warre* called 'the profession of
arms a vile and damnable occupation'. William Cecil, Lord Burghley,
arguably the most powerful peer of his time, told his son that a member
of the military profession 'can hardly be an honest man or a good
Christian'.[122] A few writers countered such criticisms by arguing that war
was divinely ordained. John Elliot, the translator of Bertrand de Loque's
Discourses of Warre (1591), claimed it was 'grounded on God's Holy
word'.[123] Just as God 'hath appointed Life and Death, Summer and
Winter, Day and Night,' wrote James Achesone in *The Military Garden: or*

Instructions for all Young Soldiers (1629), 'so hath he made Peace and War.' Sometimes military men countered attacks on their profession by adopting such a high moral tone that they appeared ridiculous. 'Serve God daily, love one another, preserve your vittles, beware of fire, and keep good company,' commanded Sir John Hawkins's standing orders for his 1562 slaving expedition. No wonder, on reading them, Queen Elizabeth sniffed, 'God's Death! This fool went out a soldier and came home a divine.'[124]

The second paradox concerning war was that soldiers and sailors were conservative folk, who plied their trade in the hierarchical and deferential society of Tudor England. They studied past wars to win future ones. In their manuals writers such as Barnaby Rich, Thomas Proctor, Thomas Digges, Edward Hobby, John Smythe and Thomas Styward looked back to Greece and Rome for inspiration as well as legitimacy. At sea Sir Francis Drake compared his 1587 attack on Cadiz to Hannibal's achievements.[125] Yet war is usually won by the side with the latest technology and methods. 'Through mutation of time, and invention of man's wits the practice of war changes,' noted Henry Barret in 1549. A generation later Thomas Lodge agreed: 'All things change, the means, the men, the arms. Our strategies now differ from the old.'[126] When a gentleman praised the old ways of fighting, Robert Barret reproved him in 1598: 'Sir, that was then and now is now.' The art of war had 'greatly altered, the which we must follow,' wrote Captain Roger Williams, 'Otherwise we must repent it too late.'[127]

Like modern social scientists, military writers and practitioners tried to define war as a science with its own theoretical and historical foundations— what Captain Fluellen in *Henry V* called 'the disciplines of the war'.[128] 'It is not only Experience and Practice which maketh a soldier,' wrote 'Captain J. S.' in his *Military Discipline and Practice, or the Art of War* (1589), 'but the knowledge most specially learned by reading History.'[129]

The officer corps was growing not just in expertise but in size. Whereas in 1569 there was hardly a captain ready to train the militia, within nineteen years there were at least two hundred available, all veterans of the Irish and continental wars. 'The place of the captain is not lightly to be considered,' wrote Giles Clayton in *The Approved order of Martial Discipline* (1591), 'for that upon his skill and knowledge depends the safety or loss of men's lives.' The—quite literally—vital need for skill and knowledge of war from self-made captains in a society that during peace valued birth and hierarchy, produced conflicts between civilians and those whom Professor Manning has called 'the swordsmen'.[130] Humphrey Barwick's experience at the Siege of Leith in 1560 illustrates these tensions. Having joined the army as a private, through hard work and merit Barwick became a captain in twelve years. During the siege he suggested to the future Lord Grey de Wilton 'in a courteous manner' that he had sited his camp in a dangerous position. 'Whereat he seemed to be offended,' telling him to mind his own business. Soon afterwards the Scots attacked: Grey was wounded and his men were routed—much to Barwick's *schaden-freude*.[131]

Notwithstanding the claims of old soldiers, such as Francis Markham, that 'the fittest man to make a soldier is a perfect gentleman', most officers did not enjoy great social prestige.[132] The percentage of peers with military experience fell from 75 per cent in Henry VIII's reign to 25 per cent in Elizabeth's. The well-born who did serve were sometimes too arrogant or careless to take the proper professional precautions. Because Sir Philip Sidney refused to wear his armour, he died in great agony at Zutphen in 1586 three weeks after a musket bullet shattered his thigh bone.[133] Thomas Moffett, who had fought with Sidney and Essex (two other puissant peers), once rhetorically asked whether the sprigs of the nobility were 'the sons of Mars'. 'Nay, the nephews of Venus,' was his answer.[134] No wonder Humphrey Barwick, who in 1594 described himself a 'Gentleman, Soldier, Captain', sardonically observed that 'it is better for a man to be accounted a good soldier in the court than to be the best soldier in the field.'[135]

The queen was ambivalent towards soldiers. Personally she was very attached to John and Edward Norris, and Peregrine Bertie, baron Willoughby, adding notes to them in her own hand to state letters. She was fond of—some say in love with—Leicester, was infatuated with Essex, and charmed by swashbucklers such as Raleigh. But at the same time she resented those military men who used her purse to prove their masculinity. While Essex might boast that 'No nation breeds a warmer blood for war' than the English, Elizabeth was the one who footed the bill both financially and politically. So she forbad the London printers on pain of death from publishing pamphlets that Essex had hacks scribble glorifying his achievements during the Cadiz expedition.[136] Occasionally, Elizabeth sympathized with the rank and file. 'It frets me not a little that the poor soldiers who hourly venture life shall want their due,' she wrote to Leicester on 19 July 1587.[137] More common was the view she once expressed to the French ambassador that soldiers were 'but thieves and ought to hang'.[138] Soldiers filched her money, either through embezzlement or strident demands. They were uncouth. When Captain Roger Williams was allowed into court to present a claim for back pay, the queen, tiring of his arguments, cut him off. 'Faugh, Williams, I prithee thee be gone. Thy boots stink.'

'Tut, madam, tis my suit that stinks,' the old soldier replied.[139]

After the queen's death, Sir Walter Raleigh (who had sense enough not to do so while she was alive) grumbled that if Elizabeth had 'believed her men of war as she did her scribes', England would have thrashed Spain. 'But Her Majesty did all by halves.'[140] Later historians and warriors have

agreed. Sir John Fortescue said she did not like soldiers and treated them
badly. Field Marshal Montgomery thought that 'England's part in the
history of land war in the sixteenth century was practically nil'. According
to G. R. Elton the cost of war was as monumental as its benefits were
meagre. He blamed the queen, who 'displayed qualities of indecisiveness,
procrastination, variability of mind, cheeseparing that went far to ensure
the failure of the various enterprises attempted'.[141]

Recently, such negative views of the last third of Elizabeth's reign have
been challenged.[142] During these years England beat the Spanish,
completed the conquest of Ireland, and, by helping the Dutch win independence, may well have ensured the survival of Protestantism. Englishmen
recognized that the Royal Navy dominated the seas and the implications
of seapower. 'Whosoever commands the sea commands the trade,' wrote
Raleigh, 'whosoever commands the trade of the world commands the
riches of the world, and consequently the world itself.'[143] Elizabeth not
only laid the foundations of English hegemony, but did so remarkably
cheaply—at least in comparative terms. To be sure, the £4.5 million–5.5
million that England spent on war in the last third of the queen's reign
was no paltry sum. Yet it represented just 3–4 per cent of its Gross
National Product, as compared to the 8–9 per cent the Spanish and the
16 per cent the Netherlands expended. During the 1540s Henry VIII
spent £650,000, or 260 per cent of his annual income of £250,000, on the
French war; in 1600 Elizabeth spent £320,000, or 86 per cent of her
annual income of £374,000, conquering Ireland. In sum, Elizabethan
warfare obtained great results at a sustainable cost—something that was
to elude the queen's immediate successors.

CHAPTER 4

WHY MEN FOUGHT

That he which hath no stomach for this fight,
Let him depart; his passport shall be made
And crowns for convoy put into his purse:
We would not die in that man's company.
Henry V, IV, iii, 40–43

A S THEY ANTICIPATE THEIR FIRST EXPERIENCE OF COMBAT MOST
soldiers ask themselves two fundamental questions. First, what really
makes a person fight when he—and today she—is in combat, and, second,
will I fight and not run away? To paraphrase Shakespeare, they ask what
gives humans the stomach to fight, and do I have it? These question are
very different from asking why nations or groups go to war, or why individuals join the armed forces in the first place. They relate to why people
actually fight, kill and run the risk of being killed. The answers are complicated and consist of two components. The first is external: it depends on
good leadership, and is mainly coercive. Far from letting men depart home
with 'crowns for convoy', armies do all they can, including inflicting the
death penalty, to stop men from running away. The second is internal,
being based on a person's sense of self-worth as a human being—on what
has been called 'honour'—and on the fact that as social creatures we crave
the respect of the small group in which we live. If we lose either or both,
we are so shamed that we come to fear that no man would wish to die in
our company. Just before a skirmish in Flanders, Thomas Churchyard, the
Tudor captain, played on this sentiment. 'I asked of my company if they
would fight, and desired such as would be in their houses to depart.' All
stayed and fought.[1]

The challenge of getting men—for until recently fighting has been an
overwhelmingly male activity—to face the test of battle is as old as war
itself. William Patten, a veteran of the Battle of Pinkie (1547), noted that
fighting was 'quite against the quiet nature of man'. 'A rational army,'
thought Charles-Louis, baron de Montesquieu, the seventeenth-century

French philosopher, 'would run away.'[2] Captain Roger Williams thought three things made men overcome their natural fear and stay: 'a good chief, a good purse, and good justice'.[3]

A few men knew no fear: happy warriors, they loved fighting and killing. At the Siege of Rouen (1591) Sir Thomas Coningsby enjoyed watching cannon balls smash houses, pass through walls, and ricochet all over the place: 'It was a pleasure to behold,' he noted in his diary. George Lauder, the author of *The Scottish Soldier* (1629), revelled in carnage:[4]

> Let me still hear the Cannons thundering Voice,
> In terror threatening ruin; that sweet noise
> Rings in my ears more pleasing than the sound
> Of any music consort that can be found . . .
> Then to see legs and arms torn ragged fly
> And bodies gasping all dismembered lie.

A contemporary called Sir Simon Harcourt, who was killed fighting in Dublin in 1642 after twenty years of very active service as a soldier of fortune, a man 'who loved always to be in action'. After his fourth campaign Colonel Blackadder wrote to his wife: 'I still have reason to say that the time of fighting and action, and the prospects of danger, are the pleasantest times I have.' Corporal Matthew Bishop wrote to his spouse, 'My Dear, you cannot conceive the Pleasure I have enjoyed in the last campaign.' He continued, 'I longed to be in action, for my nature was such that without it my Spirits fell.' After surveying the carnage at Malplaquet, where the allies lost 26 per cent dead and wounded, Matthew Bishop was more stoical, taking consolation in Williams III's adage that 'every ball that kills or wounds has his commission before it is fired'.[5] Some soldiers welcomed war. In 1630 Ensign Edmund Verney, a mercenary on the continent, wrote home, 'We hear that you are likely to have war with France. Tis brave news. 'Twere sport for us to hear that all the world were in combustion, then we would not lack for work. O 'tis a blessed trade!' Sir Thomas Birch recalled that during the Civil Wars some of his comrades actually opposed negotiations that might end the war 'too soon'.[6]

'Pay well, hang well'

Sir Ralph Hopton, the royalist Civil War commander, was convinced that two of the best ways to make men fight were to 'pay well' and to 'hang well'.[7] Carrots and sticks have always been good ways of motivating people. Pay was particularly efficacious. From the Scots campaign of 1560

Sir Ralph Sadler wrote to Queen Elizabeth that when soldiers 'lack their wages, they will serve with the worst will'.[8] During the Siege of Denbigh in May 1646, a group of parliamentary officers described their troopers as 'most unreasonable men if they are disappointed in pay'. Francis Gamull, a royalist colonel, sardonically observed, 'money best stoppeth all discontented men's mouths.'[9] Most mutinies were, in truth, strikes against poor or no pay.

The military historian Sir John Keegan once remarked that alcohol and the prospect of plunder played a much larger part in getting the British soldier (and sailor) to fight than most commanders would care to admit.[10] In addition to being high in the calories that active service requires, in war and peace alcohol makes men violent. (In the seventeenth century at least a third of civilian murders were committed under the influence of drink.)[11] Before combat getting drunk together helped men bond; during battle liquor invoked Dutch courage; and afterwards it numbed memories, soothing post-combat stress.

Once fighting started, the prospect of plunder became a much stronger incentive to fight than provisions or pay. As Rudyard Kipling, that most astute observer of the British soldier, put it:[12]

> Ow the loot!
> Bloomin' loot!
> That's the thing to make the boys git up an' shoot!

Looting was one way in which the soldier could lord it over civilians, who normally looked down upon him. It was a legitimate, or semi-legal, form of stealing—sometimes of goods that were valued more as trophies of domination than for their market worth. Ben Jonson, the playwright, boasted not just of having killed an enemy soldier in single combat during his service in the Netherlands in 1591, but of having 'taken optima spolia from him'. Jonson, like most soldiers, would admit that looting was fun. After storming Sherborne Castle, Dorset, in 1645, the roundheads started to massacre the defenders, but stopped when they discovered 'a great store of treasure'. Afterwards an observer noted that 'five shillings gotten in the way of spoil from the enemy gives them more content than twenty shillings by way of reward in an orderly manner.'[13] Looting could raise morale. During the 1589 assault on Lisbon, Sir Francis Drake reported that lack of food had demoralized the troops, 'but if God will bless us with . . . reasonable booty for our soldiers and mariners, all will take good heart again.' Bounteous booty cheered Donald McBane during the Blenheim Campaign of 1704. 'We plundered and lived a jolly life,' he wrote, 'being in an enemies country we had liberty to do as we pleased.' But looters could themselves be looted. In 1702 during the Siege of Rota, Matthew Bishop 'found' sixty pieces of eight, only to be robbed of them by comrades when he was asleep. Perhaps this explains why Bishop was so censorious of the Guards who at Malplaquet in 1709 'behaved themselves like black-guards by plundering their own dead ... before they were cold or quite dead'.[14] Sometimes looters were hanged. But proclamations threatening death failed to deter many. Too common was the attitude Captain Henry Herbert reported in 1672: 'Our men were forbidden to plunder but if they found any that was not too hot nor too heavy, they would have valued the proclamations no more than the Ten Commandments.'[15]

Those who broke the Commandments—or, more pertinent, the army's articles of war—had to be judged promptly and punished severely. When a man entered the armed forces he surrendered many of his civil rights. He had to. War is a harsh environment. Lawyers are bad enough in the barrack room: they are fatal on the battlefield. That is why John Cruso maintained that it was better 'for a soldier to meet a glorious death in battle than a shameful one at the end of a rope'.[16] Punishments worked. Sir James Turner observed with irony that in 1651, after two or three Scots soldiers had been hanged for plundering and robbery, the regula-tions against such activities 'were well enough observed'.[17] Therefore, most military crimes were punished physically, either through whipping or running the gauntlet, or with death. It was best to begin harshly. When the earl of Pembroke invaded France in 1557, he brought a 'hangman with all his necessaries'. 'Violent and bloody men' such as soldiers, wrote William Jenkyn in 1656, 'fear not hell so much as the halter.'[18] At the start of the 1596 attack on Cadiz a soldier was executed for murder and a lieu-tenant cashiered for corruption. The admiral's physician, Roger Marbeck, recorded that 'the severe execution of justice at the very first did breed such a deep terror' that there was no further trouble.[19] The expedition was a great success. Ruthless punishments not only deterred men from running away during combat, but kept them fighting, sometimes to well beyond the bitter end.

Court martials, panels of officers, administered justice quickly and without many formalities. In Hampshire between December 1643 and May 1645 court martials executed nineteen soldiers—thirteen for desertion, and two apiece for murder, robbery and mutiny. Between 22 April and 20 December 1644 in Sir William Waller's parliamentary army, court martials tried thirty soldiers—nine for plunder or robbery, six for mutiny, five for desertion, five for neglect of duty, three for murder and two for disobedience. Of those convicted, eleven were sentenced to be hanged, one was shot, six were cashiered, while eight suffered physical punishment. In order to coerce men to fight, executions were more common in war than in peace. For instance, between September 1651 and January 1652 a court martial in the Dundee area tried fifty-five men, of whom only two were executed. Of the rest it reprimanded ten, cashiered two, imprisoned three, referred two to higher authority, flogged twenty-eight (with a rather high average of forty-one lashes), and acquitted eight.[20] Over half a century later, in 1708 in the Low Countries nineteen soldiers were court-martialled for desertion. Seven were acquitted, twelve were sentenced to death, seven of them with recommendations of clemency. General John Churchill, duke of Marlborough, accepted the court martial's recommendations. He spared John Muddy's life because it was his first offence and, as his captain Alexander Ruthven wrote, he was 'a weak and silly man'. But Marlborough signed Samuel Cluse's and John Hill's death warrants since this was their third conviction for desertion.[21] For home-based troops the monarch determined who would get clemency. Queen Anne preferred to leave the decision to chance. Of a group of forty-five deserters in the Isle of Wight condemned to death, she used the roll of the dice to determine the six who would suffer the ultimate punishment. George I reviewed the records, pardoning twenty-four of the forty soldiers sentenced to death in 1716.[22]

Court martials and executions were dreadful for all concerned. In 1708 Captain Blackadder wrote in his diary, 'Attended a court-martial, a very unpleasant part of my duty, prosecuting a deserter for his life.' The trooper, a member of Blackadder's own company and a repeat offender, was sentenced to death. 'Awoke most of the night, my thoughts taken up with that poor wretch,' his diary ran. 'I attended the poor creature at his death. He seemed penitent.'[23]

More effective than the death penalty in stopping men from running away in battle was putting them in a position where it was almost physically impossible to do so. In the early modern battlefield men were never on their own. Infantry stood in lines several dozen long, and from two to six deep. To use a phrase from the American Civil War, they were in effect locked in a moving iron box from which it was very hard to escape, with battle-proven veterans on the flanks, the enemy to the front and sergeants to the rear with poleaxes to dispatch any who tried to make a break. Because soldiers were part of a group, who fired together, there was no problem about the reluctant failing to discharge their weapons.[24]

'Lead well'

In addition to rewards and punishment, Sir Ralph Hopton believed that a third factor made men fight, advising his officers to 'Lead well'. Leadership has always been crucial in persuading men to remain in combat, which as Clausewitz observed is 'the province of danger'. Leaders must also make their troops take actions, such as firing weapons or manoeuvring, and prevent them from becoming paralyzed by terror. 'Sometimes fear doth seize men,' recalled the veteran James Touchet, earl of Castlehaven, in 1690, 'that they know not what to do.' Conquering panic was so crucial to a leader's job that an Elizabethan military manual advised 'Let every great commander vomit at the scent of fear.'[25]

The question of effective leadership has always preoccupied military thinkers—by the mid-1980s some four thousand volumes on the topic had been published, and a 2009 Google search came up with twenty-four million hits for 'leadership'.[26] Leadership is hard to teach and even harder to define: yet most soldiers know it when they see it, especially when displayed by their own officers. Sometimes attempts to define leadership can be so broad as to lack utility. John Keegan argued that the 'big man', the larger than life person, makes a good leader. Charles Wilson, baron Moran, who served as a front-line medical officer in the First World War (and as Churchill's doctor in the Second), observed that 'The art of command is the art of dealing with human nature.' Again, the British Army's adage that 'There are no bad soldiers, only bad officers' is as vague as Roger Boyle's comment of 1677 that 'I very seldom saw the English soldiers flinch if their officers were good.'[27]

What, then, makes a good officer? In 1944 the US Army asked that question of its soldiers. Thirty-one per cent replied courage and example; 26 per cent pep talks, humour and keeping subordinates informed; 23 per cent concern for their men's welfare; and only 5 per cent friendliness and informality.[28] Remarkably, this tallies with the definitions of leadership from prominent Elizabethan military thinkers. Roger Williams listed first, combat experience; second, bravery; third, loyalty to one's own men; and fourth, liberality and generosity, as the qualities most needed for a successful leader. John Cruso listed experience, valour, authority and felicity, with which Barnaby Rich agreed, adding four more of his own: justice, fortitude, prudence and temperance.[29] Thus war (as I have argued in this book and elsewhere) in many ways remains remarkably constant. Take, for instance, one aspect of junior leadership. In 1727 Major General Humphrey Bland, a veteran of the Wars of the Spanish Succession, advised young lieutenants 'that the private soldiers when they are about to go into Action form their Notions of the Dangers from the outward appearance of their officers. . . .In Order to dissipate their Fears and fortify their Courage, the Officer should assume a Serene and Cheerful air.'[30] A Second World War platoon commander said almost the same thing. He described his role in battle as 'essentially histrionic . . . to feign a casual and cheerful optimism to create an illusion of normality and make it seem as if there was nothing in the least strange about the outrageous things one was asked to do.'[31]

Courage is the first quality demanded from all leaders, no matter their rank. Proven bravery helps a junior leader convince men to follow him into danger, while it gives a senior commander the moral authority to send men to their deaths. Lacking long-distance communications, such as radio, early modern leaders at all levels were expected to be heroes, getting involved in the actual fighting to inspire their troops. As Sir Philip Sidney, perhaps the most heroic figure of Elizabeth's reign, noted: 'A brave captain is a root, out of which, as branches, the courage of his soldiers doth spring.' Sir Francis Vere recognized this at the Battle of Nieuport (1600). Wounded in the leg and, fifteen minutes later the thigh, he refused to complain or see a surgeon, 'for I knew if I left the place my men would instantly quail.'[32]

Courage in itself was not enough. Anticipating the duke of Wellington's adage that 'There is nothing on earth so stupid as a gallant officer,' Barnaby Rich observed in 1578 that 'It is not requisite that every private captain … should rashly enter into attempts.' Yet a first-rate commander must know when to take action, for as James Touchet noted in 1680, 'Great Advantages in War are rarely offered, and for the most part soon past.'[33] A good leader must share like dangers with his men. 'I will run the same fortunes and hazards with you,' Major General Philip Skippon promised the London trained bands in November 1642 before the Battle of Turnham Green.[34] Half a dozen years later, in 1648, Oliver Cromwell reminded the roundheads how 'he had oftimes ventured his life with them, and they with him.'[35] Marlborough always rode into battle on a white horse wearing a shining scarlet uniform with a sash, not, as he explained to his wife, from vanity, but 'to deserve and keep the kindness of this army, I must let them see that when I expose them I would not exempt myself.'[36]

A good leader not only courted danger: he scorned it. For instance, at the Siege of Maastricht in 1673 the Prince of Orange (later William III) was hit in the arm, which nigh panicked his soldiers. So, George Carleton recalled, 'he took off his hat with the wounded arm, and smiling, waved it to show those there was no danger.' He displayed similar sangfroid in the face of peril, admitting on being wounded at the Battle of the Boyne (1690) to have lost 'near half a spoonful of blood'. William also empathized with his men. During the same battle, as he watched the Dutch Guards receive an attack from James II's cavalry, he whispered, 'My poor Guards, My poor Guards, My poor Guards.'[37]

Leaders paid a price—in their own blood. One way of showing this is to compare the ratio of killed and wounded among officers and other

ranks. The higher the ratio the more intense the fighting, and the degree
to which officers hazarded their lives. During the Civil Wars, of a sample
of seventy-six senior commanders 30.3 per cent were killed and 36.8 per
cent wounded, a 1.21 ratio. The injury rate for cavaliers, 41.4 per cent, was
much higher than that for roundheads, 31.4 per cent. This is to be
expected. Cavalier officers had a strong sense of honour which made them
more likely to press home an attack, while medical services tended to
break down on the royalist side, especially after it was losing. Improved
medical care may explain why during the Nine Years War (1688–97), and
the War of the Spanish Succession (1701–14), the rate fell. Yet officers
continued to die more often than other ranks. For instance, at Steenkirk
(1692) the killed/wounded ratio for the former was 2.28 and 0.71 for the
latter, and at Blenheim (1704) it was 2.44 and 1.59 respectively.[38]

Soldiers had nothing but contempt for cowardly leaders. Elis Gruffudd,
the Welsh captain, scorned Thomas Hussey, whom the duke of Norfolk
appointed his second in command during the 1544 Boulogne Campaign,
calling him 'a fat-bellied lump of a man, big in body and authority, lacking
in sense and a coward'.[39] As they campaigned on the continent in 1672,
Captain Henry Herbert's regiment were unhappy, the officers' mess being 'a
cabal of eating and drinking as well as finding fault with our colonel'. Their
colonel, Sir Herbert Jones, was a coward, or, as Captain Herbert more tact-
fully put it, 'His Laundress observed that the knight's linens have a stronger
smell after a fight than at other times.' This, the captain continued, explained
why Colonel Jones kept on sliding off his horse, his saddle being so well
lubricated.[40] Before Blenheim, an unpopular major in the 14th Foot (The
West Yorkshire Regiment) apologized to his men, and begged them not to
shoot him. After the fighting, much relieved to survive, he called for three
cheers, and was promptly shot dead by a nameless marksman.[41]

Many argued that courage and competence proven by combat experience
were the criteria for good leadership. 'He therefore that judgeth or directeth
against experience, is not in deed a man, but a fool more ignorant than a
beast,' wrote Geoffrey Gates in 1579. 'It is impossible for any state to know
the worth of their Captains without being in action against great enemies,'
observed Roger Williams. Captain John Baynard wrote to Elizabeth I in
1599 that 'It is most necessary that there be no commander employed to
have command of men in the wars, but such as are of experience.'[42] 'If you
choose godly honest men to be captains of horse, honest men will follow
them,' believed Oliver Cromwell, adding that 'I would rather have a plain
russet-coated captain that knows what he fights for and loves what he
knows, than that you would call "a gentleman" and is nothing else.'[43]

Such views could be subversive, as those plain russet-coated captains
demonstrated when the army executed Charles I in 1649 and took over the

government. Early modern society was based on hierarchy rather than ability. To be sure, military incompetence could be fatal. Thomas Churchyard, who took part in the botched assault on the walls of Leith in 1560, where many English troops died because the scaling ladders were eight feet too short, bitterly observed that this mistake took place 'with blood the poor men bought'. Captains, as James Achesone noted in 1629, 'hath the charge of men's lives'.[44] But so long as not too many men's lives were at hazard, competence took a back seat to deference. Elizabeth's senior commanders were aristocrats. Charles I chose the viscount Wimbledon to lead the disastrous attack in Cadiz in 1626 because of his court connections and loyalty rather than his abilities and experience. Two years later the king selected his favourite, the duke of Buckingham, to lead the expedition against the French island of Rhé, where—once again—in the decisive assault on St Martin's Fort the scaling ladders were too short. At the start of the Civil War even parliament chose as their generals men such as the earl of Essex, more for their pedigree than proficiency. But as the war went on, and as casualties mounted, soldiers increasingly volunteered to serve under officers with a proven record of success. During the war officers such as Oliver Cromwell, John Lambert and Henry Ireton rose on their abilities. After the war they established military rule, perhaps even a military dictatorship.[45] In reaction, after the restoration of the monarchy in 1660, a system developed in which officers purchased their commissions, ensuring that the establishment was financially linked with the officer corps. Surprisingly, this produced competent leadership for nearly two centuries.

The qualities needed to be a good leader change according to rank. At the lower levels leadership is a face to face business, in which decisions are fairly simple and limited. At the top it becomes impersonal: as they become more senior, leaders have a problem projecting their personalities and objectives to those they command in an increasingly complicated milieu. Surprisingly little attention was paid to the qualities required for a good non-commissioned officer—perhaps because such aptitudes were assumed, or else did not find their way into manuals that appealed to the more literate officer class. Certainly in the highly structured early modern battlefield, the role of NCOs was rather limited. However, towards the end of the seventeenth century and during the eighteenth, as battle tactics and movements became more complicated, and long-term enlisted infantrymen required extensive training, the task of NCOs grew. Increasingly, they acted as intermediaries between the officers and other ranks. The purchase system meant that inexperienced officers required more guidance from veteran sergeants, who had been promoted on merit. One late seventeenth-century cartoon portrayed a boy officer advancing into battle secured by baby's reins held by an old NCO.

Young officers received scant respect. In 1707 Edward Ward wrote that[46]

An Ensign's usually a young gentleman who passed through all the classes of his education handsomely enough, and was ripe for the university, being designed for a clergyman, but unfortunately happened to be caught abed with one of his mother's chambermaids. . . . The young spark was doomed to the army.

The key leader was the captain. 'The charge of Captains is of so great importance,' wrote John Cruso, the Cambridge don, in his best-selling manual *Military instructions for the Cavallerie* (1632), 'that it should not be given to any but to men of singular valour and experience.' A captain must maintain discipline, ensure orders are carried out, and know every man by name. This was very important because, explained Cruso (who possessed military insights rare amongst academics), soldiers had left their friends and family to follow their captain to a foreign country. Thus the captain must be a father to his men. Sir John Smythe, a veteran, made a similar point about general officers: in 1590 he wrote that they must 'win the love of their soldiers by taking great care of their healths and safeties', and by treating them like 'their own children'. They must, Smythe continued, 'preserve by all means possible the lives of their soldiers, and not to employ and hazard them on every light occasion'.[47]

'I shall die in honour'

In 1651, just before his execution for loyalty to the crown, James Stanley, seventh earl of Derby, explained that 'I was born in honour, have lived in honour and hope I shall die in honour.'[48] Honour was critical in explaining why men fought. In life and death, in peace and war, honour played an immense part in motivating early modern men, especially the gentry and aristocracy. Honour is as old as manhood itself, although the concept can change over time. Today it is seen in terms of disrespecting a man as a man. In the middle ages it was connected with the idea of chivalry, even platonic love, in which unattainable women were valued all the more because they were unavailable. The Reformation affected the concept of honour in three ways. First, the Church tried to sanctify honour. In *The Mirror of Honor* (1597), John Norden declared that 'no man can become honorable without divine inspiration.' Second, a group of intellectuals, known as the humanists, attempted to civilize honour by making it less bellicose. Third, the crown tried to control it by becoming honour's official dispenser: in 1555, for instance, Mary Tudor took over the College of Heralds.[49]

Honour had two components—lineage and masculinity. It had two outcomes—winning it gave pride and self-respect, while losing it inflicted a shame that was hard to assuage. Honour was something one's family compounded like interest over generations, endowing its possessors with pride and potency. Maintaining the honour of one's dynasty was a compelling obligation. Keeping one's honour was a matter of keeping faith with one's predecessors, be they members of the same regiment or corps, or blood ancestors. As he stood before a firing squad in 1649, Arthur, baron Capel, declared, 'I die, I take it, for maintaining the Fifth Commandment.'[50] He was honouring his father and mother: cowardice would have disgraced them. In his *Booke of Honour* (1625) Francis Markham argued that 'The Fittest Man to make a soldier is a perfect gentlemen, for generous spirits are apt for great dangers.' Perhaps that was the case. Certainly perfect gentlemen, who knew and were proud of their ancestors, had more to lose if they lost their honour. This, it was argued, made them better leaders than 'men of obscure birth'.[51] The higher they were, the harder they fell. While a gentleman could not earn honour in the same way as a merchant could grub for money through compound interest, he could lose it in a single act far more precipitously than a townsman could go bankrupt. As Iago pointed out:[52]

Who steals my purse steals trash—'tis something, nothing . . .
But he that filches from me my good name
Robs me of that which not enriches him
And makes me poor indeed.

Loss of honour made a gentleman a figure of scorn. When Henry, the fifth earl of Northumberland, and his son (also Henry) failed to behave bravely, the poet John Skelton contemptuously wrote in 1522:[53]

The earl of Northumberland
Dare Take nothing in hand
Our Barons be so bold,
Into a mouse hole, they would
Run away and creep
Like a mainy of sheep.

Death was preferable to dishonour. Before sailing to fight on the continent, an English colonel told his regiment that 'when honour is gone the soldier dies, although the man may drag on in a miserable despised life.'[54] Cowards lost their caste, for as Shakespeare put it, 'True nobility is exempt from fear.'[55] That was the trouble with honour. You could fall—hard and fast. Arduously won over generations, through many manly feats of valour, honour could be lost in a trice, and regained, if at all, only with much difficulty. But, unlike female honour, which was usually connected with virginity, male honour could be recovered.[56] Before the Battle of Brentford (1642), Charles I addressed Sir Thomas Salisbury's Denbighshire Regiment, which had broken in battle three weeks earlier: 'Gentlemen,' said the king, 'you have lost your honour at Edgehill. I hope you will regain it again here.'[57] And they did, routing three crack parliamentary regiments. Salisbury's men would have agreed with the motto of the Royal Regiment of Wales: 'Gwell Angau na Chiwilydd—Better death than dishonour.'

Honour was also linked with masculinity. In 1562 Gerard Leigh pronounced honour as 'glory got by courage of manhood'.[58] In the seventeenth century Sir Francis Bacon defined winning honour as 'the revealing of a man's virtue and worth'.[59] In Francis Beaumont and John Fletcher's 1607 play *The Knight of the Burning Pestle* (a pestle being a metaphor for the male organ), Ralph urges his comrades 'bear yourselves . . . like men, valiant men.'[60] In battle, troops were constantly reminded of the biblical injunction to 'play the men'. In August 1588, as the Armada was approaching, a ballad, 'The Great Galleazzo', urged all to 'play your parts like men'.[61] In 1660, expecting battle, Lieutenant Thomas Browne wrote to his father, 'I hope you shall hear we behaved ourselves like men.'[62] After the Battle of Worcester (1651), one of the victors boasted that their triumph was 'done by us as men'.[63]

Those innocent of combat were considered incomplete men, being dubbed virgin or maiden soldiers. In 1647 John Corbet criticized the militia as being 'effeminate in courage'. Those who would not fight were frequently described as being sissies—'fellows unfit for women and war'.[64] The link between sex and combat, between honour and manhood, can be found in the poetry of Richard Lovelace. In the well known explanation of why he was going to the wars, he tells his Lucasta that he was choosing a new mistress—combat—because: 'I could not love thee, dear, so much, Loved I not honour more.' Afterwards, having lost, and having thus left the wars, in 'To Lucasta from Prison' he reverts to more traditional ways of realizing his masculinity, dreaming of lying 'tangled in her hair'.[65] Cowards lost their manhood. 'To abandon my honour,' declared Colonel Joseph Bampfield in 1685, would be 'womanish'.[66] Those who did so were reckoned not to be real men worthy of respect: they were scorned as cuckolds, the worst of all insults.[67]

In early modern Britain men craved honour, and war was the circumstance in which it was best won. Lucy Hutchinson remembered that her father was 'in love with true honour'. Philip Massinger, the playwright, advised that[68]

If 'ere my son
Follow the war, tell him it is a school

Where all the principles tending to honour
Are taught.

All too often, honour might be a soldier's sole reward. Unpaid, unpen-
sioned, unappreciated, wounded in mind and body, many a veteran would
agree with George Monck that 'He that chooseth the profession of a soldier
ought to know withal that honour must be his greatest wages.'[69]
Military honour was largely a male concept with little appeal to women,
especially as they were the ones who during wars were raped, widowed,
and left to bring up orphaned children. When in *Henry IV, Part II*
Northumberland tells Lady Percy 'my honour is at pawn,' his wife berates
him 'for God's sake, go not to these wars.' In her poem 'The Soldier's
Death', Anne Finch, countess of Winchilsea (1661–1720), complained:[70]

Ye Silent, ye dejected men of war
For see! Where on the bier before you lies,
The pale, the fallen, the untimely Sacrifice
To your mistaken shrine, to your false Idol Honour.

Not surprisingly, there was little room for women in military honour. As
recent debates suggest, many men find the presence of women in war
threatening. Even females of the highest status had to be very careful
of male sensitivities when they took part in combat. For instance,
Charlotte, countess of Derby, refused to surrender Latham House in
1644 because it would lead to 'the loss of her honour'. But she went on to
add that as an obedient wife, and loyal subject, she would give up the house
if her husband, who was away in the Isle of Man, or her king ordered
her to do so.[71]
Disguising women as men has long had a prurient appeal: it featured in
ninety-nine of some three hundred plays performed on the London stage
from 1660 to 1700.[72] Because combat was the apex of being a real man,
and cowardice the sanctuary of sissies, men found women disguised as
soldiers or sailors especially disturbing. The House of Commons was
horrified in 1643 to hear a report that Prince Rupert had women dressed
as male soldiers, and got even more upset when they were told he used a
couple of them as whores.[73] Jane Ingleby, the daughter of a Yorkshire
yeoman, is said to have charged with the king's cavalry at Marston Moor
in 1644 and, wounded, escaped back to the security of her father's farm.
In 1651 it was reported that a drummer boy stationed at the Tower of
London was found out to be a drummer girl—after she had a baby.[74] 'John
Brown', a black soldier in the Royal Africa Company, was discovered to be
a woman, when she fell ill aboard the *Hannibal* in 1693.[75]

Perhaps the best-known she-soldier was Christian Davies (1667–1739), better known as Mother Ross. On finding out that her husband had got drunk and had been shanghaied into the army to fight in Holland, she immediately cut her hair, put her children into her mother's care and enlisted as a man—apparently she had a boyish figure. She served in the Scots Greys, was wounded, demobilized, re-enlisted and fought at Nijmegen, Venlo and Blenheim—all in order to find her husband. Eventually she found him—in the arms of a Dutch woman. Their ensuing conversation is not recorded. Christian returned to the colours, and on being wounded at Ramillies, her secret was revealed when the surgeon removed her shirt to treat a wound and 'saw my breasts, and by the largeness of my nipples, concluded that I had given suck'. She became a regimental suttler, selling provisions to the soldiers. On finding her husband's corpse on the field of Malplaquet, she was free to marry a Grenadier, and after the war was presented to Queen Anne, who awarded her a shilling a day. Eventually, she died an out-pensioner of Chelsea, being buried with full military honours. Although partly fictional, Christian's behaviour was more acceptable in a male world, because—like the countess of Derby at Latham House—she was acting as a good wife, trying to rescue her husband.[76]

Stories of she-soldiers and sailors should be taken with more than a pinch of salt. Take the Maiden Lillard, who, to avenge her slain lover, reputedly fought and died at the Battle of Ancrum (1545):[77]

Upon the English loons she laid many thumps
And when her legs were cut off she fought upon her stumps.

According to a popular ballad, after Mary Ambree had watched the Spanish murder her lover, Sir John Major, in Ghent, she raised three thousand troops in order to exact revenge. In fact, there is no evidence that the Maiden Lillard or Mary Ambree ever existed. She-soldiers (and sailors) were found far less often in battles than in ballads. Between the reigns of Elizabeth and Victoria over a thousand ditties record the deeds of over a hundred heroic heroines: in contrast, only one of the 236 surviving military diaries was written by a woman.[78]

'My dearest friends were there'

Religion played an important part in war—as it did in every activity in early modern Britain. Before battle it comforted men, and during it assuaged combatants' fear of death if only by reassuring them there was an afterlife. But it would be wrong to exaggerate the role of religion in making men fight. After the Battle of Naseby (1645) a parliamentary chaplain described 'the greatest part of the common soldiers' in the victorious New Model Army, that supposed 'army of saints', as having 'little religion'.[79] Religion became even less important in the standing army of the late seventeenth and early eighteenth centuries. For instance, in 1703 eleven of the twenty chaplains attached to Marlborough's army as it campaigned on the continent were absent. 'They were either in England, Ireland or in the Colonels' pockets,' Chaplain Samuel Noyes complained to the Archbishop of York.[80] Faith could have little effect on making even the most religious men stay and fight. Richard Baxter, one of the seventeenth century's leading theologians and pastors, and chaplain to Colonel Edward Whalley's parliamentary regiment from 1645 to 1647, might have been expected to rationalize his behaviour in battle in religious terms. Far from it. He explained what made him stay in a fight:[81]

> Many of my dearest friends were there, whose society had formerly been delightful to me, and whose welfare I was tender of, being men that had a deeper interest in my affections than any in the world had before those times. . . . It was they that stuck to me, and I to them. . . . I would not forsake them . . . my faithful people that purposedly went through with me . . . so many wars and dangers.

In other words, what contained his fears and stopped him from bolting is what today we call small group loyalty, which was crucial in enabling men to confront the face of battle. In combat men felt intensely towards their comrades, mates, oppoes, buddies, or butties.[82] They experience a sentiment as ardent as love: directed towards people they may not even like, it can be more intense than what they feel for their families. The key that makes a man fight—not just join up or campaign but stay and fight, slay and be slain—is loyalty to the small group to which he belongs. 'Man is not a killer, but the group is,' wrote Konrad Lorenz in his study *On Aggression* (1963). We may or may not be naturally aggressive animals, but without doubt we are gregarious ones.[83] We take comfort—especially in battle where comfort is sorely needed—from the close proximity of our friends and comrades.[84] Amias Steynings, a veteran of the Thirty Years War, was convinced that it was comradeship that made fighting possible. From Lord Vere's camp in Maastricht he wrote home, 'If one man or two should endure alone, and not thousands, there would be no wars.'[85] Robert Monro justified writing his memoirs of mercenary service in the Thirty Years War 'because I loved my comrades'. He explained why men fought:[86]

> Nothing therefore in my opinion, more worthy to be kept next unto Faith, than this kind of friendship, grown up with education, conformed

by familiarity, in frequenting the dangers of war. And who is more worthy to be chosen as a friend than one who has shown himself both valiant and constant against his enemies.

After his regiment mustered at Saffron Walden in June 1645, Ralph Josselin, a parliamentary chaplain, wrote in his diary that 'The Colonel was pleased to honour me to be his comrade. I shall never forget his great love and respect.' After surrendering at Limerick in 1690, Captain John Stevens refused to leave his unit. He wrote in his journal, 'I could not live from my regiment, which was all the home I had and all the friends.' Of course, this feeling could become a two-edged sword: the death of a friend could be so traumatic that it could produce a nervous breakdown or an uncontrollable desire for revenge.[87] When those bonds of friendship, that glue of unit cohesion, broke down or never developed, the results could be calamitous. Sir Richard Fanshawe, the British ambassador, explained why the expeditionary force sent to Portugal in 1662 disintegrated: he wrote that there 'appears to me to be no cement at all in our troops, being admirable individuals, but the worst body that ever was'.[88]

Men have always asked themselves: Do I have the stomach to fight? Honour, a sense of manhood, small group loyalty, punishments, rewards, all combine to make them do so, as does the shame of failure. What is remarkable is that most men find that they have the stomach. They do not run, they acquit themselves bravely, perhaps because they lived up to the expectations that they will do so. As a best-selling seventeenth-century ballad put it:[89]

> We are no cowardly shirkers, but Englishmen true bred,
> We'll play our parts like valiant hearts and never fly for dread.

CHAPTER 5

THOSE WERE GOLDEN DAYS: EARLY STUART WARFARE, 1603–1639

Plenty and Peace breeds cowards
Cymbeline, III, vi, 24

IN RETROSPECT, AT LEAST, THE PERIOD BETWEEN JAMES I'S ACCESSION to the English throne in 1603 and the outbreak of the British Civil Wars in 1639 seems a pacific interregnum between two periods when war was dominant. From the perspective of the Civil War, it could have been seen as a lull before the storm. 'O those were golden days!' recalled Peter Hausted, an Oxford don.[1] For the first half of this interval such an interpretation is valid. James pursued a largely peaceful policy because he disliked war; because England needed to rest after the huge military effort of the last third of Elizabeth's reign; and because time was required to allow the conquest of Ireland to take hold. Between 1624 and 1628, when the king's heir, Charles I (r.1625–49), and his favourite, the duke of Buckingham, dominated policy, England become involved in four military expeditions. All of them failed catastrophically with considerable political ramifications.[2] In the last decade of this period, from 1629–39, Charles recognized that he could not wage an expensive continental war without calling parliament—something he was not prepared to do. So he used his energies to reform the navy and militia. During this period of relative peace, very large numbers of men from the British Isles served overseas as mercenaries.

'The most cowardly man'

Sir John Oglander, a gentleman from the Isle of Wight, thought that King James I of England and VI of Scotland was 'the most cowardly man that

I ever knew. He could not endure to see a soldier, to see men drilled, to hear of war was death to him.'[3] During a tour of the Bodleian Library, James declared that had he not been king he would have been a don. His personal motto (which one can still see emblazoned above his statue outside the Bodleian) was 'beati pacifice—blessed are the peacemakers'. As king of Scotland he had shown some courage: at the Bridge of Dee in 1589, when his army expected an imminent attack from the rebel Catholic earls, James walked amongst his troops, perhaps with 'a little touch of Harry in the night', encouraging them, not taking off his clothes for two days. In his *Works*, which were first published in 1616, the king may have been thinking of the Bridge of Dee when he advised commanders to 'once or twice in your own person hazard yourself fairly,' but also 'conserve yourself thereafter for the weal of your people.'[4] But by the time he inherited the English crown in 1603, James had lost whatever martial urges he might have had, finding excitement instead in the hunting field.

James also recognized that after the stresses of Elizabethan warfare, England needed to conserve her resources. Thus he made peace treaties with France and Spain that allowed the settlement in Ireland to take root. When Sir Cahir O'Doherty rebelled in April 1608, having been insulted by George Paulet, the governor of Derry, the City of London sent two hundred troops to Ireland, but the rebellion petered out of its own accord before they could arrive.[5] The Union of England and Scotland under a common monarch also needed a period to take hold. James tried to integrate the two kingdoms, but the English parliament thwarted him, leaving Anglo-Scottish relations a contentious issue for generations.

James I sorely neglected the navy. Spending on it fell from £70,000 in 1590 to £30,000 in 1608. The system of having cadres of skilled warrant officers, such as a carpenter and boatswain attached to each ship when it was laid up, broke down, being replaced by night watchmen whose quality left much to be desired. Of the ninety-three watchmen at Chatham, only ten knew the Lord's Prayer, and even fewer the points of the compass. 'The Navy is for the greatest part manned with aged, incompetent, vagrant, lewd and disorderly companions,' reported a royal commission in 1608. 'It become a ragged remnant of tapsters, tinkers, cobblers, and many common rogues which will never prove good seamen.'[6] Although the Royal Navy was able to perform routine duties, such as patrolling the North Sea and transporting dignitaries, it could not stop the Dutch in 1605 from attacking some Spanish ships that had sought refuge in Dover Harbour.[7]

Corruption was rife in James's reign, especially during the administration of Charles Howard, first earl of Nottingham. As Lord Admiral he showed the same enthusiasm for plundering the English navy as he had as a commander for defeating the Spanish Armada. Bills were padded, dead men paid, repairs double-billed, positions sold. It has been estimated that between 1605 and 1608 naval fraud cost the king £40,000.[8]

Many attacked James's policies as fraudulent, ineffectual and utopian.[9] Foreigners concurred that the English had become 'effeminate, unable to endure the fatigations and travails of a war: delicate, well-fed, given to tobacco, wine, strong drink, feather beds; undisciplined, unarmed, unfurnished of money and munitions'.[10] Sir Walter Raleigh snidely observed that the only sounds of war came from the playhouses on London's South Bank. The playwright Thomas Dekker confirmed this denunciation in *The Artillery Garden* (1616):[11]

Boys blush that men should loiter out an age
Never to hear drums beat but on a stage.

Who was to blame? In 1604 Barnaby Rich, that old soldier, dedicated his memoirs to Prince Henry, the king's son and heir, explaining that 'in a prince there is nothing so glorious as to be called a great Captain or a worthy soldier. . . . The affair of war [is] a knowledge behoveful for the greatest monarch.'[12] The implications were obvious: that James I (r.1603–25) was a mediocre monarch especially when compared to his predecessor Queen Elizabeth I of blessed memory. Sir Francis Bacon was blunter. Alluding to the homosexual monarch's lack of masculinity (as well as his appalling personal hygiene), he wrote that 'a slothful peace both courage will effeminate and manners corrupt'.[13]

There is no doubt that James loved men, making his paramours, such as George Villiers, duke of Buckingham, his chief ministers. Before women and gays were allowed into fighting units, soldiers connected toughness and courage with being real men. Those who lacked these attributes they deemed sissies, effeminate, or to use the words of John Corbet, the seventeenth-century military historian, 'fellows unfit for women and war'. So it was a short step for contemporaries to use the king's homosexuality as an explanation for his cowardice.[14]

Four Failed Expeditions

As James aged his timidity grew, and he may have suffered from dementia. He in effect handed over the control of politics to Buckingham, on whom he became cloyingly dependent. Within half a dozen years after Prince Henry's death in 1612, Buckingham managed to control the new heir, Prince Charles, retaining his dominance from 1625 to 1628 during the first three years of King Charles's reign. Together, Charles and Buckingham launched four military expeditions against Spain and France.

Why they did so is a bit of a mystery. Until his marriage to Henrietta Maria, a French princess, on 20 June 1625, Charles was almost certainly a virgin, so he may have hankered after war to prove his masculinity.[15] Charles did not suffer from that desperate yearning for military glory that had afflicted Henry VIII. To be sure, he was determined to restore his sister, Elizabeth, and his brother-in-law, Frederick, to the Palatinate, the territory from which they had been expelled in 1618 at the start of the Thirty Years War. If there was a constant in Charles's foreign policy, this was it. Yet it is hard to see how any of these four expeditions could have done much to further that goal. Charles was angry with the Spanish for having humiliatingly spurned his efforts as prince to woo their king's sister during his madcap visit to Madrid in 1623. When he arrived home in October, Charles received such an ecstatic welcome that it was not exceeded by any British emissary back from a botched mission abroad until Neville Chamberlain returned from Munich in 1938. The jubilation at the prince's return—bonfires, bell ringing, fountains flowing with wine for all to drink—may well have encouraged him later to go to war with Spain. During their stay in Madrid, Buckingham lost his influence over the prince, so he may have egged on Charles's military ambitions as a means of controlling him.[16] Both believed that success in war overseas would able them to overcome parliamentary opposition at home.[17] Had, for instance, they been able to capture the Spanish silver fleet on its way home from the Americas, any constitutional reservations that parliament might have had about waging war without its approval would have been drowned by the noise of counting coins. Yet the fact remains that apart from personal considerations, Charles and Buckingham had little real reason for going to war with Spain and France. There was no doubt Charles enthusiastically supported the war. Anyone hampering the war effort, he declared, 'deserves to make their end at Tyburn'.[18] With the king's enthusiastic support, Buckingham, who was as able an administrator as he was an inept military commander, raised large expeditionary forces. For example, the expedition sent to the Rhine Delta under Count Mansfeld consisted of 16,399 men on 85 ships.[19] In contrast, in the 1588 Armada, Spain, with a population three times larger than England's, dispatched 30,000 men on a 130 vessels. When the considerable expeditions of the 1620s failed, their size magnified the extent of Britain's military defeats and the ensuing political fallout.

The first expedition was commanded by Count Peter Ernst von Mansfeld, a freebooter whom the Spanish ambassador called 'an infamous man that had long wasted the empire by his spoils and robberies'.[20] The illegitimate son of the governor of Luxembourg, he felt the stigma so bitterly that he became one of those bully boys who bloomed during the

Thirty Years War. As liable to plunder his own employer as he was the enemy or neutrals, Mansfeld raised a ragtag expeditionary force, which rendezvoused in late December 1624 at Dover. At the end of January 1625 the Mansfeld expedition set sail, much to the relief of Dover's mayor and citizens, without much idea of where they were headed. When the French refused to let them land at Calais, they cruised aimlessly around for several days, before finally going ashore near Breda in the southern Netherlands. Lacking rations, warm clothing and ready cash, they perished in a Rhine Delta winter. 'We die like dogs,' wrote one commander from his regimental headquarters (a pigsty the tenancy of which he had most likely obtained by eating the previous occupant), 'and in the face of an enemy we could not suffer as we now do.'[21] As spring melted the snows of the Rhine Delta, so disappeared a British army. Within six months only one in twenty of Mansfeld's men were left alive.

The record of the next expedition was even more catastrophic. The attack on Cadiz was commanded by Edward Cecil, Viscount Wimbledon— 'the general,' sniffed a contemporary, 'from whom as little could be expected as he performed.'[22] Chosen for his court connections, rather than for any military experience or competence, on 2 October 1625 Wimbledon sailed out of Portsmouth Harbour at the van of eighty-five ships. Then they anchored for a council of war, which decided to attack Cadiz. The British bombarded the port on the 20th. To avoid getting hit, they opened fire beyond the range of the enemy's cannon. Since the range of the Spanish cannon was equally limited, the Royal Navy accorded the enemy a similar convenience. Two days later two thousand British infantry landed on the beach a few miles south of the castle guarding the entrance to Cadiz Harbour. Having forgotten to fill their water bottles, they were delighted to stumble across a warehouse just outside the castle containing six hundred tuns of wine. 'No words of exhortation, nor blows of correction would restrain them,' one of their officers wrote, 'but breaking with violence into the rooms where the wines were, crying out that they were King Charles's men and fought for him, caring for no man else, they claimed the wine their own ... till in effect the whole army, except the commanders, were drunken and in common one confusion.'[23] Seeing the opportunity, the Spanish sallied out to slaughter the intoxicated British troops. 'I must confess,' reported Wimbledon, displaying that sangfroid so characteristic of British commanders after a debacle, 'that it put me to some trouble.' But he excused the incident by saying that even when sober the troops were 'incapable of order' and had never obeyed him.[24] The expedition sailed home in defeat and disgrace, with one-third of its ships lost to battle, gales, incompetence and disease. One ship lacked enough men to row the longboat, another sufficient to ply the pumps. The horror was not over when they reached port, where many died of the plague. The expedition ended, John Rous told his diary, in 'a shameful return'. Lord Delaware, one of its leaders, agreed, confessing to a friend, 'Never an army went out, continued, and returned with so much disorder as this.'[25]

Delaware's forecast that the record of the Cadiz expedition for ineptitude could never be beaten lasted less than two years. Charles and Buckingham learned nothing from their mistakes, except, perhaps, not to let minions make mistakes for them. Thus in June 1627 Buckingham personally led a fleet of 100 ships from Portsmouth, carrying six thousand infantry and a thousand cavalry, to capture the Isle of Rhé, just off the French port of La Rochelle, where Louis XIII was besieging the Huguenots, his rebellious Protestant subjects. The landings on 12 July went well, two thousand men wading ashore, with Buckingham at their head.[26] One commander described his troops as 'the mere scum of our provinces'.[27] In fact, they fought robustly: it was their leaders who did badly. Five days after landing, the British started to besiege the main French position at St Martins. By September it seemed as if the French would capitulate, the St Martins' garrison being down to a couple of days' rations. On the night of 28 September, however, the French managed to relieve St Martins by using the small fort of La Prée on the mainland side of the island that Buckingham had neglected to take in the initial landing. The mistake cost the British dear. The besiegers became the besieged. 'Our army grows everyday weaker,' an officer wrote home, 'our victuals waste, our purses are empty, ammunition consumed, winter grows.'[28] On 27 October the British made one last desperate effort to take St Martins. They failed, largely because the scaling ladders were five feet too short—an inexcusable piece of negligence considering that the besiegers had been staring at the walls for over three months, during which they had plenty of time to measure them. Two days later two thousand French troops sallied out of La Prée, forcing the British to pull back. Thanks to Buckingham's decision to place the rearguard on the wrong side of the bridge to Loix, the small island from which the main evacuation took place, the retreat turned into a rout. A few weeks later the jubilant French king and his victorious officers heard a Te Deum sung in Notre Dame, Paris, beneath forty captured British colours hung from the cathedral walls.

Had not John Felton, an army lieutenant deranged at being denied promotion, assassinated Buckingham in August 1628, the duke would surely have led the second expedition to relieve the Huguenots at La Rochelle. Instead, the following month under the command of Robert Bertie, earl of Lindsey, the fleet sailed from Portsmouth. 'Such a rotten, miserable fleet, set out to sea no man ever saw,' thought John Ashburnham.[29]

They arrived off La Rochelle on the 10th. First they tried to bombard the French forts into surrender, 'with the expense of much powder on our side and little blood', Captain Dawtry Cooper noted in his log.[30] Finding the entrance into the horseshoe-shaped harbour blocked by a boom of large tree trunks chained one to another, a captain tried to blow it up: instead, he blasted himself to smithereens. Five days later the British attacked, losing six men. Even more faint-hearted was the next day's assault, in which neither side suffered a single fatality. Several days afterwards, as the anchored fleet watched through their telescopes, the four thousand surviving members of La Rochelle's original garrison of fifteen thousand surrendered to the French king, having eaten all of the city's horses, dogs, cats, and most of its rats. On 1 November Lindsey's ships departed for home.

For sheer ineptitude it would be hard to find such a quartet as the expeditions that left England during the 1620s. Admittedly, amphibious operations are extremely difficult to mount and prone to disaster. Yet if such was the case, why then were the six most senior officers on the Cadiz raid all soldiers? Without doubt bad weather played a crucial role in all of the expeditions, but tardy planning meant that they set out far too late in the year, many troops having hung around billets in England since the spring, untrained and undisciplined. Instead of eating fresh food, they consumed preserved rations, such as salted beef and pork, which were less healthy, more expensive, and should have been left for the expeditions.

For their limited objectives, Charles and Buckingham's expeditions were too large, and thus took too long to assemble: Mansfeld took twelve thousand men to the Rhine delta; 16,399 sailed for Cadiz. True, the British lacked the one quality that Napoleon demanded all his generals possess—luck. The Spanish treasure fleet, replete with gold and silver from the Americas, sailed into Cadiz a few days after the British had left. Soon after Lindsey's fleet headed home, a Biscay storm broke the boom at La Rochelle. Yet bad luck does not excuse the fact that in all of these expeditions leadership was inept, command was fractured and goals were poorly defined. Senior commanders issued orders that made those given to the Light Brigade seem like models of clarity. Intelligence—both in the psychological and military sense of that word—was in short supply, none of the four targets, for instance, having been adequately reconnoitred. Even though equipment was old and lacking, surely someone could have issued water before the landing at Cadiz, measured the height of the walls at St Martins, or fabricated a waterproof charge to blow up the boom at La Rochelle?

The results of incompetence were profound. Perhaps a fifth of the fifty thousand men drafted for the four expeditions made it home alive: of the rest some succumbed to enemy action, and more perished from disease, poor food and miserable accommodation. Initially, the public did not feel the loss too badly. Many welcomed the departure of the first drafts, which 'rid the county of these straggling vagrants,' as Thomas Barnes preached at Great Waltham, Essex, 'which do swarm amongst us'. It was far better, he continued, 'for loitering fellows and lewd livers' to be 'fighting in the field than playing in the tap-houses'. But after good riddance had been bidden to bad rubbish, to what Francis Markham called these 'filthy base and debased creatures', and honest young fellows were being conscripted and killed, public opinion hardened: the not insignificant support for war in 1624 quickly evaporated.[31] The monstrous behaviour of troops stationed in England before they left to fight overseas further estranged the public. Sir John Oglander recalled that the Scottish regiment commanded by William Douglas, earl of Morton, billeted in the Isle of Wight before the La Rochelle expedition in 1627, committed 'murders, rapes, robberies, burglaries, the getting of bastards and almost the undoing of the whole island'.[32] In addition, the growing tax burden that per capita was 47 per cent higher in 1628 than it had been in 1618, and 14 per cent higher than in 1598–1603 (when England was fighting in Ireland, the Netherlands, and at sea against Spain), further alienated people, especially when one expensive disaster followed another—the Rhé expedition alone cost over half a million pounds.[33]

The Halcyon Days

After the failure of the La Rochelle expedition, England remained at peace from 1628 to 1638, a decade that from the purview of the Civil Wars many Englishmen, such as the poet Thomas Carew, thought of as the 'halcyon days'.[34] Like most of Charles's policies, having ten years of relative peace was not one consciously decided upon, but one into which he drifted. Buckingham's murder, and the king's growing dependence on his French wife, Henrietta Maria, made foreign wars less attractive. During the next decade there were four main motifs in British military history. First, an anti-war one in which the government, artists and poets extolled the blessings of peace. The second was an effort initiated by the king to improve the militia and trained bands. The third was a huge exodus of mercenaries from not just England and Wales, but also from Scotland and Ireland, to fight in the Thirty Years War. And finally there was ship money, which the crown used to expand the navy, ostensibly to deal with piracy, but more as a royal status symbol.

Many Englishmen were grateful for having been spared the horrors of the Thirty Years War. Best-selling pamphlets reported a continental

conflict of unmatched brutality, in which promiscuous plunder, rape, sack-
ings and atrocities led to famine, disease, cannibalism and untold miseries.
For instance, *A True Representation of the Miserable Estate of Germany*
(1638) illustrated the horrors with crude woodcuts that can still sicken
modern stomachs hardened by photographs of Dachau or Cambodia.
One woodcut showed soldiers using a minister's library of rare books to
roast him alive. In another the troops had just torn a baby from its mother's breast, and tossed it into the air to be caught on a pike. A third illustration depicts troopers stripping a victim's muscles from his hands. The
caption to a fourth reads 'Men's guts pulled out of their mouths.'[35] Horror
stories of the Thirty Years War reached the British Isles through private
correspondence. 'The whole army,' Sydenham Poyntz, the mercenary,
wrote home about the Swedish capture of Wurzburg, 'in a fury breaking
in the Town pillaged it, Cloisters and Abbies, committing great disorders,
using much tyranny towards the clergymen, cutting off their members,
and deflowering the nuns.'[36] No wonder after looking at such material and
reading reports from abroad, Nehemiah Wallington, the London artisan,
wrote how fortunate he was to live in England, and not famine-torn
Germany where 'they did boil whole pots and kettles of frogs and did eat
them with their entrails.'[37]

Charles used official royal propaganda to extol the blessings of peace.
'Look up,' Ben Jonson advised people as they entered the Banqueting
Hall at Whitehall, 'to read the king in all his actions.' Above them
they could see Peter Paul Rubens's masterpiece, one of whose three
great central panels Charles had commissioned, acclaiming his father
as a peacemaker.[38] More obvious was the message in Ruben's *Saint George
and the Dragon*, a painting (see ill.11) that pleased Charles so much
that he gave the artist a diamond ring. It portrays Charles as St George,
England's patron saint, who has just rescued a maiden (who bears
an uncanny resemblance to Queen Henrietta Maria) from the Dragon
of War. On the left two women support a third who has apparently
just survived a fate worse than death. In the foreground amid corpses,
civilians beg for mercy—all victims of the Thirty Years War, from
which Charles has spared a happy nation, depicted by the idyllic
rural background and the heavenly choir of cherubs fluttering above.[39]

Painting was not the only form of court-sponsored art that celebrated
the advantages of avoiding the Thirty Years War. Poets identified the king
with peace:

Welcome Great Sir, and with all the joy that's due,
To the return of Peace and You.

Thus wrote Abraham Cowley on Charles's return from a state visit to Scotland in 1633.[40] The same year the court put on a masque entitled *The Triumph of Peace*. Thomas Carew joined in the chorus:[41]

> But let us that in myrtle bowers sit
> Under secure shields, use the benefit
> Of peace and plenty, which the blessed hand
> Of our good king gives this obdurate land.

And if England did have problems, then they were due to a surfeit of peace. *Salmacida Spolia*, the Twelfth Night court masque for 1640, opens with a Fury fomenting a storm over England:[42]

> And I do stir the humours that increase,
> In thy full body, overgrown with peace.

Notwithstanding the work of officially sponsored artists, poets and playwrights, Charles I's commitment to peace was marginally thicker than the paint upon the ceiling of the Banqueting Hall. The king would have loved to bow to public pressure to join the Thirty Years War, and thus restore Elizabeth and husband Frederick to the Palatinate. In 1632 the ballad 'Gallants to Bohemia' urged:[43]

> The true religion to maintain
> Come let us to the wars again.

But going to the wars meant going to parliament for taxes, and parliament inevitably meant a renewal of the constitutional crisis (caused mostly by military failures) that had bedevilled the 1620s—and this was a price Charles was not prepared to pay.

The Militia and Trained Bands

In much the same spirit of making the best of a bad job, Charles turned his efforts—which were far from considerable during the 1630s—to reforming the militia and its more skilled component, the trained bands. On paper they appeared to be formidable bodies. A muster roll of February 1638 for England and Wales listed 93,718 infantry and 5,239 cavalry, ranging from 130 soldiers from Rutland to 12,641 from Yorkshire.[44] In reality, the militia was far less impressive. These 'weekend warriors' frightened few foreigners, and impressed even fewer Englishmen. John Corbet described Gloucester's militia as being 'incapable of discipline'. Thomas Palmer, vicar of St Mary Redcliffe, Bristol, told the city militia that their training was more like 'a May-game than a battlefield'.[45] Professional soldiers were particularly caustic. Lieutenant Colonel William Barriffe began his widely read training manual *Military Discipline for the Young Artilleryman* (1643) by lamenting that the trained bands were 'called forth to exercise their postures and motions every four to five years. Whose fault it is I know not, but I pray God it will be amended.'[46]

Soon after becoming king, Charles attempted to amend the situation by using the brief *Instructions for Musters and Armes and their Use* that the Privy Council had issued in 1622. He ordered that only 'householders of good condition or yeomen's sons be allowed to join the militia'.[47] Far more significant was the cadre of eighty-nine sergeants, all veterans of the Thirty Years War, whom the crown dispatched to the counties to train the local volunteers. The presence of these seasoned soldiers, known as muster masters, did much to expose civilians to military realities, particularly those who served in the infantry. Cavalry soldiers, who provided their own horses, and thus came from gentry or richer yeomen families, tended to be less amenable to the advice of hoary veterans. In 1630 the king had to cancel the summer regional musters that he had scheduled for cavalry regiments because their basic training was not up to this fairly simple operation.

Charles's attempts to create what he called 'a perfect' or 'exact' militia failed. They were symptomatic of his propensity for grandiose objectives that exceeded both his resources and his attention span. The king's goals were mostly conservative, and sometimes degenerated into the trivial. He had an obsession for detail that would have been creditable in a regimental sergeant major but not a commander-in-chief. He deplored the introduction of the newfangled continental style of marching, issuing a warrant in 1632 to retain the traditional English march, as 'the best of all marches'. He urged the militia to revive the use of the longbow, a weapon that had seen its glory days two centuries earlier in the Hundred Years War.[48]

During the 1630s there was no obvious threat from abroad to stimulate enthusiastic training, or to prompt local governments into spending vast sums of money on defence. With the repeal in 1603 of the Tudor militia legislation, the crown's right to compel subjects to attend musters fully equipped at their own expense rested on custom and the prerogative, rather than the firmer foundation of statute law. In 1635 the mayor and aldermen of Norwich contested the king's right to raise a militia. More important than legal challenges was the refusal to turn up. 'There is no law to enforce him,' explained John Bishe of Brighton for having skipped musters for three decades.[49] Magistrates were less inclined to prosecute the recalcitrant, especially if they were also friends. During the 1630s, as the government demanded more and more in unpaid services from local elites, it became harder to find volunteers to serve as company officers. One muster master, Gervase Markham, complained that he got no respect, only contempt and impudence, from those he tried to train. In addition, muster masters often had to wait for years for their wages: the only way that Somerset could pay Captain Thomas Carne was from the county's maimed soldiers' fund. By the end of the 1630s both the Somerset militia and the Sussex trained bands were in such bad shape that even if they had wanted to fight they could not have done so.[50]

There were exceptions. In 1633 Captain Anthony Thelwell, a veteran of the Thirty Years War, reported that Lancashire's forces were 'reasonably well exercised . . . and able bodied', the county having spent £10,000 over fifteen years to produce a fairly proficient militia.[51] Two years later Lieutenant Hammond watched the 'ready exercised and well disciplined' Isle of Wight militia skirmishing along the River Medina: 'A brave show there is, and good service performed,' he concluded.[52] Captain de Eugaine, a continental veteran hired to train the Yarmouth Artillery Company, reported after their 1638 field day that 'although I have seen good service in the Netherlands and other places, yet never I saw a better thing'. Another observer agreed that Yarmouth's gunners were 'well schooled', and exercised in 'a soldier-like manner'.[53]

Without doubt the best part-time soldiers were London's trained bands. Their permanent staff were regularly paid; on weekends and summer evenings young men enthusiastically marched north out of the city to drill and fire their weapons in the Artillery Ground—which Ben Jonson boasted was a 'seed plot of the war'.[54] Londoners supported their trained bands so ardently that when Francis Beaumont and John Fletcher satirized them in *The Knight of the Burning Pestle* (1613), the audience hissed the play off the stage.[55] Puritan ministers, such as William Gouge, praised the trained bands, preaching in 1626, 'I do love it, I admire it, I honour it, I praise God for it.'[56]

Mercenaries

It has been calculated that, between 1620 and 1649, 170,537 men from the British Isles fought overseas as mercenaries.[57] Roughly half of the troops were English and Welsh, about a fifth were Scots, and the rest Irish. The vast majority of the English and Scots fought for the Protestant anti-Hapsburg forces. Overwhelmingly, the Irish served Spain, then France, and finally the German emperor. English soldiers tended to go out in formations recruited at home with official approval. Typical were the 5,013 men Charles sent in 1627 to help his brother-in-law, Christian IV of Denmark. As a result of mismanagement, the worst their commander Sir Charles Morgan had seen in twenty years' service, many died of disease. In April 1628 Morgan had to surrender his forces, now reduced to about 2,800, to Marshal Tilly. They were held in houses 'so nasty and ill kept,' wrote Morgan, that 'they seemeth more fit to keep hogs than brave soldiers.' Only 2,472, or 49 per cent, of his men survived. The six thousand men the marquess of Hamilton raised with royal sponsorship in 1631 to fight for Gustavus Adolphus, the king of Sweden, were so ravaged by disease (a third died from dysentery within a month) and so poorly trained that the Swedish king sent the useless survivors home before they had a chance to fight.[58]

The Scots have had a long and glorious tradition of foreign service. One seventeenth-century Dutch pamphlet called them 'sure men, hardy and resolute'.[59] Between 1619 and 1624 fifteen thousand Scots fought as mercenaries for France, while in the following eighteen years twenty-five thousand of them served in foreign armies.[60] So many Scots fought for the Dutch that at times they comprised 7 per cent of their army. The majority of the Scots entered Swedish service, making up about a quarter of its army, the relationship between the two nations being so close that one author has described it as an 'An unofficial alliance'. Many Scots died in foreign service. Between 1626 and 1634 half of the 105 gentlemen volunteers in Lord Reay's Regiment lost their lives fighting for Gustavus Adolphus. Scots mercenaries made love as well as war: a third of the widows of Scottish officers drawing pensions in 1635 were foreign born, mainly Dutch.[61]

Not surprisingly, Irish mercenaries chose to fight for Catholic monarchs. From 1605 to 1641, 32,660 such mercenaries served overseas. Between 1634 and 1636, 13,800 fought in the Netherlands for their Most Catholic Majesties of Spain. In the next decade this number rose to an average of 26,487.[62]

Typical of a mercenary's experiences were those of James Turner, a minister's son, who was educated at the University of Glasgow from which he graduated with an M. A. in 1631 at the age of eighteen (see ill.13). Defying his father's wishes that he become a Presbyterian minister, the following year Turner volunteered to serve Gustavus Adolphus. He landed in Denmark in 1632 and after marching to Mecklenburg 'fell grievously sick'. It was five weeks before he was able to walk. In the early winter of 1632 Turner took part in the Siege of Nuremberg, in which four thousand were killed and six thousand wounded, and in June fought at Hamelin, where nine thousand imperial soldiers perished. In his memoirs he recalled the horrors of war. 'After this battle I saw a great many killed in cold blood by the Finns, who professed to give no quarter.' Campaigning was nearly as bad. 'My best entertainment was bread and water,' he wrote, adding with the dry humour which has kept many a soldier going that he had 'abundance of the last, but not so the first'. After a couple of years service he had become a seasoned campaigner so capable of fending for himself under all circumstances that 'I wanted for nothing—horses, clothes, meat nor monies.'[63] Neither did he want for brutality, for those who served overseas endured an especially cruel form of warfare. For instance, in August 1612 within three weeks of landing in Norway (then part of Denmark), a contingent of three hundred Scots from Caithness was ambushed by the local peasants at Skottereien. Half were killed, 134 taken prisoners, of whom 120 were shot in cold blood the following day. A grateful Danish government rewarded the peasants with grants of land.[64]

The Ship Money Fleet

After Buckingham took over as Lord High Admiral in 1619, the administration of the Royal Navy improved enough to support the four continental expeditions. Their failure, and Buckingham's assassination, left the navy exhausted. So Charles tried to fight on the cheap by commissioning privateers. Legitimated by Letters of Marque, English pirates preyed on French and Spanish merchant ships, taking enemy vessels worth £780,000 between 1625 and 1630. But privateering was a two-edged sword. It has been estimated that from 1616 to 1642 foreign pirates and privateers captured four hundred English ships worth a million pounds, and took eight thousand men, women and children prisoner.[65]

North African pirates were an especially vexatious problem: thirty Salle vessels took two hundred captives from Cornwall; Yarmouth was bombarded; King's Lynn lost twenty-five ships worth £9,000 and Ipswich five valued at £5,000; even the queen's dwarf and midwife were captured in the Channel. The former's abduction upset Henrietta Maria so much that an unfeeling courtier noted it caused 'more upset at court than if they had lost a fleet'. The thousand women who petitioned Charles in 1651 to free their husbands held as slaves in North Africa had more cause for complaint. In August of that year Henry Hendy, master of the Dover mail packet, wrote that in the past seven weeks pirates had boarded his ship, robbed and beaten him up seven times. When, on the last occasion, the long-suffering seafarer showed the pirates his *laissez passer* signed by the Secretary of State, Sir John Coke, they told him 'to keep it to wipe his breech'.[66] Perhaps the most humiliating episode of all took place in 1639 when Charles agreed to protect a large Spanish fleet carrying ten thousand soldiers and much treasure to Dunkirk to fight the Dutch. Off Dungeness a Dutch fleet under Maarten Tromp attacked the Spanish ships, forcing them to take refuge in Dover Harbour. Charles offered to protect them for £150,000, and then started to negotiate with the French for their help to regain the Palatinate for his sister, Elizabeth, and brother-in-law, Frederick, while at the same time offering to have the Royal Navy convey Spanish troops to the Netherlands at thirty shillings a head. On 11 October, Tromp put an end to this triple dealing by sailing his fleet into Dover Harbour, and cutting out the Spanish, only ten, perhaps eighteen, of whose ships escaped to Dunkirk.[67]

Charles built up the navy less to avenge such insults than to enhance his prestige. As the poet Edmund Waller flattered:[68]

Wherever the navy spread her wings
Homage to thee and peace to all she brings.

The king described his efforts to expand the navy as 'his proper vanity'. After art collecting, it was his favourite hobby. When some nobles questioned the high costs of building the *Sovereign of the Seas*, Charles retorted, 'Why should he not be admitted to build that ship for his own pleasure?'[69] The *Sovereign of the Seas* was a supership of 1,500 tons, 100 cannon and at least 1,000 crew. Her stern was elaborately carved and gilded, adding to her total cost of £65,000. Balladeers foretold that she would[70]

Curb the Pope and scourge the Turk
And ferret those that thieving lurk.

In fact, she did no such thing. While the vessel was big enough to range the seven seas, England lacked the support systems for a blue-water navy. Anyway, the ship was far too large to chase North African or Dunkirk pirates. Smaller, shallow draft, fast vessels known as 'whelps', such as the ones the Dutch possessed, would have been far more useful than this floating status symbol. Status symbols do not come cheap. To pay for the navy, which in the 1630s was far more important than the army, the crown introduced ship money. Originally this had been a levy on coastal counties to cover maritime defence. In 1633 it was extended to all English counties, producing much more money. Within two years the ship money assessment reached £217,184, and even though parliament had never approved the tax, only 2.3 per cent remained uncollected.

Military activities in the three and a half decades before the outbreak of the British Civil Wars were limited. Until 1623 James's reign had been pacific, and devoid of fighting. Afterwards the military developments between 1623 and 1638 were more significant in the way that they influenced the Civil Wars, the most important conflict in our period. Take the four military expeditions, all of which were spectacular failures. For the thirty thousand Englishmen who died in them, and for their relatives, they were of course catastrophic. As each failed expedition limped home, it engendered more anger at its incompetency, financial cost and loss of life. Parliament, the body that voted taxes, became the forum for dissatisfaction: here many of the ideas and attitudes that came to a crisis during the Civil Wars were debated and developed. For instance, when parliament, angry at the Cadiz debacle, refused to vote money to attack Rhé, the king levied a forced loan, in which subjects were required to lend the same amount of money they would have paid in a legal tax on the promise that they would be paid somehow and sometime in the future. Many were sent to prison for refusing to pay; even more debated the limits to the king's prerogative. It is no accident that those Englishmen who came of political age during the wars of the 1620s were more likely to be roundheads, whereas those who did so during the 1630s tended to be cavaliers.[71]

Ship money played a similar role in the radicalization of many members of parliament. In the Grand Remonstrance of 1641, as relations between the king and parliament deteriorated, the Commons cited ship money as one of their major grievances. Such may have been the case—but only in retrospect. Notwithstanding the objections to the tax from those such as John Hampden, the vast majority paid, if not cheerfully. With the acuteness that only hindsight bestows, some historians have argued that the crown's inability to raise enough money to pay the ever-increasing costs of war in the first half of the seventeenth century inevitably led to a confrontation between king and parliament. However, the failure of the four expeditions was not due to a lack of finances. For instance, the assault on St Martins failed not because someone was trying to save a pound or two on lumber for the scaling ladders. In truth, as ship money showed, Charles could in fact raise large sums to build a large fleet without a widespread public refusal to pay. The failure of James's and Charles's military policies was due to bad planning and bad luck, poor leadership and downright incompetence. The seeds they planted in the 1620s were harvested in the 1640s.

Even though Charles spent much time and not a little money on the trained bands and militia, the state of those units that marched off to fight the First and Second Bishops' Wars (described in Chapter 7) was proof positive of the failure of his policies. Such weakness notwithstanding, the militia had exposed a very high proportion of the king's subjects to military matters. As the officers and men drilled, perhaps with little enthusiasm, and afterwards as they drank, with certainly far more gusto, they got to know each other better, and the bonds of civilian life were strengthened into comradeship. The militia was a firm enough foundation for parliament to use as a basis for their army, which, with many a change, won the Civil War.

Considering the ineptness that preceded that war, the conflict itself was fought with a surprising degree of competence. This was mostly due to the mercenaries who returned home in the late 1630s and early 1640s to offer their skills to whomever would pay. Many mercenaries were not too particular for whom they fought. Sir James Turner recalled that when in August 1640 he reached the harbour to take ship to return to Scotland, there were two vessels, one carrying mercenaries to fight for the king, and the other for the Scots Presbyterian rebels known as covenanters. He did not much care which one he boarded. 'I had swallowed without chewing in Germany a very dangerous maxim,' Turner explained; 'so long as we serve our master honestly, it is no matter which master we serve.'[72] When in May 1639 the Royal Navy captured a vessel carrying twenty Scots veterans home to fight for the covenant, they all promptly volunteered to fight for the crown. Returning from the Thirty Years War, Colonel Edward Massey went to York to seek a command in the king's service, but finding he lacked sufficient connections rode on to London where there was more money and fewer officers: he soon found a colonelcy in the parliamentary army.[73]

During the thirty-six years between the accession of James and the outbreak of the Civil Wars, large numbers of men from the British Isles served overseas as foreign mercenaries. The absence of such a large group of young violent males may have helped make the British Isles more pacific. In these years there were no rebellions, and only a few small revolts, such as those in the Fen country. In Ireland the period between 1603 and 1641 was also remarkably peaceful, especially when compared to the previous and ensuing six decades. While the absence of so many young men may have made the British Isles more peaceful, without doubt the return home of so many mercenaries skilled in the latest techniques for killing their fellow creatures made possible the bloody Civil Wars of the mid-seventeenth century. In October 1640, less than two years before the outbreak of that war in England, a letter writer sardonically observed that these mercenaries 'took up the trade of killing men abroad, and now are returned to kill, for Christ's sake, men at home'.[74]

CHAPTER 6

LOW-INTENSITY COMBAT: CAMPAIGNING

'tis the soldiers' life,
To have their balmy slumbers wak'd with strife.
Othello, II, iii, 220–21.

MOST OF THE TYPICAL SOLDIER'S TIME WAS NOT SPENT IN BATTLES or sieges, but in the dull, usually arduous routine of campaigning and garrison duty. The former was sometimes punctuated by guerrilla attacks, skirmishes and ambushes. The latter could become a siege if the enemy made a concerted attack (see Chapter 9). In what Winston Churchill called 'a well-written, soldierly account', Sergeant John Millner of the Royal Regiment of Ireland described his experiences. They were typical of a veteran soldier. Between 1701 and 1712 Millner served in a garrison or was on furlough for 45.5 per cent of the time, mostly in the winter or early spring. During the summer and autumn he took part in twelve campaigns, being in the field for 73 months, and marched at least 5,082 miles on 446 days, an average of 11.25 miles per diem. The only year, recorded Millner, when 'we had neither battling nor sieging' was 1707; even so, 'we were somewhat employed in marching.'[1]

Garrisons

During the winter or early spring most soldiers spent their time in garrison duty, or else went home, either on paid or unpaid leave, or without leave. In foreign-based units, especially towards the end of our period, sergeants and junior officers would be sent home to recruit. In the spring most troops, as well as recruits, would return to their garrisons for training, and then go off to campaign, wage battles and fight sieges. During the seventeenth century 87 per cent of the battles were fought between April and November.[2] Some troops would remain in garrisons during the campaign season, protecting strongpoints. Up until 1558, for instance, there was a large English garrison in Calais. During the Thirty Years War and the British Civil Wars about half the troops were in garrisons.[3] The proportion decreased during the late seventeenth and early eighteenth centuries.

Garrison duty could be pleasant. Accommodations in barracks, churches, private or (better still) public houses were certainly more comfortable, and kept out the weather more effectively than tents or barns, or even the bare earth used on the march. Food was usually superior and more plentiful. There were opportunities for graft. During garrison duty in the War of the Spanish Succession (1701–14), Captain Richard Kane was in charge of collecting rent from his garrison's suttlers, those private merchants who supplied the troops. 'The part of my office I liked very well, judging at once that something would stick to my fingers,' he confessed. At the same time Peter Drake devised an equally profitable fiddle. He got a general to sign blank warrants for twenty-five soldiers, whose pay he collected. 'In for a penny, in for a pound,' he chortled, happy to make 'sixty ninepences' from the scam and not to be caught.[4]

Garrison troops could invite their families to come and stay with them, or they found pleasures elsewhere. Some liaisons were casual: in 1715 Christine Forbes, a deformed Edinburgh beggar, without any legs, had a child 'begotten in fornication with a soldier who went North'.[5] Other entanglements were less fleeting. In 1675 Ensign John Bernardi met a young gentlewoman, worth £6,000, who wanted to marry him. 'But she being of so prodigious a size,' he confessed, 'he had not the courage.'[6] James Turner, the Scots mercenary, was billeted in Oldendorpe in the house of a Dutch widow. 'She was very handsome, witty and discreet,' he fondly recalled.[7] With equal pleasure Captain Richard Kane looked back on garrison duty during the War of the Spanish Succession: 'I spent my time between lace and the bottle' (both apparently paid for by extorting from the suttlers). The Dublin garrison became so notorious that a Jacobite who spent the winter of 1690/91 there called it 'a seminary of vice, an academy of luxury or rather a sink of corruptions, and a living emblem of Sodom'.[8]

Some English soldiers were less enterprising in looking after their creature comforts. For instance, during the French winter of 1522/23 Elis Gruffudd, the Welsh veteran, reported that many of his comrades did not bother to build themselves warm shelters, lying instead on the earth under hedges, as they moaned they wanted to be back home in bed with their wives. Some tried to keep warm by sleeping beside fires: one unfortunate got so close that he burned his shoes and feet without waking, so tired was he. Some died of the cold. Gruffudd, who believed in the old soldiers' adage that 'any fool can be uncomfortable,' had found himself a warm bed 'where I was as snug as a small pig'.[9] In late October 1642, Captain Nathaniel Rich, who was serving with Essex's parliamentary levies in Lincolnshire, wrote that 'The winter is already come, and our lying in the field hath lost us more men than have been taken away either by the sword or the bullet.'[10] During their invasion of Scotland in 1650 most of Cromwell's army lacked tents, and thus lost four and a half thousand men to sickness.[11] During the winter of 1689/90, unlike the Dutch and French regiments in William III's service, the English soldiers did not build themselves cozy huts of timber lined with straw. As a result, Captain Kane recalled, three-quarters of the raw recruits 'died like rotten sheep'.[12] Most men were not provided with tents on campaign until the War of the Spanish Succession.

Crowded conditions in garrison promoted accidents and disease. In Dublin in the winter of 1597, 140 barrels of prime gunpowder exploded, killing 126 people.[13] At a siege in 1704 a pig destined for the slaughter escaped, and a soldier fired his pistol at it: he missed, hitting forty-five barrels of gunpowder instead. An officer sleeping beside the magazine was blown to smithereens, his limbs 'being found separate a vast distance from each other'.[14] The pig's fate is unrecorded. Men often slept in promiscuous proximity, with scant sanitation. Germs readily spread, leading to outbreaks of typhus, influenza and pneumonia—the latter being known as 'leaguer sickness'. Latrines overflowed, contaminating drinking water. Between March and August 1600 the sick rate for the English garrison at Lough Foyle, Ireland, rose from virtually zero to 60 per cent. It fell to 14 per cent by the following July, rising to 32 per cent in September. Of the fourteen thousand soldiers sent to the West Indies in 1740–42, only a thousand died in combat: tropical diseases killed 93 per cent of the victims.[15]

Going to the Wars

Most of those who left home to go and campaign and fight had to part from loved ones, a painful experience, since many rightly feared that they would never meet again—at least in this world. Soon after he left for the War of the Spanish Succession, Corporal Matthew Bishop wrote to his wife, 'My Dear! It grieves my soul to part from you.' His commander, the duke of Marlborough, wrote to his spouse, 'It is impossible to express with what a heavy heart I parted with you, when I was by the water's side. I could have given my life to have come back.'[16] A few contemplated what might happen after their death. To 'My Dearest Betty,' R. W. wrote in 1678, 'I do not know what ghosts do or where they inhabit after Death: but I am sure, that if they retain any tincture of our souls, whilst you live, mine would sometime be so kind, as if to whisper in your ear, that I died yours.'[17]

Wives, of whatever rank, desperately missed and feared for their husbands off fighting. As a ballad put it in 1743:[18]

Oh, there he goes, my dear is gone
Gone is my heart's desire
Oh, may the bullets miss my John
That's all that I require.

Susan Rodway was terrified that her husband, Robert, a private in the London Trained Bands, who was fighting at the Siege of Basing House, Hampshire, in 1644, would be killed, and she be left a widow. She ended a letter to him: 'So I rest ever praying for your safe return.' At the other end of the social scale Mary missed her William with equal fervour. 'My heart is ready to break every time I think in what perpetual doings you are,' she wrote to her consort, William III, away at the Irish wars. Being the queen, she confessed, Mary II could not show any weaknesses or fears for his survival in public, but in private 'my heart is ready to break . . . I cannot sleep nor eat.' King William outlived his Mary; almost certainly, Private Rodway never made it home, and Susan never knew how and when her Robert died.[19]

Going to the wars not only produced countless widows and orphans, but deprived many women of the opportunity of getting married, and enjoying what was thought to be the natural and most felicitous state for females. The death of so many mainly unmarried males in battle left behind roughly as many women for whom there were no mates. In addition, a huge number of young men, mostly unmarried, left their native lands to serve overseas, where they might take foreign wives, have families and never come back home. Perhaps as many as a hundred thousand did so. According to one estimate, during the first half of the seventeenth century one in five young males fled Scotland as mercenaries.[20] In August 1644, when Civil War casualties peaked, John Denton wrote to his great aunt Isham, 'I think if these times hold there will be no men left for women.' And as if to prove the point his aunt Susan, a middle-aged spinster long past making a good match, fell in love and married Captain Jeremiah Abercrombie, a rugged Ulsterman. 'I think few of her friends like it a bit, but if she had not him she would not have any,' sniffed great aunt Isham.[21] Abercrombie was killed a few months later, leaving Susan a widow. In the early modern period men believed that once awakened in marriage, a woman's physical appetites continued undiminished in widowhood. So by making large numbers of lusty widows they feared that war could result in sexual tumult. This did not, of course, take place, but the large number of pamphlets written on the subject shows that, while they were fantasies, men's fears were real.[22]

Apart from the Civil Wars, going to the wars meant going overseas—a psychological as well as a physical transition. The movement usually began with typical military chaos. 'This day our regiment embarked' for Flanders, Captain Blackadder wrote in his diary for 7 March 1707, 'all has been noise, bustle and confusion.'[23] Most troops had never before left their native land or sailed across the sea. Some died; more were frightened and seasick; all found the voyage arduous. When Elis Gruffudd left for Calais in 1527, a storm blew up, not unusual for January. The sailors threw out the anchor, but it would not hold, prompting them to beseech various saints for succour. Gruffudd joined the chorus, promising to go on a pilgrimage to St Winifred's Shrine, North Wales, if God saved him. The vow seemed to do the trick. After the ship ran aground on the Goodwin Sands, where the crew jettisoned most of the cargo, the storm abated, enabling them to reach Calais. (Gruffudd never visited the shrine.) Lieutenant Richard Pope had a similar experience in 1702. On his way to join Marlborough's forces on the continent, a storm killed forty horses and nearly wrecked his ship on the Goodwin Sands.[24] Private John Deane's five-day trip from Scotland in 1707 was less perilous, although equally unpleasant. Jam-packed aboard, the Grenadier Guardsman slept on the deck, short of food. Landing in Flanders, Deane recalled, 'we bid adieu to the wooden world, being translated from Purgatory to Paradise, from pinch gut to whole allowance'.[25]

'A bad irregular way of living'

To get into combat men had first to campaign, an experience that the majority of them regarded as the most wretched part of military life—worse, in many ways, than battles or sieges. Thomas Raymond, an English veteran of the Thirty Years War, made this point: 'I cannot but think that the life of the private or common soldier is the most miserable in the world, and that not so much because his life is always in danger—that is little or nothing—but for the terrible miseries he endures in hunger and nakedness, in hard marches and bad quarters.' In 1581 Barnaby Rich wrote that campaigning was 'nothing but pain, travail, turmoil, disquiet, cold, hunger, thirst, penurie, bad lodging, worse fare, unquiet sleep'.[26] A decade later Robert Hitchcock, a grizzled captain of pioneers who had served under the Holy Roman Emperor Charles V, described campaigning as 'sharp services, penury, hunger, cold lying on the ground, and a hundred hazards, dangers and hard adventures'.[27] Writing from Maastricht to his uncle and aunt back home in 1631, Amias Steynings, an officer in the regiment (The Buffs) of Lord Horace Vere, baron of Tilbury, lamented, 'We have passed through a great many miseries both by sea and land since we left England, and are now in great want for lack of victuals.'[28] 'Long and quick marches in hot summer weather,' agreed Donald Lupton in 1641, 'cannot but be wonderfully burdensome.' George Carleton recalled, 'We had little to do but marching, and countermarching all the campaign' in the Low Countries in 1691.[29] 'Done nothing this campaign but march and countermarch, to very little purpose,' wrote Captain Roger Pope in August 1703. Two years later John Blackadder wrote in his diary, 'Sabbath. Marching all the day.' 'Still marching,' began his entry for 10 June. It continued, 'One day too much heat, another too cold, a bad irregular way of living.'[30]

Four things made campaigning such a bad, irregular way of living: foul weather; numbing tiredness; poor accommodation; and lousy food, drink and clothing.

Even though campaigning took place roughly from April to November, this was no guarantee of decent weather. Although it was early May, the weather in the Mourne Mountains, Ireland, in 1642 was the worst Sir James Turner had ever known, notwithstanding his experiences on the continent during the Thirty Years War. Rain, hail and wind blew down the tents, making sleep, a fire, and even warm food, impossible. Several troopers died of hypothermia. 'Great fatigue and toil, a very spare diet, lying on the ground, little sleep, constant watching,' was Turner's verdict.[31] From Derry in 1600 Captain Nicolas Dawtry complained to Robert Cecil, earl of Salisbury, that in twenty days' campaigning his clothing had never once been dry. 'Such weather was not known by the age of man,' a dragoon wrote to his family from Portugal in March 1703, 'with rains, and winds we could keep no tent standing.'[32] From Flanders at midsummer of the same year the Reverend Samuel Noyes reported enduring 'the worst day's march I ever saw: 'twas very cold, winds very high.'[33]

Sometimes campaigning in bad weather was deliberate. Charles Blount, Lord Mountjoy, completed the conquest of Ireland in 1603 because he fought during the winter, giving the enemy no respite. Neither they nor his own men liked this. In December one of Blount's soldiers, Nicholas Dawtrey (a putative prototype for Shakespeare's Falstaff), wrote home that the weather was the worst for thirty-seven years, that his clothes were always wet, and that although he 'plied his troops with whiskey and wine, I could not stop them from dropping from the country disease'—most likely dysentery or malaria.[34]

With its exhausting marches, carrying heavy loads over bad roads, getting by on little sleep and few vittles, campaigning was very tiring. No wonder Napoleon observed that the first quality demanded from a soldier is enduring fatigue, the second being courage.[35] Colonel Blackadder made this point to his wife in September 1709. 'Danger, though it be great, yet soon over,' he wrote, 'seems to me a small thing in comparison of a constant trial of fatigue either of body or mind. The former rouses the spirits, the other sinks them.'[36] In another letter, written after riding for thirty-four hours non-stop, Blackadder called exhaustion 'a hell on earth'. Tiredness wears men down, being a chief cause of post-traumatic stress disorder. Pikeman Raymond recalled how a season's campaigning turned the enthusiastic gallants who had volunteered to fight in Sir Philip Pakenham's company during the Thirty Years War into worn-out hulks of their former selves.[37] Practically every day from May 1689 to October 1690, Trooper R. Alexander was on the move, being involved in many skirmishes and ambushes, in one of which he was wounded. Eventually, he broke down and attacked the Sergeant of the Guard, but seems to have escaped punishment, pleading what we would call 'combat fatigue'.[38] Campaigning wore out even the best of units. 'I verily believe,' wrote Charles Croke, a member of the five cavalry troops sent to Portugal in 1662, 'there was never a more gallant company sent out from England . . . they came into the country full of money and gallantry, and those which survived it left as full of poverty and necessity.' Three months later Croke was cashiered for desertion.[39]

An obvious result of fatigue was being unable to stay awake. During the Siege of Guienne (1588) some English Troops fell asleep during combat. On the retreat from Devizes in 1643 Richard Atkyns, the royalist captain, admitted:[40]

I fell off my horse twice upon the Downs, before I came to Farringdon, where I reeled upon my horse so extremely that the people took me to be dead drunk. When I came to my house I desired my wife's aunt to provide a bed for me: the good woman took me to be drunk too. I slept at least fourteen hours together without waking.

Most soldiers went into battle bone-tired. Afterwards the victors could enjoy a good night's rest. Following their triumph at the Boyne in 1690 one of Williams III's men recalled, 'We shifted as well as we could without tents and servants and slept very heartily upon the ground.'[41]

On campaign the ground was frequently a man's bed—sometimes his sickbed. Four weeks of sleeping rough, out in the open, in 1643 cost Sir Thomas Barrington's regiment more men than they had lost in combat. The following year, during a sixty-nine-day campaign, Sir William Waller's army slept outside on twenty-one nights.[42] At least the ground was firm. 'For our comfort at night we had a base bog to lie upon,' recalled Captain Stevens about campaigning in Ireland.[43]

In theory, soldiers on campaign were supposed to be billeted in peoples' houses, churches, taverns, or warehouses. A quartermaster with his assistants would go ahead of the army, and place tickets (or billets) on the doors of buildings, listing how many men they could accommodate, and from which units. Here troops might spend the night in relative comfort, cooking a warm meal. In practice, things could be very different. Private James Sharloe remembered being billeted in a hut behind an alehouse in March 1698. They had no fire, there was hardly room for his eight-man squad to lie down, the two bundles of straw they were issued were not enough to sleep on, and the innkeeper's wife would not let them use her kitchen until all her other customers had eaten. That night it rained, and unable to sleep Private Carter amused himself by killing rats with his bayonet.[44] Richard Coe had a different problem in 1644. Billeted in a salt cellar in Salwich, Worcestershire, we 'grew so dry that we drunk the town dry'.[45]

'Lack of food,' observed Brigadier Bernard Fergusson, the Chindit commander, 'is the biggest single assault on morale.' Marlborough agreed that 'No soldier can fight unless he is properly fed on beef and beer.'[46] The anonymous author of *An Essay on the most effective way to Recruit the Army* (1707) boasted that 'The English are the best soldiers in the world so long as their Beef and Pudding lasts.' In theory, troops were supplied with two pounds of bread and one pound of meat a day plus two bottles of beer, amounting to 4,800 calories—plenty enough to support rigorous exercise. In addition, soldiers needed shoes, uniforms and ammunition. To maintain an army of sixty thousand men on the continent during the War of the Spanish Succession required 245,274 tons of food and fodder, including 15,155 tons of bread. If all these had to be exported from England, 441,339 tons of shipping were needed.[47]

Since tea, coffee and chocolate were unknown until the end of our period, when they were very expensive, troops did not often enjoy hot drinks. Frequent 'brew ups' were unknown. Unlike twentieth-century soldiers, who constantly smoked, there are few mentions of the use of tobacco in combat. The most poignant comes from the Siege of Rathbury Castle, Ireland, in 1642, when Christopher Rosgill, a tenant farmer, and one Tantalus, a barber, were so desperate for a smoke that they slipped out of the castle to scrounge tobacco. As they were sitting on a riverbank enjoying a puff, thirty royalists surprised them, hanged Tantalus, and speared Rosgill with a pike.[48] Even in those days smoking could kill.

Unlike a modern army, where as few as one soldier in sixteen actually fights, and logistics comprise 90 per cent of the organization's efforts, in early modern armies practically every soldier was engaged in combat. Supply and support were the responsibilities of civilians, such as soldiers'

'wives', or suttlers and carters hired for the campaign. Yet until the development of railways, supplying armies remained an intractable problem. It
depended on horse or ox-drawn carts which, often moving on bad roads,
could only make a dozen or so miles a day, and required huge amounts of
fodder, further compounding supply problems. During the Nine Years
War and the War of the Spanish Succession armies tried to pre-position
supply dumps, which limited their mobility, while increasing their size.
Sometimes, as in the conquest of Ireland or during attacks on Scotland,
armies tended to march along the coast or rivers, so as to be supplied by
ship.[49] Frequently, soldiers had to live off the land. They issued IOUs for
requisitioned goods, which might or might not be honoured. All too often
they resorted to outright plunder. As the Elizabethan soldier, Sir John
Smythe, put it, unpaid and unfed soldiers had to survive 'on the spoil and
misery of the common people'.[50]

But who could blame them? Ellis Gruffudd remembered having to eat
'old butter grown so mouldy, and of so many colours that a man had to
hold his nose'. Unable to find any food, Thomas Raymond tried tobacco,
but 'it made me sick and ill all day', so he switched to brandy, which, as
the equally hungry Private Bishop observed eighty years later, 'nourished
the inner man'.[51] Usually, generals faced less onerous privations. Echoing
generations of future Englishmen overseas, on the march to Blenheim
Marlborough complained he could not get a decent cup of tea. The earl of
Leicester's tribulations were more serious. 'We starve on every side,' he
wrote to Sir Francis Walsingham during the 1586 Netherlands campaign,
'If our people should be no better relieved, I look for the foulest mutiny.'[52]

Until the medical advances of the First World War, disease killed more
men than the enemy.[53] As 'Pestilence' boasted in Thomas Dekker's play
Dialogue Between Ware, Famine and Pestilence (1604):[54]

> Say that an army forty thousand strong
> Enter thy crimson lists, and of that number
> Perchance the fourth part falls, marked with red death.
> Why I slay forty thousand in one battle.

For one thing, soldiers were poorly fed and subject to intense physical
demands. 'By continual drinking of water, they cannot but be made weak,'
observed Queen Elizabeth, as she urged her troops fighting in Ireland to
drink beer.[55] Medical care was often poor, even non-existent: not a single
surgeon accompanied the thirty-two thousand troops during the 1544
Boulogne campaign. Some soldiers resorted to patent remedies. Barnaby
Gouge claimed to have cured himself of dysentery by drinking water out
of 'a rusty skull'. More pleasant was James Cathcart's medication. In

command of Fort Phillipina in Flanders in 1702, 'a melancholy spot' where 'my men died like rats', he attributed his survival to drinking a bottle of claret a day.[56] Poor weather, cold, rain, even snow added to men's miseries, especially when they could not change into dry clothes or find warm shelter. So as a rough rule of thumb, for every six months a unit spent in the field it could expect to lose half its strength, most to disease and a few to desertion. In the spring of 1585 Thomas Digges reported that over half the soldiers who had landed in France the previous August and September were dead, while many of the rest were so sick and feeble they would be better off in hospital at home, rather than drawing soldiers' pay abroad. Statistics do not convey the human cost of war-related disease. Take Colonel Christopher Codrington of the 1st Foot Guards (the Grenadiers), who caught a fever during the 1702 Guadalupe expedition. He was ill for four months in considerable pain, and lost his sight from taking too much laudanum. 'I am so spiritless,' he scribbled to a friend, 'that I am not able to hold up my head.' Codrington never fully recovered his health, dying eight years later.[57]

'For many of us never better'

Notwithstanding its stresses, privations and horrors, campaigning had its satisfactions. 'We live well and eat and drink all that we can get and lie upon the straw, and for many of us never better,' Thomas Coningsby wrote home from Rouen in 1591.[58] Of his service in the Thirty Years War, Thomas Raymond concluded 'so long as money lasted we had a merry life.'[59]

Campaigning, especially overseas, brought new experiences, which some soldiers lapped up as avidly as modern tourists. Pikeman Raymond found the Catholic churches and friars in the Spanish Netherlands especially intriguing. During the First Bishops' War in 1639 John Aston thought the parish church architecture in the north of England particularly pleasing (although he did complain that as they got closer to the border, 'the price of drink increases').[60] Richard Symonds's diary often reads more like a travelogue than the military journal of a cavalier captain.[61] The same might be said of the memoirs of Ensign Charles Croke of the Horse Guards, who fought in Portugal in 1663. Like devotees of the *Michelin Guide*, he and his brother officers made detours to see particularly worthwhile sights, which added variety and made their perambulations more enjoyable. They ate new foods, such as figs, olives, oranges, lemons and pomegranates, and were fascinated by papist hermits 'wearing nothing but hairy gowns'.[62] As a younger son, Captain Henry Herbert had been denied going on a Grand Tour. Yet his service in the British Brigade in the 1670s made up for it—at least in part. Of Cologne he wrote, 'The cathedral here is not so great nor so sumptuous as we expected.'[63] Everything about the country impressed another English officer who campaigned in the Netherlands in 1689, except for the women: 'Fat, burly and unsightly' was his judgement.[64]

More than anything else, what made campaigning bearable, even pleasant, was the friendship of comrades. Captain John Hodgson remembered that during the Scots campaigning of 1650 someone found a large barrel full of cream, which he brought to the officers' mess. They drank it by the dishful, some filling their hats with cream. When the churn grew low two officers turned it upside down over a third's head, so he could lick the inside as the cream dribbled down all over his clothes. Everyone thought it hilarious, including Oliver Cromwell, who paused to watch the fun.[65] Captain Josiah Bodley fondly recalled a New Year's Eve he spent with two brother captains, Caulfield and Constable, in Governor Richard Moryson's lodgings, during the brutal conquest of Ireland. Having taken off their coats they talked of various things, Caulfield on food, Constable about hounds, as they drank mulled Spanish wine laced with nutmeg, ginger and sugar. An hour later they went into dinner, a magnificent feast, after which they retired to a bedroom for pipes of tobacco and more drink. 'The wine also had begun to operate a little upon us, and everyone's wits became somewhat sharper: all gabbling at once.' They all said many witty things that afterwards they could not recall. Finally, they played what might best be described as 'officers' mess games', laughing until tears streamed from their eyes.[66]

The company of women brought a different sort of pleasure. In 1633 in the Netherlands a soldier had a 'pretty young wench, which lay with him in his hut'. A comrade—if that is the right word—under the impression that the man was on guard duty stole into the hut, to steal a kiss, if not more. Feeling a set of hairy lips, he leapt out of bed, chased by the hirsute trooper who stabbed him a couple of times in the buttocks.[67] But women were much more than a source of discord or bawdy humour. On the march, in garrisons, during sieges, and even battles, they were a means to survival. Whether or not blessed by the clergy, army 'wives' were a source of vittles and succour. They nursed the sick and wounded. They foraged for food and firewood. As Sir James Turner recognized, 'As woman was created to be a helper to man, so women are greater helpers in armies.' Quite simply, without camp followers early modern armies could not have functioned.[68]

Atrocities

Shortage of food, and a blindly malicious sense of fun, led soldiers to steal from the civilians through whose territories they marched. Captain Henry

Herbert recalled about the 1672 campaign in Holland that both the French and English 'loving mischief for mischief's sake, would kill cattle and leave them to lie to infect the air having no need for them.' Chaplain Noyes wrote that 'We plundered and burnt almost all the villages to right and left,' as Marlborough's men marched through Germany in July 1704, 'our men could not be restrained from plundering.'[69] Sometimes troops stripped the land bare. 'The country is so wasted there is nothing to destroy,' observed Captain John Brende, as he trekked through the Scottish Lowlands in 1548.[70]

Irish troops were particularly eager plunderers. During the 1544 Boulogne campaign they ranged the French countryside to find a bull, which they tormented with flaming torches. The poor creature's bellows attracted cows, who were led back to camp for slaughter.[71] This—and their habit of cutting the heads off enemy prisoners of war—prompted the French to torture and mutilate any Irish they could lay their hands on.[72]

Afterwards soldiers had the problem of disposing of the loot, for unlike sailors they could not transport it home on their ships. Stolen food and drink were readily consumed. Gold, silver coins and precious stones could be sown into the linings of uniforms. But most goods were too heavy to be carried on the march. Sometimes a market would be held after a city had been sacked, at which troops disposed of their spoils at knock-down prices. Cattle, sheep and horses were easily moved, so in localities such as Ireland or the Scottish Borders, where they were a significant form of wealth, rustling became endemic.

Civilians could react to plunderers in two ways: by trying to pay them off or by fighting back. During the 1591 Rouen expedition peasants deserted their villages, leaving food and cider on their tables in the hope the English invaders would take them and do no further damage. Or else, like the Clubmen, a group of neutrals during the English Civil War, they could resist. As one of the Clubman ballads warned:[73]

If you offer to plunder or take our Cattle,
Be assured we will bid you battle.

George Carleton remembered that in the 1680s the Dutch peasants used their bread ovens to bake alive any marauders they caught. Three decades later Chaplain Noyes recalled that many plunderers became detached from their units, and that those captured by enemy hussars 'were not only killed, but left miserably mangled'.[74] Such a fate discouraged desertion, which during the War of the Spanish Succession fell to 5 per cent a year.

Plundering provoked atrocious reactions, which in turn could be followed by even bloodier reprisals. None was worse than that at Molain,

Belgium. At the end of the War of the Spanish Succession six hundred British soldiers advanced on the town, hell-bent on booty. When the inhabitants opened fire, killing several troops, the British went berserk, and drove the inhabitants into the church, which they set alight, burning four hundred alive. They plundered and then set fire to the town, before getting royally drunk.[75]

Skirmishes and Ambushes

As they campaigned, soldiers had to deal not only with hunger, tiredness, bad weather and hostile civilians, but constant small-scale enemy assaults. 'There did hardly one week pass in the summer half year,' wrote Captain Richard Atkyns of the English Civil Wars, 'in which there was not a battle or skirmish.'[76]

Skirmishes are little battles, which usually occur when two sides bump into each other. Because of their almost spontaneous nature, and because there is rarely time beforehand to assemble large forces, few men on either side are involved. Unlike major battles or sieges, which are deliberate events to which both sides must agree and contribute considerable resources, skirmishes happen by accident. While they are less well known than battles, they could produce many casualties. For instance, only two of the 179 petitions submitted by wounded royalist veterans in Devon after the Civil Wars were for injuries suffered during a battle.[77] Skirmishes often involved cavalry, who, as scouts, were often the first to come into contact with the enemy, usually another horse patrol. Thomas Churchyard described an especially brutal melee that occurred in France in 1557:[78]

> The English band provoked the skirmish, and so the blood broil began hotter and hotter, and came to hand strokes, where many a lance was broken, and many a man lay grovelling on the ground, some under their horses.

When he was a schoolboy growing up in Myddle, Shropshire, during the Civil War, Richard Gough saw a skirmish similar to hundreds, perhaps thousands, of others during the early modern period. Cornet Collins, an Irishman from the royalist garrison at Shrawardine Castle, stopped in the village that the king's men considered their territory, having plundered it the previous day, to have his horse shod. Unfortunately for him, a patrol of eight roundheads from Morton Corbett, under the command of Richard Maning, entered Myddle ostensibly to arrest one Nat Owen for theft and desertion. (Maning also suspected that Owen was having an affair with his wife.) The two patrols bumped into each other at Allen

Chaloner's smithy. Collins jumped on his horse and galloped away, but was shot, toppling into the village pond. His two troopers fired at the roundheads, killing one of their horses, but managed to escape—only to be captured soon afterwards. Being Irish, they were hanged. The villagers pulled Collins from the pond, and carried him bleeding profusely to Chaloner's house, where they dumped him on the floor. Collins begged for a soft mattress to relieve the pain. There was none, Mrs Chaloner replied, presumably with a degree of satisfaction, explaining that when he plundered her house the previous day, he had thrown the mattress into the village pond out of spite. Nonetheless she retrieved the tattered, sodden paillasse and slid it under the officer, before summoning the local minister. 'I went with him,' recalled Richard Gough, 'and saw the Cornet lying on the bed, and much blood running along the floor.' That night a party took Collins back to Shrawardine, where he died the next day.[79]

Lieutenant John Creighton never forgot the equally brutal skirmish that took place at about five in the afternoon of 22 July 1680 at Ayr's Moss, Scotland, when his cavalry troop came across some covenanters under a Captain Fowler:

> I gave him such a blow on the head with my broad sword, as would have cleaved his skull, had it not been defended by a steel cap. Fowler, turning about, aimed a blow at me, but I warded it off, and with a back stroke cut the upper part of his head off from the nose upwards.

In his haste to pursue the fleeing rebels, Creighton rode into a bog. With cuts to his back and ribs, he broke his own sword on a rebel's head, before being shot and hit on the head. He fell off his horse, and was left for dead. Recovering consciousness he tried to lift himself up, attracting the attention of a covenanter, who cackled, 'God, the dog is not dead yet,' and tried to run him through the belly. Creighton managed to deflect the blow, even though his sword was broken, prompting his enemy to run away. In great pain he staggered to his feet, and using a carbine as a crutch hobbled to find his horse. But it had been stolen by a rebel (who, Creighton noted with much pleasure, was captured and hanged the following year). It took Creighton a long time to recover from his wounds because some green cloth had been forced into one of them, presumably by a sword blow, and sewn inside by an incompetent surgeon. The gash festered. So lead tubes were inserted to allow the pus to escape, and to introduce brandy, which sterilized the abscess. Eventually the cloth seeped out, and the wound healed. Nonetheless, Creighton recalled, 'I was never afterwards so able to bear fatigue.'[80]

Skirmishes were fast and frenzied. James Wallace, a covenanter, described one such encounter: 'The two parties meet, and after fire given

on both sides, they fall to it with their swords,' until one side broke and
ran. Captain Carleton knew how brutal skirmishes could be. In 1704 in
Spain a Scottish dragoon, a fairly small man, used his huge broadsword to
strike the head off an enemy as easily as lopping a poppy. For Carleton the
definition of a skirmish depended on its size. 'Although the common
vogue has given it the name of a Battle,' he wrote about the fighting that
took place near Senoff, 'in my humble opinion, it might rather have
deserved the name of a confused skirmish. I found it impossible to distinguish one part from another.'[81]

Ambushes were different from skirmishes since they were deliberately
set by one side to catch the other unawares. Captain Roger Williams
described how his unit ambushed a Spanish convoy moving from Ghent
to Bruges in about 1573. He positioned his men at dawn. As the convoy,
with fifty cavalry in the front and as many in the tail, and infantry
guarding the cannon and supplies in the middle, entered the ambush
zone, the allies fired a musket volley, their cavalry charged the infantry,
who ran, allowing the allied foot to capture the artillery and ammunition
with little loss. Being ambushed was utterly terrifying. Sergeant Henry
Foster remembered how the royalists surprised the London Trained
Bands, retreating through narrow lanes near Aldermaston in September
1643. The roundheads panicked. Up went the cry, 'Away, Away, everyman
shift for his life, you are all dead men.' Horses bolted, overturning carts,
blocking the narrow road. An ammunition wagon caught fire, blew up,
killing ten men: it scared the rest, and illuminated targets for the royalist
snipers hiding in the hedgerows. Amazingly, the London Trained Bands
(an elite parliamentary unit), regrouped, and following classical military
procedure, charged the surprised ambushers who fled or were captured. In
hot blood, helpless from terror, yet relieved to be alive, the Londoners
smashed in the prisoners' brains with musket butts.

Soon after Donald McBane enlisted in 1687, the Clan MacDonald
ambushed his unit at Keppoch. 'I was sadly affrighted, never having seen
the like before,' he confessed. 'I took to my heels and ran thirty miles
before I looked behind.'[82] McBane (who has been described as 'a soldier,
pimp, thief, gambler and duelist') ran away to fight another day.[83] In fact,
over the next half century he fought in fifty-two sieges and sixteen battles,
where he discovered all too well what it was like to experience high-
intensity combat, which will be described in Chapter 9.

CHAPTER 7

ALL DISEAS'D:
CIVIL WARS AND
COMMONWEALTH: EVENTS,
1638–1660

We are all diseas'd,
And, with our surfeiting and wanton hours
Have brought ourselves into a burning fever
And we must bleed for it.
Henry IV, Part 2, IV, 1, 61–64

IN APRIL 1786 THOMAS JEFFERSON AND JOHN ADAMS WERE TOURING
England, the nation from which the United States had just won a war
of independence. They made a pilgrimage to Edgehill, the first battle in the
first of three British revolutions that culminated in their own. Adams was
irate at the locals' ignorance of what had happened at Edgehill. 'Tell your
neighbours and your children that this is holy ground,' the future president
declared, 'all England should come in pilgrimage to this hill once a year.'[1]

Now each year many thousand people do come to Edgehill, and to the
other Civil War battlefields, not as pilgrims but as re-enactors (and spectators). It is no accident that today the largest and most consistent groups
who commemorate the past in the United Kingdom are the members and
fans of the Sealed Knot and the English Civil War Society, who every
summer dress up to refight the battles of the mid-seventeenth century.
They do so both because it is fun and because war has an enduring fascina-
tion. But they could choose to re-enact other conflicts, such as the
Napoleonic Wars (a fight in which the British played a distinguished role)
or the Second World War (clearly a struggle between good and evil). Yet
they select the British Civil Wars because—even after over three and a
half centuries—these wars still speak to numerous audiences.

No event in the history of the British Isles had a greater effect on world history than the Civil Wars which broke out in Scotland in 1639, continued until the restoration of the monarchy in 1660, and were in many ways unresolved until the Glorious Revolution of 1688–92. These wars were a defining moment: G. M. Trevelyan argued that they were the most important happening in our history; Simon Schama called them 'the crucible of our modern history'. But in order to assess the impact of these wars (which will be the subject of Chapter 8), we must first examine their nature, causes, outbreak and progress.

The Nature of the Civil Wars

Almost since the first shot was fired, historians have differed over what to call these wars. At the time phrases such as 'these unnatural wars' or 'civil wars' were commonplace. Soon they became known as 'The Great Rebellion'. Great because it was significant; rebellion because it was illegitimate. This view predominated until the nineteenth century when Thomas Babington Macaulay argued that the Civil Wars were essentially a Herculean struggle between liberty and despotism, which the former won, thus making possible the glories of Victorian England. Towards the end of the century, S. R. Gardiner portrayed the turmoil as a Puritan Revolution, in which Godly Protestants resisted the Counter-Reformation of pseudo-Catholic royalists. In more recent times Karl Marx and his followers have interpreted the breakdown of mid-seventeenth-century England as the first great Bourgeois Revolution. During this period the gentry supposedly rose—or at least the mere gentry came to the top—as the aristocracy experienced a crisis. Lately, revisionist historians have stressed the short-term, even accidental nature of events, in which the acts of individuals played a more important role than the seemingly inevitable and impersonal forces that the Reformation set in motion a century before. Some have suggested that the Civil Wars were essentially Wars of Religion; others that they were the last great baronial revolt.[2]

Whatever to call them has been, and still is, a matter of much debate. Contemporaries recognized the conflict's complex nature, the first use of the term 'Civil Wars' being in a pamphlet of 1643.[3] Yet two points are crystal clear: that the conflicts affected every part of the British Isles, and that they were a series of wars. They opened with the First Bishops' War of 1639 and the Second Bishops' War of 1640. The First English Civil War lasted from 1642 to 1646, the Second took place in 1648, while the Third lasted from 1649 to 1651. Fighting in Scotland started with the First Bishops' War in 1639 and ended in 1651 with the Battle of Worcester. The Irish Revolt of 1641 began the Wars of the Confederation, which lasted until 1653, being followed by the brutal Cromwellian Settlement in which hundreds of thousands lost their lands, being forced to move to the barren province of Connaught or driven into exile. Since many died— more in relative terms than in any British war before or since—describing them as wars is obvious. They should also be called British, because they affected every corner of the isles, being the first major event in the history of England, Scotland and Ireland together. These events were, first, caused by conflicts between the three kingdoms, and, second, resulted in funda- mental changes in the relations between them.[4] Thus I prefer to call this multinational and complicated conflict 'the British Civil Wars'.

Naming the events of the middle of the seventeenth century is not a tidy process—which is appropriate, since they were far from tidy events. In most Civil Wars there have been clear determinants of each side, be they regions (as in America), sects (as in Ulster or Lebanon), ethnicity (as in Sri Lanka or Nigeria), or ideology (as in Russia or China). While such determinants prevailed in the Irish and Scots Civil Wars, they were not as clear-cut in the English ones. Except for Middlesex, in no English county were all the members of parliament, including those who represented boroughs, on the same side. As Lucy Hutchinson, the wife of a leading parliamentarian, recalled, 'Every Country had the civil war, more or less, within itself.' The way in which 'the flame of war broke out', she believed, confused her contemporaries.[5] Richard Ward used the same simile of fire in his *Anatomy of Warre* (1642) to blame the eruption of the conflagration on a lack of understanding. 'As children through ignorance of the nature and peril of Fire often fall thereinto and are burnt, so men not acquainted with the nature and danger of war, too often desire it and too soon rush into it.'[6] A roundhead song, 'The Zealous Soldier', written in August 1642, before the fighting really began, expressed a sense of innocent, even naive enthusiasm:

For God and his cause I'll count it gain
To lose my life. Oh can one happier die
Than to fall in battle to maintain
God's worship, truth, extirpate Papacy?

John Taylor, the water poet (and retired naval veteran), had a ready explanation for such misplaced zeal:[7]

Methinks the proverb should not be forgot
That wars are sweet to those who know them not.

Another poet, Samuel Butler, confessed that people could not explain the outbreak of war:[8]

When Civil Fury first grew high
And men fell out, they knew not why.

Bulstrode Whitelock, a lawyer and member of parliament, reflected this
sense of puzzled ignorance when he wrote to his wife in July 1642:[9]

It is strange to note how we have insensibly slid into the beginnings of
a civil war, by one unexpected accident after another, as waves of the sea,
which have brought us thus far, and scarce we know how.

Thomas Knyvett, a Norfolk gentleman, knew whom to blame. 'The one
party now grows as resolute as the other is obstinate,' he told his wife in
May 1642. But he did not know where to go, adding 'Oh Sweet heart, I
am now in a great strait what to do.' Eventually he fought for the king,
because, as the inscription on his tombstone explained, 'Here lies loyal
Knyvett, who hated anarchy.'[10]

The Bishops' Wars

It was the fear of anarchy that disturbed most Englishmen, as the British
Isles drifted into a war that first began in Scotland in 1639. The outbreak
of two wars between England and Scotland, known as the Bishops' Wars,
can be traced back to 1603, when James VI of Scotland became James
I of England, thus giving the two nations a joint monarchy but little else
in common. His successor, Charles I, aimed at strengthening the links
between the two nations by enhancing the Scottish system of bishops
(hence the wars' nomenclature), and attempting to force the Scots to
accept a new prayer book. They refused to do so, rioting in St Giles
Cathedral on 23 July 1637, the day the new liturgy was first used. Some
Scots even threw stones at black and white dogs, whose coats allegedly
resembled bishops' copes, to show their contempt for episcopacy. Tens of
thousands of Scots signed (some with their own blood) a covenant vowing
to reject the new prayer book as well as bishops, both of which they saw
as English and—worse still—papist innovations. Thus they became
known as covenanters, who, as one of their pamphlets explained, 'are
driven in such straits as we must either . . . . Suffer the ruin of our estates,
or else . . . fall under the wrath of God'.[11]

Charles rejected the advice of John Stewart, earl of Traquair, that it
would take a permanent garrison of forty thousand English soldiers to
make the Scots accept the new liturgy. To do so, he wrote, underlining his
words to show the strength of his feeling (the only time but one he ever
did so), was because it would quite literally be '*damnable*', jeopardizing his

immortal soul.[12] Charles, as was his wont, attributed the worst of motives to his enemies: their real objective, he convinced himself, was to establish a banana republic, as ludicrous as, say, that of Venice, which would condemn his dominions to anarchy. Once Charles accepted this specious argument, war became both logical and inevitable.

The Bishops' Wars were far more important politically than militarily because they were waged incompetently, and because both sides shied away from hard fighting. When they came to unwelcome blows, they shadow-boxed with great restraint and scant enthusiasm.

Charles's plans for the First Bishops' War were ambitious. A contingent of Irish Catholics were to land near Carlisle, as their fellows in Ulster harassed the province's Scots settlers. With an expeditionary force of five thousand troops James, marquess of Hamilton, invaded the Firth of Forth region, but failed to prevent the covenanters from taking either Aberdeen or Edinburgh Castle. After routing the royalists at the 'Trot of Turriff', a Scottish force commanded by Sir Alexander Leslie, a veteran who had fought as a Dutch and Swedish mercenary, invaded England. On 30 May 1639 Charles joined his army of twenty thousand men at Berwick. Neither side wanted to fight: few Englishmen were willing to hazard their lives for an unpopular king; most Scots shrank from fighting their divinely anointed sovereign. On 4 June Henry Rich, earl of Holland, led a mixed army of a thousand cavalry and three thousand infantry on a reconnaissance into Scotland. Since the former could ride faster than the latter could march, particularly on hot summer days when most foot soldiers lacked water bottles, the cavalry were on their own when they came across Leslie's men at Kelso. Unwilling to attack, Holland retreated. This pusillanimous episode shattered the morale of the English forces. Before Kelso an English officer boasted, 'here is a gallant company of cavaliers as brave in courage as in clothes.' Afterwards a captain quaked, 'The Scots are very strong ... our army is very weak.'[13] Negotiations opened on 10 June, and a week later both sides agreed to start demobilizing within forty-eight hours.

Charles's defeat forced him to call a parliament in April 1640, the first in over eleven years. Relations between the king and commons rapidly broke down, and early on the morning of 5 May Charles suddenly dismissed parliament, confident that he could use Irish troops to quell both the commons and the covenanters. Thus he started the Second Bishops' War.

The king left London on 20 August 1640 to join his northern army. The same evening a huge Scottish army crossed the Tweed at Coldstream and advanced towards Newcastle. Forty thousand strong, it amounted to 4 per cent of the total Scottish population.[14] Even though Charles had at least twenty-five thousand men arrayed on the border, they were poorly trained. 'We were never disciplined, nor mustered,' one of them wrote in his diary.[15] Sir Edward Conway could only collect three thousand infantry and fifteen hundred cavalry to march the four miles from Newcastle to Newburn to try and stop the invaders from crossing the Tweed. Like many battles, that of Newburn began on 28 August in a haphazard way. Each side was on one bank of the river, waiting for the tide go out to let them cross. An English trooper, annoyed by the arrogant way in which a Scots officer stared at him, opened fire, wounding the fellow. Fighting mad, the covenanters waded across the river, routing the enemy. The only heroes of the Second Bishops' War were a couple of Welsh soldiers who stood and fought to the death, as their English comrades skedaddled for Newcastle.[16] The Scots easily seized the counties of Northumberland and Durham, forcing the king to sign a treaty at Ripon on 26 October.

At times during the Bishops' Wars it seemed as if a madness swept the land. Many English draftees tried to dodge fighting the Scots. One hung himself. In Kent, Henry Oxinden got two of his tenants exempted. In Lincolnshire and Essex conscripts cut off their big toes so they could not march north.[17] The troops that did so were poorly led. An observer noted that their commander, Thomas Howard, the earl of Arundel, 'had nothing martial about him but his presence and looks'.[18] The marquess of Hamilton, leader of the amphibious attack on the east coast, did not want to go to Scotland, telling the king 'next to hell I hate this place'. He became even more loath to fight after his mother vowed personally to shoot him if he ever set foot in their native land.[19]

The royal army was as poorly equipped and fed as it was led. Unlike the Scots, only senior English officers had tents, leaving the men to sleep on the ground. Many of the pistols issued to the soldiers had broken butts, or ones that had been poorly glued together. In theory, this made them far more lethal to the firer than the target: in practice, the point was moot because the firing mechanisms rarely worked, and many pistols lacked touch holes. When soldiers' pay was docked to cover the cost of repairing the deficiencies in their weapons, some of them mutinied, for which two were hanged. Others resorted to fragging. 'Our soldiers are so disorderly that they shoot bullets through our own tents,' an officer wrote home, 'the king's tent was shot through once.'[20] 'Most of them beggarly fellows,' wrote one officer about King Charles's bad bargains. Sir John Poulett agreed that the king had 'the fewest volunteers that I ever saw in any army'. Sir Edmund Verney told his son that 'Our men are very raw, our arms of all sort naught, victuals scarce and provisions for horses worse. I daresay there was never so raw, so unskillful and so unwilling an army brought to fight.' Lord Conway agreed that the troops were 'more fit for Bedlam or Bridewell' than the king's service.[21]

So scared was one company of recruits of being ambushed by latter-day Robin Hoods that as they marched north through Sherwood Forest they doubled their guards.[22] Yet the most disturbing thing about the English troops was not their poor fighting ability, but the crimes they committed which, noted Sir Jacob Astley, proved that they were 'all the archknaves in the kingdom'.[23] In Selby, Yorkshire, soldiers beat up their own officers and civilians. In Derbyshire they tore down enclosures. In Marlborough, Wakefield, Derby, London and Cirencester, they broke into jails to free comrades and those who had refused to pay taxes to fight the Scots. In Essex levies murdered a pregnant woman, and plundered several houses. They mutinied in Royston, Beccles and Cambridge. Troops beat up Oxford undergraduates, whom they despised as both draft dodgers and as the privileged progeny of an Anglican bastion. Pressed men from Staffordshire tore down fences around a game park in Uttoxeter for kindling.[24]

The religious context of many outrages was obvious. In Suffolk conscripts started wearing white sheets to parody bishops' surplices. In churches in Hertfordshire and Essex troops chopped up the recently installed altar rails for firewood. The most notorious outrages were the murder of officers whom conscripts suspected of being Catholics. At Faringdon, Oxfordshire, recruits, outraged at Lieutenant William Mohun (who was rumoured to be a papist) for almost cutting off a drummer's hand after the lad hit him with his stick, attacked the officer when he was upstairs in a tavern having dinner. They forced him to crawl out on the beam from which the inn sign hung, beating and stoning him until he fell to the ground. Convinced he was dead, they tossed him into a dung heap. Barely alive, Mohun crawled out. So they stabbed him, cudgelled his brains, and dragged the lieutenant's corpse through the town to place it in the pillory. At Wellington some conscripts from Devon suspected that their officer, Lieutenant Compton Evers, was a papist, so they murdered him and looted his body, on which they found a crucifix, which confirmed their worst suspicions. The only way that Francis Windebanke, scion of a distinguished Catholic family, could convince his new company that he was a Protestant, and thus get them to obey him, was to order them to kneel and sing psalms, before issuing them with drink and 'stinking tobacco'. Thus Captain Windebanke convinced 'the Godly' that he was such a jolly good fellow that he could not possibly be a papist.[25] Many ordinary folk protested vehemently against such crimes. 'We find ourselves oppressed with the billeting of unruly soldiers, whose speeches and actions tend to the burning of our villages,' declared a Yorkshire petition, 'as we cannot say that we possess our wives, children and estates in safety.'[26]

The Irish Rebellion, 1641

Nonetheless the impact of the Bishops' Wars in preparing the king's subjects for Civil War was limited. What changed attitudes—with the decisiveness of the 1914 invasion of Belgium, Pearl Harbor, or 9/11—was the outbreak of the Irish rebellion in October 1641.

Admittedly, this sea change would not have been possible had not Charles's defeat in the Second Bishops' War, and his need to raise the £860 a day he had agreed in the Treaty of Ripon to pay the Scots army for their costs of occupying Northumberland and County Durham, forced him once again to call parliament in November. Known as the Long Parliament (since it sat on and off from 1640 to 1660), during its first year it tried to devise a constitutional form of monarchy that limited the king's power and ensured parliaments were called at least every three years. All that this excellent plan lacked was a king who was willing to be a constitutional monarch.

Matters came to a head in late 1641 with the outbreak of a rebellion in Ireland, which more than anything else, at least in the short term, precipitated the Civil War. As we have seen, the English conquest of Ireland was comparatively recent, being completed with the earl of Tyrone's surrender in 1603. Most Irish Catholics resented the English and Scots, especially those Protestant settlers who had stolen their lands. In Ireland religion was the cursed divide. 'I see plainly,' explained Thomas Wentworth, earl of Strafford, Charles I's Lord Lieutenant of Ireland in 1634, 'that so long as this kingdom continues popish, they are not a people for the crown of England to be confident of.'[27]

As has so often been the case, England's difficulties were Ireland's opportunity. In the autumn of 1641, with king and parliament deadlocked over a constitutional settlement, throughout Ireland Catholics spontaneously rose against the alien oppressors. 'The crisis has burst upon us with the suddenness of a violent torrent,' wrote Sir John Temple, Irish Master of the Rolls, as he cowered inside Dublin Castle: inflamed by Jesuits, the rebels 'march on furiously destroying all the English, sparing neither sex nor age, most barbarously murdering them, and that with greater cruelty than was ever used amongst Turks or Infidels'.[28]

Thousands were massacred with a brutality that became more gruesome with every telling. Babes were reported snared on pikes, or cut from their mothers' wombs, children were roasted on spits, daughters were raped—all as parents and spouses were forced to watch. According to *Treason in*

Ireland for blowing up of the King's English Forces with 100 Barrels of Gunpowder (1642)—a pamphlet whose title aroused memories of Guy Fawkes—at Rockoll, accompanied by bagpipes, which 'they played exceedingly loud', the rebels 'cruelly murdered' an English family. At Nassey they slew Henry Orell, his wife and daughter 'in the most barbarous manner that ever was known'.[29] At Athy they hanged an English woman by her hair from her door, and boiled a maidservant alive in a beer vat. At Kilkenny they raped Mrs Atkins, who was heavy with child, before ripping open her womb, and then tossing mother and child into a fire. In County Tyrone sixteen Scots children were purportedly hanged alive, and a fat Caledonian killed, to be rendered into candles. The rebels tied another victim to a tree, slit open his belly, pulled out his intestines to see whether 'a dog's or Scotchman's guts were the longer'.[30]

Such atrocity stories lost nothing in the telling as they crossed the Irish Sea to England, particularly when they were brought by thousands of terrified refugees, and illustrated by cheap stomach-churning woodcuts. Estimates as to the number of victims grew exceedingly. Devereux Spratt, a clergyman from Tralle, reported that the papists had massacred a hundred and fifty thousand Protestants; both Richard Baxter and Lucy Hutchinson put the figure at two hundred thousand, while in 1646 Sir John Temple thought three hundred thousand had died. Since there were fewer than a hundred thousand Protestants in Ireland, contemporary estimates were grossly exaggerated, twenty, thirty, perhaps fortyfold.[31]

Even so, it would be hard to overstate the effect their deaths had on the rest of the British Isles. Like the massacres in 1857 at the start of the Indian Mutiny (or, if you prefer, the First War of Indian Independence), these killings united Englishmen in righteous anger to punish the perpetrators. In April 1642, 37 per cent of the pamphlets published in England touched on the rebellion in Ireland.[32] Four days after its outbreak, Secretary of State Sir Edward Nicholas wrote from London to the king that 'the alarm of popish plots amaze and fright the people here more than anything'.[33] 'O what fears and tears, cries and prayers, day and night, was there then in many places, and in my dear mother's house in particular!' remembered Joseph Lister of Bradford, 'I was about twelve or thirteen years old, and though I was afraid to be killed, yet was I weary of so much fasting and praying.' Looking back, Richard Baxter, the minister from Kidderminster, agreed that 'the terrible massacre in Ireland, and the threatening of the rebels to invade England were the chief reasons why the nation moved to a state of war'.[34]

It took nearly a year to do so.

All Englishmen agreed that an army must be raised to exterminate the Irish rebels in a war of virtuous revenge.[35] But they could not agree who should control it. Many no longer trusted the king, particularly after

5 January 1642 when he demonstrated his disdain for any constitutional limits on his authority by staging a military *coup d'état*. At the head of a company of heavily armed soldiers, Charles marched into the commons chamber to arrest the five members whom he believed were the ringleaders hell-bent on treason. But, as the king plaintively noted, looking around the chamber from the speaker's chair, 'the birds have flown'. Forewarned, they had taken refuge in the City of London. Frustrated, the next day, like a dazed driver staggering away from a road accident, Charles and his family left London for Windsor. Their departure was so hasty that there were no bedsheets for them at the castle. It was the first of many uncomfortable nights the king was to endure as England drifted into Civil War.

The nation did so over what Charles called 'The Fittest subject for a king's quarrel'.[36] Fearful that he would use the army, which was being raised to put down the Irish Rebellion, to crush them first the House of Commons passed a Militia Bill depriving the king of his long-standing right to appoint army officers. Charles refused point-blank. 'You have asked of me that was never asked of a king and with which I would not trust my wife and children,' he angrily told the parliamentary deputation who begged him to sign the bill.[37]

So it was over this fundamental issue—the control of the army—that the king and parliament went to war. Both would have fervently agreed with Mao Zedong that political power came out of the barrel of a gun— or, at least, a musket. Without the control of the armed forces, declared Charles, 'Kingly power is but a shadow.'[38] So on 23 April 1642 he tried to seize the muskets and other weapons held in the arsenal at Hull. In the first clear act of military rebellion, the governor, Sir John Hotham, refused to open the city gates. Humiliated, Charles toured the north of England seeking support. After watching the king trying to raise troops, William Salisbury, a distinguished soldier from Denbighshire, lamented that we 'are like to embroil the kingdom in a perpetual war'.[39]

Writing to his wife that summer, Bulstrode Whitelocke, the parliamentarian lawyer, ruminated about what such a war would be like: 'We must surrender up all our laws, liberties, properties and living into the hands of insolent Mercenaries, whose rage and violence will command us.' Among the first casualties, Whitelocke was sure, would be 'reason, honour and justice'. The world that he and his wife had loved would be turned upside down, with base folk lording it over the noble, the profane usurping the pious; fields would be laid waste, goods pillaged, and the land would bleed itself to death. Whitelocke concluded that 'you will hear other sounds, beside those of drums and trumpets, the clattering of armour, the roaring of guns, the groans of wounded and dying men, the shrieks of deflowered women, the cries of widows and orphans'.[40]

One key event mitigated the horrors of Civil War, by preventing it from becoming an international conflict in which foreign troops intervened. Between 1634 and 1640 without parliamentary approval Charles had extended the levy of ship money to inland counties, raising £880,000. The ship-money fleet was well built. Its officer corps, personified by Sir John Pennington and Captain William Rainsborough, made the Royal Navy 'an increasingly coherent and professional force'. Naval officers were a distinct group with their own character, whom Charles ignored—at his peril.[41] Thus in early 1642 parliament was able to seize control of the navy since the commissioned and warrant officers believed the king favoured popery. According to Edward Hyde, earl of Clarendon (Charles's counsellor who later wrote a *History of the Rebellion and Civil Wars*), the loss of the navy was of 'unspeakable ill consequences'.[42] Control of the navy would have allowed the king to bring Irish troops to England, and to internationalize the Civil War by getting help from fellow European monarchs. He could have used the navy to blockade London, decimating parliament's trade and thus their customs revenues. He might even have taken the capital, ending the war by capturing (to use Clausewitz's phrase) the enemy's 'centre of gravity'.[43] But it was not to be. The Civil War was bad enough without becoming—like, say, Vietnam or Afghanistan—the cockpit for the ambitions of great powers. It remained a British conflict, in which parliament used the navy to support land operations, such as the invasion of Scotland, and to mop up royalist strongholds such as Tenby, south Wales. With the loss of the navy, the worst the royalists could do was to encourage Irish privateers.[44]

The First English Civil War, 1642–46

Charles formally declared the First English Civil War at Nottingham on 22 August 1642, when he raised the royal standard bearing his coat of arms as well as the motto 'Give Caesar his due,' and ordered all rebels to return to their allegiance. For the king the war was a matter of retaining what was his by right, and punishing those subjects, perhaps misled by wicked agita- tors, for their treasonable follies. By formally going to war, Charles found a cause, something in which an uncertain man could believe, giving him much wanted certainty. The night after he planted his standard in the ground, the hole being hastily dug with knives and hands, a wind blew it down into the mud. Quite clearly, putting down a rebellion would not be as easy as the king anticipated. The First English Civil War lasted for nearly four years, the campaigns being determined by the seasons.

Because the war broke out in the autumn, the 1642 campaign was rela- tively short. By declaring war, Charles forced trimmers off the fence, the

3. Major battles in the British Isles, 1486–1748.

majority of whom—once they had gathered in their harvest—came down on his side. This gave him enough men to fight the first pitched battle at Edgehill, Warwickshire, on 23 October 1642. The roundheads and cavaliers were evenly matched: the king had 2,800 cavalry, 10,500 infantry, 1,000 dragoons, and 20 cannon; parliament fielded 2,150 horse, 12,000 foot, 720 dragoons, and from 30 to 37 artillery pieces.[45] Initially, the royalists had the strongest position, having drawn up the bulk of their forces at dawn on Edgehill Ridge. This long escarpment, 350 feet high (then denuded of trees), dominated the rolling country to the north-west, where the rebel forces assembled. Because the commander of the parliamentary forces, Robert Devereux, third earl of Essex, refused to budge, the king (perhaps provoked by a short and ineffective roundhead bombardment) ordered his troops to move down the slope. Here they faced the enemy a thousand yards away. On both sides infantry were stationed in the middle, with the cavalry on the flanks, artillery between formations, and the few dragoons posted behind bushes as sharpshooters.

The royalists did not complete their move down the slope until about two in the afternoon, when the gunners fired at the massed ranks on the

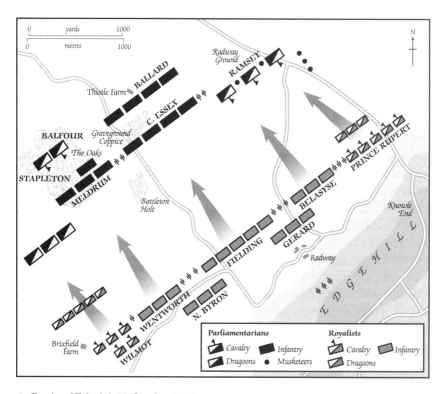

4. Battle of Edgehil, 23 October 1642.

other side. Cannon did little damage, especially to the roundheads, since the soft ground absorbed many balls. At about three o'clock Prince Rupert, the king's nephew and crack cavalry commander, ordered his troopers on the right flank to charge. They advanced at the trot for about two hundred yards. Trumpeters sounded the gallop. The royalist horse swept through Sir James Ramsey's cavalry, stationed on the parliamentary left, hacking and slashing the fleeing enemy for two miles until they reached Kineton, where they stopped to plunder the parliamentary baggage train. Much the same thing happened on the royalist left flank, where Henry Wilmot's horse broke Sir William Balfour's and Sir Philip Stapleton's cavalry, chasing them to Kineton, where they also joined in the plunder. By the time Rupert was able to regroup his men, and return to Edgehill, he was too late to play any further part in the fighting.

With the parliamentary cavalry shattered, and his own horse lost to looting, Sir Jacob Astley ordered the king's infantry to advance. They did so, remembered the future James II (who as a young boy watched the battle from the ridge), 'with a slow steady pace, and a very daring resolution'.[46] Seeing the royalists move towards them, Essex's infantry brigade broke and ran. Edward Montagu, Lord Mandeville, begged his soldiers to stay and fight, beating some of them with a cudgel, but to no avail. Only 6,400 foot remained to meet the advance of over 10,000 of the king's men.

The battle came to what contemporaries called 'push of pike'. Clarendon recalled, 'the remaining foot on both sides stood their grounds with great courage.' Although many of the king's soldiers were armed only with clubs, they stayed in their ranks, picking up muskets from the dead and wounded. 'And the execution was great on both sides,' reported Clarendon.[47] Yet neither side came apart. 'The foot being engaged in such warm and close service, it were reasonable to imagine that one side should run and be disordered,' Prince James recalled. 'But it happened otherwise, for each side, as if only by mutual consent retired some few paces.' What occurred next was, concluded the king's second son, 'A thing so very extraordinary.'[48] Those few musketeers who had not expended the dozen or so rounds they had been issued continued firing in a desultory fashion. A few of the remaining parliamentary infantry bolted. But the rest stood. The two sides gazed at one another, and did nothing. Like two punch-drunk pugilists, the infantry had fought themselves to exhaustion. They could no longer move. Their burn-out was both physical (most men having been up marching since four or five that morning) as well as psychological. The result was inconclusive. For the overwhelming majority who fought there, Edgehill was their first experience of combat.

It took the royalists a fortnight to follow up their advantage. They marched towards the capital, stopping on 12 November to brush aside parliamentary forces at Brentford. The sack of the town—mild by continental standards, or even by those that took place later in the war—so terrified Londoners that the following day the trained bands came out en masse to Turnham Green to protect their city. 'Remember the cause is for God and the defence of yourself and your children,' General Philip Skippon reminded them. 'Pray heartily and fight heartily, and God will bless us.' That evening, after much praying and little fighting, both sides heartily withdrew, the royalists having concluded that 'it had been madness' for them to try and take London.[49] Here the king lost his best chance of capturing the rebels' main base, of crushing parliament and perhaps establishing an absolute monarchy. Thus Charles's reverse doomed the British Isles to a decade-long Civil War, a commonwealth, even a Glorious Revolution. Turnham Green was a turning point in the Civil War—for it was not bloody enough to be called a battle. So the aptly named Turnham Green deserves to be commemorated by more than an underground station on the District Line, and a couple of signboards put up by the local council. After Turnham Green, both sides returned to their winter depots—London and Oxford—to rest, and prepare for the coming campaign season.

During 1643, the war's first full year, there were numerous battles including Braddock Down, Stratton, Lansdown and Roundway Down in the western theatre and Adwalton, Winceby and Hull in the northern one. The central campaign, however, revolved around Prince Rupert's capture of Bristol on 26 July. While inspecting this prize, England's second city, Charles learned that Colonel Sir George Massey, the governor of Gloucester, thirty-five miles up the River Severn, was willing to yield the city so long as he could salve his honour by doing so personally to his sovereign. When the king arrived at Gloucester, Massey reneged. Determined to teach him a lesson, Charles insisted on capturing the city. The earl of Essex responded by mobilizing his forces around London post-haste to relieve Gloucester, the key point that controlled the River Severn and access to South Wales.

Unable to take Gloucester, Charles raised the siege on 5 September, and pursued Essex back to London. Having slowed the parliamentary withdrawal at Aldbourne Chase on 18 September, two days later the royalists managed to block their retreat at Newbury, fifty miles west of the capital. The two sides were evenly matched, the king having eight thousand foot and six thousand horse, and Essex ten thousand infantry and four thousand cavalry. Because the First Battle of Newbury was fought in hedgerow country, the king's superiority in cavalry was not as advantageous as it would have been in open terrain such as Edgehill. At seven in the morning of 20 September, fighting began for control of the field's central feature, Round Hill. Newbury was an incoherent melee in which artillery played an unusually important role. When nightfall ended the fighting, there was no clear-cut winner. Having exhausted all their eighty barrels of powder (four times more than fired at Edgehill), the royalists had to withdraw to Oxford, permitting Essex and his men to retire to the security of London.

Both sides used the winter to regroup and prepare for the 1644 campaign season. Realizing that it was losing, parliament signed an alliance, known as the Solemn League and Covenant, with the Scots, who in early 1644 invaded the North of England. Charles dispatched Prince Rupert to capture Newark so as to secure his lines of communication with his northern army under the earl of Newcastle. On 14 June the king sent Rupert with an ambiguous set of orders to relieve York, which he did on 21 June, setting the stage for the war's largest battle.[50]

Forty-six thousand soldiers met at Marston Moor, five miles west of York, on 2 July 1644. A contestant called the battlefield 'the fairest ground for such use as I have seen in England'. Marston Moor was set in open

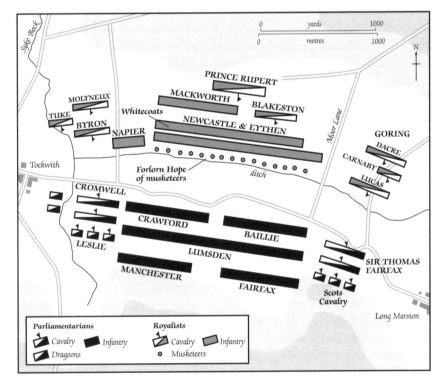

5. Battle of Marston Moor, 2 July 1644.

country, with few natural defensive features. The troops were drawn up in the usual fashion, with the infantry in the centre and the cavalry on the flanks. Between the two sides a road and a ditch gave cover for a line of royalist musketeers, known as the 'Forlorn Hope'. Determined to force a confrontation, Rupert lined up most of his men by nine in the morning. The allied army of Scots and parliamentary troops arrived much later. Indeed by early evening, sure that the enemy would not be ready until the next day, Rupert withdrew for a meal and Newcastle retired to his coach for a smoke. 'About half an hour after seven o'clock,' recalled Leonard Watson, the parliamentary scoutmaster,[51]

> we seeing the enemy would not charge us, we resolved by the grace of God, to charge them, and so the sign being given we marched down to the charge. In which you might have seen the bravest sight in the world: two such disciplined armies marching to the charge. We came down the hill in the bravest order, and with the greatest resolution that was ever seen.

After the allied army moved forward across the road, winkling the 'Forlorn Hope' from their ditch, the battle took place in three sectors virtually at the same time and independently of each other. On the west flank Cromwell's horse clashed with Rupert's. At first it seemed as if the prince had the advantage, particularly after Cromwell had to withdraw to have a superficial neck wound dressed. When the Scots commanded by David Leslie (an able general who had learned his trade under Gustavus Adolphus) charged on their wiry little ponies, the balance swung towards the allies. Cromwell was able to rout Rupert's cavalry, and (most important), by retaining control of his own troopers, regrouped so as to return to continue fighting. On the eastern flank things were not going so well for the allies. Sir Thomas Fairfax's troops found the ditch in front of the enemy's position a serious obstacle. Although four hundred parliamentarians managed to cross it, they could not break the enemy in almost an hour's hand-to-hand fighting. George Goring's cavalry charged the allies, who ran in panic and confusion. Meanwhile, in the centre the main battle was taking place between the ranks of infantry. It was a chaotic, bloody shoving match. As General Lawrence Crawford's parliamentary foot managed to gain the upper hand, Newcastle's infantry, aided by Sir William Blakeston's cavalry managed to drive a wedge through the middle of the allied line. The battle hung in the balance. Suddenly, as night was about to fall, Cromwell's regrouped cavalry attacked the king's infantry in the rear. Many royalists panicked, a few surrendered. For an hour or two in the moonlight three thousand of Newcastle's Whitecoat Regiment fought on stubbornly, refusing all quarter.

Marston Moor was, as Cromwell exalted, 'an absolute victory obtained by the Lord's blessing'.[52] Fifteen hundred allied soldiers had perished, as had three thousand—perhaps as many as four thousand—of the king's men. Except for the Whitecoats, the majority of those who died were hacked to pieces as they broke and tried to escape from the field.

But the king made up for his loss in the north with a victory in the south-west.

On 29 March 1644 General Sir William Waller's parliamentary army of ten thousand men had beaten Lord Forth and Sir Ralph Hopton's six thousand royalists at Cheriton. Greatly encouraged by parliament's first real victory, Essex marched his field army from London towards Abingdon, which he captured on 26 May, threatening the king's main base at Oxford. With only two weeks' food left, Charles withdrew his troops from Oxford west to Worcester. The roundheads followed in hot pursuit, but their generals, the earl of Essex and Sir William Waller, quarrelled and parted company. The former went to the West Country to fight Prince Maurice, Rupert's brother; the latter pursued the king, who had advanced on Buckingham, thus threatening the parliamentary heartland of East Anglia. At this point Charles lost his nerve. Turning back, he brushed against Waller's army at Cropredy Bridge on 29 June, as the two armies were marching almost parallel on either side of the River Cherwell. Waller lost seven hundred men, including deserters, which broke his army's morale, and allowed the king to turn west to pursue Essex's troops.

The Lostwithiel campaign of 1644 was Charles's most brilliant military achievement. Perhaps Cropredy had endowed him with enough self-confidence to eschew his habit of accepting the advice of the last person to give it. Anyway, he skilfully coordinated his forces on a wide front, where thick hedges and sunken roads (similar to the Bocage that bogged the Allies down in Normandy in 1944) rendered communications extremely difficult. Charles drove Essex's forces westwards through Devon to Cornwall. Taking Lostwithiel on 21 August, he trapped the enemy in the peninsula on the west bank of the River Fowey. The capture of Castle Dore ten days later convinced Essex that he was beaten. It was, he admitted, 'the greatest blow we have ever suffered'.[53] That night, as his cavalry under Sir William Balfour slipped through the royalist lines, Essex escaped in a fishing boat, leaving Sir Philip Skippon to negotiate a surrender.

Charles let victory slip through his fingers, allowing the roundheads to lay down their arms and march away to fight another day. They recovered with amazing speed, forcing the king to chase them back to London. Once again their paths crossed at Newbury. Because parliament had combined its forces, the two sides were evenly matched with fifteen thousand men apiece. The earl of Manchester's roundheads blocked the king's advance on London, as Waller's men, having made a fifteen-mile flanking movement around the enemy, attacked their left on 27 October. The two forces failed to coordinate their assaults, and Cromwell, for some unexplained reason, did not charge with his usual elan. That evening, after sunset ended the fighting, Charles extricated himself from a dangerous situation by a night march through a fifteen-hundred-yard gap in the enemy's lines. He reached the safety of Oxford on 1 November.

The third full year of fighting, 1645, turned out to be decisive. The king suspected as much, confiding to his wife that 1645 might be 'the hottest for war of any that has been yet', adding that it would be determined by 'the battle of all for all'.[54]

Realizing that the war was going badly, that they had fought poorly at the Second Battle of Newbury, and that 1645 would be the decisive year, parliament established a New Model Army. It was a mighty force, largely because in April 1645 parliament had passed the Self-Denying Ordinance that stripped high-born but incompetent officers of their commissions, leaving the New Model to be commanded by men chosen, not for their pedigrees, but for proven professionalism. The other ranks, especially the horse troopers, were well trained, superbly led, promptly paid and highly motivated.

When he left his base at Oxford on 7 May, Charles clearly under-estimated this New Model Army, because he divided his own forces, sending three thousand men under Lord George Goring to the West Country, while retaining the remaining eight thousand. To maintain communications with Ireland, the king moved north to relieve Chester, which Sir William Brereton was investing. On hearing that the Siege of Chester had been raised, and in order to thwart Fairfax—the parliamen-tary commander-in-chief, who had just encircled Oxford—Charles shifted east, capturing Leicester, and thus threatening Essex and Suffolk, the parliamentary base. This reverse forced Fairfax to give up the Siege of Oxford and join Cromwell to confront the royal army.

Forewarned, Charles was not forearmed. He was out hunting when he learned of the New Model's approach. Although outnumbered by ten thousand to fifteen thousand, the king had little choice but to stand and fight on a gentle ridge about a mile north of the village of Naseby.[55] By about nine on the morning of 14 June the sun burnt off the morning mists to reveal both sides drawn up in the traditional formation, with infantry in the centre and cavalry on the flanks. Since the roundheads were in dead ground south of Broad Moor, the royalists moved forward at about ten or eleven (the accounts vary). Soon the horse got too far ahead of the foot, and had to wait for them to catch up, as the parliamentary troops, screened by a 'Forlorn Hope' of musket men, moved over the rise, where they could look downhill at the advancing foe.

Coming under fire from Colonel John Okey's dragoons on their right flank, Rupert's horse charged and broke Henry Ireton's cavalry. Once again the stag-hunting squires tallyhoed too fast and much too far. The royalist cavalry did not stop until they reached the enemy baggage train, a little to the north-west of Naseby, which they spent the rest of the battle plundering. On the right flank Cromwell advanced his cavalry at a steady pace, so as not to lose control on the difficult muddy ground. For about an hour the Ironsides fought hand to hand with Sir Marmaduke Langdale's Northern Horse. Seeing that his horse troopers were about to break—the first of the fear-stricken men having already galloped past him—Charles wanted to lead his cavalry reserves in one last desperate charge. The war, however, was not to have a Hollywood ending, with Charles and Cromwell fighting it out hand to hand. Grabbing his sovereign's bridle, Robert Dalzell, earl of Carnwath, shouted 'Will you go unto

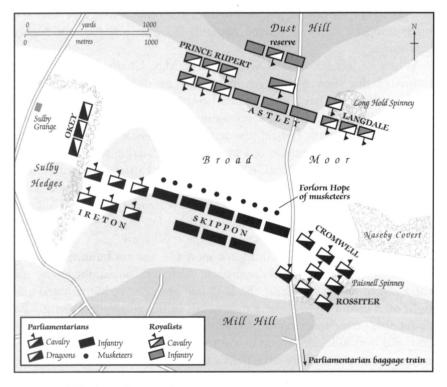

6. Battle of Naseby, 14 June 1645.

your death?' This gesture, combined with an ambiguous order, panicked the reserves who rode hell for leather back to Leicester, leaving the infantry to their fate.[56]

All this time the foot had been slugging it out in the centre. At first it seemed as if the more experienced royalists, who included the king's superb Welsh infantry, would prevail over the larger numbers of the New Model Army. But after an hour, as Fairfax sent in his own fresh regiment of foot, and Cromwell's horse and Okey's dragoons attacked, the king's infantry disintegrated so precipitously that most were captured.

For parliament, Naseby was a famous victory: the roundheads killed five hundred royalists, took three hundred wagonloads of booty worth a hundred thousand pounds, and captured four thousand royalist prisoners, whom they paraded through the streets of London. The parliamentary army jammed 680 prisoners into Lambeth Palace, and caged the rest in the open on Tothill Fields, where they suffered the further indignity of having to listen to puritan sermons—in Welsh! For the king, even more serious than the loss of men and materiel was the capture and publication of his private correspondence, which revealed the full extent of his perfidy. Charles had schemed to have French and Irish troops intervene in England, while he offered the Orkney and Shetland Islands to Sweden in return for its help.[57]

Even though the First English Civil War dragged on for nearly another year, after Naseby the royalists lost much support and all hope of winning: from then on everything else was a mopping-up. Clarendon rightly called Naseby 'a battle for a crown'.[58] In July 1645 Goring gave up the west at the Battle of Langport. Rupert surrendered Bristol on 10 September. Two weeks later, after the parliamentary forces beat a royalist army commanded by the king at Rowton, Charles lost Chester, his main link to Ireland. In May 1646 Charles had surrendered himself to the Scots, the last royalist garrison to capitulate being Harlech ten months later.

Even if the First English Civil War petered out more with a whimper than a bang, the loss of life had been enormous and the fighting ferocious. Surprisingly, the war had been fought with relatively few atrocities, especially when compared with the wars in Scotland and Ireland or most other Civil Wars. Sixteen massacres are known to have taken place during the First Civil War, in which perhaps a hundred and fifty parliamentarians and five hundred royalists were murdered. As the fighting dragged on, as soldiers got more war weary, and as propaganda became harsher, atrocities, especially by parliamentarians, tended to become more common, setting a pattern for the Second Civil War.[59] At Basing House a hundred royalists were killed in hot blood following a horrific assault. The cold-blooded massacres of prisoners—as at Holt Castle, Denbighshire, Hopton Castle,

Shropshire, and Barthomley, Cheshire—were unusual. For one thing, Englishmen spoke the same language and could negotiate a surrender— unlike the Welsh camp-followers whom the roundheads slaughtered after Naseby, who, unable to speak English, could not explain that they were not Irish.[60] To be sure, parliamentarians routinely hanged Irish prisoners, soldiers and civilians, even bilingual ones. At Lyme Regis it was reported that a mob killed an old Irishwoman by rolling her over a cliff in a nail-studded barrel.[61] After parliament passed an ordinance on 24 October 1644 that 'no quarter shall henceforth be given to any Irishman, or Papist born in Ireland' captured on land or at sea, things got even more brutish. When Sir Thomas Mytton took Shrewsbury in February 1645, and hanged a dozen Irish prisoners of war, Prince Rupert retaliated by stringing up an equal number of parliamentarians. The commons were outraged. They ordered the earl of Essex to explain to Rupert—who as a foreigner apparently did not appreciate the nuances of English lynching— that 'there was a very great difference between an Englishman and an Irishman'.[62]

Civil War in Scotland

Back on 26 October 1640, at the end of the Second Bishops' War (and twenty-two months before the outbreak of the First English Civil War), Charles had signed the Treaty of Ripon, in which he conceded almost all of the Scots demands. Afterwards he went to Edinburgh to confirm his concessions. But peace with Scotland was fleeting, lasting less than three years. North of the border there were two wars. The first broke out after the Lowland Presbyterians made an alliance, the Solemn League and Covenant, in September 1643 with the English parliamentarians, which led to their invasion of the North of England and subsequent decimation at Marston Moor. The second was a Civil War within Scotland, a conflict between the Lowlanders and the Highlanders, who were divided by geography, culture, language and religion. The Lowlanders were more economically advanced, spoke English and were Presbyterians; the Highlanders were organized into clans, lived on the economic margins, spoke Gaelic and tended to be Catholic.

The two wars came together during the campaigns of James Graham, marquess of Montrose. The scion of one of Scotland's leading families, Montrose had initially supported the covenant. By 1643 he was so disillusioned with the ambitions of the kirk that he sent the king an offer to raise the Highlands. After the covenanters invaded England in 1644, Charles accepted. Montrose's first rising was a fiasco: he was lucky to escape to England with his life. In August 1644, in disguise, he returned to the Highlands with a couple of companions, having a silk royal standard hidden around his waist. This time he was far more successful. Clansmen flocked to the king's colour. In September at Tippermuir they confronted a contingent under John Elcho, earl of Wemyss, whose battle cry was 'Jesus and no Quarter!'[63] Defeated, the covenanters got what they proffered. Although outnumbered two to one, at Inverlochy the following February, Montrose's troops slew fifteen hundred covenanters for the loss of eight of their own. In May they killed half of Colonel John Hurry's covenanters at Auldearn; in July and August they defeated General William Baillie at Alford and Kilsyth.

In some respects Montrose's campaigns were less a struggle between dour Lowlanders and free-spirited Highlanders than they were a clan feud between the earl of Argyle's Campbells and the MacDonalds, many of whom were Ulstermen led by the earl of Antrim. Such feuds were very common: between 1573 and 1625 there were 365 of them. They were also very costly: half of Alistair Moir MacLeod's twenty-eight male dependants died in a single feud.[64] Because these feuds got caught up in a wider conflict, war in Scotland was far bloodier than it was south of the border. After routing the covenanters outside Perth, Montrose's men boasted that they could walk the three miles back to the town using the enemy dead as stepping stones without once touching the ground. An eyewitness of their plunder of Nairn 'saw no man in the street but was stripped naked to the skin'.[65] After accepting the surrender of some Campbells commanded by Zachary Malcolm at Lagganmore in Glen Euchar, Montrose's troops locked them and their women in a barn, then set it alight, roasting all but two alive.[66] No wonder at Auldearn the covenanters stood their ground: unfortunately, they did so on a bog and thus lost half their men. After the Battle of Inverlochy where casualties were just as high, the poet Ian Lom MacDonald surveyed the corpse-strewed field and the loch bloody with floating carcasses:[67]

> You remember the place called Tawney Field?
> It got a fine dose of manure
> Not the dung of sheep or goats,
> But Campbell blood well congealed.

Ancient clan hatreds robbed the bard of all pity:

> To Hell with you, if I cared for your plight
> As I listen to your children's distress,
> Lamenting the band that went into battle
> The howling of the women of Argyle.

Alasdair MacColla, Montrose's kinsman and second in command, was just as callous: jubilant at the slaughter of sixteen Campbell lairds, he lamented that their pregnant wives had been spared.[68] All sides committed atrocities. In 1645 the covenanters butchered a hundred rank and file of the garrison of Asiog Castle, Ayrshire, who surrendered on promise of quarter, saving the thirty-six officers to be hanged later at leisure. A couple of years afterwards General David Leslie, Lord Newark, meted out a similar fate to the royalist defenders of Dunaverty Castle.[69]

Montrose was a born leader: energetic, an outstanding guerrilla warrior, he inveigled the enemy into fighting on his terms. Two-thirds of his men were veterans, either of the Ulster campaign of 1641–42 or the Thirty Years War. Fighting in all weathers, they set the Highlands ablaze. Yet his men were outnumbered, especially after David Leslie's covenanters returned home following their victory at Marston Moor. The two armies met at Philiphaugh, where on 13 September 1645 Leslie's men surprised and routed Montrose's forces. Many of them were slaughtered; their leader managed to escape to Norway.

Civil War in Ireland

As we have seen, the Irish Rebellion of 1641 produced a tremendous backlash in England. In the following year Charles sent an army to crush the rebels, who united to form a Catholic confederate government, based in Kilkenny, which established a quasi-independent Irish state. For eleven years the highly complicated Wars of the Confederation took place in the island, where as many as four armies operated at the same time. The outbreak of the English Civil War in August 1642 saved the Confederation of Kilkenny because Charles had to withdraw his forces to fight parliament in England. Twelve months later the king signed a peace treaty with the confederation, which soon after sent a few Catholic Irish troops to England to fight on Charles's side. In 1645 Pope Innocent X dispatched Archbishop Giovanni Rinuccini to Kilkenny with a large supply of arms and money to help the confederates win toleration for Catholics and what would much later become known as 'home rule'. The confederation became increasingly divided and in desperation made a secret treaty with the king using Edward Somerset, earl of Glamorgan, as an intermediary. Charles, realizing he had conceded much too much, promptly repudiated the treaty. Parliament's victory in the First English Civil War sealed the confederation's fate. Unable to unite the Irish, Rinuccini returned home in February 1649. Six months later Oliver Cromwell landed in Ireland.

Compared to England, or even Scotland, Civil War in Ireland was much more savage and complicated. The English were determined that the Irish should pay—in as many ways as possible—for the 1641 rebellion. In March 1642 parliament passed the Adventurers' Act, which hoped to raise a million pounds from the sale of two and a half million acres of land confiscated from the rebels, thus setting the pattern for the 1650s.[70] To enforce the act an army of twelve thousand Scots invaded Ulster in August. They were commanded on alternate days by Sir Robert Munro and Edward, Viscount Conway—which did little to enhance the effectiveness of the troops, whom an English officer correctly called 'the scum of that country'. For instance, John Erwyn, with a gang of Scots soldiers, broke into Mary Mullen's house, grabbed her, slashing her head and fingers with his sword, as she screamed repeatedly, 'Dear John, do not kill me, for I have never offended you!' Then he thrust his sword under her right breast into her heart, stripped her naked, and—just to make sure she was dead—placed a live coal on her forehead.[71]

Such savagery was encouraged at the very top. Charles told his forces in Ireland to 'prosecute the said Rebels and Traitors with fire and sword'.[72] The Lords Justices in Dublin instructed James Butler, marquess of Ormonde, 'to burn, spoil, waste, consume, and demolish all the places, towns, and houses where the said rebels are . . . and to kill and destroy all the men there inhabiting able to bear arms'. The earl, who had just hanged the defenders of Naas, had few scruples about obeying such commands, particularly as the rebels held his wife and children hostage. When Secretary of State Conway ordered Colonels Crawford and Gibson to lead a punitive expedition to ravage Counties Wicklow and Kildare he wrote, 'you are to kill, slay and destroy all the rebels you can there find.'[73] The king's soldiers needed little official encouragement, 'so earnestly did they desire to have the killing of more of the rebels,' a journalist explained. Another related that after the rebels called 'our men English dogs and Scotch dogs', they 'put them all to the sword'.[74]

The full horror of the fighting in Ireland, which British forces conducted with the casual cruelty characteristic of a S.S. Einsatzgruppen on the Eastern Front, can be seen in the diary of an anonymous officer who took part in a search and destroy mission through County Wicklow in November 1641 (see ill.9).[75] On 28 November the English caught two spies, whom they hung on the castle wall at Newcastle. The next day 'were taken and hung some men and women'; their numbers and offences the diarist apparently felt not worth recording. Later that day two more Irish were hanged, and one shot for trying to stop the troops rustling his cattle. When the English reached Wicklow on the morrow, they hanged three people, including a pregnant woman. After being ambushed on their way to Bray, they killed eight prisoners, and nonchalantly shot and killed a peasant as he was innocently ploughing his fields.

Such expeditions were the bloody norm, since the English preferred to destroy rather than search. For instance, William Damon's diary of a two-week foray against the rebels—which was published in 1642 in England under the title *Welcome news from Ireland*—reported how 'we marched . . . burning and pillaging all the way'. This eyewitness account of atrocities becomes numbingly tedious.[76] On every day but two the English burned villages and hanged rebels—a couple on 5 April, four on the 6th, eight on the 7th, fourteen on the 8th, and on the 12th 'We rested at Malborough, and that night hanged 3 poor Rogues . . . all dying without any show of penitence.' After helplessly watching the Irish kill parliamentary prisoners at the Battle of Knocknanoss in 1647, an English officer cheerfully noted how his troops made the rebels 'pay the price of their insolent attempt by putting the greatest part of them to the sword'. Day after day the slaughter continued. 'We were killing till night as fast as we could,' the officer concluded.[77] An English diarist recorded that at Clontarf the 'soldiers got very good pillage, and so left the town burning'. The following summer Roger Boyle, earl of Orrery, reported that at Limerick 'We had a fair execution [i.e. massacre] for about three miles, and indeed it was bloody, for I gave order to kill all, although some prisoners of good quality were saved.'[78] Colonel Michael Jones, the parliamentary commander in Ireland, ordered six hundred prisoners killed in cold blood on the grounds that they were deserters: he even hanged his own nephew, Elliot, for going over to the crown.

In many respects Ireland became one huge 'free fire zone' in which, as Ulick Bourke, the earl of Clanricarde admitted, English troops murdered, plundered, mutilated and ransomed to their hearts' content. Apart from an English lieutenant who was reported hanged for murdering a woman in May 1642, they did so virtually unchecked, and with an excess that horrified even hardened veterans of the Thirty Years War, such as Sir James Turner. Such behaviour, both Turner and Clanricarde warned, was counter-productive because it encouraged further resistance and atrocities from the other side.[79]

Pleas for humanity fell on deaf ears because the fighting in Ireland had got out of control. Neighbour fought neighbour to settle old festering feuds. Irish warfare not only brutalized the conflict in England, but exacerbated the intensity of feelings throughout the rest of the British Isles. It led to violent and spontaneous iconoclasm, the destruction of religious images by soldiers.[80] The parliamentary practice of hanging the Irish they took prisoner in England led to further outrages that augmented animosities on all sides, and encouraged the conviction that they were fighting a holy war in which there could be no compromise. Take for instance the evidence of a woman—known as MW—whom Irish troops captured in June 1644. She alleged that they 'killed my husband and my child, both before my face, and stripped and wounded me and a child of five years old: and it was thought that I could not live. . . . But our cause was God's.'

The Second English Civil War, 1648

Even if Charles I never gave up believing that his cause was God's, by the spring of 1646 he had come to realize that it was lost—if only for the time being. Early on the morning of 27 April he slipped out of his main base in Oxford in disguise, recognizing that the First English Civil War was over. It had left hundreds of thousands dead and wounded, without producing a solution—or at least one the king would accept. By now a growing number of parliamentarians were coming to the dreadful conclusion that Charles could not be trusted. Thus on 10 June Sir Charles Erskine, a Scots commissioner to the Westminster Assembly, wrote to his wife, 'We are in no less expectation of troubles than when you left us, every hour producing strong effects and changes in affairs, so that honest men can hardly know what way to walk.'[81]

Certainly on leaving Oxford Charles hardly knew what way to walk. After skirting the north of London, the king meandered through East Anglia, and then Nottinghamshire, where in early May he surrendered to the Scottish occupying army just outside Newark. Here he was, Charles told his wife, 'barbarously baited' by Presbyterian preachers, who tried to convert him. Since their missionary efforts were as ineffectual as their purses were empty, in February 1647 the Scots transferred the king to parliament in return for a promise that their debts be paid.[82] The following June Cornet George Joyce abducted Charles from parliament's custody at Holdenby House, Northamptonshire, handing him over to the army, who held him at Hampton Court, from which he escaped in November. Once free, Charles dithered over where to go next, before opting for the Isle of Wight. Here on Boxing Day 1647 he signed a secret Engagement with the Scots (who had become terrified by the growth of radicalism south of the border), promising to accept Presbyterianism for three years if they invaded England and restored him to power. Thus, with a stroke of his pen, 'Charles R' began the Second Civil War, and, in effect, signed his own death warrant. He did so, as he had told the army commanders in August 1647, because he was convinced that 'You cannot be without me. . . . You will fall to ruin if I do not sustain you.'[83] The king banked on the growing dissatisfaction with parliament and the army, and the strong popular desire to return to a sense of normality which Martin Parker voiced that year in his best-selling ballad:[84]

... all things will be well,
When the King enjoys his own again.

Fighting in the Second Civil War started in Wales. Angry that his men had not got their arrears of pay, Colonel John Poyer seized Pembroke Castle, prompting other disgruntled roundheads to commandeer Tenby and Chepstow, and declare for the king. On 1 May 1648 parliament ordered Cromwell to take eight thousand troops to crush the rebellion, which he did at St Fagans on 8 May. It took him until 11 July to capture Pembroke Castle. Poyer was sent to London, where he was court-martialled and shot.

During the Second Civil War, the roundheads were disinclined to treat prisoners kindly—as Michael Hudson learned. A quiet, even plain-spoken man, Hudson studied at Oxford, where he graduated as a Doctor of Divinity, before becoming a royal chaplain. After helping the king escape from Oxford in April 1646, Hudson went into hiding, was arrested by the army, escaped, and was re-arrested. He escaped once more disguised as a porter balancing a barrel of apples on his head. The Second Civil War enabled him to show his true colours. In June 1648 at Woodcroft House, Northamptonshire, he staged a royalist rising, which two roundhead companies under Colonel Thomas Waite, a local MP and later regicide, easily put down. Since one of Waite's kinsmen had been killed in the fighting, the colonel denied 'that rogue Hudson' quarter, driving him up to the roof of Woodcroft House where he was pushed off the edge. Hudson clung for dear life to a battlement. So, royalist hagiographers claimed, the roundheads hacked off his hands at the wrist. Hudson fell to the moat, and, as he tried to use his stumps to swim to the bank, they smashed in his head. Afterwards Trooper Wood, a grocer from Stamford, bragged that he had cut out the reverend doctor's tongue as a souvenir.[85]

Horrible as such incidents were, they pall beside the brutality of the Siege of Colchester.[86] At Blackheath on 30 May seven thousand men under Sir Thomas Fairfax routed a group of royalists, mainly from Kent, and two days later drove the remnants back to Rochester, where 'huddled into a crowd of confused destruction', an eyewitness recalled, the royalists 'were overwhelmed'. The survivors fled, some to be slain in St Neots, the rest seeking refuge in Colchester, where Fairfax's army surrounded them. The fighting quickly became savage. After capturing the house of Sir Charles Lucas (a veteran royalist commander) a few hundred yards south of Colchester's walls, the roundheads ran amok. They burst into the family vault, tearing open Lady Lucas and her daughter Lady Killigrew's coffins, and dismembered the corpses of Sir Charles's mother and sister, throwing arms and legs about the vault, and clipping hair to wear as favours in their hats.

Two weeks later, at three in the afternoon of 13 June, Colonel Marchmount Needham's regiment assaulted the Headgate, where the London Road entered the city wall. The struggle went on until midnight. 'Here you might see the limbs of men, horses, fire, dust confused together in one horrid Chaos,' an eyewitness reported.[87] Having lost their colonel, two captains and a hundred other ranks, Needham's roundheads went berserk, slashing and killing like lunatics. They took no prisoners. But they did not win the day. Their defeat heartened the king's men. 'I earnestly desire you not to be dismayed, for we trust in God,' the royalist Robert Vesey wrote home to his wife the next day, before, more mundanely, asking her to send him some clean linen.[88] On 6 July, Sir Charles Lucas and Sir George Lisle (veteran of the Thirty Years War) led a large raiding party across a narrow footbridge over the River Colne to recapture the parliamentary stronghold at East Mill. It was as neat a piece of action as the war had ever seen. One observer noted that the royalists sallied out 'as if it had been a sporting skirmish amongst tame soldiers at a general muster', killing nineteen enemy and pitching their cannon into the river, before making a dignified withdrawal. In return, Fairfax paid three grenadiers three shillings apiece, and twenty assault troops half a crown each, to storm the gate house, which they did. After a grenade blew up a magazine the ninety royalist defenders surrendered.

A week later, stories that the royalists were using poisoned shot started to circulate: 'Our soldiers,' observed a parliamentary officer, 'were exasperated with the loss of blood of their fellow soldiers, many being slain with chewed or poisoned bullets.'[89] In cold blood the roundheads executed twenty prisoners taken with suspect ammunition. John Rushworth, a member of parliament who acted as a war correspondent, reported that the royalists had amputated the fingers of several wounded officers, including a colonel, to loot their rings and were using scythes to cut off the enemy's feet.[90]

After eleven pitiless weeks Colchester's garrison of 3,531 surrendered on 28 August, with but a barrel and a half of powder left, having devoured the last dog, cat and most of the horses. 'It was a sad spectacle to see,' remembered Rushworth, 'so many fine houses burnt to ashes, and so many inhabitants sick and weak.'[91] Fairfax immediately arrested Lisle, Lucas and Sir Bernard Gascoigne (a Tuscan mercenary). By two the next afternoon a court martial had condemned them to death. Five hours later Lucas and Lisle were shot for breaking the parole they had given after surrendering in the First Civil War. Gascoigne, the Italian, was reprieved so as not to upset overseas opinion. Even though they had broken their word as gentlemen, Lucas and Lisle instantly became royalist martyrs: it was said that the grass never again grew on the spot where they fell (not

true, but there is a marker there today). Within a few days eight pamphlets
appeared condemning this 'most barbarous unsoldierly murder'. People
were horrified that England had sunk to the abyss of the Thirty Years War,
where such killings were accepted. Edmund Verney, who was himself to
be murdered three years later during the sack of Drogheda, called the
shootings 'horrid and barbarous'.[92] It was to set a precedent for another
execution that was to take place outside the Banqueting Hall in Whitehall
the following January.

On 8 July 1648 a Scottish army invaded England to fulfil the Engagement they had signed the previous December to restore Charles, who had
agreed to accept Presbyterianism for at least three years. Thus, a parliamentary newspaper complained, the Scots brought 'their lice and their
Presbytery' with them. Six weeks later the Scots fought a climactic battle
at Preston. Unlike Naseby, Marston Moor or Edgehill, Preston was a long
drawn-out, dispersed and extremely confused battle that lasted from 17 to
19 August. Cromwell reported he had never seen his troopers 'so exceedingly battered'. On the battle's opening day his men fought Marmaduke
Langdale's English royalists among the hedgerows and narrow lanes of
Ribbleton Moor. According to Captain John Hodgson, a roundhead
veteran, the initial Scots resistance was slight. The first enemy his
Lancashire militia company encountered were huddling in a ditch. Soon,
however, the going got tough. 'There was nothing but fire and smoke,'
Hodgson remembered, adding that 'The bullets flew freely.'[93] Gradually,
the royalists were pushed west into Preston, where around the bridge
across the River Ribble fighting lasted until nightfall. That evening the
Scots commander, the duke of Hamilton, decided to withdraw towards
Warrington, where he hoped to take up a strong defensive position behind
the River Mersey. At Wigan Sir James Turner's Scots cavalry refused to
charge. When Trooper Patrick Grey shot his captain, whether deliberately
or by accident, he was executed on the spot. But that did not stop the
Scots retreat turning into a rout.[94] Hours later, using the same phrase he
had employed after Naseby, Cromwell told William Lenthall, Speaker of
the House of Commons, 'Surely, Sir, this is nothing but the hand of
God.'[95] By now the army was convinced that the king must die and that
God's hand was behind the trial and execution of Charles I on 30 January
1649 for, *inter alia*, waging two cruel and unnecessary wars against His
people.

The Third Civil War, 1649–51

The execution of Charles I did not bring peace. Far from it. Instead it
precipitated two brutal conflicts, first between England and Ireland, and

then England and Scotland. But the death of the king did in a way make a clean sweep, allowing the new republic to try and settle the Irish question. Within six months Oliver Cromwell, who had come to dominate the army, which in turn had taken over the government, set sail for Ireland with a large expeditionary force. In August he assured his senior officers that God wanted them to crush those papist savages, and told the rank and file to think of themselves as Israelites ordained to extirpate idolatry from Canaan. Crossing the Irish Sea was a far more turbulent going-over than that of the Red Sea, for according to Chaplain Hugh Peters (who prided himself on being something of an expert on both maritime and mortal transitions), Cromwell was sicker than any man he had ever seen. In Dublin the general announced that 'God hath brought him thither ... for the carrying out of the great work against the barbarous and bloodthirsty Irish.'[96]

Cromwell wasted no time starting His great work. On 10 September he began the Siege of Drogheda, the strategic town that controlled the mouth of the River Boyne.[97] Well protected by a wall a mile and a half long, twenty feet high, six foot thick at the base and four at the top, dotted with 29 guard towers and defended by 319 cavalry and 2,221 infantry, Drogheda was a tough nut to crack. 'He who could take Drogheda could take Hell,' boasted its governor, Sir Arthur Aston, the peg-legged veteran. (He had lost his leg five years earlier in a riding accident while trying to impress some ladies with his equestrian prowess.) Aston spurned Cromwell's demand to surrender, so after a heavy bombardment the English stormed the town. It was a Promethean struggle. When a cannonball struck off his legs, Colonel William Warren continued fighting on his stumps. The third assault, which Cromwell led in person, succeeded. Several thousand roundheads poured through the breach. They beat Aston to death with his wooden leg, and set fire to St Peter's church, where a thousand enemy had taken refuge. 'We refused them quarter,' Cromwell reported, 'we put to the sword the whole number of defendants.' The thirty or so of those who were spared were transported to Barbados. Cromwell's chaplain gloated that over 3,500 enemy perished at Drogheda for the loss of sixty-four roundheads.[98]

Half as many enemy died the following month at Wexford. After a traitor opened the gates on 11 October, Cromwell's men charged into the town. Without orders they ran amok. Two boatloads of refugees sank, drowning 330 folk, many of them civilians. Without mercy the roundheads butchered priests and friars, who approached them brandishing crucifixes, naively assuming that this would mollify the enemy rather than infuriate them. Cromwell's men also massacred two hundred women at the Market Cross as they begged for quarter. 'Seeing thus the righteous hand of God upon such a town and people,' explained Cromwell, 'we thought it not good nor just to restrain our soldiers from right of pillage nor doing execution upon the enemy.'[99] But there was no excuse for the massacre at Wexford, which took place during surrender negotiations, unlike that at Drogheda, which could be justified according to the rules of war because the garrison had rejected a demand to capitulate.[100]

The Irish bloodletting continued. In early November four hundred men were killed at Carrick, where the defenders hurled stones down from the walls. Tired and ill, Cromwell's troops continued to campaign through the winter. 'I tell you,' their commander reported to parliament, 'a considerable part of your army is fitter for a hospital than the field.'[101] In February 1650 the army massacred the two hundred defenders of Callan who had refused to surrender. After taking the small outpost of Thomastown, Cromwell hanged a sergeant and a corporal, since they were the most senior soldiers left alive. After Gowran Castle surrendered a few days later, all but one officer was shot and a Catholic priest hanged.[102]

But the roundheads did not have everything go their way. After an eleven-day artillery bombardment had breached the walls at Clonmel, County Tipperary, at eight in the morning of 9 May, a thousand of them stormed through the gap, to find themselves trapped: the defenders had built a corral of stones, timber, and even dung, in front of which was a six-foot trench. As those in the front cried 'back!' and those at the back shoved forward, the defenders stabbed at the roundheads with pikes, slashed them with swords, and raked them with muskets and grapeshot.[103] Cromwell was as angry 'as ever he was since he first put on a helmet against the king', observed an officer in Sir John Clotworthy's regiment, 'for he was not used to being thus repulsed.'[104] A fortnight after the worst defeat of his career, Cromwell sailed for home to deal with the growing problem of Scotland.

As the Montrose campaign had demonstrated, fighting in Scotland was far more vicious than that in England (although less so than in Ireland). But the cruelty of Cromwell's 1650 invasion of Scotland came less from a policy of deliberate brutality and more from arrogance compounded by desperation. The Ironsides who marched north across the border that summer did not think much of the Scots. Their streets were empty, their women were poorly dressed 'pitiful sorry creatures', who constantly whined that the lairds had drafted their menfolk.[105]

The two sides met at Dunbar on 3 September. The Scots seemed to have the upper hand for Cromwell's forces were trying to retreat south. As a cold wet dawn broke, and a thin moon waned, Cromwell unleashed his infantry against the centre of the Scots lines. 'I never beheld a more terrible charge of foot than was given by our army,' reported a veteran correspondent. The roundheads caught the enemy unawares: many Scots officers had left their units to bed down in more comfortable billets; most soldiers lacked lighted match to fire their weapons. An observer wrote:[106]

The Foot threw down their Arms, and both Horse and Foot Ran several ways....We pursued them as far as Haddington, killing, wounding them all the way, there were about 4,000 slain in this place, and in the pursuit about 10,000 taken Prisoners, most of which are wounded.... We lost not forty men.

In many ways, down even to the date of its climactic confrontation, 3 September, the Worcester campaign was a replay of Dunbar. A year after his father's execution, Charles II returned to Scotland where on New Year's Day 1650 he was crowned king. With ill grace he took the covenant, and converted to Presbyterianism. Confident that the English would flock to join his standard, on 3 August 1651 he crossed the border at the head of sixteen thousand Scots troops. They were a ramshackle lot: the soldiers plundered with an enthusiasm that their senior commanders reserved for quarrelling amongst each other, or for making pessimistic predictions. General David Leslie was convinced that his army 'would not fight', while the duke of Hamilton considered the invasion 'very desperate'. The Scots reached the strategic city of Worcester on 23 August, and had less than a week to rest and mend the city's crumbling walls before Cromwell arrived with twenty-eight thousand men. He attacked at five in the morning of 3 September. After about two hours' fighting, royalist resistance collapsed. The slaughter was appalling, 'what with the dead Bodies of the Men and the Dead Horses of the Enemy filling the streets,' remembered Bulstrode Whitelocke.[107] The Scots paid a terrible price for their loyalty to the king, two thousand, perhaps three thousand of them perishing in the campaign, while Charles, after many an adventure, managed to escape to France. The victors, who claimed to have lost only two hundred men, had no doubt whom to thank. 'We are the people that the Lord hath done all this for,' exulted one of them. 'The Lord of Hosts was wonderfully with us,' thought Robert Stapleton. Oliver Cromwell boasted that 'the Lord appeared so wonderfully in His mercies.'[108]

Cromwell's rejoicing was, however, more than a little premature.

CHAPTER 8

TALK YOU OF KILLING: CIVIL WARS AND COMMONWEALTH: IMPACT, 1638–1660

Desdemona: Talk you of Killing?
Othello: Ay, I do.
Desdemona: Then heaven have mercy on me
Othello, V, ii, 37–40

IN 'THE CIVIL WARS', A POEM WRITTEN IN 1609 ABOUT THE WARS OF THE Roses in 1609, over a generation before the actual British Civil Wars, Samuel Daniel observed:[1]

O war! begot in pride and luxury,
The child of malice and revengeful hate,
Thou impious good and goodly impiety
That art the foul refiner of a state.

Daniel was using the word 'refiner' as a metallurgist might: to enhance, strengthen, even purify the state. Between 1638 and 1660 war was the crucible that forged several key issues of the British experience: the relationships between the component parts of the British Isles, between authority and freedom, between rulers and the ruled, between liberals and conservatives, between religious faith and scientific rationality. Since killing is the central act of war, and it is killing—more than anything else—that makes wars decisive, it seems logical that there was a relationship between the number of war deaths and the impact of war. So this chapter will first assess how many British people were killed directly and indirectly as a result of the Civil Wars. It will then look at how individuals died, the effects of their deaths on family and friends, and the experience of being wounded. Then it will investigate the wider effect of the killing, and how it radicalized people, especially soldiers. Finally, the chapter will show how at the macro level war strengthened the English nation, which used its new-found military power over Scotland and Ireland to form a British state.

How Many Died

As we saw in Chapter 3, trying to establish war casualties is notoriously difficult, particularly when records are not as copious as they are today. Tricks of memory, as well as the needs of propaganda, produced wildly different estimates. For instance, the nineteen contemporary accounts of the assault of 15 June 1644 on St Mary's Tower during the Siege of York estimate from twenty to over three hundred casualties.[2] Occasionally, physical evidence supports contemporary accounts. A nineteenth-century road widening near Aylesbury dug up a mass grave with two hundred skeletons, confirming the estimates given by Civil War newsletters. The best way of getting a total picture of how many died is to enter into a computer every incident found, ranging from Marston Moor, the wars' bloodiest battle, to a fracas in Doncaster in which one man perished. Mindful of the cliché 'lies, damned lies and statistics', in doing so I have tried to be conservative: long ago as an intelligence officer I was trained that underestimating the numbers of the enemy could be literally fatal, especially if they attacked! The trouble is that by producing precise figures computers give a misleading sense of accuracy. On the other hand they enable one to analyse data by asking, for instance, how many people died per month or year, or in battles or skirmishes. Since it is impossible to assess the nationality of those who died, casualties are be listed in the place there they did so. Thus the 6,120 Scots who died fighting in England, mainly at Marston Moor, Preston and Worcester, are listed under England, just as Cromwell's round-heads who died at Drogheda are put in the Irish column.

During the 1640s perhaps a thousand died from combat deaths at sea. In the 1650s large numbers died in foreign expeditions such as the conquest of Jamaica, privateering, the Dunkirk campaign, and naval warfare off the Spanish coast. Rather arbitrarily, these have been estimated at 40 incidents, with 3,000 combat casualties. Since pestilence and accidental deaths at sea tended to be far more frequent than on land, and the West Indies were notorious for yellow fever, a three to one ratio for non-combat to combat deaths would not be unreasonable, giving us a total of twelve thousand.[3] Adding the thousand who died in the 1640s gives us thirteen thousand, so if we allocated this in proportion to the relative populations of England (62.5 per cent), Scotland (12.5 per cent), and Ireland (25 per cent), we get 8,125, 1,625 and 3,250 for each nation respectively.

Between 1639 and 1640 some fifty thousand English and Scots troops took part in the two Bishops' Wars. If we assume a 10 per cent death rate (a conservative one), and split the deaths equally between the two kingdoms, we get 2,500 English deaths for the Bishops' Wars. Between 1642 and 1651 the computer analysis shows that 34,105 parliamentarians and 51,645 royalists died in England in combat in 647 incidents. Violence declined in England during the years from 1651 to 1660 when 25 roundheads and 300 royalists died in ten incidents such as the Sealed Knot conspiracies, and Penruddock's (1655) and Booth's risings (1659). This gives us a total figure of 86,075 dead in combat.[4]

Estimates as to the ratio between the number of people who died in combat and those who succumbed indirectly to disease vary. Jacques Dupâquier, the French demographer, calculated that during the seventeenth century only 10 per cent of military deaths were due to battle. Geoffrey Parker put the figure at 25 per cent. During the years 1642–45 the annual death rate for the Banbury garrisons averaged 10 per cent, while burials in the parish church rose three and a half fold. Death rates in more crowded cities such as Oxford, Bristol and Exeter could well have been twice or even thrice as high.[5] Joseph Bampfield, the royalist governor of Arundel, attributed the majority of the five hundred deaths of its nine-hundred garrison during the siege to 'the bloody flux and spotted fever'.[6] An archaeological finding supports this diagnosis. Fewer than half, three, or perhaps four of the nine members of the royalist garrison of Sandal Castle, Yorkshire, who were buried in the same grave during the siege, were killed in combat.[7] Applying a conservative ratio of 1.5 disease to combat deaths to our total of 86,075 combat deaths produces 129,113 disease deaths.

While disease-related fatalities are rare in modern war, accidental deaths, particularly those from aircraft crashes and friendly fire, are far more common than they were in early modern conflicts. For instance, of the 162 alumni of North Carolina State University who died during the Second World War, 98 (60 per cent) were killed in action, 59 (36 per cent) died from accidents, and 5 (4 per cent) from disease.[8] The earliest firm figures we have for the ratio of combat to accidental deaths is for the American Civil War, where for every hundred soldiers who died directly in combat, five did so by accident.[9] So if we apply this ratio to the 86,075 English combat deaths, we get 4,303 accidental ones.

In addition, after the Battle of Worcester in 1651 the army sent about thirteen hundred prisoners of war—about half of whom were English—as slaves to Barbados, where they were cruelly treated. Since the mortality rate for Europeans crossing the Atlantic and in Barbados was so terrible, we could safely estimate that half perished prematurely, giving 325 English dead from transportation. 'No one, but myself, as far as I know, came out again,' recalled Heinrich von Uchteritz, a German mercenary, who was ransomed for eight hundred pounds of sugar.[10] Only two others were known to have returned home: John Heywood, from Devon, and Thomas Jackson, from Kendal. Fourteen years in Barbados seems to have addled Jackson's brains. After he was arrested in April 1665 for speaking 'treasonable words' against Charles II, the local magistrates dismissed the case explaining that 'The fellow seemeth but simple.'[11]

Table 2 below summarizes the totals for war deaths in England, suggesting that 230,441 died directly or indirectly as a result of war between 1638 and 1660.

While it must be remembered that these figures are only estimates (their illusory precision notwithstanding), they do accord roughly with the views of contemporaries. 'Scarce a month, scarce a week without the sight or noise of blood,' recalled Chaplain Richard Baxter. Cromwell told parliament in 1645 the conflict was 'a vast burden upon the people'. Four years later Nicholas Lockyer called the wars 'a time of slaughter, fields, cities, towns, dipped and dyed in blood'.[12] Thomas Hobbes reckoned that a hundred thousand people had perished during the fighting and from war-related disease, while both an anonymous English officer and Sir William Petty, the father of English demographics, put the English casualties at three hundred thousand.[13]

Scottish casualties are even harder to estimate because records north of the border were sparser than in England. During June 1640 the earl of Argyle led five thousand Campbells in a six-weeks' expedition to pillage royalist clans in the Highlands, in which perhaps a thousand perished. In addition, another 2,500 died as a result of the two Bishops' Wars (see above). The computer-based analysis shows that 16,245 parliamentarians and 11,765 royalists died in forty-six incidents between 1642 and 1651.[14] This does not include Glencairn's Rebellion of 1653–54, in which nearly twenty thousand roundheads were involved. So perhaps four thousand died in thirty incidents. This gives a total of 32,010.

Table 2 War deaths in England, 1638–60

Bishops' Wars	2,500
Combat	86,075
Disease	129,113
Accident	4,303
Overseas/at sea	8,125
Transported	325
Total	230,441

Disease ravaged both sides in Scotland. Perhaps four to five thousand died from plague in 1644, while as many may have perished in the war-related famine of 1648–49. During the 1650 invasion of Scotland, 4,500 of Cromwell's army died from sickness. Thus, if we apply the English ratio of battle to non-battle deaths, 48,015 died from disease in Scotland. To this we must add 5 per cent of the combat deaths to account for accidents, making 1,601. In addition, as many as ten thousand Scots prisoners were transported as slaves, of whom perhaps half died on the Atlantic crossing or were worked to death in the West Indies.

Table 3 War deaths in Scotland, 1638–60

Bishops' Wars	3,500
Combat	33,010
Disease	48,015
Accident	1,601
Overseas/at sea	1,625
Transported	5,000
Total	92,751

If the figures for England are estimates, and those for Scotland inspired guesses, those for Ireland are—it must be admitted—miracles of conjecture, and cannot be broken down into categories as can those for England and Scotland. Sir William Petty estimated the loss of life in Ireland between 23 October 1641 and 23 October 1652 as follows:

Table 4 Petty's war deaths, Ireland, 1641–52

Protestants dead through plague, war and famine (including 37,000 massacred at the outbreak)	112,000
Roman Catholic dead	504,000
Total	616,000

Without doubt Petty grossly exaggerated the number of Protestants massacred in 1641: most likely six thousand, about 4.8 per cent of Ireland's Protestants, died. But his totals do not include the forty thousand 'wild geese' who were driven into exile, some to die in Spanish or French military service, others to settle abroad. Charles Blount, Lord Mountjoy, estimated that after the Elizabethan wars only one in four Irish mercenaries made it back home. In addition, during the commonwealth six to twelve thousand of the wives and children that the wild geese left behind in Ireland were deported as indentured servants to the Americas.[15] Very few of the Irish sold as indentured servants in New England (where many prospered) or in the West Indies (where most perished) returned home. In the parish of Kilcormick a surveyor reported, 'There is no house or church.' The population of North Wexford fell by 80 per cent, many parishes having become 'free-fire zones'.[16] As early as 1642 Owen Roe Neil related that County Donegal 'not only looks like a desert, but like Hell'. Having travelled extensively throughout Ireland in 1652 and 1653, Colonel Richard Lawrence, governor of Waterford, stated that 'the plague and famine had swept away whole counties that a man might travel twenty or thirty miles and not see a living creature, either man, beast or bird'.[17] Lawrence was reporting before the Cromwellian settlement during which Petty estimated that the English confiscated eleven million acres, out of twenty million, to give them to Protestants. Between 1641 and 1688 the Catholic share of the profitable land in Ireland fell from 59 per cent to 22 per cent.[18] On pain of death tens of thousands of Catholics were ordered to the rocky province of Connaught, or into foreign exile. The English threat to kill those who refused to leave was not a hollow one. Colonel Daniel Axtell, the officer who commanded the guard during Charles I's trial, smashed the brains of six women he found near Athy outside their reservation in Connaught.[19] Fighting in Ireland was, as usual, extremely bloody: while 10 per cent of the partici- pants died in an average battle in England, three times as many did so in Ireland, where prisoners of war—and civilians—were routinely massacred.[20]

As recently as 1974 a leading Irish historian described Petty's estimate that 618,000 people—or 38 per cent of Ireland's population—died due to the Civil Wars as 'the best we have'.[21] Since then Petty's figures have been questioned. Scott Wheeler put the dead at between 125,000 and 200,000 (6.25 per cent to 10 per cent) of the total population. David Scott put the number at 500,000 (25 per cent). Robin Clifton suggests that 400,000, or 19 per cent of Ireland's population, perished.[22] The most recent—and most convincing—estimate comes from Padraig Lenihan, who argued that the population of Ireland fell by between 15 per cent and 20 per cent to 1.3 million. In other words 230,000 to 325,000 people died out of a total population estimated from between 1,530,000 and 1,625,000. Since Lenihan's research focused on the years from 1649 to 1653, his higher number of 20 per cent, or 325,000 deaths, seems more probable for the longer period, and will be used.

Even though Petty's figures have been proven too high, one thing no one—not even English historians—can doubt: that during the middle of the seventeenth century Ireland suffered a bloodbath of major proportions, which Lenihan has rightly called 'a demographic catastrophe'.[23] In comparison to the fifth of Ireland's population who died because of war between 1641 and 1660, 18.6 per cent perished during the Great Famine of the 1840s—a far better known cataclysm.

In Table 5 the numbers for England, Scotland and Ireland have been combined to give a total tally of 648,192 dead in the British Isles from 1638 to 1660.

Even though it must be stressed that these figures are very rough estimates, and should be taken with a pinch of caution and a pound of scepticism, they do suggest that the loss of life the Civil Wars inflicted on the British Isles was immense, even when set into context of calamities such as plague or other horrors.

Let us put these figures in context with other wars. In gross numbers the bloodiest conflict in history, with as many as seventy-eight million dead, was the Second World War, followed by the Taiping Rebellion of 1850–64, when twenty million Chinese perished. In proportionate terms the worst conflict in history was the War of the Triple Alliance (1864–70) in which three hundred thousand (60 per cent) out of half a million Paraguaians died. About 20 per cent of the population died in the Thirty Years War, as compared to 5.5 per cent and 6.05 per cent in Europe in the First and Second World Wars. Compared to these figures, those for the Civil Wars in England (4.6 per cent) and Scotland (9.7 per cent) seem high, and for Ireland (20.6 per cent) catastrophic. Perhaps a more accurate context would be to compare these proportions to other British wars and other Civil Wars. The effects of the Wars of the Roses, England's other great Civil War, have, for instance, been exaggerated, being nowhere as devastating as Shakespeare would have us believe.[24] In the American Civil War 3 per cent of the total population died.[25] In the First World War, out of a British population of thirty-five million, officially 765,399 people lost their lives. If we include as war-connected deaths the 183,577 people who died in 1918–19 from Spanish flu, then 2.61 per cent of the population

Table 5 British war deaths, 1638–60

	Dead	Population	Percent of nation	Percent of British
England	230,441	5,000,000	4.6	66
Scotland	92,751	1,000,000	9.2	13.2
Ireland	325,000	1,575,000	20.6	20.8
Total	648,192	7,575,000	8.6	

died directly or indirectly as a result of the war. By comparison 'only' 0.94 per cent of the British population died in the Second World War.

So, in other words, the British Civil Wars were not just the bloodiest conflict in British history, but rank high in the sad story of man's inhumanity to man.

How People Died

Unlike modern wars, we do not have figures for the Civil Wars of how men died, or of what sort of weapons did the most damage. In the Second World War, for instance, artillery caused 75 per cent of British wounds, compared to the Civil Wars, when cannon were so primitive and slow that they had comparatively little effect.[26] Then, many men died in pitched battles as the infantry stood in line facing each other, exchanging volleys, before advancing towards each other. As pikemen came within range of the enemy's weapons, about a dozen feet, their pikes went up, and they drew their swords. Like musketeers they stabbed, hacked, clubbed and trampled the enemy to death. Even more perished when one side broke and ran. In this butchery the cavalry were terribly lethal. A horseman could readily outrun a footsoldier, and from his saddle bring his sword down on the victim's vulnerable head, back and neck.

Surprisingly, only 15 per cent of casualties occurred in the nine largest and best known battles in which over a thousand perished. In conflicts, 37 per cent did so with between 200 and 999 dead, while almost half (47 per cent) lost their lives in small battles or skirmishes in which two hundred or fewer were killed. There seems to have been a fair amount of almost random killing, unreported by military authorities, or newsheets, but noted in parish registers when corpses were found and given a Christian burial. For instance, between 1644 and 1645 Guy Carleton, vicar of Bucklebury, Berkshire, recorded four such deaths, which cannot be attributed to any known skirmish or battle.[27]

The reasons why many more people died from disease than enemy action are obvious. From the crowded royalist base of Oxford, Lady Anne Fanshawe wrote that 'the sad spectacles of war', plague and sickness came 'by reason of so many people being packed together'. John Taylor, the poet, who was appointed water bailiff for the besieged city, vividly recalled the bestial condition of the River Thames:[28]

Dead hogs, dogs, cats and well flayed carrion horses
Their noisome corpses soiled the water sources;
Both swines' and stable dung, beasts' guts and garbage,
Street dirt, with gardeners' weeds and rotten herbage.

And from this water's filthy putrefaction,
Our meat and drink were made, which bred infection.

Such poor water caused dysentery, which could kill a third of those infected. Typhus, which contemporaries called camp fever because it was associated with the crowded military accommodations, had a 25 per cent fatality rate.[29] Even more devastating was that perennial seventeenth-century scourge, the bubonic plague, with a 50–70 per cent death rate. Between 22 June 1647 and 20 April 1648, 2,099 people died of the plague in war-torn Chester. Plague so devastated Stafford that it took a generation for the town's population to recover.[30]

Accidents by definition were episodic. Weapons are inherently dangerous machines, especially in the hands of ill-trained troops or careless conscripts, such as those involved in accidents in late 1642, right at the start of the First Civil War. On 17 September during an argument with a couple of Oxford undergraduates, Captain Staggar's musket went off—accidentally, said he—hitting a woman who happened to be shopping at the butcher's stall next door.[31] In November 1642 Thomas Hollamore, a member of Sir Ralph Hopton's troop, was 'killed by the going off of a musket'. Hopton's men must have been a careless bunch, for the following month 'the going off of a musket unawares' killed Christopher Awberry, one of Hopton's gentleman volunteers.[32] Mistakes made during the stress of combat could kill. Colonel John Hampden died at Chalgrove when his overloaded pistol blew up.[33] Gunpowder is extremely dangerous, as Thomas, earl of Haddington, and several of his staff officers discovered when they called for candles, and the servant set them down on a conveniently placed powder barrel![34] At the Siege of Gloucester, Captain James Hurcus stepped out of his trench to see whether the grenade he had just thrown at the roundheads had gone off. It did. He died.[35] After Captain Starker captured Hoghton Tower, Lancashire, he and his troops inspected the loot. One soldier was so impressed with the huge stash of gunpowder that he lit his pipe, blowing up the arsenal, as well as himself, his captain and sixty of his comrades.[36] Major Bridges, and twenty-three other royalists, drowned in the Avon when a partially demolished bridge collapsed.[37]

Compared to the huge loss of life, property damage was far less extensive. Seventeenth-century weapons were not nearly as destructive as, say, modern artillery or strategic bombers. Nonetheless the war destroyed two to three hundred country houses and damaged uncounted medieval castles. Perhaps as many as a tenth of townspeople were made homeless, especially when defenders pulled down buildings to give them better fields of fire in a siege: it took sixty years to completely rebuild Exeter.[38] Irish property damage was far greater. In *The Political Anatomy of Ireland* (1672),

Sir William Petty estimated that the value of people, stock, houses and land in Ireland fell from £13,500,000 to £5,200,000—a plunge of 61.4 per cent.

Radicalization

All wars to some extent radicalize those who survive them. As an American song popular after the First World War put it:[39]

How yea gonna keep 'em down on the farm
After they've seen Paree?

Parliament's soldiers had seen Edgehill, Marston Moor and Naseby, plus dozens of sieges and countless skirmishes. They had seen their friends killed and wounded, and themselves survive. They had no wish to get back to the farm, workshop or apprenticeship, with their arrears unpaid. They did not want to be sent to fight in Ireland, where, if they were lucky enough not to be killed or die of disease, they might end up farming that island's barren and hostile soil. War had—as it does to all who take part in it—fundamentally changed 'the boys'. Keeping them down was to be a difficult, perhaps an impossible, challenge.

At the time many soldiers realized the effect combat was having upon them. 'An Army is a harsh, cruel world, a brutal self-seeking power,' wrote the roundhead Chaplain William Sedgwick in his memoirs, adding that 'Many are wholly taken off from wars by the great experience we had of the beastly deceits, the horrible cruelty and corruption that attended it.' Preaching in 1646 Hugh Peters, another parliamentary chaplain, reminded the victorious roundheads that in the army they had found a way to exercise their talents as human beings, sinking their differences to unite to achieve common goals: thus 'men grow religious and more spiritual'.[40] Later the same year, Peters told the troops that in the military 'Men are not in their proper work, which eccentric motions produce many things untouched.' And then, as if the effects of combat were as obvious to those who had endured it as they had been painful, Peters enigmatically concluded, 'I need not particularize.'[41]

Immediately after combat, survivors' emotions came to the surface. Time and time again roundheads gave God full thanks for their victory and His favour. 'Thus the Lord of Hosts hath done great things for us, to whose name be ascribed all the glory,' wrote Sir Thomas Fairfax after capturing Nantwich in 1644.[42] Immediately after Naseby in June 1645, Colonel John Okey, whose regiment of dragoons had just taken heavy casualties, wrote to a friend, 'Now what remains but that you and we should magnify the name of our God that did remember a handful of despised men, whom they had thought to have swallowed up before them.' Okey embellished God's victory by portraying His (and his) soldiers as the underdogs, although in fact they had outnumbered the royalists: 'And I desire you that you would, on our behalf, bless God that hath made us instruments for our kingdom's good,' Okey concluded.[43]

Taking part in and surviving combat changed the way in which many troopers thought of themselves. 'I speak not now of our Army of soldiers,' wrote William Erberry, 'but of the army of saints.'[44] In *Orders from the Lords of Hosts*, a sermon first given to Colonel Rossiter's Regiment, Edward Reynolds described this process:[45]

> Because there is death in the camp soldiers carry their lives in the hand, and look death in the face daily. . . . Soldiers stand in most need to be very holy men because they may be taken away very suddenly . . . a holy army is victorious and successful. . . . Yea, is this not to be clearly seen . . . in our new model?

This view that victory had somehow sanctified the survivors was not just something preachers handed out like medals of approval. While in the past the victors believed that God had brought them victory (as after the Spanish Armada for instance), this was the first time the victors became convinced that God wanted them to use that victory to do His work—whatever that might be. This was a firm conviction that many of the New Model Army, especially the cavalry, accepted and, in several ways, originated. It might be seen as a way of dealing with post-combat stress. 'Sir, you may speak against the preaching of Soldiers in the Army,' a young cavalryman told Chaplain Thomas Edwards, 'but I assure you that if they may not have leave to preach, they will not fight.' Indeed, the trooper went on to argue that 'God hath blessed' His soldiers so bountifully that He had enabled them 'within these four months to rout the enemy twice in the field'.[46]

These new-found saints did not want to become suckers. They were adamant that the army's 'harvest should not end in chaff, and what it had won in the field should not be thrown away in the Council Chamber'. In their songs soldiers voiced the fear that they would be betrayed: that having won the war they would somehow lose the peace:[47]

> That if our Armies lay down Arms
> Before the work is at an end,
> We may expect worse Harms
> More precious lives and Estates to spend.

Their fears came to a head in late 1647 when the senior army officers debated with representatives of the rank and file, in Putney parish church. 'Do you not think,' asked Edward Sexby, 'that we fought all this time for nothing? All here, both great and small, do think that we fought for something.'[48] Colonel Thomas Rainsborough went further. He argued that after winning a war, and seeming about to lose the peace, many soldiers had been radicalized into a new concept of self:[49]

I think that the poorest he that is in England hath a life to live, as the greatest he: and therefore truly, Sir, I think it's clear that every man that is to live under a government ought first by his own consent put himself under that government.

Rainsborough's magnificent phrases still blaze down across the centuries as an inspiring declaration of the rights of man, the rule of law, the consent of the governed—even of democracy. It had an appeal to another victorious British Army, that of 1945 which helped elect a Labour government. Just as in 1945, when junior officers, such as Lawrence Stone, helped radicalize their men, they did the same thing during the First English Civil War.[50] All in all, those plain russet-coated captains, who knew what they fought for and loved what they knew, had created what Richard Baxter, the parliamentary chaplain, called 'a very extraordinary army'.[51]

It was also an army that decisively won its wars. On the continent sieges were the dominant form of warfare. But in the British Isles, where the science of fortification was less advanced, and there were few foreign experts to import the latest technology, battles predominated. By their very nature, the results of battles tend to be more definitive, which meant that a radical army had fewer restrictions on putting their programmes into effect.[52] This would in part explain why the army executed the king. The trial and execution of Charles I were one of the most dramatic episodes in British history. The day the king was publicly beheaded before a crowd of thousands outside the Banqueting Hall in Whitehall, 30 January 1649, was one of those dates which everyone remembers what they were doing when they heard the news. 'That the king is executed is good news to us: only some few honest men and a few cavaliers bemoan him,' wrote Cornet John Baynes to his brother Adam. His callousness is understandable for Baynes was writing from Pontefract, where he was besieging the last royalist holdout, and thought the news that the king was dead would induce the garrison to surrender.[53] While posterity has seen the king's trial as a clash between absolutist and representative government, many parliamentary soldiers (like Cornet Baynes) regarded it more as the trial of a war criminal: they believed that having reneged on his surrender, Charles was no longer entitled to the protections granted prisoners of war. By breaking his parole, the indictment against Charles at his trial declared he had inflicted 'the needless loss of much blood'. The indictment went on to list specific battles—Edgehill, Caversham, Gloucester, Newbury, Cropredy, Bodmin, Leicester, Naseby—where he had been present, and at which consequently 'much innocent blood of the free people of this nation has been spilt, many families undone'.[54] The execution of Charles I made a political solution to end the war all the more difficult to achieve because it radicalized parliamentarians, the army and royalists.

Afterward the royalists could do little except lie low, hope for the best, and turn Charles into a martyr. Reading *Eikon Basilike*, purportedly written by the king just before he died, might provide comfort as they had to deal with the real business of the day. Royalists—or their wives if they had fled into exile—had to negotiate fines with parliament to keep their estates. A few, such as the poet Abraham Cowley, hoped that 'the Royal Blood which the dying Charles did sow' would one day become 'the seed of Royalty'. In despair, many, like the poet Robert Herrick, must have asked themselves:[55]

O times most bad
Without the scope
Of Hope

Where shall I go
Or whither run
To shun
This public overthrow?

State Formation

Practically the first thing the army had to do after executing the king was to create a new form of government known as the commonwealth. But in chopping off the king's head and ending the monarchy, the new regime cut off a link with the past that would have given it legitimacy. The commonwealth never resolved this problem, remaining constitutionally and politically unstable, while being militarily strong. Yet during the 1650s through that military strength the commonwealth laid the founda-tion for Britain's lucrative Caribbean empire, the British Army won a reputation as exalted as it had enjoyed in the Hundred Years War, the Navy beat the Dutch, and England forged a British state.

After most wars the armed forces are demobilized as quickly as possible to save money and let the men go home to their families and freedom. But during the 1650s the commonwealth retained a large standing army averaging forty thousand men that peaked at seventy thousand men in 1652, and a large navy of over two hundred ships.[56]

'An army is a beast that has a great belly, and must be fed,' a pamphleteer complained in 1653.[57] He was right. A huge standing army and a growing permanent navy were extremely expensive, costing an average of £2,700,000 a year, which was about nine-tenths of the government's revenue. Such a financial burden could not have been borne by the pre-1642 tax collection system in which the king was, in peacetime at least, expected to live off his own. Parliament only voted taxes—and then grudgingly—in the extraordinary time of war. Afterwards the costs of war moved from being a royal responsibility to a national one backed up by a government increasingly founded on parliament. They also became a more indirect levy, shifting away from property and income taxes (assessments that could be easily abused) to direct revenue taxes on items such as beer and salt, that were cheap to collect, hard to evade, and extremely productive. They laid the foundation for the fiscal sinews of war that enabled Britain to become a world power.[58]

The commonwealth used its considerable armed forces to fight two sorts of wars: internal ones, which were in effect continuations of the Civil Wars of the 1640s, and external ones, which were traditional conflicts fought between nation states. The distribution of troops in 1655 suggests the relative importance of each: of 55,500 men, 23,000 (41.4 per cent) were in Ireland, 19,000 (34.3 per cent) in Scotland, 11,000 (19.8 per cent) in England and 2,500 (4.5 per cent) in the West Indies.[59]

In England the army had to deal with the Sealed Knot, a secret royalist society intent on overthrowing the government. In this it had about as much chance of success as its namesake (the Civil War re-enactment society) does today. Of the eight attempts the Sealed Knot made, Penruddock's Rising of 1655 in Salisbury was the most serious: it began as a farce and ended in tragedy; the leaders were executed, their followers transported. As a result of the rebellion, Cromwell divided England into ten, later eleven, military districts each run by a major general with orders to 'promote godliness and virtue, and discourage ... all profanities and ungodliness'.[60] Lucy Hutchinson called the major generals 'a company of silly mean fellows ... these ruled according to their wills, by no law.' In fact, even though one of the major generals, William Boteler, advocated stoning blasphemers, their rule was neither as tyrannical nor unpopular as posterity would have us believe: it was an indication of the growing power of the armed forces.[61]

The most immediate challenge facing the commonwealth was dealing with Ireland. Ever since the 1641 rising, many Englishmen had been convinced that the Irish papists must be harshly punished. The savagery of Cromwell's conquest (described in Chapter 7) was followed by the confiscations of the 1650s when the English appropriated the land of six thousand Irishmen, forcing untold thousands more to move on pain of death to the barren west of the country. 'To Hell or Connaught' were the alternatives the English offered papists whom they could not imagine going anywhere but down in the next life. As we have seen, perhaps a fifth of Ireland's population lost their lives as a result of the wars. No wonder the Irish have never forgotten the brutality of Cromwell's conquest. In 1972 a song (which topped the charts in Dublin) protested the introduction of internment without trial in Northern Ireland:[62]

Through the streets of Belfast
In the dark of early morn.
British soldiers come marauding
Wrecking homes with scorn . . .
Round the world the truth will echo
Cromwell's men are here again.

Cromwell's men did not make quite such a lasting impression on the Scots. In the three years between the battles of Preston (17–19 August 1648), that of Dunbar (3 September 1650) and Worcester (3 September 1651), the Scots had taken fearful casualties. They could no longer boast of being an unconquered nation. In 1651 Robert Blair, a minister of the kirk, described his country as 'a poor bird', whom 'the hawk . . . hath eaten it up'.[63]

Many of the Ironsides who had won the Civil War were sent overseas to fight foreign enemies. The most important expedition captured Jamaica in 1655. Led by William Penn and Robert Venables with 38 ships and 2,500 men, its original target was Hispaniola, a nest of privateers, which they failed to take, snapping Jamaica up as a consolation prize. An ungrateful government reprimanded Penn and Venables, not realizing that they had laid the foundations for the highly profitable British West Indies. In June 1658 four to five thousand Ironsides routed a Spanish army at the Battle of the Dunes, near Dunkirk. England's standing as a land power had not been higher since the days of Henry V and Agincourt, nearly two and a half centuries before.

The Navy and the First Dutch War, 1652–54

Many have argued that the New Model Army that parliament created, that Cromwell perfected, that won the Civil Wars at home and beat the

Scots, Irish and French abroad, was the progenitor of the British Army. If this was the case, then in large part it was due to the army's victory in the Civil Wars, which produced a well run, well financed, confident and aggressive English state. In much the same way the Civil Wars and commonwealth helped produce England's first modern navy: ironically the Royal Navy became a blue-water navy at the only time it was not royal. During this period England's power and prestige increased greatly at sea, due in part to Charles I's ship money, that hated tax levied in the 1630s which helped bring about the First Civil War. From 1640 to 1655 the English navy grew from 43 to 133 ships, as the proportion of armed merchant vessels in military service fell from a half to a quarter. Naval expenditures increased from two to three hundred thousand pounds. After a purge of incompetent officers in 1649, Cromwell's sea captains were as dedicated as their plain russet-coated comrades on land.[64]

It is from these years and from these men that Daniel Baugh dates the origins of a blue-water British navy, one able to operate for long periods away from its home bases. In 1652 the system of rating seamen as able and ordinary was introduced; the former were paid twenty-four shillings a month, and had to be over twenty with at least five years' sea time. The same year the navy adopted the single line-ahead tactical formation that required ships to be able to fire port and starboard broadsides at roughly the same time, increasing the need for standardization and better training. The preamble to the 1652 Articles of War stated that 'It is upon the Navy, under the providence of God, that the safety, honour and welfare of this realm do chiefly attend.' Some would argue that the institution of a daily rum ration three years later did much to achieve this goal.[65]

The navy demonstrated its new-found capabilities, the result of the army's victory in the Civil Wars, during the First Dutch War of 1652–54. By 1651 years of intense Civil War had severely damaged trade. As a contemporary ballad put it:[66]

Our ships are all taken, our merchants all stripp't
Our tradesmen all taken, our money all clipped.

So parliament passed a Navigation Act. Its objectives were simple. 'The Dutch have too much trade and the English resolved to take it from them,' observed General at Sea, George Monck, explaining, 'what we want is more of the trade the Dutch have.' By enacting that cargoes to and from British ports must be shipped in British vessels, parliament intended to destroy the Dutch merchant fleet, the largest in the world. The Dutch War (the first of three) was a new sort of war, a global war—fought not like

Henry VIII's for glory, nor Elizabeth's for religion, nor Charles I's continental expeditions for dynastic honour, but for trade.[67]

The war began in May 1652 when Admirals Robert Blake and Maarten Tromp met in the Channel in an exchange in which the British got the best. In August an action off Plymouth was inconclusive, while the English won an engagement off Kent the following month. In December, Tromp defeated Blake off Dungeness because many cowardly British commanders refused to fight. After several 'shy' captains were dismissed and rates of pay and victuals were improved, the British Navy performed well off Portland Bill in May 1653, and at Texel in July, where Tromp lost 20 of his 100 ships as well as his own life.

In his *Panegyric to My Lord Protector* (1655), Edmund Waller, the balladeer who could trot out best-sellers with equal facility for either Charles or Cromwell, praised Britain's naval mastery:[68]

The sea's our own! And now all nations greet
With bending sail, each vessel of our fleet.
Your powers extend as far as wind can blow
Our swelling sails upon the earth may go.

Two years later Waller celebrated the capture of a Spanish galley in the Jamaica campaign:[69]

Others may use the ocean as their road,
Only the English make it their abode.

During two decades of the Civil Wars and the commonwealth, the English made an abode not just of the oceans but of the British Isles. Like many European states in the first half of the seventeenth century, Britain was 'a composite state', made up of three nations (and a principality), which shared a common monarch and little else.[70] Indeed, the attempt by one of those monarchs, Charles I, to create a more unified state precipitated the Civil Wars. As Charles Tilly has pithily observed about this European-wide process of state formation, 'War made the state and the state made war'. R. A. Brown agreed that 'the origins of Modern Europe were hammered out on the anvil of war', while John Lynn has argued that 'warfare and military institutions' should be placed 'at the center of our understanding of the creation, character and domination of the state'.[71] Oliver Cromwell—astute as ever—recognized, in part at least, the role war had in forming the state. 'Sir,' he wrote to Major General Lawrence Crawford, 'the state in choosing men to serve it, takes no notice of their opinions. If they be willing faithfully to serve,—that satisfies.'[72]

The soldiers who forged this British state did not do so consciously. The troops who invaded Scotland in 1650 dubbed themselves 'The Army of England'.[73] Yet within three years, their general, Oliver Cromwell, had himself proclaimed the Lord Protector, of 'the Commonwealth of England, Scotland and Ireland, and the dominions thereunto belonging'.[74] The navy made the same point less subtly. The figurehead of the parliamentarian flagship, *The Naseby*, nicknamed 'The Great Oliver', showed the Lord Protector trampling over England, Scotland and Ireland as well as Spain and the Netherlands.[75] Half a century before the 1707 Act of Union, England and Scotland shared a common parliament, common rights, the same council of state, and religious toleration.

Yet this war machine, which had achieved so much, ultimately failed. In many ways it was not the republic's fault. Cromwell did not provide for an effective succession; thus when he died in 1658, and his son Richard, the aptly nicknamed 'Tumbledown Dick', was made Lord Protector, things immediately fell apart. Law and order broke down; the economy was in chaos. So unpopular was the army that as the Sheriff of Oxford proclaimed the new Lord Protector, the undergraduates pelted the guard of honour with turnips and carrots. The cost of maintaining a large standing army nearly brought England to financial ruin. Bankrupt of both money and ideas, the army restored the monarchy in May 1660, hopeful that Britain would return to the status quo ante *bellum civile*.

CHAPTER 9

HIGH-INTENSITY COMBAT:
BATTLES AND SIEGES

Hotspur: But I remember, when the fight was done,
When I was dry with rage and extreme toil
Breathless and faint, leaning upon my sword ...
Henry IV, Part I, I, iii, 33–35

HOTSPUR HAS JUST SURVIVED A BATTLE, WHICH (WITH SIEGES) ARE the most intense experiences that war inflicts upon its participants. He is extremely dry for, as a veteran of the Battle of Kohima (1944) recalled, 'fighting is the most dehydrating experience known to man.'[1] Thus, during the Four Days' Battle (1666), Lieutenant Thomas Browne had a stock of beer handy so he could grab a bottle as needed.[2] Hotspur is physically exhausted, breathless, even to the point of fainting, because combat is hard labour, demanding intense physical effort. 'It was very hot work for about two hours,' Colonel Blackadder told his wife about Ramillies.[3] Hotspur is also exhausted with a rage that goes beyond sanity. So great is the chasm between battle and normal human behaviour that William Manchester, who fought as a US Marine in the South Pacific, concluded 'No man in battle is really sane.'[4] In battle, observed Hugo Grotius, the Dutch jurist, 'frenzy had been openly let loose'. In Martin Parker's ballad 'The Maunding Souldier' (1629), a veteran, reflecting on his experience in combat confessed, 'I laid about me as I were mad.' A British officer remembered that at Culloden, 'Our lads fought more like devils than men.'[5] Perhaps this explains why just before the Battle of Edgehill, Sir Jacob Astley, a veteran of the Thirty Years War, prayed, 'O Lord. Thou knowest how busy I must be this day. If I forget thee do not forget me.'[6]

Battle: The Epitome of War

As General S. L. A. Marshall rightly observed, the experience of battle is 'the epitome of war'.[7] Battle deserves this designation not just because it is so intense and terrifying, transporting men into 'an epidemic of insanity' so violent that those who fail to make the transition usually fail to survive.[8] Battles are decisive because they are invariably consensual. By agreeing to fight, both sides believe that it is greatly in their interest to do so. Battles are extremely confusing, and hard to reconstruct. Between 1485 and 1746 they normally took place over a day between dawn and dusk. The only major battle to last longer was Preston (17–19 August 1648), which was more a long drawn-out, large-scale ambush. It was not consensual since the Scots did not want to fight, but were trying to escape back home. Battles took place in a cycle with stages. They started when both sides agreed to fight; in the second stage they approached one another, choosing their ground and drawing up their forces; in the third they came into contact, fought it out, until one side usually broke and ran; the final stage, pursuit, was the bloodiest. In battle the three main arms, infantry, cavalry and artillery, played different roles, which changed during the early modern period mostly due to improved weapons.

'The battle decides all,' declared Field Marshal Montgomery. Roger Boyle, earl of Orrery, agreed in 1677 that they 'are the most Glorious and commonly the most important Acts of War, wherein usually the moments to obtain the victory are so few'. Unless they cannot help it, generals only commit their forces to battle when they believe they will win. As George Monck wrote, 'I should have such to know that soldiers go into battle to conquer and not be killed.'[9] In his *Treatise on Modern War* (1639), John Cruso, the best-selling military author, affirmed that 'Of all the actions of war the most glorious and most important is to give battle.'[10] That is why commanders staked as many forces as they could afford on a battle, since they were convinced that the benefits from winning were considerable. Conversely, the costs of losing were as great, if not greater, for not only have the losers hazarded all the men they can afford, but in the rout that normally follows a victory, many, if not most, of their troops are killed, wounded or captured.

Battles are extremely risky. 'There is nothing,' declared John Taylor, poet and veteran of the 1596 Cadiz and 1597 Azores expeditions, 'more unsure than the success of a battle.'[11] In battle everything is at hazard. 'The loss of a battle is many times the loss of a kingdom,' noted James Touchet, earl of Castlehaven. Thus Charles, Lord Cathcart, a brigade major who fought in the War of the Spanish Succession, observed in 1710 that 'when there's a battle our all's at stake.'[12]

Even the most experienced soldiers had difficulty making sense of intense combat, which, as General George S. Patton put it, 'is an orgy of disorder'.[13] Wellington agreed. 'The History of a battle is not unlike the history of a ball!' the duke admitted after Waterloo, 'Some individuals may recollect all the little events of which the great result is the battle lost or won: but no individual can recollect the order in which, or the exact moment at which, they occurred.'[14] 'It is not an easy thing to describe a battle,' Lord George Murray wrote about Falkirk (1746), 'Springs and motions escape the eye ... add to this, the confusion, the noise, the concern that the people are in.' William Patten recalled the fighting in 1547 was 'terribly confused'.[15] After the Battle of the Boyne (1690), Captain John Stevens, a Jacobite, wrote, 'I shall not presume to write all the particulars of this unfortunate day's transactions, the confusion being such that few can pretend to do it.'[16] Sir Richard Bulstrode came to the same conclusion when he tried to make sense of his own experiences at Edgehill:[17]

> There is always great difference in relation of battles, it is certain that in a battle, the next man can hardly make a true relation of the actions of him that is next to him; for in such a Hurry and smoke of a Set Field, a man takes notice of nothing but what relates to his own safety. So that no man can give a clear account of particular passages.

Even today, when there are far better records (the first organized collection of personal memories was after Waterloo), it is still hard to make sense of battles. Peter Paret, the distinguished military historian, tried to trace the stages of an engagement in which he had fought as a staff sergeant in the American Army near Luzon in the Philippines, 'but found that as a participant I could never fully reconstruct so much as a skirmish'.[18]

Why is combat so confusing?

First of all, people are frightened and concentrating on their own survival in the milieu William Patten remembered at Pinkie in 1547:[19]

> Herewith waxed it very hot, on both sides with pitiful cries, horrible roars, and terrible thundering of guns besides. The day darkened above head, with smoke of shot. The danger of death on every side, the bullets, pellets and arrows flying each were so thick and so uncertainly lighting, that nowhere was there any surety of safety.

Finding out what was happening in such an environment, particularly for troops experiencing it for the first time, is extremely difficult, if not impossible. Jammed in ranks, neighbours blocked one's view, as did helmets and raised weapons. Sometimes men could not see the enemy until they were almost upon them. Gunpowder smoke from muskets and cannon limited visibility: it was a rolling white stinking fog, interspersed with red and orange flashes of exploding weapons. When the enemy emerged from this fog they seemed to be taller and thus more threatening. By the late seventeenth and early eighteenth centuries armies adopted tall hats, which added to this impression. So commanders tried to stay up wind of the other side. The noise of weapons firing was intense and disorientating, particularly when discharged by ranks, with the muskets of the men behind going off almost beside one's ear. Innocent of I-pods, rock bands, jet planes and jackhammers, our ancestors lacked our familiarity with such ear-drum shattering noises. Captain John Campbell could not remember recapturing his regimental colour at Ramillies (which today would have won him a Victoria Cross), 'the fire and smoke being so thick'.[20]

Battle is both literally and figuratively a fog. Little wonder mistakes occur. At Aughrim (1691), William III's left wing mistook a bog for firm ground, sinking into the mud up to their buttocks (none the less they won the battle). Fourteen years later, during the assault on Barcelona 'our guides mistook the way', recalled Colonel John Richards, 'The Grenadiers went one way, the musketeers another, and the Prince and My Lord [Peterborough] the third.'[21] Modern soldiers might call such an event a 'SNAFU' since confusion is the norm in combat. Clausewitz used another 'F' word, 'friction', to describe this. In war, he explained, even the simplest things are difficult. Unforeseen obstacles—the weather, miscommunications, misunderstanding, fear, stress, a failure to reason why—all slow things down, degenerating the impact of an operation over time.

The historian is also trying to understand what combat was *really* like during a dissimilar age hundreds of years ago. Now everyone admits to being frightened: then hardly anyone did so. Today men and women use the first-person singular frequently: then it was rarely employed. Hardly anyone wrote autobiographies (the word was not coined until 1806), which were invariably religious self-examinations. Early modern men were very concerned for their 'public face', which they were loathe to lose by, for example, admitting to fear. In his preface to Captain Roger Williams's *Actions in the Low Countries* (1618), his comrade John Hayward praised the author, for using the third-person singular: 'he hath wrote so modestly of himself, that some might happily esteem him a looker on.'[22] Military diaries, particularly before the last third of the seventeenth century, tended to be day-to-day descriptions of what happened with hardly any analysis or personal details.[23]

The Cycle of Battle

Battles usually start when both sides agree to fight. Sometimes there can be a ritual to them. The Battle of the Spurs (1513) resembled the fights of the New Guinea Stone Age tribesmen, where many insults are exchanged, and perhaps a few spears and arrows are thrown, until someone gets hurt and the proceedings end. If one side withdrew there could be no battle. For instance, on the morning of 4 May 1704 at Dursburg Hill, Sergeant Millner remembered that the French advanced, but after coming within allied cannon range pulled back. The two sides stood staring at each other until four o'clock, when the enemy withdrew, 'leaving us the Honour of the day,' the sergeant bragged.[24]

As both sides approached each other they would send out scouts, usually cavalry, to discover the other's position and strength, and a good site for engaging him. Once the sides had implicitly agreed on a place, they had to draw up their forces in what was known as the 'close order battlefield'. This compact area, usually a mile wide and a mile deep, revealed itself slowly, as each side deliberately arranged their positions.[25] The process could be agonizingly slow. At Ramillies on 11 May 1706 the allied scouts were sent out at one in the morning. Two hours later the main body marched off in a heavy fog, which cleared at about ten to reveal the enemy. At noon cannon opened sporadic fire, which by two in the afternoon had become fairly sustained. At three the infantry advanced, pausing frequently to dress their lines, to ensure they were straight. Fighting continued until just before sunset (9.19 p.m.), when the enemy was routed. It took twenty hours to arrange the forces for Malplaquet (11 September 1709). The night before that engagement the English and French camped so close to each other that they had many frequent and friendly communications. 'But at last each man being called to his respective post,' remembered Sergeant Millner, 'our commerce was turned to and swallowed up and drowned in Blood.' George Hamilton, earl of Orkney, thought that 'it really was a noble sight to see so many different bodies marching' into battle at Malplaquet.[26] Colonel Blackadder thought Malplaquet 'the most deliberate, solemn and well ordered battle I ever saw'. Every man was in his place and boldly advanced with speed, resolution and a cheerfulness that showed confidence in victory. 'I never had such a pleasant day in all my life,' concluded Blackadder about an action in which 35 per cent of the participants died or were wounded.[27]

Few soldiers possessed such sangfroid. As they waited for battle to begin, men would have to relieve themselves as they remained within their positions, because it was too risky to let them break ranks to nip behind a convenient bush. Officers might try to steel their men with a pep-talk.

'Gentlemen you are come this day to fight ... for ... your king, your religion, your country,' Viscount Dundee told his troops before Killiecrankie (1689), adding that he expected them to behave 'like true Scotsmen'.[28] Waiting men might smoke or talk, tell jokes, or sleep or eat—all good means of calming nerves. Alcohol was another way of doing so. Donald MacBane greatly appreciated the dram he was served before Malplaquet. Most were very tired. Before the Battle of Roundway Down (1643), Captain Edward Harley had not slept in a bed for twelve days. Before the fighting began at Culloden fifteen hundred Highlanders were reported 'nodding with sleep in the ranks'. Often men had no food. Henry Fowler had not eaten for forty-eight hours before the Battle of Selby (1644), while the London Trained Bands were so hungry that halfway through the assault on Basing House they paused to loot a barn containing vittles: as they stuffed and drank themselves silly, they were massacred. Before Malplaquet the Cameronians had had nothing to eat for five days. Nonetheless they went into action cheerfully singing psalms.[29]

Infantry were the key: they were the 'Queen of Battles', not just because before mass artillery and air power they tended to decide battles, but because there were so many of them. Foot soldiers were easier to recruit and draft, and cheaper to equip and train than were cavalry or artillery.[30]

During the sixteenth and seventeenth centuries the normal practice was to line up the infantry, several ranks deep in the centre of the formation, with cavalry on the flanks and artillery scattered throughout between infantry battalions. Infantry consisted of pikemen and musketeers. Heavily armoured pikemen would hold their sixteen-foot iron-tipped weapons out, with the end clamped to the earth by a boot. The pikemen's job was to protect the musketeers from cavalry as they reloaded their slow-firing weapons. Matchlock muskets, which used a glowing match cord to light the charge, were especially dangerous, since the cord could ignite the bandoleers of gunpowder charges that musketeers hung around their chests, burning them alive. In the early seventeenth century the musket, or harquebus, was so heavy that it required a forked stand on which to rest the barrel as it was pointed at the enemy. As muskets got lighter, and cheaper, the proportion of musketeers to pikemen increased from a third to two thirds.

Once lined up facing each other, the infantry opened fire, supported by slow-firing light cannon, whose balls were lucky to kill a man or two. Infantry fire was ponderous (and the pikemen could not fire at all), so first volleys produced few casualties, even though the wound that a heavy, slow-moving musket ball inflicted was appalling, with an exit hole perhaps a foot in diameter. After a few desultory rounds, one or, rarely, both lines would advance. As they came into contact, in what was known as a 'push of pike', the pikemen did not impale each other like suicidal hedgehogs, but lifted their weapons up, and drew their swords. Musketmen reversed their weapons, turning them into clubs. Matchlocks were so slow and inaccurate that it has been suggested they were far more lethal as cudgels than as muskets.

In a huge heaving, screaming, smoke-filled, acrid, broiling, bloody scrum the two ranks of infantry hacked and slammed each other. They did not break into small groups independent of each other (as films often suggest), but remained within their ranks. In this ghastly experience they were helped by a disposition common to many animals who, when frightened, tend to 'incline much to crowd in upon another',[31] as the earl of Castlehaven, a veteran of the Irish and French wars, noted in 1680. In the *Arte of Warre* (1591) William Garrard reported that in combat ranks of infantry could press so hard upon each other that it was impossible for a wounded or dead soldier to fall down. Today bunching together is dangerous, for it allows a single shell to kill many. In the early modern period this tendency to keep together was used so men would stay in ranks and lines, supporting each other as a unit. To survive units had to remain united: they must not become a mob. The purpose of hand to hand combat was to disintegrate an enemy formation, turning it into a mob of individuals to be killed at will. 'Whatsoever may cause fear in your enemy, ought not to be omitted by you,' advised Roger Boyle in his *Treatise on the Art of War* (1677). 'Fear is truly said to be a Betrayer of that Succor which reason also might afford.' In other words, Boyle urged creating 'a panic fear'.

Panic Fear

Panic fears often started after lines of infantry had been fighting each other in hand to hand combat, usually within a quarter of an hour, for this sort of fighting was as terrifying as it was tiring. The front rank of each line pressed one against the other, as those behind pushed forward. Units about to break would start oscillating, ranks moving in waves, as individuals on the sides and rear of the formation started to run away. At a certain tipping point all panicked. Illustration 5 shows how this process took place at the Battle of Pinkie (1547).

Once a unit broke, the true horror of battle began. Men ran, being pursued by cavalry who hacked them down. Arthur Trevor recalled the madness of the rout after Naseby:[32]

In the fire, smoke and confusion of that day I knew not for my soul wither to incline. The runaways on both sides were so many, so breathless, so speechless, and so full of fears that I should not have taken them for men.

James Ure, who ran in the panic fear after the Battle of Bothwell Bridge (1679), confessed, 'The Lord took both courage and wisdom from us.' In other words fear had made them foolish, for it was well known that staying to fight rather than running away was a far less dangerous option. As the earl of Castlehaven explained, 'For though man in his reason be the most excellent of creatures on earth, yet having lost it by the passions of fear, is one of the least.' Most of the 179 casualties the Cameronians took at Steenkirk in 1692 occurred as they ran. Their chaplain, Alexander Shields, noted that at Lander the following year 'there were more killed by running than by standing.'[33] Statistics bear this out. Of a sample of eleven battles in the early modern period, the winning side lost 4 per cent of its men, compared to the defeated who lost 16.7 per cent—over four times as many. In a drawn battle, such as Edgehill, each side lost 13 per cent, as they fought one another to a stalemate, neither side breaking in a panic fear.[34]

For pursuers a panic fear was a killing spree, a binge of elation, of blood lust; it was an orgasm of carnage. Unable to see his fleeing victim's face, the horseman could swing his sword down against his back, neck or head, usually with fatal results. Perhaps the origins of this blood lust go back to man's earliest roots as hunter-gatherers, when we chased some huge beast, to relish its capture, death and consumption. Certainly there were links between combat and hunting. As Thomas Dekker observed in his poem, 'The Artillery Garden' (1615):

Of war hunting is but the Ape,
Doing her tricks in less fearful shape.

After Flodden in 1513, where hundreds of fleeing Scots were murdered in hot blood, an English poet boasted 'we killed them like cattle.'[35] An English officer described how Colonel Jean Martinet's regiment ran in 1706 'like lost sheep'.[36] Gideon Bonnivert remembered how after the Boyne 'we killed but an abundance of their men, and pursued the rest until nine o'clock.' Sergeant Millner wrote in his diary how after Oudenarde (1708), 'We drove the enemy from ditch to ditch, from hedge to hedge . . . in great Hurry, Disorder and Confusion,' until nightfall ended the slaughter.[37] 'Our men,' William Patten wrote about the rout at Pinkie, 'with an universal cry "They Fly! They Fly!" pursued and thereunto so eagerly and with such fervours that they overtook many and spared indeed but a few.' Looking back on his own and his comrades murderous behaviour, Patten marvelled 'we had used so much cruelty, and that we had killed so many'. With dry humour he described the enthusiasm with which they looted the enemy corpses stark naked: 'Many hands make light work.'[38]

Humour has always served as a means of dealing with our fears—hence jokes about AIDS or mothers-in-law. It steadies men, helping them to brush aside the awful sights and sounds of combat. Humour often relied on understatement. 'I went to visit Monsieur Hallard,' Sir Thomas Coningsby wrote in his diary of the Siege of Rouen, 'and beheld the dressing of his wound, which in common opinion is not deadly, but will mar his dancing.'[39] Humour was often sardonic, almost to the point of cruelty—which can be characteristic of the best jokes. The Reverend William Dillingham described the death of the lord of Chatillon at the Siege of Ostend (1601), when a cannon ball hit his teeth, cutting his head off and spraying his brains all over his colonel, as 'an unhappy mischance'. After the French opened fire at Blenheim early in the morning, Sergeant Hall of the Coldstream Guards told his friend Sergeant Cabe, 'We had an indifferent breakfast, but the Mounseers never had such a dinner in their lives.'[40] During the Siege of Derry in 1689, the Reverend George Walker recalled that the defenders were so short of food that some suggested cannibalism, much to the concern of 'a certain fat gentleman' who, noticing that 'several of the garrisons look on him with a greedy eye, thought fit to hide himself'.[41]

Scottish fighting tended to be less regimented, especially with troops who were more independent and, although brave, inadequately trained. In the 'Highland Charge', the Scots, after exchanging a round or two, discarded their muskets—and sometimes their clothes—and with drawn claymores charged the enemy, screaming blood-curdling Caledonian curses. They did not do so in ranks, but as individuals, which lessened their effectiveness particularly against soldiers trained to fire rapid accurate volleys. 'They came with cries and sound of Drums and Bagpipes,' Fynes Moryson wrote of a fight that took place in Ireland in 1601, where General Mountjoy 'had lodged in a trench some four hundred shot [musketeers], charging them not to shoot till the rebels approached near. And after that our own men had given them such a volley in the teeth, they drew away and we heard no more of their Drum and Bagpipes.' When the Highland charge worked, as it did at Killiecrankie in 1689, where the Williamite infantry could not remove the bayonets that plugged into and not around the barrels of their muskets, the resultant sounds were very different. 'Nothing was heard,' wrote Sir Ewen Cameron of Lockiel, 'but the sullen and hollow clashes of broadswords, with the dismal groans and cries of dying and wounded men.'[42] When the Highland

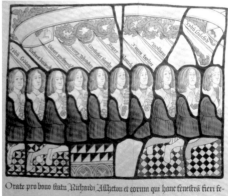

1 Memorial stained glass window to the sixteen locally recruited archers killed during the Flodden Campaign of 1513, in St Leonard's Church, Middleton, Lancashire. This may be England's first war memorial.

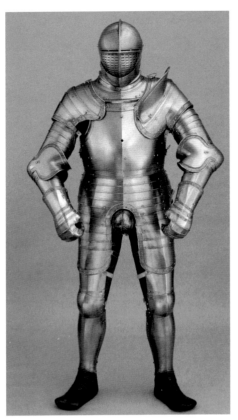

2 Henry VIII's field and jousting armour, 1540. The size of the suit shows the king's bulk, while the codpiece might help explain his marital problems.

3 Henry VIII at the Siege of Boulogne, 1544. While the king declared his ambition was 'to exceed the glorious deeds of his ancestors', this engraving shows how chaotic the face of battle really was.

4 Richard Schlecht's painting, *The Sinking of the H.M.S. Mary Rose* during the French attack on Portsmouth in 1544, shows that the sea is no place for the incompetent.

5 John Ramsay's contemporary illustration of the Battle of Pinkie between the English and Scots in 1547 shows a classic 'panic fear'. Scots soldiers are starting to run from the rear and sides of their formation. Afterwards a victor recalled, 'nowhere was there any surety of safety.'

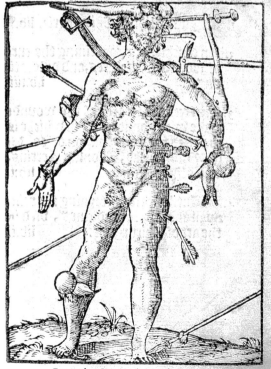

CERTAINE VVORKES
of Chirurgerie, nevvly compiled and published by Thomas Gale, Maister in Chirurgerie.

Prynted at London by Rouland Hall.

6 'A wound man', illustration from, *Certaine workes of Chirurgerie*, 1563, by Thomas Gale who served as a doctor in the French wars where he recalled, 'there was a great rabblement that took upon them to be surgeons. Some were sow gelders, and horse gelders, with tinkers and cobblers.'

7 The poet, soldier and military historian George Gascoigne (1525–77) presents a manuscript to Elizabeth I. He observed 'how sweet war is to such as know it not.' She once told the French Ambassador that soldiers were 'but thieves and ought to hang'.

8 The English attack on Cadiz in June 1596 has been described as 'one of the most efficient acts of war carried out by any Tudor government'.

9 English soldiers in Ireland 'burning and pillaging all the way', parade in triumph, carrying severed Irish heads and leading a captive by a halter.

10 Early seventeenth-century matchlock musket with stand; although slow to fire, its heavy ball made an exit wound the size of a dinner plate.

11 Peter Paul Reubens' painting of St George and the Dragon made the case for peace at a time when Charles I wanted to go to war.

March with your rest in yowr hand.	March and with your Musket carrie yo'rest.	Unshoulder your Musket	Poize your Musket.
Joyne your rest to yo' Musket	Take forth your match	Blow off your Coale.	Cock your match.
Try your match.	Guard, blowe and open your pann.	Present.	Giue fire.

C

12 An illustrated drill manual from Henry Hexham's *The Principles of the Art Militarie*, 1637; 'now we have obtained the handsome skill, by order, method, and by rule to kill.'

13 Sir James Turner, the Scots mercenary who believed that 'so long as we serve our master honestly, it is no matter which master we serve.'

14 Dirck Stoop, Charles II's entry into London, 1660; the king being restored 'by that very army that had rebelled against him'.

15 The Dutch sack the English naval base at Chatham, 1667. 'I think the Devil shits Dutchman,' babbled Sir William Batten, the Surveyor of the Navy.

Severall of ẙ Rebells hang'd upon a Tree

16 Several Rebels hanged from a tree after the Battle of Sedgemoor, 1685, from a set of playing cards.

17 Battle of the Boyne, 1 July 1690, painting by Benjamin West. Afterwards a victor boasted, 'we killed but an abundance of their men, and pursued the rest'.

18 *The Manner of the ship Sampson in Stress of Weather*, by Edward Barlow, the seventeenth-century mariner, from his journal, showing how cruel the sea could be.

19 'Brown Bess' musket; the standard infantry weapon for over a hundred and fifty years, which inflicted 40 per cent of battle casualties.

20 *The Recruiting Sergeant*, painted by John Collet (1725–80). 'If any gentlemen, soldiers or others have a mind to serve Her Majesty...if any have severe masters...undutiful parents...too little wages... or too much wife, let them repair to the noble Sergeant Kite'.

21 Colonel John Blackadder, the Scots soldier who after the Battles of Blenheim and Malplaquet 'went down into the field of battle, and there got a preaching from the dead.'

22 Captain Robert Parker, the army officer who fought on the continent and in Ireland, where he recalled 'the miserable effects of war appeared in a very melancholy manner'.

23 Christian Davie, aka Mother Ross, the 'she-soldier', who fought during the War of the Spanish Succession. She died an out-pensioner of Chelsea Hospital, being buried with full military honours.

24 The Battle of Culloden, 16 April 1746. 'I laid about me as I were mad', recalled a British officer, adding that 'Our lads fought more like devils than men.'

Charge failed, as it did at Culloden, the groans and crying were on the other side.

The Thin Red Line

Culloden was the culmination of military changes that took place in the late seventeenth and early eighteenth centuries for three reasons, helping produce what would become known as the 'thin red line'.[43] First, the invention of the bayonet meant the musketeers now could defend themselves, and no longer needed pikemen. Second, the development of a flintlock musket, which used a flint on steel to strike a spark that ignited the weapon, increased reliability and rates of fire. With the steps needed to reload decreased by almost a half, a well-trained infantryman could fire five shots a minute. Flintlocks, which were first issued to the guards regiments between 1670 and 1683, were universal by 1708, and over the next century and a half nearly eight million of these sturdy weapons were manufactured (see ill.19). They had a long triangular-shaped bayonet, which made a wound that was hard to stitch closed.[44] Third, improvements in discipline and training meant that ranks of the long service professional infantry of a standing army stood unflinching, taking huge casualties before breaking. At Blenheim, recalled Sergeant Millner, 'We stood within sixty paces of the enemy, neither side making any motion.' He explained that 'The whole burden of the battle fell chiefly and solely on our Foot, as it often and commonly happened,' adding, with more than a hint of bitterness, that 'our Horse and Dragoons sustained very little or no Loss throughout the whole war.'[45] Compared to the Civil Wars, bodies of infantry were less liable to close with each other to fight hand to hand. For three hours during the Battle of Oudenarde 'we were obliged to stand in cold blood, exposed to the enemy's shot,' recalled Colonel Blackadder, who kept up his morale by silently singing Psalm 103 over and over again:[46]

> As for man, his days are like grass: as a flower of the field, so he flour-isheth.
> For the wind passeth over it, and is gone: and the place thereof shall know it no more.

The much increased firepower of infantrymen meant that units tended to break before coming into hand to hand combat. This explains why bayonets inflicted only 2.2 per cent of wounds at Malplaquet. Breaking was especially common when an advancing unit was ordered to withdraw. An Irish captain in French service described how at Ramillies 'We had not gone forty yards in our retreat when the words *sauve qui peut* went through the great part, if not the whole army, and put all to confusion.'[47]

Infantry versus Cavalry

The job of the cavalry was twofold. First, scouting for intelligence or provisions, when they might stumble across another patrol and skirmish with each other. Second, pursuing an enemy who had broken in panic fear. Occasionally, cavalry charged each other; even more rarely were they able to break infantry. One such occasion was at the Boyne. 'The horse came on so unexpected and with such speed, some firing their pistols,' Captain Stevens recalled, that 'all took to their heels'.[48]

So long as well trained infantry stood they won. Horses will not charge a standing object, be it a wall or a line of determined foot soldiers, shying aside at the last moment. 'And having received their fire without much damage,' recalled Private John Deane of the Grenadiers at Oudenarde in 1708, 'we gave them a merry salute firing directly at the enemies' faces, which caused them to immediately turn tail.' Deane, however, was outraged because there was no allied cavalry to exploit the rout, and the 'poor bloody infantry' had to mop up the enemy from hedge to hedge, breast work to breast work. 'The fighting was very desperate,' the Grenadier sergeant concluded.[49]

It would be nice to think that this triumph at Oudenarde confirms the view that 'of all the world's great heroes, there's none that can compare ... To the British Grenadiers.' But statistics, not patriotic songs, really explain why infantry beat cavalry. On a line of equal length there were many more foot than horse soldiers, the latter usually charging in ranks at least two deep, against as many as six of the former. Even packed so close to each other that one man's knee was tucked behind that of the comrade beside him, horse troopers were spread at least twice as wide apart than infantry, and with their mounts presented large targets. Thus, if in the early seventeenth century on a sixty-foot front, 30 horsemen in two ranks charged 150 infantry (half of whom were musketeers), during the twenty seconds it would have taken the cavalry to trot two hundred yards (the effective musket range), each side would have been able to fire a single volley. The infantry would have shot five bullets at each horseman, while the cavalry fired one at every five foot soldiers. Or to put that another way, the ratio of bullets fired at the enemy favoured the infantry 12.5 to one. If we take into account the fact that the infantry fired much heavier rounds from a stable position, not a moving horse, the figure could be at least twice as high.

These estimates are for the middle of the seventeenth century when infantry used slow-firing matchlocks. By the end of that century and the start of the next, three developments augmented the infantry's advantage. First, the introduction of the flintlock meant that infantry, who were becoming much better trained, could fire two instead of one round at the approaching cavalry, the number of steps for reloading being reduced from 43 to 26. Flints reduced misfires by 40 per cent. Second, as just mentioned, the bayonet made pikemen redundant, increasing the number of musketeers. Third, the combination of flintlock, bayonet and rote training permitted much thinner and thus longer lines, three or even two ranks deep.[50] Together these quadrupled the infantry's fire ratio from one in 12.5 to perhaps as high as one in fifty.

What do all these numbers mean? Well, to put it crudely they explain why during the late seventeenth and early eighteenth centuries the infantry came to dominate the battlefield. If the British Civil Wars had taken place half a century later, it is hard to see how a cavalry commander, such as Oliver Cromwell, could have risen to preeminence or how his radicalized horse troopers could have become so politically important.

Sieges

Sieges are one of the oldest forms of total warfare. The earliest fortifications that archaeologists have discovered are at Jericho, built seven thousand years before the birth of Christ, and perhaps five and a half millennia before Joshua and the Israelites made the walls come tumbling down.[51] Forts are built to guard places of key strategic importance, such as river crossings or mountain passes: they are sited on features such as hills, river bends or cliffs, which give the defenders an advantage. Soldiers, like all human beings, are drawn to the comfortable and familiar, which means they are attracted to fighting from forts and castles. Being protected behind walls, firing through slits, they are far less exposed than the attackers, who must approach in the open with their whole bodies vulnerable. They can get trapped in killing zones as they assault a heavily defended and geographically well located site. Shakespeare instinctively grasped Clausewitz's adage that 'the defensive is the stronger form of war', when he has Macbeth boast from the walls of Dunsinane:[52]

Our castle's strength
Will laugh a siege to scorn: here let them lie
Till famine and the ague eat them up.

Sieges did not require the consent of both parties, for the defenders were confined within their positions. This gave the initiative to the attackers: cut off, defenders tended to react. It also meant that sieges could be long drawn out—for weeks, even months—with disease and starvation costing far more lives than combat. That can become the defenders' objective: to hold a place not just because of its strategic importance, but to wear the enemy down. As General Monck observed in 1671, 'Long sieges ruin armies.'[53]

Sieges took place in a cycle that was in many ways less flexible than that of battles. The cycle began with reconnaissance. Joshua started his Siege of Jericho by sending two spies to the city to discover the strength of the defences and the enemy's morale. On the basis of such surveillance, and after ensuring that he had enough resources and that reinforcements could not break the siege, a general would start the process by surrounding the fort. He would then invite the defenders to surrender. At this stage few took up the offer, since doing so would be utterly dishonourable. For ceding Bristol prematurely in 1643, Colonel Nathaniel Fiennes was widely denounced as 'that bloody Coward', court-martialled and sentenced to death.[54]

If the enemy refused to surrender, the attackers had three options. First, they could mount an immediate attack. Second, they could make a breach in the walls through which they could storm. Third, they could invest the fort, starving the defenders into capitulation. At any time, of course, they could give up, and march away.

The first option, an immediate attack, had the advantage of catching the defenders unprepared. On the other hand, the attackers might be similarly situated. Scaling ladders, as we have noted, were sometimes too short and too weak. At Burick, Rhine-Westphalia, in 1590, as Sir Francis Vere's troops started to climb, the rungs broke, scattering the English to the ground. Vere was desperate to avoid a long and costly siege, such as the one he had waged at nearby Litkenhoven, after which he had executed the 350-man garrison. So when he reminded Burick's defenders of that fate, they surrendered.[55] Because of their slow, deliberate nature, sieges were rife with such calculations, which altered as a siege progressed. Attackers had to balance the costs of a siege with its chances of success. Defenders had to offset the likelihood of holding out until relieved, or of having their surrender accepted, with the likelihood of being put to the sword.

The second option in a siege was to breach the walls. This required huge resources. Marlborough's siege train consisted of eighteen heavy cannon and twenty mortars, drawn by three thousand wagons and sixteen thousand horses, which occupied thirty miles of road.

Engineers and gunners were the keys during an investment. In order to bring guns within range to batter a breach in the wall, as well as provide cover so the infantry did not have too much open ground to charge across, engineers built trenches. They were zigzagged to thwart enfilading fire, and constructed with a sense of inevitability as infantrymen advanced towards the breach. The other contribution engineers made was to strengthen the design of forts. Star-shaped forts, which subjected attackers to enfilading fire, as well as sloping earthen walls that deflected or absorbed cannon balls, became dominant towards the end of the eighteenth century. So much so that in 1677 Roger Boyle observed that 'Battles do not decide national quarrels, and expose countries to the pillage of conquerors as formerly. For we make war more like foxes than lions, and you will have twenty sieges for every one battle.'[56] Although the British Army won four major battles in the War of the Spanish Succession (1701–14)—Blenheim, Ramillies, Oudenarde and Malplaquet—it also took part in eighteen sieges, with the average regiment fighting in three of them. A typical siege lasted from forty to sixty days (that at Liège in 1702 dragged on for 120), with most resulting in a victory for the besiegers.[57]

Once the trenches had been completed, gunners had to breach the walls. Artillery, to be sure, had a fearsome reputation. Miguel de Cervantes called cannon 'devilish instruments'. Ben Jonson thought that 'From the devil's arse did guns beget.' John Milton agreed they were 'a devilish machination'. So in keeping with the wicked image of artillery, Sir John Meldrum's roundheads nicknamed their heaviest piece, a twelve-feet-long thirty-two pounder, 'Sweet Lips' after a notorious whore from Hull.[58] In fact, the impact of artillery could be limited. During the Siege of Pontefract from 17 to 21 January 1645, the roundheads fired 1,359 rounds killing only eight defenders. Rates of fire were slow, artillery was heavy to transport, and thus more suited to long sieges than pitched battles. Nonetheless, given time cannon invariably made a breach.

At this point, as the infantry were poised to storm, the defenders were given one last chance to surrender and avoid the horrors of a sack: 'shrill-shrieking daughters . . . naked infants spitted on pikes . . . mad mothers with howls confused'.[59] The surrender terms could be generous: at best the defenders could march out, bands playing, colours flying, and keep their own weapons and possessions. At worst they gave up unconditionally, with the hope that the lives of soldiers and civilians might be spared.

Unlike most battles, civilians were caught up in sieges. Sometimes they actively supported the soldiers, helping dig fortifications, cook food, nurse the wounded, even reload snipers' weapons. They might demand that soldiers keep on fighting. When Barnard Duffield urged the garrison to surrender during the Siege of Exeter (1547), his daughter Frances, 'contrary to the modesty and shamefastness required of a woman, especially young and unmarried, runs most violently upon him and struck him in the face'.[60] More often, civilians favoured surrender, for most modest and shamefast maids knew only too well the awful consequences of a successful storm.

Soldiers knew equally well its dangers. 'He must wade to it in blood,' wrote Colonel John Hutchinson about storming castles. It was so horrible that the storm troops, known as the 'Forlorn Hope', were often paid a bonus, or plied with alcohol.[61] They would advance, heads down, as if they were walking into a blizzard. Often the assault failed, for the attackers were crammed into a narrow, rubble-strewn breach, as the defenders fired and hurled grenades down on them. In August 1632 at Venlo six to seven thousand Italians assaulted the British defenders, charging through a churchyard to the top of the trenches, where they stabbed with their swords and pushed the enemy with their sixteen-foot pikes. 'But our men gave them such a welcome, and did so repulse them, that some were slain upon the breast work, and tumbled down into the ditch, and together were knocked down,' Captain Henry Hexham, Vere's quartermaster, gloated, 'and had their brains beaten out.'[62] In another failed storm at Maastricht in 1676, the English soldiers suddenly leapt out of their trenches and charged across a hundred yards of open ground to the breach, as their cannon fired in support. When they reached the top of the breach the enemy replied with grenades and a small cannon. 'Everyone was struck with a panic fear,' confessed George Carleton, as they bolted pell-mell back to their own trenches, losing in the rout more men than they had in the assault.[63] Even successful storms were chaotic. The earl of Essex described the one he led on Cadiz in 1596 as being executed 'with more courage than order'.[64]

The best description of a full-fledged storm is from Major John Blackadder, who commanded the Cameronians, plus four hundred Grenadiers, in the assault of Lille in September 1708. On receiving his orders 'I was easy and calm, committing myself to God.' The attack was postponed for twenty-four hours, allowing the assault troops to rest on the hospital beds prepared for the wounded. Blackadder drifted off to sleep, thinking of those 'groaning with wounds and broken bones' who would fill his berth on the morrow. At noon he went into the trenches to brief his men. They did not attack until seven that evening, when, without warning, they went over the top, scattering grenades at the enemy. The first wave was beaten back in confusion. So Blackadder led the second. Hit in the arm, with all the other officers wounded, 'I thought it my duty to stay a while and encourage the Grenadiers to keep their warm post.' After quarter of an hour's fighting, which grew more intense by the minute, Blackadder was hit in the head. It took him three hours to get through the trenches, which were jammed with men and supplies hustling forward and the wounded and broken trudging back, before the major found a house and bed to rest for the night and allow his wounds to stop bleeding.[65]

No wonder those who survived a successful storm took their fears and relief out on the defenders. 'Three hours plundering is the shortest rule of war,' Marshal Tilly said of the Siege of Magdeburg in 1633, adding that 'A soldier must have something for all his toil and trouble.'[66] What did he get? Once the order 'havoc' was given, the dogs of war enjoyed unlimited rape, pillage and mindless vandalism without restraint, untold murder and torture, as much liquor as fetid brains could stand, as much loot as spent bodies could carry, and sights that would haunt men who possessed but a shred of decency until their dying days. In 1691 a diarist described Athlone after its sack:[67]

> I think there was never a more tragical scene in so short a time and small a place. One could not set foot at the end of the Bridge or the Castle, but on Dead Bodies. Many laid half buried under the rubbish, and more under faggots ... the stink is insufferable.

The sack of Leicester in May 1645 was notably vicious, especially because it was inflicted against fellow countrymen. The royalists hanged Mr Raynor, 'an honest religious gentleman'. They killed Mr Sawyer in cold blood. They massacred many prisoners of war, and they 'put diverse women inhumanly to the sword'. Perhaps seven hundred died and uncounted more bore the scars of abuse. William Summers declared that having lost her son and all her possessions his 'wife hath been distracted ever since'.[68] By nightfall, remembered Captain Richard Symonds, one of the attackers, there was 'scarce a cottage unplundered ... and no quarter given to any in the heat'.[69] Over the next few days the royalists left the city carrying their loot in a couple of hundred wagons.

If a storm failed, or could not be mounted, the attackers could either raise the siege or else resort to the third option, starving the defenders into surrendering. The latter was a desperate course. Both sides got little rest, constantly alert for an enemy attack. 'We slept like hares, with open eyes,' recalled Sir Thomas Coningsby of the Siege of Rouen.[70] 'Am very heartily fatigued,' Captain Nicholas Haddock wrote to his father from the Siege of Alicante (1706). Two years later during the eight-week Siege of Lille, James Cathcart spent only six nights in bed, took part in eight assaults and was one of only twenty-two of his 212-man company to survive unhurt.[71] Artillery, particularly mortars, also sapped the enemy's morale, inflicting gruesome damage. Elis Gruffudd recalled that the smell of dead rotting horses killed during the Siege of Boulogne (1544) made the air loathsome to breathe, and promulgated pestilence. Disease ran rampant. During the five weeks' Siege of Le Havre (1563), 2,600 of the 7,500 defenders died of sickness: death rates during the Siege of Dieppe (1591) ranged from 40 per cent to 56 per cent.[72] Limerick in 1690 was one of the nastiest of sieges. The Williamites catapulted corpses and dead horses into the city to spread infection. Crows and ravens flew from the surrounding counties to grow fat on decaying bodies, and on amputated limbs from the field hospital, becoming so contemptuous of human beings that they would walk among them like domesticated chickens. After artillery set the hospital on fire, charred bodies could be seen strewn all over the place, some by the doors to which men, women and children had desperately crawled to escape the flames.[73] Soon afterwards Limerick surrendered.

Even if after all their suffering a garrison surrendered on conditions, there was no guarantee that the victors would keep their promises, so intense were the feelings on both sides. After parliamentary forces surrendered at Bristol in 1643 and at Lostwithiel in 1644, royalist troops and outraged civilians ignored the terms, assaulting and plundering the enemy. 'I saw them strip a woman,' an eyewitness at Lostwithiel wrote, 'she had lain in but three days before. They took her by the hair of her head and threw her into the river, and there almost drowned her. The woman died within twelve hours.'[74] When the Carrickfergus garrison surrendered in 1689, William III's forces granted James's troops the privilege of marching out, colours flying, drums beating, permitting them to enter French mercenary service. A mob of locals had other ideas. Irate at the damage the Jacobite artillery had inflicted on the town, they attacked the garrison, stripping them of their clothes.[75] Such hatred was all too much part of the insanity of intense combat.

CHAPTER 10

RESTORATION TO GLORIOUS REVOLUTION, 1660–1688

> They have a king and officers of sorts;
> Where some, like magistrates, correct at home,
> Others, like merchants, venture trade abroad,
> Others, like soldiers, armed in their stings,
> Make boot upon the summer's velvet buds.

Henry V, I, ii, 196–203

'I STOOD IN THE STRAND AND WATCHED IT AND BLESSED GOD,' WROTE the diarist John Evelyn on 29 May 1660, for he, like millions of his fellow subjects, was thanking his Maker for the restoration of Charles II. Five days earlier the king had sailed from Holland aboard *the Naseby* (hastily rechristened the *Royal Charles*) and landed at Dover, ending fourteen years of exile on the continent. His journey to London was a triumph. At Dover, Canterbury, Rochester, Deptford and Southwark, commoners and the quality welcomed their new king with universal enthusiasm. So crowded was London Bridge that the king and his entourage could hardly push through into the City, where the Horse Guards and five regiments of infantry were waiting to escort him to his palace at Whitehall (see ill. 14). As Evelyn watched the soldiers, their plain russet-coats being adorned with silver cloth and lace to make them look less Cromwellian, he wryly observed that the restoration 'had been done without one drop of blood shed and by that very army that had rebelled against him'.[1]

This chapter will examine the role of the armed forces from the restoration of the monarchy to the Revolution of 1688. The army got little thanks for putting Charles II back on the throne, if only because many blamed it for the crises of 1659–60 that made a restoration necessary. Distrust of a standing army remained strong. Quickly, however, it was realized that the country could not survive without one, so the practice of purchasing commissions was instituted to ensure that the officer corps was tied to the establishment and would never again be tempted to take over the government. Since the navy had largely stayed aloof from politics during the Civil Wars, it did not adopt a similar system. Indeed, reforms, such as exams, were introduced to encourage the promotion of the competent, resulting in the navy's creditable performance in the Second and Third Dutch Wars. The accession of the Catholic James II in 1685 changed everything. Initially, the army was loyal to the new king, who had a stellar military record, and crushed Monmouth's rebellion. But when James packed the army with Catholic officers, and increased the size of the armed forces, fears about a standing army increased, being one of the reasons why William and Mary were invited over from Holland to restore Protestantism. They were successful, and England was saved from another Civil War because at the crucial moment the army, led by John Churchill, changed sides.

The Restoration Army

When John Evelyn noted in his diary how the same army that had executed Charles I eleven years later restored his son to throne, he added 'It was the Lord's doing!'[2]

To be fair, George Monck deserved as much—if not more—of the credit. Born in 1608, the son of Sir Thomas Monck, a member of the Devon gentry, Monck had been a professional soldier for the whole of his life. He saw action during the expeditions to Cadiz in 1625 and to Rhé two years later. In 1637, in Dutch service, Monck led the 'Forlorn Hope' at the Siege of Breda. In 1640 he returned to England, taking part in the Second Bishops' War, before fighting for the king in Ireland. In 1644 soon after Monck returned to England, the parliamentarians captured him at the Battle of Nantwich, and held him prisoner in the Tower for two years. They released him to fight on their behalf in Ireland. In 1650 he went with Cromwell to Scotland, being appointed commander of a regiment, which he led with great distinction at Dunbar. After a brief secondment as one of the three sea-generals of the navy, where he fought brilliantly in the First Dutch War (1652–54), Monck returned to Scotland to crush Glencairn's Rebellion. He was widely respected by the army. Cromwell thought him an 'honest general ... a simple hearted man'.[3]

After Cromwell died in 1658 everything unravelled. In January 1660, at the head of an army seven thousand strong, Monck marched his troops from Coldstream, on the Scottish border, to London which he entered a month later. In March he recognized that military rule was not the solution, telling a General Council of officers that 'nothing was more injurious to discipline than their meeting in military council to interpose in civil things'.[4] So after a couple of months of growing disorder General Monck opened negotiations with the king, which were completed on 1 May.

Charles II was grateful to the man who had restored him, awarding Monck the Order of the Garter, making him earl of Albemarle, Captain General and Commander-in-Chief, giving him a pension of seven hundred pounds a year, an estate in Essex, and—as if that were not enough—much of the Carolina colony. The king was not so bountiful towards the army, which had after all executed his father and forced him into exile. Indeed, the army was most unpopular. In the summer of 1660 a ballad declared:[5]

Make room for a honest Red-Coat
(and that you'd say's a wonder),
The Gun and the Blade
Are his tools—and his Trade
In for pay, to kill and Plunder.

Parliament disbanded the forty thousand-strong New Model Army, paying the troops their arrears of £835,819 8s. 10d. Officers and men went quietly back to civilian life. Perhaps some roundheads had had enough of war and military service; others felt it safer to lie low in case they attracted the attention of the new regime.

The restored monarch swiftly realized that he could not remain in power without an army. In November 1660 Charles II ordered the raising of the King's Regiment of Guards (now the Grenadiers), composed mostly of men who had served him on the continent. Its commanding officer, Colonel John Russell, an ultra-royalist member of the Sealed Knot, quickly recruited twelve companies of a hundred men. The rising of the Fifth Monarchists, an extreme puritan sect, in January 1661 convinced the king that these forces were not enough. In February he reconstituted Monck's New Model Regiment as the Lord General's Regiment (later the Coldstream Guards), and formed a regiment of horse (later the Life Guards). Within two years the army increased from five thousand to eight and a half thousand regular troops. It remained that size for most of Charles's reign, falling to 6,797 men in 1680. In the 1670s the army consisted of two cavalry regiments (the Life Guards and the Horse Guards), of 1,080 troopers, three infantry units, the First Foot Guard, the Coldstreams, the Marines, and Holland's Regiment (The Buffs, or East Kent), with seven thousand men, plus another thirteen hundred in thirty garrisons.

The restoration army had two main duties, internal security and external defence.

Policing was its main internal role. The army patrolled roads to suppress highwaymen, many of them reputedly cavalier officers who could not settle down after the Civil Wars. Every month a squadron of cavalry escorted gold and silver from the Naval Office in London to Portsmouth and Chatham to pay sailors and dockyard workers. Soldiers were stationed outside London theatres before and after performances, and at Tyburn and Newgate during executions. After the government ended the practice of farming out the collection of customs to private entrepreneurs, replacing it with the Board of Customs in 1671, the army was extensively used to curb smuggling.[6] In Scotland an Anglo-Scots force under the duke of Monmouth, the king's illegitimate son, dispersed a rising of Glasgow covenanters at Bothwell Bridge in 1679, massacring a couple of hundred afterwards. Soldiers do not, however, make good policemen, especially when dealing with civilians, such as the Oxford undergraduates who disdained troops as their social inferiors. In May 1678 fighting broke out between soldiers, who were billeted in student housing, and undergraduates, who were affronted that the former had attacked the proctors. Happily, this unique example of student affection for the university's police did not end in death or serious injuries.[7]

Within two years of coming to the throne Charles dispatched troops overseas. In 1662, as part of his marriage treaty to Catherine of Braganza, Charles agreed to send (and pay for) an expeditionary force to Portugal. A year later one of its officers, Sir Henry Bennet, wrote home that 'The English forces ... do daily molder away' for want of pay, food and accommodation. The king used foreign service to get rid of New Model Army veterans, especially officers, who might be a threat to his regime. His plan was lethally effective. Only a fifth of the five thousand British troops sent to Portugal over the next five years returned home, while 43 per cent of Thomas Dongan's regiment (most of them roundhead veterans) sent overseas as part of the British Brigade in French service, died or deserted within two months in 1678.[8]

Britain's involvement with Tangier—part of Catherine's dowry—was equally ruinous in men and money. When the first military governor Henry Mordaunt, earl of Peterborough, arrived there in 1662 he found a derelict town, with no defences or harbour, being invested by several thousand Berbers. Within a few months the garrison grew to two thousand foot and five hundred horse, and work started on the defences and building a harbour wall. The Tangier Regiment (Queen's Royal West Surrey Regiment) were the first long-term garrison, being sarcastically known as 'Kirke's lambs' after their colonel, Percy Kirke, and his banner, a paschal lamb. Maintaining Tangier was dreadfully expensive, costing £140,000 a year in 1676. When parliament refused to vote money for the garrison, it was evacuated in 1684. In some ways the Tangier garrison anticipated future imperial bases, such as Gibraltar, Malta, Suez and Aden. It was the first one that included wives on strength, as well as a schoolmaster. But unlike later imperial bases it failed, basically because it lacked an empire to support. The restoration army had bitten off more than it could chew.

The Purchase System

With too many enemies in Tangier, the restoration army lacked friends at home. For one thing it was composed of the dregs of society, who were missed little, if at all. In 1672 someone described its recruits as 'gaolbirds, thieves and rogues'. Six years later a letter writer called soldiers the 'scum of our nation'.[9] Lord Macaulay, the historian, described the Tangier Regiment, which returned to England after the evacuation, as 'the rudest and most ferocious in the English army'.[10]

Fear and loathing of soldiers lasted for a remarkably long time. Colonel Silius Titus told the House of Commons in the 1660s that 'In peace there is nothing for an army to subdue but Magna Carta.' 'There is no more disagreeable thought to the people of Great Britain,' wrote Joseph Addison in 1708, 'than that of a standing army.' Daniel Defoe agreed that 'A standing army is inconsistent with free government.' Edmund Burke declared that a disciplined army is 'dangerous to liberty', just as an undisciplined one 'is ruinous to society'. Across the Atlantic the ghost of Oliver Cromwell lurked behind the Founding Fathers as they wrote the Constitution which made a civilian, not a soldier, commander-in-chief of the armed forces.[11]

The English gentry preferred to keep commands in the restoration army in the hands of their own sort, men whom Charles II called 'the most ordinary fellows that could be'.[12] During the Civil War the militia and trained bands had become thoroughly professionalized: some believed too much so. Afterwards the gentry, amateur soldiers, regained command, and admittedly ran their regiments and companies with a passable efficiency. 'Our security is the militia,' boasted Sir Henry Capel to the House of Commons in 1673, 'that will defend and never conquer us.'[13]

The problem was that a part-time militia was not strong enough to protect the nation, which anyway had a standing army several thousand that, unchecked, could once again take over the government. So unplanned and haphazardly, and in spite of many objections, a solution was found in the system of purchasing commissions.

While the origins of the purchase system may be traced back to the middle ages, it did not become widespread until after the restoration.[14] In 1681 Charles II spent five thousand pounds on a colonelcy in the

Grenadier Guards for his illegitimate son, Henry Fitzroy, aptly ennobled
as the duke of Grafton. Four years later the king ordered that to be valid
all purchases of commissions should be registered with the Paymaster
General, thus recognizing and regularizing the system. Even so, Charles's
closest advisers opposed the process. 'I sell no offices,' the earl of Clarendon
boasted, 'I wish the officers of the army did not: then there would not be
so much sharking from the poor soldiers as there is.'[15]

In spite of such protests, the purchase system took hold for several
reasons. During the commonwealth many cavalier officers had served in
the French Army, reputedly the finest in Europe, where purchase was the
norm. Selling a commission on retirement, death or wounding provided
an officer, or his widow, with a lump sum that could be used to buy an
annuity. Buying commissions reduced the pool of candidates, particularly
among penurious ex-roundhead officers.

The chief attraction of purchase was that it kept army officers chosen for
their merit and zeal from taking over the government as they had in the
commonwealth. After the restoration the nobility and gentry were determined that the army would never again turn against them. So by making
commissions available only to the wealthy, the gentry and nobility ensured
that their sons—usually the younger ones—dominated the officer corps,
and that the army was thus no longer a threat to the political order. The
two were intimately linked. For instance between 1714 and 1769, 152 or
40 per cent of all regimental commanders were also members of parliament. Money and family connections not only enabled the aristocracy (and
to a lesser extent the gentry) to control the system of military promotions
at the regimental level, they also permitted them to dominate the electoral
system, managing British politics until the Great Reform Bill of 1832
at least.

That a generation after the abolition of the House of Lords in 1649, the
peerage was able to control British politics as well as the British Army, was
an amazing comeback.[16] During the middle ages, through the heavily
armoured knight, the aristocracy had dominated the battlefield. The development of the longbow, and then gunpowder weapons, ended their
mastery. Siege artillery, which only the crown could afford, made noble
castles with their vertical stone walls far more vulnerable. By Elizabeth's
reign the aristocracy had become domesticated; the view that the Civil
Wars were a last desperate baronial revolt is unconvincing: certainly the
men who actually fought them did not think about it in such terms.[17] Yet
within twenty years of a standing army becoming recognized as a necessary evil, the aristocracy and gentry had taken over the officer corps. In the
sixteenth and seventeenth centuries 23.6 per cent of English army officers
were the sons of nobles. The aristocratic grip on the system increased with

each rank. Between 1660 and 1701, 38 per cent of regimental commanders were peers, while many more were their sons. By 1769 over 43 per cent of regimental and 50 per cent of garrison commanders were from aristocratic families. Of a sample of 188 officers who served from 1661 to 1685, 39 were peers or sons of peers, 73 were knights or baronets, 53 were esquires or gentlemen, 89 served in the House of Commons, 69 in the Lords— while only 18 (10.4 per cent) were of humble birth. No wonder Peter Drake, the eighteenth-century soldier of fortune, complained that the gap between officers and NCOs had widened.[18]

Purchase was not only an insurance that the army would never take over the establishment: it morphed into a vast system of outdoor relief for the titled classes that meshed with their gentleman's code of honour. Younger sons, debarred by primogeniture from inheriting the family estates, found a rewarding career in the infantry and cavalry. Jobs for the well-born boys increased. While a Civil War regiment of foot had approximately one officer for every sixty men, by the eighteenth century this figure had risen to one in nineteen.[19]

The purchase system had another, less recognized advantage. By permitting a free market, it meant that the monarch could not control who became lieutenants, captains, majors and colonels. Admittedly, the king could—and did—determine appointments to general-level commands. Had the post-restoration monarchy been able to control who became an officer, and who could buy and sell commissions, and thus be promoted, then it might (as had Charles I and the earl of Strafford in Ireland during the 1630s) have created an army whose first loyalty was to the crown.[20] Such armies were the norm on the continent. Charles I had been utterly opposed to surrendering his right to appoint army officers. 'By God, not for an hour,' he vowed in 1642 when parliament demanded that he do so.[21] And it was over this immediate issue, more than any other, that he fought a Civil War. Yet his eldest son, Charles II, always the realist, gave up this right with nary a protest: when his younger son, James II, tried to regain it, he provoked yet another revolution.

For most of the 271 years the purchase system was in place it worked reasonably well. By and large the British officer corps studied its profession, and had a sincere, if distant, regard for their men.[22] Of course, having to stand in rank during battle to give and receive volleys of musket fire at a range of one to two hundred yards did not demand much intelligence from an officer. (Indeed, the lack thereof might have been a distinct advantage.) During this period casualty rates for officers were similar to other ranks (unlike the wars of the twentieth century). Between 1660 and 1871 two-thirds of commissions were purchased. The proportion declined during wars when the expansion of the army increased the demand for officers. For example, it fell to 25 per cent in 1810 at the height of the Napoleonic Wars.[23]

In its favour the purchase system allowed younger, and thus more vigorous, men to buy regimental command in the infantry and cavalry more quickly than in the artillery or engineers where promotion was by seniority. It may have also helped produce the 'amateur' tradition of the British Army. This not only prevented the officer corps from becoming a caste, set apart from civilians, but encouraged the idea, perhaps the myth, that through manly pluck the British officer played up and played the game, and by muddling through the gentlemen somehow beat the players in the last innings.[24]

Commissions could not be purchased in the corps of artillery and engineering, where special skills were required, but had to be earned by studying at a military academy, such as Woolwich. The scientific element of these military arms was strong. From 1661 to 1687 a tenth of the projects investigated by the Royal Society related to military sciences, mostly ballistics.[25]

Throughout the entire army, and not just among sappers and gunners, there was, however, a growth of standardization and professionalism. In 1675, 1,800 copies were issued to both the regular army and militia of the standard drill manual, *The Abridgment of Military Discipline*, which among other things ordered that all drill movements were 'to be performed with a graceful readiness and exactness'. Further editions of the manual appeared in 1680, 1685 and 1686.[26] Officers were encouraged to go abroad to study foreign armies. Many had learned much from their service as mercenaries with the Dutch and Swedes, particularly about the importance of training. For instance, at Hounslow Heath a mock fort was built to make exercises more realistic.[27] In 1681 Charles II founded the Royal Hospital, Chelsea, which by 1690 housed 595 army veterans. Grenadier companies developed in each infantry battalion composed of the strongest soldiers, who carried three to four bombs in addition to their flintlocks.

To augment the distinction (in both senses of that word) of officers, gorgets were introduced after the restoration. These small plates hung around the neck over the chest mimicked the armoured breastplate worn by medieval knights. A royal warrant of 1684 ordered that 'for the better distinction of Our officers' captains should wear gold gorgets, lieutenants black ones studded with gold, and ensigns silver. By 1702 all gorgets had the royal coat of arms engraved upon them, underscoring the officer corps' links with the crown.[28]

The adoption of uniforms, which started in the Civil Wars and became standard after the restoration, also reflected the army's growing identification with the monarchy and, more so, the state. In the past only servants had worn uniforms. Thus, when the state issued them to its soldiers it claimed them as its servants. Uniforms drew a clear distinction between the military and civilians. Uniforms have other practical advantages. They might frighten the enemy by enhancing intimidating physical attributes such as height or broad shoulders. They could enhance the wearers' self-confidence, establish a hierarchy, reinforce unit *esprit de corps*, and distinguish friend from foe in the gunpowder-induced fog of battle. Red coats, some have argued, were a clever choice, since their colour masked the extent of bloody wounds, limiting panic and clinical shock. Others, perhaps more familiar with the military mind, have pointed out that red may have been selected since it was the cheapest dye on the market.[29]

The purchase system worked astonishingly well, helping produce both Marlborough's and Wellington's armies—perhaps the best in the history of the British Army. It lasted a remarkably long time, ending in 1871, mainly because of the monumental incompetence of the officer corps during the Crimean War (1853–56). Charging Russian artillery into the valley of death—doing and dying without reasoning why—was almost as stupid an exploit as, say, marching one's infantry company like lemmings off the edge of a cliff. While no record has been found of an army captain actually doing the latter, many a naval captain has wrecked his ship on the rocks below.

The Restoration Navy

As the Royal Navy expanded after the restoration, it managed to find ways of balancing the need for competence while ensuring that the naval officer corps remained loyal to the establishment, largely through the work of Samuel Pepys.

This new navy was a mighty and growing force, consisting of vessels owned by the crown and dedicated to military service. In the past the state had often requisitioned or chartered merchant vessels, there being little structural differences between merchant and naval ships since both carried cannon. Local coastal communities might also provide vessels for their own defence (as was the original purpose of ship money), or else the state could license privateers so entrepreneurs could seize enemy ships for profit. Privateering, legalized by letters of marque, continued to be an important adjunct to naval warfare for well over a century. But the strategic responsibility for making war at sea increasingly became the task of the Royal Navy, an indication of the crown's growing monopoly of frigates and ships of the line.[30] Between 1660 and 1688 the number of Royal

Naval vessels over a thousand tons increased from 88 to 132, the average size of ships growing by 40 per cent.[31] They required a vast complicated support system. Naval bases were the largest industry in the land, with sophisticated operations, such as rope making, food preparation and preservation, shipbuilding and repair.

The tensions between naval officers appointed for their lineage and those for their competence went back a long way. Sir Francis Drake, it will be remembered, insisted that the gentlemen and mariners must work together, since the cruel sea was no place for the dilettante no matter how blue his blood. This was in direct contrast to the land, where pedigree counted as much if not more than proficiency. In the Royal Navy the contest between lineage and competence was seen in terms of the 'gentlemen' and the 'tarpaulins', those hoary-handed and often hoary-mannered officers who had risen by ability. The dichotomy may be simplistic. 'Gentlemen', wrote Nicholas Rodger, was a code word for royalist officers, just as 'tarpaulins' was for commonwealth ones, who had been mostly been ex-warrant officers or owner-masters from the merchant marine.[32] Tarpaulins often disdained gentlemen. William Bull, the master of the *Hector*, who started his career as a captain's apprentice, wrote that the gentlemen knew nothing about the sea, and cared less about their crew, 'the poor sailors being made a slave and vassal to every supposed gentlemen'.[33] Gentlemen ofttimes sneered at tarpaulins as parvenus. It was said that Admiral John Benbow started life as a butcher's boy, and that Admiral Shovell had been a shoemaker's apprentice, while Pepys claimed to know four or five captains who had been footmen.[34] Compared to the army, few naval officers were the sons of the nobility, especially in Scotland and Ireland. During the sixteenth and seventeenth centuries 6.9 per cent of Englishmen who served as officers in the navy and 23.6 per cent in the army were from aristocratic families, as compared to 6.3 per cent and 37.5 per cent of Irish officers and 1.7 per cent and 38.3 per cent of Scots. In other words, army commissions were nearly four times more popular than navy ones among English aristocratic officers, six times more so among the Irish, and twenty-three times more so with the Scots.[35]

Over time the gap between tarpaulins and gentlemen narrowed. In 1665 the duke of York had Lieutenant Mansell of the *Rainbow* court-martialled and cashiered for reproaching his captain for having been a Cromwellian, and ordered that in future no reference be made to a man's previous service.[36] The public image of the naval officer as both a competent tarpaulin and courteous gentleman developed. For instance, in William Congreve's play *Love for Love* (1695), Captain Ben Legend is an uncouth bluff fellow. He hails the heroine, Miss Prue, as if she were a frigate several cables away, suggesting they 'swing in a hammock together'.

Understandably, she turns him down. Fifteen years later, in Charles Shadwell's play, *The Fair Quakers of Deal: or the Humours of the Navy*, Captain Worthy beats Captain Flip, a 'most ignorant Whappineer-Tar', and Captain Mizen, 'a cynical sea fop', to get the girl.[37] The play's hero blends both breeding and gentility, a combination that in real life owed much to Samuel Pepys. Pepys was, without doubt, the greatest English diarist. Some have suggested that his importance as such may have exaggerated his significance as a naval reformer. But there is no question that he loved the Royal Navy and its honest sailors. 'This day,' he wrote in his diary for 12 March 1667, 'a poor seaman, almost starved for food, lay in our yard a-dying. I sent him half-a-crown and we ordered that his ticket [for arrears of wages] to be paid.'[38]

Born a London tailor's son in 1633, Pepys was a bright, ambitious boy who went to St Paul's School and then Cambridge University on scholarships. Through a connection with a distant cousin, Edward Montagu, first earl of Sandwich, he sailed as the earl's secretary to the Baltic in 1659. The following year he was aboard the fleet that went to Holland to bring Charles II back for the restoration. In July 1660 he was appointed to the Navy Board at the munificent salary of £350 per annum, starting a connection with the Admiralty that, on and off, would last twenty-nine years.

Pepys was a very hard worker, often at his desk by four in the morning. He studied every detail and constantly harked back to the good old days of Elizabeth's navy.[39] In 1670 he reprimanded Sir Anthony Deane, the shipwright, for using iron braces to strengthen the *Royal James*, a newfangled practice that soon became the norm. By the standards of his time he was honest, despising those who were corrupt. Thus Pepys dismissed Charles II as being 'only governed by his lust, and women and rogues'.[40] He had a much higher opinion of the king's younger brother, the duke of York, with whom he worked closely to reform the navy. James wrote standing orders that defined everything from petty officers to petty discipline—'those who pisseth on the deck' were to receive ten lashes.[41] So when James complained that there were no clear job descriptions for the Navy Office, Pepys drafted some, which the duke presented to the Privy Council as his own. British naval administration was more centralized and efficient than the Dutch. With the help of Sir William Penn, Pepys composed *The Duke of York's Sailing and Fighting Instructions*, which, it has been asserted, are 'still the basis for naval discipline'.[42] Pepys allowed pursers to claim the full value of supplies according to the ship's authorized complement, lessening their opportunities for fraud. By letting them buy local, and thus better (and cheaper) food, instead of issuing more expensive stored vittles, such as salted meats, Pepys not only saved money but many men's lives.[43]

His most important reform came in 1677 with the introduction of examinations for promotion to lieutenant. Naval officers had already started to think of themselves as a separate profession: since the commonwealth they had been required to keep professional journals; the first club exclusively for naval officers was founded in 1674; tables of seniority appeared in 1692.[44] Exams took this sense of being a special, exclusive fellowship further. Candidates for the exam had to be at least twenty years old, with a minimum of three years sea service, including one as a midshipman. The effects were instantaneous. For one thing exams decreased the influence of the 'gentlemen', a group Pepys disliked; for another they lessened the number of lieutenants begging for a ship. 'I thank God,' Pepys wrote two months after their introduction, 'we have not half the throng of those bastard breed pressing for employment.'[45]

Exams did not, of course, end patronage. Friends at court were an immense help in securing employment once the minimum sea time (which was doubled in 1703) had been served and the exam passed. Patronage helped get lieutenants seagoing appointments, and promotion to command ships as captains, and fleets as admirals. Because the main foreign enemy shifted from Spain to the Netherlands, the navy became concentrated at Chatham and Portsmouth, much nearer to London than Plymouth. This meant that officers were in closer contact with the capital, although they were too far away to stage a *coup d'état*. Fortunately, Charles II and James II promoted competent sea officers. Admittedly, gentlemen still held a distinct advantage, because they had the social skills and familial links to impress patrons and the powerful. Gentlemen were commissioned fifteen years sooner than tarpaulins, having served less time as volunteers and midshipmen than the latter, who had worked their way up as petty and warrant officers.[46] Rather like the purchase system on land, the advantages that the gentlemen enjoyed ensured that the naval officer corps remained loyal to the establishment. Nonetheless the navy remained the career most open to talents. It required neither the purchase of a commission nor (unlike the church or law) a long and expensive education at the universities or Inns of Court.

The Second and Third Dutch Wars

Recently, historians have questioned whether trade was the real cause of the Dutch Wars, suggesting that their roots might lie in domestic factions and passionately held ideological differences. Pepys had no such doubts. 'The trade of the world is too little for us two,' he wrote in his diary for 2 February 1664, 'therefore one must down.'[47]

The Second Dutch War broke out the following year as a result of trade disputes in the East Indies. Balladeers bragged:[48]

Dutchmen beware, we have a fleet,
Will make you tremble when you see't.

On 3 June 1665 the English and Dutch fleets met off Lowestoft. James, duke of York, came off best, but failed to follow through his victory. A year later the Dutch secured an advantage at the Battle of the North Foreland. The following month Prince Rupert and the earl of Albemarle won the Battle of St James's Day, which they followed up with an attack on Texel, destroying 150 enemy ships. A songster urged:[49]

Rejoice, brave English boys,
For now is the time to speak our joys;
The routed Dutch are run away;
And we have clearly won the day;
We are
now masters of the seas
And may with safety take our ease.

Foolishly, the government took the advice of such bombastic balladeers. Overconfident, it started to demobilize, neglecting defences, such as those at Chatham, which the Dutch sacked on 8–15 June 1667, destroying several ships of the line, and towing the flagship, the *Royal Charles*, back home in triumph (see ill.15). The subsequent blockade of the Thames terrified Londoners. 'I think the Devil shits Dutchmen,' Sir William Batten, the Surveyor of the Navy, babbled to Pepys.[50] John Evelyn was so scared that he removed 'my best goods, plate, etc., from my house to another place in the country'.[51] After both sides had fought themselves to exhaustion, they signed a peace treaty at Breda in 1667.

The origins of the Third Dutch War may be found in another treaty, a secret one, signed at Dover on 1 June 1670, in which Charles accepted a £200,000-a-year subsidy from Louis XIV of France in return for fighting the Dutch. Hostilities began in 1672. On 28 May Admiral Michiel de Ruyter defeated the duke of York at the Battle of Solebay, thwarting an English landing in Holland. Even though James fought with great courage, having two flagships sunk under him, the public was horrified by the defeat. 'We hear nothing but dismal news of death about the Fleet,' wrote a lady friend to Philip Stanhope, earl of Chesterfield.[52] During the Third Dutch War Britain lost 731 merchant ships to the Dutch (90 per cent of them to privateers). But the navy's fortunes improved enough by

1673 for Charles to sign a peace treaty the following year. No one deserved more credit for the navy's success in fighting the Dutch than James, duke of York, a brave admiral and a competent administrator.

The Revolution of 1688, England

It was a pity that James did not demonstrate similar abilities after he became king in 1685. Of course, his basic predicament was apparent long before then—he was a Catholic ruling an England in which at least 95 per cent of the population were Protestants. Unlike his brother, who kept his faith ambiguous, James did not hide his Catholicism, especially after being unfairly blamed for the sack of Chatham. Parliament attempted to exclude James from the throne, but Charles thwarted their efforts by dissolving it. To further facilitate his brother's accession he even sent the duke of Monmouth (the first of his sixteen acknowledged illegitimate children) into exile.

On 6 February 1685 Charles died and James came to the throne. Four months later Monmouth returned to England, landing in Lyme Regis with eighty-two men. Monmouth, a brave and experienced soldier, marched to Taunton, where the local ladies' seminary presented him with a Bible, and the mayor proclaimed him the legitimate king on the spurious grounds that Charles had actually married Monmouth's mother, Lucy Walter. After failing to capture Bristol, the key to the west of England, Monmouth's army, now 3,700 strong, retreated to Sedgemoor in Somerset.

Today Sedgemoor is a quiet pastoral place, much drained, with cornfields, green pastures and wedges of swans. An anodyne plaque honouring those 'WHO DOING THE RIGHT AS THEY GAVE [UNDERSTOOD] IT FELL IN THE BATTLE OF SEDGEMOOR, 6 JULY 1685' masks the horrors that took place. In the small hours Monmouth attempted a night attack, which lost its surprise when someone accidentally discharged a weapon. Coming within range of the royalist forces, most of whom were behind a drainage ditch, the rebels fired but with little effect. In the ensuing rout Monmouth's army lost 1,400 killed and 500 taken prisoner compared to 80 killed and 220 wounded of the 2,500–3,000 royal forces. Many of the rebels did not die in combat but were murdered in hot or cold blood afterwards. 'Our men are still killing them in the corn and the hedges and ditches, whither they are crept,' wrote Captain Phineas Pett three hours after the battle. Adam Wheeler, a drummer in Colonel John Windham's company, saw one rebel, who 'was shot through the shoulder, and wounded in the belly, he lay on his back in the sun stripped naked for the space on ten or eleven hours, in that scorching hot day to the admiration of all the spectators. And as he lay a great crowd of soldiers came about him and reproached him calling him "The Monmouth dog".' The treatment of the rebels immediately after Sedgemoor was shameful (see ill.16). Six prisoners were stripped naked and strung up from the sign of the White Hart Inn, Glastonbury. During his 'bloody assizes' the notorious Judge George Jeffreys sentenced four hundred people to death (including the burning alive of a pregnant woman accused of sheltering a rebel), and twelve hundred more to transportation.[53] Acting in concert with Monmouth, Archibald Campbell, marquess of Argyle, sailed from Amsterdam to land on the Mull of Kintyre, Scotland, on 20 May. He brought three hundred followers, hoping that the Highlanders would flock to his standard. Few did, and Argyle was captured within the month, to be executed soon afterwards.

The rapid collapse of the Monmouth and Argyle Rebellions, plus the apparent approval of the harsh punishment of the rebels, suggested widespread support for the new regime. Yet within three years and three months James II had squandered all the goodwill that he had enjoyed at his accession by his quest to promote, if not restore, the Catholic faith. The king started by purging and packing powerful institutions. He called a parliament whose election he had much influenced: yet, unable to work with it, James dismissed it. He turned on his natural allies, the Tory party (descendants of the cavaliers), removing members of the established church and Oxford University from high offices. Yet nothing did the king greater harm than his policy towards the armed forces. The French ambassador, Paul Carillon, an astute observer of English affairs, thought that fear of James's armies was the greatest single grievance in the nation.[54]

James expanded his armies' size and increased the number of Catholic officers. By 1686, 40 per cent of officers in the Irish Army were papists, prompting John Brenan, the Catholic bishop of Cashel, to gloat that the king 'has made the army all Catholics'.[55] Similar policies were pursued in the Scottish Army, where highly Protestant units were sent on foreign service to get them out of the way. All this confirmed the widely held impression that the English army and navy were riddled with papists (particularly among the officers), and the number of Catholics was growing. The actual picture is more complicated. While the percentage of Catholic army officers increased from 10 per cent to only 11 per cent, the proportion of them rose with seniority, with 27 per cent of the field officers and most of the regimental commanders being Catholics. Of other ranks, 15 per cent were papists, many of them being Irish troops brought over to England.[56] The total number of Catholic officers increased with the enlargement of the army, which, thanks to rapidly expanding customs revenues from sugar and tobacco, grew during James's reign from 8,565 men to over 34,000. In relative terms the army was as large as Louis XIV's. Many feared James yearned to become as absolute a monarch as the French king. Two decades earlier Pepys had noted that 'The design is, and the duke of York is hot for it, to have a land army, and so make the government like that of France.' James confirmed such fears by ordering that some cannon cast in Scotland bear the motto 'Haec est Vox Regis' ('Here is the Voice of the King').[57]

James's policies towards the army played on three of the public's profoundest suspicions: the distrust of a standing army, which went back to Cromwell; the loathing of Catholicism, which started with the refor-mation; and a dread of absolutism, which Louis XIV's growing power fostered. Relations between soldiers and civilians deteriorated quickly before the Revolution of 1688. One member of parliament alleged that the king's troops were allowed 'to outrage and injure whom they pleased'. Daniel Defoe complained about 'the unspeakable oppression of the soldiery'.[58] When the London magistrates tried to curb such excesses, the soldiery called them 'cuckolds and should be made so by them', adding that their worships 'were not worthy to kiss their Arses'.[59] By October 1687 relations became so bad that publicans started taking down their signs to avoid the unwelcome patronage of the three and a half thousand Catholic troops the king had just brought over from Ireland.[60]

Matters came to a head in 1688 over the king's attempt to suspend laws that discriminated against those who were not members of the Church of England. James appointed Sir Edward Hales, a Catholic, commander of an infantry regiment, while waiving the requirement that he take the Test Oath abjuring the Bishop of Rome that the law required from all accepting office under the crown. Hales's coachman, Arthur Godden, brought suit, hoping to collect the £500 fine that the law levied on offenders. In *Godden* v. *Hales* the judges found for the master not the minion. Lord Chief Justice Sir Edward Herbert explained that the king could dispense penal laws for 'necessary reason', of which he 'is the sole judge'.[61] The king exercised this power when he issued a Declaration of Indulgence that suspended laws penalizing non-Anglicans, and by ordering it read aloud from the pulpit on two successive Sundays, forced every Anglican priest, deacon and bishop in England into an act of humiliating obedience. Many refused. On the second appointed Sunday, 27 April, the hated Declaration was read in fewer than two hundred out of over nine thousand churches.[62] In the face of such massive disobedi-ence James ordered the seven bishops who petitioned against the Indulgence to be tried for seditious libel. After a London jury acquitted them on 30 June 1688, they were the heroes of the hour. As they were rowed up the Thames in triumph, crowds on either bank cheered them, their enthusiasm doubtless fuelled by the free wine and beer put out in the streets by substantial citizens.

Many soldiers shared their feelings. Indeed, before the trial, as the seven bishops were being led into the Tower, many of the guards asked for their blessings. After their acquittal James's main army, camped on Hounslow Heath, celebrated. The king, who was there dining with Lord Louis Feversham, an old comrade from the Battle of Southwold Bay, asked why the men were cheering. 'It was nothing but the joy of the soldiers at the acquittal of the Bishops,' their commander replied. 'And you call that nothing?' retorted a disheartened monarch.

For a man who less than a fortnight earlier had become father to a long-awaited male heir, James was in surprisingly low spirits. On 10 June, after eleven years of failure, the king's second wife, Mary of Modena, gave birth to a son. Yet the overwhelming majority of the people could not accept the baby's legitimacy, because a male heir meant the continuance of Catholic rule for the foreseeable future. Instead, they preferred to contend that the baby was a foundling, smuggled into the royal bedchamber in a warming pan. 'Where one believes it, a thousand do not,' wrote Anne, James's daughter, about her stepbrother's legitimacy.[63] Seven members of the aristocracy—soon dubbed the 'Immortal Seven'—sent William of Orange, the Stadholder of the Netherlands (who was married to Mary, James's eldest daughter), a letter inviting him to invade England and free its people from papist rule.

William landed at Torbay on 5 November 1688 with fifteen hundred men, only a quarter of whom were English mercenaries in Dutch service. Initially, few locals joined his army. Eight days after the landing a correspondent explained why: 'most of our Western people having ever since Monmouth's time been troubled with dreams of gibbets'.[64] To meet William's forces, the king's marched thirty thousand men west to Salisbury, leaving another nine thousand in reserve in garrisons. The odds were on James's side.

The same, however, could not be said of James's men. As they marched west tasked with repelling the invaders, their Catholic officers could not stop them from singing the wildly popular 'Lillibullero', an anti-papist satire in which a comic Irishman threatens:[65]

But if dispense do come from the Pope,
We'll hang Magna Carta and dem in a rope.

Bishop Gilbert Burnet, the contemporary historian, observed that 'perhaps never has so slight a thing had so great an effect'. Its author, Thomas Wharton, boasted that it 'sung a deluded prince out of three kingdoms'.[66] James was expelled in a revolution that was in England, at least, a largely bloodless one, with about 150 deaths. It was also a surprising revolution—

'one of the strangest catastrophes that is in history,' thought Bishop Burnet, adding that 'a Great King with strong armies and mighty fleets, a vast treasure and powerful allies, fell as at once.'[67] Neither James nor his army wanted to fight.

On 16 November James left London to join the bulk of his forces at Salisbury, which he reached three days later. Lord Charles Middleton, the Secretary of State, reported him 'in perfect health'. Suddenly, the king had a copious nosebleed, which lasted for at least forty-eight hours. Nothing could stem it. The 'prodigious bleeding' made him lethargic and incapable of taking decisions, a condition that his doctors worsened by medical bleeding, the cure-all of the day. James's disintegration was not combat fatigue: a reaction to too many days or weeks of intense fighting. He was a proven hero, his service under the French General Henri Turenne having earned him 'a reputation for his undaunted courage'.[68] In exile James rationalized his collapse as punishment for having broken his marriage vows so often and enthusiastically, warning his son that 'Nothing has been more fatal to men, and to great men, than the letting themselves go to the forbidden love of Women.'[69]

Whatever its causes, the results of James's breakdown were immediate. Early in the morning of 23 November, hours after a council of war advised the king to retreat from Salisbury to London, John Churchill, his best and most influential general, deserted to William, taking half the royal army with him. The king fled to France. William warmly welcomed—yet never fully trusted—the turncoats. Parliament—or rather the Convention House of Commons, so called because true parliaments require a sitting monarch to call them into being—had William and Mary approve a Declaration of Right, before offering them the throne, which they accepted. The new monarchs conceded that 'the raising or keeping of a standing army within the Kingdom in time of peace unless it be with the consent of parliament' was 'against Law'.[70] To enforce this proviso parliament, fully mindful of recent mutinies, passed the Mutiny Act, which established a system of court martials. Since the act was set to expire within twelve months, it had to be re-enacted every year. Thus, in England, parliament made a standing army, and the army made a standing parliament.

The Revolution of 1688: Scotland and Ireland

In Scotland and Ireland events were very different. North of the border during the summer of 1689 John Graham, Viscount Dundee, raised three thousand Highlanders in King James's name. On 27 July they beat General MacKay's army at Killiecrankie. Dundee, however, was killed, leaving his men without a leader, to be defeated at Dunkeld on 21 August, and finished off at Cromdale the following May.

The war in Ireland, known as the War of the Two Kings, was far more serious and brutal. Although the Catholic Irish sympathized with James (Dublin's City Council having spent fifty pounds on claret to drink the warming pan baby's health), they viewed the war as one for Irish independence. Meanwhile, James, who landed in Ireland having sailed from France in March 1689, saw war in Ireland as little more than a stepping stone to regain his English and Scots thrones. Understandably, tensions between the two sides grew. John Stevens, a captain in the Jacobite army, called the Irish 'a people used only to follow and converse with cows'.[71]

The war started in early 1689. In February Richard Talbot, earl of Tyrconnell, raised nearly forty-nine thousand troops, mostly Catholics. They invested the town of Derry, which after a siege of 105 days, the garrison having been forced to eat dogs, rats and horse flesh, was relieved on 28 July. The gallant defence of Derry helped produce the climactic Battle of the Boyne by persuading William to go to Ireland in person and confront James. Their two armies met at Oldbridge on the River Boyne, roughly a quarter of the way between Dublin and Belfast (see ill.17). Only half of William's men were British, who were neither as well equipped nor trained as his Dutch and Danish troops. Outnumbered by twenty-five to thirty-five thousand men, James was outfought by an even greater ratio. When William sent some of his forces to Rossnaree Ford, four miles to the west of Oldbridge, to cross the river and cut off James's retreat, he countered by dispatching two-thirds of his troops to stop them. It was a fatal mistake, for William had retained the bulk of his strength at Oldbridge, allowing him to cross the river and rout James's weakened army. They ran, a veteran recalled 'like sheep flying before the wolf'. At ten that night James arrived in Dublin breathless, and after a hasty meeting of the Irish Privy Council decided to return to France. Once again he had lost his nerve. No wonder the Irish called him 'Séamu an chaca'—'James the beshitten'.[72]

After being crushed at the Battle of Aughrim, 12 July 1691, the Irish made peace with William at Limerick the following October. The treaty was in fact an abject surrender, which allowed sixteen thousand troops, the so-called 'wild geese', to leave their native land for service in the French Army. The following year William destroyed James's last—and faintest—chance of regaining the throne when Admiral Edward Russell's fleet destroyed the French ships tasked for an invasion of England at Cap de la Hogue, near Cherbourg. From the cliffs James watched his hopes (plus several thousand French sailors) drown, exclaiming with a strange patriotic pride, 'Ah! None but my brave English could do so brave an action'.[73]

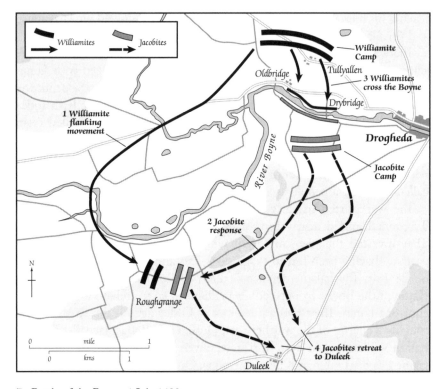

7. Battle of the Boyne, 1 July 1690.

Between the restoration and the Glorious Revolution, Britain's armed forces came of age. Even though many had wanted to abolish it, the standing army became institutionalized as the purchase system made it more acceptable, at least to the establishment. A large professional navy came into being, officered by competent men. As we have seen, after the accession of James II fears of a standing army grew as the king enlarged its size and the number of its Catholic officers. Ironically, the main contribution this powerful army made to the Revolution of 1688 was to do nothing. By refusing to fight for the old king, and by going over to the new one, it facilitated a largely bloodless revolution, at least in England. The Revolution of 1688 gave William what he wanted: the use of British forces against France to protect his beloved Holland. Had he lived longer he might have regretted his military achievements, for over the next half century they led to the decline of the Netherlands, while bringing together the forces that made Britain the pre-eminent world power.

CHAPTER 11

THE PERIL OF THE WATERS: WAR AT SEA

But ships are but boards, sailors but men: there be land-rats and water-rats, land-thieves, and water-thieves,—I mean pirates,—and there is the peril of waters, winds, and rocks.

Merchant of Venice, I, iii, 16–18

WAR AT SEA IS VERY DIFFERENT FROM WAR ON LAND. AS HAS BEEN argued, the sea is an inherently dangerous environment, where men drown in storms, or die from diseases that spread like wildfire in the crowded insanitary conditions aboard ship, or they perish from poor rations or a lack of food and water. Indeed, war marginally increased one's chances of dying at sea. Because it is such a perilous place, survival at sea requires great skills, gained only from experience. It also demands a harsh discipline, for the results of disobedience, or even negligence, can be fatal to all aboard. Yet going to sea has its attractions: seeing new places, the beauty of a tropical sunset, racing along in a monsoon gale, winning the lottery of fabulous prize money—all persuaded men to serve on ships. During the early modern period, the skills required of a sailor changed little since ships remained remarkably consistent, being built out of wood, with smooth-bore cannon, sails and three masts. Ships remained much the same, so the experience of a naval battle stayed pretty constant. Because ships were in essence floating artillery platforms, they were more man than ship killers, thus making decisive naval victories extremely hard to achieve.

The Cruel Sea

Richard Hakluyt, the Elizabethan father of British naval history, recognized the hazards of being at sea in time of peace as well as war. He wrote: 'No kind of man in any profession in the Commonwealth pass their years in so great and continual a hazard as sailors and so few to grey hairs [old age].'[1] No wonder, he added, that so few of them reached a ripe old age. Storms, uncharted shoals, rotten hulls, anchors that did not hold, masts that could not stand the strain of gale-force winds, cliffs and careless navigation could all sink a ship. On 22 October 1707 Sir Cloudesley Shovell, a popular admiral, ran his fleet aground on the Isles of Scilly in the worst naval accident in British history.[2] Lacking accurate timepieces, navigators could not precisely determine longitude. As a result, two thousand sailors drowned (and parliament offered a £20,000 prize for the inventor of a precise chronometer).

Storms could kill without pity and without survivors. Explanations, no matter how good, did not count. As Captain John Smith (the first Governor of Virginia) pointed out in his best-selling *Sea-Grammar* (1627), 'there is no dallying nor excuses with storms, gusts, overgrown seas and lee shores.'[3] Shovell's fate made this point. He not only lost his life when he sailed his fleet ashore, but a reputation built up over forty years. By failing to follow the usual practice of anchoring overnight when uncertain of one's position, and by pressing on instead, the admiral, whom Queen Anne called 'the finest seaman of his day', became a horrid warning to all who go down to the sea in ships.

The ocean is alien: we cannot drink it, and, even if we can swim, we cannot survive in it for long. To stay afloat, ships have to be kept watertight—no easy task for wooden planked vessels. To survive, food and water had to be preserved for as long as possible in barrels that were prone to leakage. A large, highly trained, professional crew was needed to work the most complicated and expensive machinery of the day. Man-made or natural accidents could strike without warning. In 1661 James Yonge, a fourteen-year-old surgeon's mate, was seated on the heads of the *Adventure* when a sudden wave turned the ship hard to starboard, pushed him under water, and nearly swept him out to sea. In 1692 another surgeon's mate, this time aboard the *Deptford*, was sitting in a similar seat of ease, when a stern-chaser was fired to celebrate the queen's birthday, blowing away his hat and head.[4]

Sailors at sea usually lived on poor, vitamin-deficient food and putrid water. They inhabited enclosed, badly ventilated, fetid lower decks that were in effect floating petri dishes, in which germs and parasites, both familiar and foreign, flourished. No wonder so many died from disease. For instance, within two years, four thousand (84 per cent) of the 4,750 sailors sent to the Caribbean in 1726 died, mostly from sickness. As the ballad 'Admiral Hosier's Ghost' lamented:[5]

Think what thousands fell in vain
Wasted with disease and anguish
Not in glorious battle slain.

The most infamous affliction was scurvy. Sir Richard Hawkins, the distinguished Elizabethan sailor, called scurvy 'the plague of the sea and the spoil of mariners', claiming that he had seen ten thousand cases during his long career at sea.[6] The estimate that scurvy killed a million sailors in the eighteenth century is greatly exaggerated, since at the very most only half a million served in the navy during this period.[7] Since scurvy resulted from a deficiency of Vitamin C over several months, it only became a widespread problem after the late seventeenth century with the growth of a blue-water navy that spent a long time at sea eating preserved foods. At the start of that century several authorities had recommended effective cures. Admiral Richard Hawkins urged the use of citrus fruits. In *The Surgion's Mate* (1617) John Woodall, the East India Company's surgeon general, advocated using limes, while Captain John Smith's *Sea-Grammar* favoured lemons. Yet it was not until the second half of the eighteenth century that the issuance of limes and sauerkraut ended the scourge.

Typhus, caused by lice, and malaria and yellow fever, spread by mosquitoes, were in fact the greater killers. The introduction of hammocks in 1586, which could be folded up and brought on deck to air and dry, replacing cots that Raleigh called 'sluttish dens that breed sickness', improved hygiene.[8] So did more efficient ventilation systems, as well as the replacement of sand and gravel ballast with stones, which were easier to wash out. Hospital ships bolstered a patient's chances of recovery. By 1704 there were four in home waters and one in the Mediterranean. That year James Christie, master surgeon of the hospital ship *Jeffreys*, urged that all sick sailors be concentrated on such vessels, which should carry live sheep and fowl to provide fresh meat. As a result, Christie boasted, he only lost one in four of his patients, a much better rate than that of fashionable London surgeons. Compared to their land-based colleagues, naval surgeons could do quite well financially. James Yonge claimed to have made an average of over £120 a year from treating sailors with the pox— physically and fiscally the mercury medication exacted a heavy price.[9] Nonetheless, surgeons were often little better than butchers, with scant concern for their patients. Edward Barlow, who served forty-three of the forty-seven years between 1659 and 1701 at sea or overseas, had little time for sea surgeons. He complained that they would not bother to see a man until he had been sick for two or three days: and then all they did was feel his pulse, ask about his bowel movements, and give him a potion 'which doeth as much good to him as a blow upon the pate with a stick'. That was one of the many reasons, Barlow concluded, why 'England was the worst kingdom in all Christendom for poor seamen.'[10]

Chaplains were another group that sailors held in contempt. As university graduates they were literate so they sometimes acted as 'war correspondents', as during the expeditions of the 1620s. Most, however, were clergymen who had failed on land. Although he was fifty-five years old, with a wife and four children, in 1676 Chaplain Henry Teonge joined the *Assistance* to avoid his creditors. Even though the Bishop of London recommended Richard Bradford for the post of chaplain on the *Swiftsure*, he got drunk in every port, cheated at cards, danced naked around the grounds of Trinity College, Dublin, and a few days later did the same with his wife around Carrickfergus at one in the morning. Chaplain Thomas Turner, another of the Bishop of London's protégés, got so drunk that he climbed a mast and fell to his death.[11]

Life at sea was undeniably tough. According to Luke Foxe, the sailor who explored Hudson Bay, it consisted of 'a hard cabin, cold and salt meat, broken sleep, mouldy bread, dead beer, want of fire'.[12] Want of pay could damage morale. John Robartes, earl of Radnor, reported that his 'ill paid' sailors 'are low in courage, but loud in complaints'.[13] Nothing could sap spirits faster than hunger. 'Sir, for God's sake,' Sir Edward Howard, captain of the *Mary Rose*, begged Cardinal Wolsey in April 1513, 'send us down our victual.'[14] Samuel Pepys knew only too well the importance of ample, good and regular food. He wrote that 'Englishmen, and more especially seamen love their bellies above all else.' If you feed them well, he added, they will do anything, overcoming 'any other hardship you can put upon them'.[15] Alcohol was vitally important. 'Nothing displeases the men as sour beer,' Lord Howard of Effingham wrote to the Admiralty during the Armada. On the other hand, 'Good liquor to sailors is preferable to clothing,' noted Captain Woodes Rogers, the privateer and first governor of the Bahamas. Barnaby Slush, the sea cook, agreed that 'liquor is the very cement that keeps the mariners' body and soul together'.[16]

In theory rations were generous. In 1565 the standard daily allowance consisted of one gallon of beer, one pound of bread, two of fresh meat or half a pound of salt beef or bacon, providing 4,257 calories, ample for strenuous labour.[17] The issue of half a pint of neat rum twice a day (which provided another thousand or so calories) was instituted in 1655 following the capture of Jamaica, the sugar island, replacing French brandy. Unlike spirits, food turned rotten particularly in wooden barrels that easily leaked, the only available containers. Complaining that their food was 'full of maggots and so rotten that a dog would not it eat', in 1658 the crew of the *Maidstone* demolished the victualling office at Rochester.[18]

War and Death Rates at Sea

In 1690 William Cockburn, one of those naval surgeons whom Barlow despised, estimated that for every sailor who died as a result of enemy action, four perished from other causes.[19] Almost certainly his estimate is far too low. The sea inflicted many more dangers and did much more damage than any enemy. For instance, between 1660 and 1666 Thomas Allin, the royalist admiral, noted twenty-four incidents in his diary in which ships on which he served lost masts or spars: only one was due to enemy action.[20] During his forty-three years at sea Barlow survived three fleet actions with only one slight wound, and was shipwrecked twice, being drowned on the second occasion (see ill.18). Only 30 of the 330 pages of dialogue on *Marine Affairs* (*c.* 1634) by Nathaniel Boteler, a retired naval captain, privateer and colonial administrator, dealt with fighting at sea; the rest were on sailing, indicating the relative importance of each activity.[21]

Early statistics on deaths at sea are hard to obtain. Of the roughly thirty thousand Spaniards who set out on the Armada, twenty thousand died— 1,500 (7.5 per cent) from enemy action, 6,000 (30 per cent) in wrecks, 1,000 (5 per cent) were murdered, mainly after being wrecked, while the remaining 11,500 (57.5 per cent) succumbed to disease. Death rates from disease for the English sailors kept on board ship after the battle were nearly as high.[22] The best statistics for deaths at sea are for the years after 1746. During the Seven Years War (1756–63) only 1,512 (0.8 per cent) out of 184,893 naval personnel died from enemy action. While increasing during the American War of Independence (1775–83), that figure remained remarkably constant: of a total of 175,990 sailors, a mere 1,243 (0.7 per cent) perished in combat and 18,541 (10.5 per cent) from disease. For the Napoleonic Wars, out of 103,660 naval deaths, 6,540 (6.3 per cent) were due to enemy action, 12,668 (12.2 per cent) were lost in ship-wrecks and 84,440 (82 per cent) to disease.[23] There is no reason to think that the figures for the earlier period were much different. To be sure, in the sixteenth and seventeenth centuries voyages were shorter, so fewer sailors would have succumbed to scurvy. Yet by the late eighteenth century, chronometers, better charts and the use of ascorbics would have improved non-combat mortality.

So it seems reasonable to infer that going to war increased a sailor's chance of dying by only 5 to 10 per cent. In comparison, it raised a soldier's odds of dying at the hand of the enemy by 50 per cent or more.

A Skilled Profession

Because the sea was so perilous it was no place for the unskilled. A ship was 'too big and unmanageable a machine to be run by novices', observed Barnaby Slush. The author of *Naval Royal: or a Sea Cook turn'd projector* (1709) went on to observe that 'good mariners grew up not like mushrooms without care or culture,' but needed 'just and generous and understanding officers'.[24] One such officer, Captain John Smith, justified writing his manual because 'I have seen many books on the art of war on land, and never any for the sea.' Apparently, he was unaware of William Bourne's *A Regiment at Sea* (1574). Written by a self-taught gunner and ship's carpenter from Gravesend, it borrowed heavily from other sources. A shortage of naval textbooks meant that some students had to go back to the classics. In 1660 Sir Thomas Browne wrote to his son, a naval officer about to fight the Dutch, 'When you first undertook this service, you cannot but remember that I caused you to read the descriptions of all the sea fights of renown in Plutarch and Aristotle.'[25]

In addition to being skilled professionals, officers had to be leaders. 'I confess the charging of trenches and the entrance to a breech are attempts as desperate as a man could think,' thought Captain John Smith: having fought both on sea and on land, he believed that the former was far more dangerous than the latter.[26] To be sure, both required similar leadership skills. For instance, during the La Rochelle expedition of 1627 a tempest forced Lieutenant Dawtrey Cooper, captain of the *Pelican*, to anchor. The lines dragged, compelling Cooper to use his cudgel to make the crew (many of whom were pressed landsmen so sick they would have preferred to drown) leave the hold 'and labour for their lives'. A week later another gale woke Cooper, who went on deck to discover the watch all asleep. 'I first gave thanks to almighty God who showed me that danger I was in, and then fetched my cudgel, and wakened my watch.' Forty years later, in the same waters, a storm brought down the *Antelope*'s main mast. She was about to flounder or run aground on the French coast. The crew was inert with fear. So, like an officer rallying his men in the face of defeat, Jeremy Roch, her first lieutenant, shouted 'Who follows me?' as he ran up the shrouds to clear away the damage. Several topmen followed and the ship was saved.[27]

The training of naval officers relied more on a practical apprenticeship than book-learned theory. Although this produced the tensions between the gentlemen and tarpaulins (which are discussed in Chapters 3 and 10), it also resulted in a very efficient navy. Indeed, an incompetent navy is in many ways an oxymoron, particularly in the days of sail: storms, unseaworthy ships, rocks and cliffs tend to sink amateurs long before they ever come to battle. When soldiers, who lacked a lifetime of experience at sea, commanded fleets, the results were usually ruinous: every senior officer of the botched 1626 Cadiz expedition was a soldier. Joining a ship as volunteers or midshipmen, aged twelve to fourteen, apprentice officers occupied the orlop between the lower deck and wardroom. Because officers and men lived so close to one another at sea, professionally they had to keep their distance. After the restoration a midshipman had to serve a set time and pass an exam to be promoted lieutenant. In contrast, army officers did not serve in the ranks, had no exams to take and mixed far more with civilians.[28]

Out of combat, army discipline could afford to be more lenient. If, for example, a sentry fell asleep while guarding some stores, the results of his neglect would not be as catastrophic as that of a look-out at sea who nodded off, missing surf breaking on a reef a few hundred yards ahead. A soldier who forgot to fix his musket strap tightly deprived his battalion of an extra weapon. A gunner who did not properly secure an artillery piece before a storm could produce 'a loose cannon' that could run wild, smashing walls and bulkheads, perhaps sinking the vessel. Sailors drunk on duty were heavily penalized because they could hazard the ship. Undisciplined crews could trigger terrible results. Just before she floundered in 1544 the *Mary Rose*'s captain called his crew 'a sort of knaves I cannot rule'.[29] Naval discipline could be harsh: the first flogging around the fleet was in 1658.[30] The 1663 Articles of War ordered that anyone guilty of lying should be hoisted to the mainstay with a shovel and broom tied to his back for half an hour, and then made to clean the ship's side immediately under the heads for a week. Harshness could be mitigated. In 1675 one Skinner of the *Assistance* was sentenced to be ducked three times for desertion. But when his officer intervened on his behalf explaining that 'he had injuries enough already having a wife a whore and a scold,' he was pardoned.[31]

The view of a harsh navy of excessive flogging was truer of the Napoleonic Wars than of the early modern period, when land-based civilian hierarchies, mainly rural ones, reinforced those at sea. Mutinies, which were in fact strikes over pay and conditions, took place within well-established procedures in which each side recognized the other's rights and limits. Navies had far more skilled enlisted men than armies, especially the corps of warrant officers, such as the carpenter, sailmaker and boatswain, who stayed with the same ship and could steady rasher hands. They were a ship's backbone: competent and solid middle-class men. Take William Bourne. As a young man he attracted the patronage of Sir William Cecil, Elizabeth's chief adviser, and became a friend of Dr John Dee, the scientist. Bourne had a distinguished naval career as a gunner and carpenter, wrote several books on seamanship, gunnery and navigation and designed a primitive submarine before retiring to his native Gravesend to serve on the town council and keep an inn.[32]

For such men—the commissioned and warrant officers—discipline grew from a consensus that authority was essential to survive at sea. This was a lesson that pressed men had, often painfully, to learn. Barnaby Slush, who as a cook was one of the *Lyme*'s key warrant officers, had little time for conscripts, two-thirds of whom, he claimed, were 'boys, pickpockets and skipkennels'.[33] A few men volunteered for the navy, recruited by those such as Matthew Bishop, who had the gift of the gab. With ready wit, and readier cash, he could induce men to take the bounty and sign up for his ship. 'Bishop, thou art the greatest artist that was ever born,' his captain congratulated him, 'for it is miraculous and inconceivable that you should get so many men and the lieutenant and mate so few.'[34] But in wartime the press was the only way to man the Royal Navy. It was an unyielding and cruel system that literally snatched men from the bosom of their families. So it is unlikely that the Admiralty granted the 1695 petition of 'two pretty seamen's wives' to have 'the enjoyment of their husbands for a month', after which they promised to return them to their ships.[35] Occasionally the press tangled with the wrong people. When late one night in 1691 it tried to seize the two footmen riding behind the earl of Denbigh's carriage, his lordship intervened, and for his pains the press beat him up. Two months later several members of the press gang were tried for assault and a couple of them were sentenced to the pillory.

Whether the mob pelted them with unwonted enthusiasm or let them off lightly, we do not know. But here is a paradox. While the press was wildly unpopular, most Englishmen retained a soft spot for Jolly Jack Tar. To be sure, most landsmen found him hard to comprehend. In 1635 Lieutenant Hammond of the Norwich militia called sailors 'half fish, half flesh, for they drink like fishes and sleep like hogs'. A 1581 ballad commented on the contrast between their behaviour at sea and on land:[36]

You live at sea a lawless life,
For murther and piracy
Which on land you do consume,
On whores and jollity.

Sailors did their dirty deeds at sea, away from the land: so there was little harm in their cakes and ale, in the raucous whoredom and unbridled jollity they enjoyed during their brief stays in port. Thus Britons saw the navy as the protector of their freeborn rights: it kept foreigners away and, unlike Cromwell's army, was not going to establish a military dictatorship. After its composition in 1740 all happily sang 'Rule Britannia! Britannia rules the waves/ Britons never never never shall be slaves.' Even pressed men—virtual slaves—joined in with surprising vigour.

But, as Pepys admitted, pressing men 'is a great tyranny'. Many men did not want to serve aboard His Majesty's ships. They joined them, admitted Sir Walter Raleigh, 'as if they were to be sent slaves to the galleys'.[37] Conditions could be even more unpleasant. 'Foul winter weather, naked bodies, and empty bellies make the men voice the king's service worse than a galley slave,' reported Captain Mervyn in 1629.[38] Many men would do all they could to avoid being drafted. Of fifty-four men pressed in Hull in May 1694, thirty-six escaped, every house in town being willing to hide them.[39] On his way back from Newfoundland in 1652 the navy stopped Edward Coxere's ship in the Thames. The able seaman hid by diving overboard, and clinging to a rope hanging down from the ship's side opposite the naval vessel. Landing at Gravesend he went via back roads to Rotherhithe, the press being very hot, and hid in an ale house, 'where we refreshed ourselves with fresh meat and good drink.' Coxere ventured out disguised as a merchant. Stopped by a press gang he persuaded the officer that he was not a sailor, and made it back to his home in Dover. Realizing that 'I could not walk the streets without danger,' he made the best of things by volunteering to join the navy. Not surprisingly, Coxere eventually became a Quaker and a pacifist, going to jail for his conviction that violence was wrong.[40]

But as far as manning the navy went, in time of war violence was inescapable. 'Our Fleets,' admitted Admiral Edward Vernon, 'are manned by violence.'[41] But there was no other way: at least in wartime. In peace the navy had few manning problems. In 1688, for instance, there were about fifty thousand sailors, of whom the navy needed to recruit twelve to thirteen thousand, a relatively easy task.[42] But when war expanded the navy to fifty or sixty thousand men, the sole way it could be manned was through coercion. Although legally only seamen were exposed to the draft, the press could snare landsmen, and caught seamen almost at random. The process was unfair, and a register of seamen subject to conscription would have made sense, but was unacceptable: like a standing army, a standing list of those liable for service was seen as a threat to British liberties.

The Attractions of the Sea

Dr Johnson thought that 'Being on a ship is like being in a jail, with the chance of being drowned,' adding that 'A man in a jail has more room, better food and commonly better company.'[43] Some sailors would have agreed. Edward Barlow, who was twice taken prisoner of war, grumbled that as a sailor he only got four hours of sleep a night, lived on bad food and rotten drink, in weather that was either too hot or too cold, before concluding that 'beggars had a far better life of it than I did'.[44] If this was the case, why then did men go to sea?

To be sure, the oceans can be beautiful and attractive. Beating into a steady tropical wind, with fluffy blue clouds, as the bow cascades warm white waves, is glorious: a full gale in a well-found ship can be exhilarating. The ocean and its denizens—who were far more common in those unpolluted days—provided enduring memories. For instance,

Barlow filled his diary with illustrations of strange creatures, and fascinating foreign places. After escaping a hated apprenticeship as a cloth bleacher in 1657, he sailed twice to the Mediterranean, twice to the Canary Islands, three times to India, four to the West Indies, and five to China. Barlow disliked the land as much as he did landsmen. 'We are spilling our dearest blood for our King and Country's honour,' he wrote after the Four Day's Fight (1666), 'whilst our traitorous country men lay at home eating and drinking.' Landsmen could find their first exposure to the sea enchanting. On his way to attack Cadiz in 1596 Dr Roger Marbeck was captivated by all the novel sights. 'First in all my lifetime, I did see the flying fishes,' he recalled, revelling in their fantastic colours as they leapt out of the water to escape bonito.[45]

Some saw service at sea as an opportunity to advance, to get away from domestic problems or to make money. As John Weale sailed off on a two-year cruise to the Mediterranean in 1654 as the *George*'s purser, in his diary he breathed a sigh of relief: 'So endeth my land troubles.'[46] Others hazarded themselves for money. Matthew Bishop first joined the navy in 1702 'with the hope of making his fortune'.[47] John Morris, an ambitious master's mate, explained in 1735 that his objective was 'either a golden chain or a wooden leg'.[48] Lieutenant Jeremy Roch, who was as good an officer as he was bad a poet, wrote:[49]

My stars to travel did incline me strong
What made me seek for an occasion long
At length domestic broils increase so
To the wars abroad, I was resolved to go.

For most sailors prize money was a major attraction. The system of paying for captured ships went back to the thirteenth century, being formalized in the fifteenth. It was a powerful motivation. As Martin Parker's famous naval ballad, 'Sailors for my Money', explained:[50]

And when by God's assistance our foes are put to the foil,
To animate our courage we all have share of the spoil.

During Elizabeth's reign a few sailors reaped vast fortunes from privateering. One of them, Sir Francis Drake, slyly observed they did not go to sea for their health but 'for some little comfortable dew from heaven'. Attempts were made in 1644, 1652 and 1689 to regulate 'the custom of the sea' over the distribution of prizes, which the 1708 Prize Act eventually codified.[51] Prizes were a lottery. For both officers and men they offered the hope of striking it rich, and retiring as country gentlemen, or prosperous tavern keepers.

The Nature of Ships

A ship is the only non-gendered object in the English language described as 'she'. Almost like a wife, the ship was a sailor's home, community, family. He ate, drank and slept in her. He spent much of his time maintaining her. She could become a man's refuge and comfort. Losing a ship could be a widowing never to be forgotten. On 28 May 1712 Sir Richard Haddock wrote to his grandson, an Oxford undergraduate, that fifty years ago to the day fire had forced him to abandon ship at the Battle of Southwold.[52] A ship could also become a prison, for it is hard to escape from one. Way out at sea a deserter could hardly jump overboard and swim for freedom. In port he had to elude guard boats and shore patrols. On long voyages the ship might be the only man-made object a sailor might see for months. The culture aboard ship depended, more than anything else, on the character of the captain, who could be a wise leader or a bizarre despot. The ship was a sailor's wooden world, a world normally devoid of women, apart from two or three warrant officer's wives who might be allowed aboard unofficially, and the occasional port-time debauch, in which whores were permitted on ship under the pretence they were 'wives'. During such an orgy Henry Teonge, chaplain of the *Assistance*, was shocked to see 'a man and a woman creep into a hammock, another couple sleeping on a chest, others kissing and clipping [hugging], half drunk, half sober'.[53]

From the reigns of Henry VIII to George III, ships changed little, as a real or virtual tour of Portsmouth Naval Dockyard will reveal.[54] If you walk the couple of hundred yards from the recovered remains of the *Mary Rose*, which sank in 1544, to HMS *Victory*, which achieved immortality at Trafalgar in 1805, apart from the size—700 to 2,151 tons—you will notice little difference: both vessels had three masts, with elaborate rigging; both were long ships with heavy cannon that fired broadsides through gun ports; both sailed at roughly the same speed, with about the same windage. True, there were technological changes: a steering wheel had replaced the tiller and capstans were more sophisticated—yet they still depended on human muscle power to lift, brace and haul. Even though *Victory* and the *Mary Rose* were launched 255 years apart, a crew member from the former would have had little difficulty in settling into the latter. But if he were to walk over the quay three hundred yards to HMS *Warrior*, the revolutionary steam-powered, screw-driven, iron-built vessel with long-range rifled guns that was constructed only ninety-five years after *Victory*, he would find himself in a completely different world.

It is appropriate that the museum for these three key vessels from the Royal Navy's history are in a dockyard, for when they sailed off to war they required huge bases to support them. Between 1687 and 1703 employment at the royal dockyards increased over fourfold, from 1,185 to 5,195. Daniel Defoe described them as 'monstrously great and extensive, resembling a well ordered city'.[55] Yet all three ships, the *Mary Rose*, *Victory* and *Warrior*, were essentially floating artillery platforms, which could move with relative speed and ease, particularly compared to armies. Sailing ships transported six times as many cannon, of much larger calibre, than an army, at a fifth of the logistical cost and at five times the speed.[56] With such massive firepower it is no wonder sea battles could be so horrifying.

Naval Battle

The battlefield at sea was very different from that on land. It was not, of course, a field with geographical features—cover, hills, dead ground, roads and rivers. Only rarely did features such as sand banks or the coast affect its outcome. The sea is featureless: the geographical forces that matter were the movements of wind and waves. But this, as the duke of Marlborough, admitted, made war at sea far more difficult than on land.[57]

Sailing ships could only sail six points, in other words, 67.5 degrees into the wind, which meant that they could not use 38 per cent of the sea around them. However, since wind was free, they did not need coal or oil from a string of refuelling bases or supply ships. Indeed, they could carry supplies for many months, becoming independent of land depots. The prevailing south-westerly winds favoured the British, enabling them to blockade continental navies, the exception being Ireland, to which it was fairly easy for enemies, particularly the Spanish, to sail.

In battle, officers and men were quite literally in the same boat. While on land, generals stayed in relative safety behind the lines, during a naval battle captains and admirals were expected nonchalantly to walk the quarterdeck in full uniform, exposed to enemy sharpshooters—unlike many of the lower deck whom the ship's sides protected. In fact—in a naval battle one's chances of being killed increased with seniority. During the St James's Day Fight (1666) splinters ripped open Admiral Thomas Allin's cheek, broke his jawbone, penetrated his arm above the elbow and dislocated his thumb. 'These put me to great dolour,' the admiral confessed.[58] As the French medieval historian Jean Froissart observed, 'on the sea there is no recoiling or fleeing; there is no remedy but to fight.'[59] When the enemy is sighted, cowards could hardly leap overboard and swim for safety. So sailors did not need the unthinking, drilled discipline demanded of soldiers. While it was hard for the latter to flee the field of battle, it was nigh impossible for the former to do so.

Fleet actions opened slowly. Since it was hard to fight in high winds, ships tended to furl their sails, or take down their lowest sails so they would not obscure the view or catch fire, meaning that vessels moved at walking pace or a steady jog. Record keeping in sea fights tended to be more methodical and complete than during land battles, although comprehensive and thorough logs did not become the norm until after the end of our period. To maintain morale and identify themselves amid the smoke of combat, ships flew large national flags and pennants designating their commanders' ranks. Many recalled how colourful were approaching fleets. Some men were lucky in having something to do as the opposing fleets ponderously sailed to be within range of each other. Gun crews would check cannon balls to make sure they were true and free of rust. Safely below in the magazine the gunner and his mate would sew new powder cartridges, and the surgeon and his mates might sharpen their instruments, while on deck the boatswain would check and recheck the rigging. Most men went ebulliently into battle, encouraged sometimes by music or psalms. ' 'Twas impossible to express the universal cheerfulness our men showed as they found they should fight,' reported Matthew Bishop before the Battle of Malaga (1704), 'joking with one another.'

Once the great guns opened fire the horror began. According to the 1711 ballad, 'Dismal Lamentations of the Widows',[60]

Legs, arms, heads, hands, feet, hips, bones, backs and thighs,
By fire and powder flew up to the skies.

The balladeer was not exaggerating. Thomas Churchyard described what happened when English ships intercepted a French convoy consisting mainly of rowed galleys in the Firth of Forth in 1557: 'our cannon made a great murder and havoc among the poor slaves, whose legs, arms and oars I saw fly about.'[61] In similar terms Matthew Bishop described the effect of a French broadside on the *Swiftsure* at the Battle of Malaga: 'like a slaughterhouse' she was 'wallowing in blood'. Since Bishop's is perhaps the best description of what it was like to be a common sailor in a fleet action, it deserves quoting almost in full:[62]

Then at it we went, loading and firing as quick as possible. We were closely engaged and for my part I loaded twelve times. . . . And would have loaded more had I not been prevented by a cannon ball, which cut our powder boy almost in two, and I thought it had taken my arm off. For it took a piece of my shirt sleeve, which caused my arm, in a moment, to swell as big as my thigh. I went down to the doctor, and he put a red plaster on it, and would have had me to have stayed below. But I said I would go up and see how my comrades sped. . . . When I came up I found four of those I had left behind killed, and another wounded. . . . He shook his head saying . . . I am a dead man.

Fleet actions, like land battles, soon became engulfed in dense white gunpowder smoke, which drifted downwind giving the side that held the wind gauge an additional advantage. An account of the Battle of Barfleur (1692) similarly stressed the noise and smoke, which 'almost stunned me'. After two hours the wind appeared to drop, and the ships could hardly manoeuvre.[63] Many sailors were convinced that gunpowder made the wind fall. There is, of course, no meteorological explanation for this, so it could be part of a common psychological experience of battle, when events appear to slow down. Like Bulstrode Whitlocke at Edgehill and John Stevens at the Boyne, Jeremy Roch, *Antelope*'s first lieutenant, found combat nigh impossible to describe or comprehend. He wrote of the Four Days' Fight that 'The Noise, the Smoke, the Fire, the Blood, was not to be expressed nor understood.' His ship suffered sorely. Fifty-five men were killed and nearly as many wounded including the captain, who lost an arm. Even though 'our mast, sails and rigging all in tatters, our deck dyed with blood like a slaughterhouse,' the *Antelope* made it back to Chatham to be refitted.[64]

The *Antelope*'s experience illustrated a paradox of naval battles. Although doing terrible things to human beings, naval cannon were not ship killers. Being made out of wood, cleverly braced and sturdily reinforced, ships were immensely strong. They had to be to withstand the forces of nature. So they could also resist artillery fire. Wood absorbed the energy of cannon, turning it into flying splinters that ravaged men's bodies. But cannon fire rarely sank ships. A thirty-two-pound ball—the heaviest in general use—would be lucky to hole a wooden hull, and even luckier to do so under water when the ship was heeled: even so the carpenter could readily plug the opening, and the crew pump the vessel. Thus it is not surprising that during the Armada cannon fire sent just the one Spanish vessel to the bottom, while it sank only three of the 179 ships that took part in the St James's Day Fight. During the Dutch Wars more ships were lost to the weather than to enemy action.

Wood was both a ship's salvation and her Achilles heel: because wood was so highly inflammable, fire was a mortal danger. When, in 1630, the gunner's mate of the *Seventh Whelp* entered the magazine with a naked candle, he blew up the vessel, killing forty-eight men, including all the officers. A cannonball hit the frigate *Duncannon* as it entered Youghal Harbour in 1645, knocked the head off a woman, who dropped the candle she was carrying in the magazine, destroying the ship with the loss of eighteen lives.[65] Fire, or at least fire-ships, and the weather, did far more than cannon to defeat the Armada.

Yet the memory of the Armada set the agenda for nearly two centuries. Afterwards the Royal Navy was determined on a climactic confrontation in which it would annihilate the enemy. Such was virtually unachievable. Not only were wooden vessels virtually indestructible, but the weather, tactics and communications made it very hard, if not impossible, to concentrate sufficient forces on the enemy's centre of gravity. Because the attacking side normally held the wind gauge, the defenders could break off by sailing downwind. While on-board communications between a captain and crew were fast and effective, until Admiral Home Popham developed a system based on numbered phrases in 1803, those between ships were slow and limited. In the sixteenth century fleets attacked pell-mell, with each vessel having a go at the closest enemy. Some were assailed by many, others escaped scot-free. By the late seventeenth century, fleets attacked each other in a line formation, sailing parallel to each other as they exchanged broadsides, which, as we have seen, killed men, not ships. Between the battles of La Hogue in Normandy in 1692 (which was won by boarding) and the Saintes in the West Indies ninety years later, the Royal Navy did not win a decisive battle.

But in a sense that did not matter, for the function of the violence at sea was not just its actual use but the threat of its use. War at sea was more a matter of amphibious landings than fleet battles, of convoys rather than ship-to-ship actions. As ships remained at sea for far longer periods, deaths from the real killers—storms, wrecks and disease—rather than at the hands of an enemy, increased.

Wounds and Capture

Unlike those wounded on land, those injured at sea were a deck or two away from medical facilities, although during a major battle surgeons in the orlop deck could be overwhelmed. Tobias Smollett, who served as a surgeon's mate, described how in 1741 after the bloody attack on Cartagena, Spain, the wounded were jammed below deck with inadequate medical attention, wallowing in their own blood, vomit and excreta, maggots in the sores, wounds undressed, legs and arms hacked off by a surgeon with a saw in one hand and a rum bottle in the other, as corpses bobbed alongside where they had been hastily tipped.[66] In truth, Smollett was exaggerating. Surgeons treated the wounded in order of arrival, and being rarely overwhelmed by the numbers of casualties seldom had to practise triage. Unlike those wounded on land, those hurt on board ship were not subject to a long agonizing journey on stretchers to medical facilities, but did run the risk of death if their vessel sank or caught fire.

When a ship sank or surrendered those of the crew who did not drown or were not murdered became prisoners. The worst fate befell those captured by Algerian pirates. Some became galley slaves, others eunuchs; a few, despairing of ever seeing home again, converted to Islam in the hope that it might improve their status, or at least save their masculinity. After being captured by Salle pirates in June 1670, and forced to row in their galleys, George Elliot, a young Oxford graduate, was auctioned off as a slave. When his master suggested 'a not-to-be-mentioned Carnality' familiar to 'the citizens of Sodom' (but apparently unknown at Oxford University), Elliot escaped, and was lucky to be rescued by some Spanish soldiers. As a prisoner in Algiers for five months in 1670, Edward Coxere was constantly beaten while being forced to work for the Algerian Navy. 'We became their slaves, a heart breaking sorrow,' Coxere recalled, dejected that he might never again see his wife, pregnant with their second child.[67] No wonder English prisoners desperately wanted to escape Turkish captivity and, better still, get their revenge. The title of a book published in London in 1627 says it all: *A Strange and True Relation of a Ship of Bristol named the Jacob of 120 Tonnes, which was about the end of October last, 1621, taken by Turkish Pirates of Algeria. And How within a few days after, four English Youths did valiantly overcome 13 of the said Turks, and brought the Ship to St. Lucia, Spain, where they sold nine of the Turks for Gally-Slaves.*

Even the Dutch, fellow Christians, treated prisoners badly. Edward Barlow remembered spending the Christmas of 1672 as a Dutch prisoner of war in Java: 'instead of good pies and roast meat, we were content with a little boiled rice and a piece of stinking beef which they gave us three days in the week, and a quart of stinking water to drink a day.' Forced to labour, seven out of every eight prisoners died.[68] Captured by the Dutch at sea in 1665, James Yonge was shackled for seven months to another prisoner, sleeping on a sack in the hold, before being landed near Amsterdam. Freed at last from his shackles, 'I went like a chicken long tied,' Yonge recalled, tending to walk in right-handed circles. He was lodged in a warehouse loft with 160 other prisoners, all lousy and smelling as badly as the overflowing latrine. Yonge admitted that 'My heart was ready to break.' Eventually he was exchanged for Dutch prisoners in British hands.[69]

At sea sailors such as Edward Barlow, Edward Coxere, James Yonge, Jeremy Roch, Cloudesley Shovell and Barnaby Slush paid a high price for British hegemony, the foundation of which will be the topic of the next chapter.

CHAPTER 12

LET SLIP THE DOGS OF WAR: AFTER THE GLORIOUS REVOLUTION, 1688–1746

> And Caesar's spirit, ranging for revenge,
> With Ate by his side come hot from hell,
> Shall in these confines with a monarch's voice
> Cry 'Havoc' and let slip the dogs of war.
> *Julius Caesar*, III, i, 296–98

DURING THE TWO AND A HALF CENTURIES BEFORE THE GLORIOUS Revolution, England—and then Britain—had never been much of a military power. To be sure, the English (and Welsh) had crushed the French in several decisive battles in the Hundred Years War (*c.* 1337–1453), and had roundly defeated the Armada in 1588. Yet for most of this period the British Isles were involved in internal warfare, dealing with rebellions and Civil Wars.

During the two and a half centuries after the Glorious Revolution, Great Britain became a—and then the—major power in European and subsequently in world affairs.

How did this revolutionary change come about and what were its results? How did the British manage—as no state had since the fall of Rome—to so effectively let slip the dogs of war?

The Revolution of 1688 put in place a number of institutional changes that made the transformation of British military might possible. Replacing James II with William and Mary turned France into the national enemy, starting what has been called the Second Hundred Years War. At the same time the power of the monarch gradually decreased. By recognizing parliament as the dominant branch of government, the British state was able to raise huge sums of money to pay for the ever-growing costs of war. This enabled it to tap the vast human resources of Ireland and Scotland to man the army and navy as well as an expanding empire. By bringing the army under the control of parliament, the public accepted the standing army, if only as a necessary evil, and in both armed forces a long-serving cadre of officers and men developed.[1]

But these institutional changes did not necessarily produce military greatness. During both the Nine Years War (1688–97) and the War of the Austrian Succession (1740–48) Britain's military record was at best undistinguished, particularly compared to its magnificent performance during the War of the Spanish Succession (1701–14). One man—John Churchill, duke of Marlborough—made the difference.

The Sinews of War

William of Orange took a tremendous risk in invading England in November 1688. The Stadholder of the Netherlands expected to sail against the prevailing westerly winds (which providentially, so many believed, became a 'Protestant Wind' from the east), while risking attack from James's navy. He was able to denude the Netherlands of troops for the invasion because Louis XIV had shifted soldiers away from the Dutch border to the Rhineland. William invaded England because he wanted to use British resources to defeat the king of France. Bishop Gilbert Burnet, who knew William III well, believed that saving the Netherlands from the French was 'the governing passion of his life'.[2]

Offering the thrones of England, Scotland and Ireland and the Principality of Wales to William and Mary fundamentally altered Britain's military policies and direction. It was a metamorphosis as momentous as the Norman Conquest. Both 1066 and 1688 shifted England/Britain's military efforts back to Europe, as the monarch used the resources of his new kingdom to defend his continental possessions. After 1066 it was Normandy; after 1688 it was the Netherlands and—following the accession of George I in 1714— Hanover. For half the years between the Glorious Revolution and the Battle of Waterloo in 1815, Britain and France were at war. While there was considerable anti-French sentiment before 1688, afterwards the French became the habitual enemy. Sergeant John Millner, who fought in the War of the Spanish Succession, called them 'proud, haughty and lofty'. Others saw the war in terms of a new framework of holding the balance of power in Europe, which has ever since been a bulwark of British foreign policy. As early as 1697 the House of Commons thanked William III for giving England 'the honour of holding the Balance of Europe'. Four years later Joseph Addison reiterated this view when he wrote:[3]

'Tis Britain's care to watch o'er Europe's fate
And hold in balance each contending state.

Ironically, the change in monarchy brought about a decline in the power of the monarch. Within a few years of the revolution the king controlled only 3 per cent of the government's revenue, as compared to the 75 per cent that Charles I enjoyed.[4] William III spent much time—as much as he could—in the Netherlands, which limited his ability to exercise power in England. As a woman, his successor Anne (r. 1702–14) was not expected to wield much authority and certainly could not lead her troops into battle. George I's (r. 1714–27) limited English and his attachment to his native Hanover lessened his influence in England. His son, George II (r. 1727–60) was the last British monarch to lead his troops into battle, at Dettingen in 1743. Dramatists reflected this change: although the warrior king was commonplace in Shakespeare, by the eighteenth century he had virtually disappeared from the stage.[5]

As the crown lost power parliament gained it, becoming the dominant political body in the land. War ensured that parliament would never again be dismissed as it had been by the Stuarts. Because the Declaration of Rights (1688) laid down that a standing army could not exist without parliamentary approval, and the Mutiny Act (1689) had to be passed every twelve months, parliament became an annual event—as it has been ever since. In addition, taxes had to be passed to service the National Debt that was created to pay for wars. Over the next half century the growth of political parties and the office of prime minister, both lubricated by patronage to manage annual parliaments, produced political stability. Large landowners, mainly peers, ran parliament by directly controlling the House of Lords and about a fifth of the seats in the Commons. Thus, those with the most representation paid the most taxation. And they did so with a surprising willingness.[6] Many felt that they were getting good value for their money. After the great victory at Blenheim in 1704, one Tory squire (a member of a party not noted for its enthusiasm for taxes, and of the class that bore the burden of the land tax) remarked that taxpayers had got 'more for the four shillings in the pound than they had ever seen before'.[7]

War was unbelievably expensive, requiring huge amounts of supplies. For instance, each day during the Nine Years War William III's 100,000-man army required 150,000 pounds of bread, 300,000 pints of beer, 120,000 pounds of cheese, wine, meat, etcetera, plus 1,600,000 pounds of fodder for the horses—making a total of 400,000 tons of provisions per annum, not including boots, ammunition, weapons or uniforms. Britain spent 9 per cent of its gross national income on the military between 1689 and 1697, and 10 per cent from 1702 to 1713: Queen Anne's wars cost fifty-six million pounds. About 40 per cent of governmental expenditures went to the army and 35 per cent to the navy.[8]

In raising money to pay for war, Britain had two advantages: an economy that had increased significantly during the second half of the seventeenth century, and the development of efficient mechanisms for tapping this expanding economy for revenue. Industries such as textiles, shipbuilding, metallurgy and mining grew. Foreigners marvelled at the abundance of cheap coal which the English burned to escape the rigours of their weather, and were most impressed by the cornucopia available for purchase in London's shops, the city having grown to become Europe's largest. The post, which only cost a penny within the capital, and numerous coffee houses, facilitated the rapid exchange of ideas and information. Thus, Lloyd's Coffee House, a popular rendezvous for merchants and ships' captains, became the centre of a new industry, mercantile insurance, which was vitally necessary to protect trade, the heart of this spectacular expansion. During this period imports rose by 600 per cent and exports by 650 per cent.[9]

The Civil War had shown how it was possible for new forms of taxation to extract large sums of money. By the end of the war Oxfordshire paid £60,000 a year in taxes—seventeen times more than it paid in the much hated ship-money assessment of the 1630s—mostly through excise duties raised on popular necessities such as beer, salt and soap.[10]

There were two ways of raising money to pay for a war: first through borrowing, and second through taxation. The two are connected since people will only lend the government money if they are confident that a stable political and revenue system will ensure that the money will be repaid.

The foundation of the Bank of England in 1694 enabled the government to borrow large sums very quickly and at reasonable rates. Lenders felt their money was being spent wisely by first-rate administrators, such as William Lowndes, the Secretary to the Treasury from 1695 to 1724, who coined the adage 'take care of the pence and the pounds will take care of themselves.' The Bank of England's first governor, Michael Godfrey, was killed in the trenches at the Siege of Namur in 1695 while discussing finances with William III, an indication of the bank's key military role. Between 1694 and 1714 the government borrowed forty-six million pounds from the bank at interest rates of 6–8 per cent. The military advantages were obvious. For instance, in 1694 the Bank of England's loan of £1,200,000 enabled Admiral Edward Russell to sail a main fleet into the Mediterranean, and use Cadiz as a winter berth—two firsts.[11]

Taxes are never popular and yet after 1688 there were remarkably few complaints about them. For one thing the size of the economy increased rapidly, so while taxes as a percentage of the gross national income grew two and half times, total revenue rose four and an eighth fold. Furthermore, excise taxes were (like VAT) hidden in the cost of goods. 'Excises seem the most proper ways and Means to support a government in a long war,' wrote Charles Davenant in *An Essay on the Ways and means of Supplying War* (1695), 'because they would lie equally upon the whole, and produce a great sum'.[12] The land tax, which was based on a proportion, usually 20 per cent, of the notional rent of a piece of land, produced an even greater amount. From 1660 to 1688 royal revenues doubled, largely due to customs on tea and sugar, averaging two million pounds a year. But between 1689 and 1702 they increased by 227 per cent to £5,530,000 a year, thanks mainly to the land tax. During the Nine Years War the land tax raised twenty-seven million pounds, nearly half the crown's revenue.

Unlike excise duties not everyone paid the land tax, which was mostly borne by wealthy landowners, notably peers. Because those who were paying the piper wanted to call the tune, parliamentary interference in military affairs increased. Whigs, many of whom were prosperous merchants, wished to spend money to protect trade, while Tories, who paid much of the land tax, tended to be more pacific. The navy came in for special attention. As Professor Rodger has astutely observed, 'The importance of 1689 to naval history is not that parliament created English sea power, but that it began to take it over.' For instance, the 1694 Supply Bill specified how many ships and of what rate should be used for convoys, while that of 1708 ordered fifty-eight vessels to be employed against French privateers. Naval officers found parliamentary interference most irritating. Admiral Sir Cloudesley Shovell grumbled that 'there is no storm as bad as one from the House of Commons'.[13] (He may have changed his mind during the 1707 gale that drove his fleet into the Isles of Scilly, with the loss of two thousands lives, his own included.)

'All Europe is embroiled in war'

In 1702 an anonymous British Army officer, who claimed several years' service abroad, published *A Military Dictionary Explaining all Difficult Terms in Martial Disciple, Fortification and Gunnery*. Looking back on the Nine Years War, which had only ended three years earlier, and forward to the War of the Spanish Succession, which had broken out the year before and was to last another dozen years, the unknown officer observed that 'all Europe is embroiled in war'.[14] In many ways the two wars were (like the Revolutionary and Napoleonic Wars) one long conflict with a break in the middle. As far as Britain was concerned the world wars were a direct result of the Glorious Revolution, and William III's assumption of the British crown to use its armed forces to protect the Netherlands from the French.

The first of these conflicts, the Nine Years War, began for Britain on 7 May 1689 when William III declared war on France. Basically, it was a war of attrition, fought in the Low Countries. After being beaten at Steenkirk in 1692 and at Landen the following year, William captured the heavily defended fortress of Namur in 1695, enhancing his military reputation. By now all sides were war-weary. The bad weather of 1693 produced the worst continental famine for centuries. Although the Treaty of Ryswick, which ended hostilities in 1697, recognized William as the British king, and gave the allies only modest gains, the British public were delighted. 'It is impossible to conceive what joy the peace brings here,' William admitted on his return to London.

During the Nine Years War, for the first time since Henry VIII's campaigns of the 1540s, England sent large forces to fight on the continent. One in seven English adult males served in the army. On the other hand that army comprised roughly 10 per cent of the allied forces. At the beginning of the war in 1689 many British officers were purged on suspicion of being loyal to James II, and several regiments mutinied because Henry Shales, the Commissioner General, embezzled £70,000 of their pay. As the war dragged on the army gradually improved under William, who introduced howitzers and heavy mortars, and trained soldiers in throwing grenades and fighting at night. While William was a brave man, he was less than a stellar field commander. But he was good at building and maintaining alliances, and thus laid the foundations for British success in the War of the Spanish Succession, which broke out in 1701.

A year earlier Charles II of Spain had died, bequeathing his throne to his grandson Philip, who was also the eldest son of the Dauphin and thus second in line to the succession of the French throne. The prospect of Spain's worldwide empire passing into French control threatened to turn the balance of power head over heels. In addition, Louis XIV reneged on his promise to recognize William and his heirs as sovereigns of Britain. Deeply concerned by these developments, Britain and the Netherlands, under William III, went to war with France. Soon afterwards, on 8 March 1702, William died. His successor, Anne, escalated the war by sending John Churchill, later duke of Marlborough, to the continent to command the allied forces fighting France. For the first two years of the war Marlborough built up an Anglo-Dutch-Imperial alliance, but could barely campaign with his forces because the Dutch were reluctant to risk their contingent. Chaffing under such restrictions, he complained to a friend that without such impedimenta 'I believe we should have had a very easy victory.'[15]

Two years later Marlborough got his victory, although it was far from an easy one. In 1704, having concentrated his troops at Coblenz on the Rhine, he marched south-east towards the Danube, neglecting to inform the Dutch government of his plans. On 13 August he met the French Army at Blenheim, on the north bank of the Danube. The two sides drew up facing each other across the River Nebel, the allies on the east bank, the French and Bavarians on the west. Their north flanks were anchored by some hills, their south by the Danube, the French having turned the village of Blenheim on the river into a strongpoint. The country was flat, and even today, driving around the battlefield, which has changed little, you can see it was the perfect site for a titanic struggle.[16]

Fighting began at eight in the morning when, Sergeant Millner recalled, 'Both Armies cannonaded each other very smartly and vigourously with several batteries.' The barrage went on until noon 'with great loss'. Then Marlborough attacked Blenheim village with fifteen cavalry squadrons and twenty infantry battalions, but failed to dislodge the French; a third of the allied troops became casualties. In the next phase fighting shifted towards the centre, where the allies threw four pontoon bridges over the Nebel, but again were pushed back with heavy fatalities. From two to three that afternoon the battle hung in the balance, tilting perhaps towards the French. 'Before three I thought we had lost the day,' recalled Chaplain Josias Sandby. Both Marlborough and the duc de Tallard, the French commander, sent in their cavalry reserves. By five it seemed the confrontation would end in stalemate. Yet within an hour Marlborough wrote to his wife asking her to tell her friend the queen 'that her army has had a glorious victory'. The allied cavalry had broken French resistance in the centre, and the infantry had captured the village of Blenheim, driving tens of thousands of the enemy in panic fear into the Danube, where many drowned.[17]

'The victory we obtained,' Marlborough wrote home that night, 'is greater than has been known in the memories of men.' Chaplain Francis Hare agreed. It was the first time the French had been beaten on land for a hundred and fifty years. Another chaplain, Samuel Noyes, boasted to Archbishop John Sharp of York that 'the number of the slain is very great ... abundance drowned in the Danube'.[18] Twenty thousand of the enemy lay dead, as compared to twelve thousand allied troops. Louis XIV's hopes of dominating Europe were equally moribund: Marlborough's reputation and that of the British Army were made.

But the war was far from over. After being beaten at Ramillies in 1706, Louis offered peace, which the allies spurned. Two years later, after a third great victory at Oudenarde, the war degenerated into a series of sieges in the Low Countries, the so-called cockpit of Europe, which became a charnel house as bloody as it was to become from 1914 to 1918. Because the Low Countries were geographically central to the warring powers, and had river and canal systems that allowed them to transport and cache

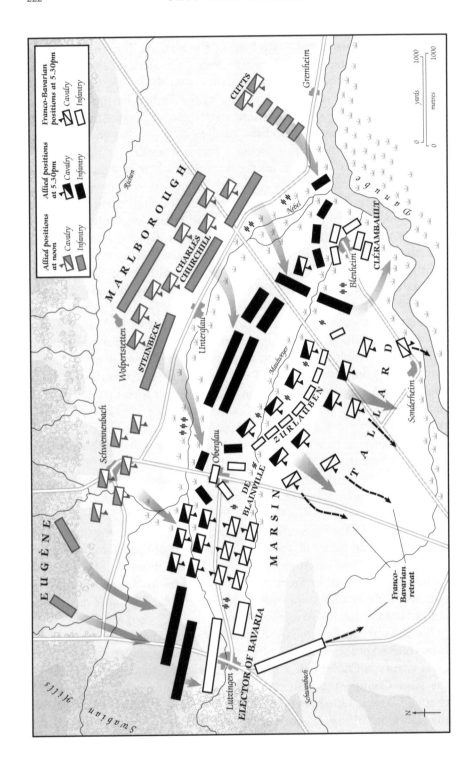

huge supply dumps, very large armies could be concentrated in the region. Thus 161,000 men were able to confront each other at Malplaquet in 1709. Claimed as Marlborough's last great victory, it was a Pyrrhic one, 'a very murdering battle' the duke admitted, in which the allies lost twice as many men as the French. But Marlborough had not lost his skills. His turning those formidable defences, the *Ne Plus Ultra* lines in northern France in the summer of 1711 was a masterpiece of military genius.

Marlborough's Military Genius

John Churchill was born in 1650. His father, Winston, was a minor gentleman whom parliament had fined heavily for fighting for Charles I. So John grew up poor, which might explain his worst vice—avarice. He was educated at St Paul's School, London, and entered the court as a page to James, duke of York. A contemporary described him as 'one of the handsomest men ever seen'. As a young man he did not let his looks go to waste, pleasuring many a mistress, including the king's, Barbara Villiers, duchess of Cleveland. According to one story Charles II discovered them in bed together. 'Go; you are a rascal,' said the king, 'but you do it for your bread.' His lovers helped Churchill's military career. At the age of seventeen he was commissioned into the Grenadier Guards. He served in Tangier and as a marine officer at sea during the Dutch Wars. Sometime in the winter of 1677–78 Churchill, by now a colonel, married Sarah Jennings, an intimate friend of Anne, later the queen. He rose in James II's favour, partly because his sister, Arabella, was the king's mistress. He played a crucial role in crushing Monmouth at Sedgemoor. But James's favour did not stop Churchill from deserting the king in November 1688, and going over to William III. Churchill explained that he had acted from 'the inviolable dictates of my conscience'. Even though William made Churchill earl of Marlborough, he never fully trusted him.[19] For instance, Marlborough's stellar service fighting the Jacobites in Ireland did not save him from being arrested for treason and briefly imprisoned in the Tower in 1692.

What made Marlborough such a great general—some say the greatest in British history?[20]

He had an excellent military education, serving as a junior officer in Tangier, at sea and on the continent. He was, it goes without saying, very brave, and his presence on the battlefield always reassured his troops. 'It is quite impossible for me to express the joy which the sight of this man gave me at this critical moment,' remembered Captain Robert Parker of the Battle of Bouchain (1711), when Marlborough posted himself next to his company (see ill.22). He did not order Parker's men to advance against overwhelming odds, for as the captain recalled, 'it was the sense of the whole army, both officer and soldiers' that their general would never squander their lives in hopeless ventures.'[21] Marlborough rarely punished, and would often give tired and wounded soldiers a ride in his coach. 'The known world could not produce a man of more humanity,' raved Corporal Matthew Bishop, who served under him.[22] Field Marshal Montgomery, who had the same knack, observed that Marlborough could keep his finger on the pulse of his army.[23] Troops esteemed Marlborough in much the same way as they were to idolize Monty, nicknaming him 'Corporal John'.

Since a corporal was then more of a quartermaster responsible for supplies, Marlborough's moniker could have been a compliment to his outstanding skills as a logistician. His army was superbly prepared, supply depots having been established along the route of march enabling them to move fast without having to live off the land. After the 250-mile march to the Danube in 1704 there were new shoes waiting for the men before they fought at Blenheim. 'Never was there a march with more order and regularity and with less fatigue,' Captain Parker recalled.[24]

Marlborough had a sense of Grand Strategy, being fully aware of the importance of sea power, and the contemporaneous campaigns fought in Spain and the Mediterranean. As a battlefield commander he was highly energetic, even in his sixties, galloping from place to place to spot the enemy's weak points. He had a good eye for the lie of the land, taking advantage of dead ground to manoeuvre his forces. He had excellent staff officers, who collected intelligence. He coordinated artillery, infantry and cavalry into effective battle groups. Always he seized the initiative, attacking the enemy to force them to concentrate their troops to hold his, and then used his reserves to assault the vulnerable spot from which the other side had withdrawn soldiers, thus shattering their line. Most important, he greatly increased the lethality of his infantry's firepower by using the new flintlock musket in a system of platoon volleys.

By the outbreak of the War of the Spanish Succession in 1701 the flintlock musket with its bayonet had completely replaced the pike. It was sturdy, reliable, used a flint to ignite its charge, being quick to reload. Its one-ounce musket ball did terrible damage. During the eighteenth century the famous Brown Bess inflicted 40 per cent of battle casualties, a much higher proportion than would later rifles (see ill.19). It even revolutionized frontier warfare against indigenous peoples such as American Indians.[25]

In addition to this new weapon the British adopted platoon firing, which Brent Nosworthy has called 'the most effective controlled fire system that would be used in the history of the smooth-bore musket'.[26] In theory, each regiment of foot was divided into eighteen platoons, who were subdivided into three groups, each of which was distributed about the lines of men three deep, that in battle were arrayed sixty to a hundred yards from the enemy. Each group of platoons would fire in rotation, producing a volley every ten seconds. This the colonel, or more often the lieutenant colonel, controlled as he stood in front of his men (except, of course, when the platoon immediately behind was about to fire). Because the lines of British infantry were only three deep, they could shift fire to the flanks far more effectively than the enemy, whose lines were four, five, sometimes six deep. Platoon firing with a flintlock demanded highly trained, long-serving soldiers, men from the bottom of society, drilled and flogged into unthinking automatons. 'Armies, which used to be full of great and noble souls,' lamented John Blackadder, 'are now turned to a parcel of mercenary, fawning, lewd dissipated creatures; the dregs and scum of mankind.'[27]

The effects of this new system can be readily seen by looking at three battles. Before platoon firing was instituted only eight thousand (or 5.6 per cent) of the 150,000 men who fought at Steenkirk in 1692 were killed or wounded. After its implementation, 32 per cent of the 109,000 men who took part at Blenheim in 1704 became casualties. The system may have reached it bloody apogee in 1709 when the British Royal Regiment of Ireland faced their compatriots in French service at Malplaquet. The former decimated the latter, killing one enemy for every fifteen rounds fired, far higher than the normal ratio of one to 250–400 shots.[28]

Statistics hide the real horror. Captain Robert Parker described the process at Malplaquet:[29]

> When we advanced within a hundred paces of them, they gave us the fire of one of their ranks: whereupon we halted, and returned the fire of our six platoons at once; and immediately made ready the six platoons of our second fire, and they then advanced upon them again, gave us the fire of another rank, and we returned them a second fire, which made them shrink: however, they gave us the fire of the third rank after a scattering manner, and then retired into the wood in a great disorder, on the which we sent our third fire after them, and saw them no more.

The comte de Mérode-Westerloo told his brother what it was like to be at the receiving end of flintlock platoon fire at Blenheim:[30]

> The men were so crowded in upon one another that they could not even fire, let alone receive or carry out orders. Not a single shot of the enemy missed its mark, while only those few of our men at the front could return the fire.

Only the best trained soldiers could withstand such punishment. Corporal Matthew Bishop was in the front rank of Sir Richard Temple's

Regiment (The Royal Dragoons) at Malplaquet. A French volley killed the men on his left and right, bowling them over, nearly bringing him to the ground. Bishop called two men from the second rank forward to fill the gap. They did. Almost immediately one was hit in the head, the other in the groin. Bishop called a man from the third rank forward, but he was so terrified that he hid behind him. Bishop harshly ordered the fellow forward, which he did 'as bold as a lion'. After taking and giving many more volleys, the French withdrew.[31]

Marlborough had an advantage that many generals fighting overseas lack—the firm support of the government back home. In part this was due to his immense popularity, the product of his charm, and, more important, his ability to win victories. During his lifetime, some 67,000 lines of verse were written in his praise. With mounting victories his army became better regarded back in England. It was 'full of excellent officers,' wrote Daniel Defoe, 'who went from the shop and behind the counter into the camp, and who distinguished themselves by their merits and gallant behaviour.'[32] Marlborough's political friends, such as Sidney Godolphin, the queen's chief minister, helped retain parliamentary support, while his wife's friendship with Anne was crucial. The intimacy, which had begun as an adolescent crush between the plain Jane of the lower fourth and the fetching games mistress, was an attraction of opposites. Anne, fourteen, chubby, awkward, and uncertain; Sarah a confident, beautiful, self-assured nineteen-year-old. The friendship survived both women's marriages, Anne's to George, a boring Danish prince, and Sarah's to John, an up-and-coming army officer.

Unlike his wife, Marlborough possessed considerable diplomatic skills. To use a modern analogy, he combined the genius of a fighting general, such as Montgomery or Patton, with those of a brilliant coalition leader, such as Eisenhower. Like Ike, everyone liked 'Corporal John'. Added to his undoubted charm was an abundance of tact and affability. 'He is as skilled as a courtier as he is brave as a general,' thought the Electoress Sophia of Hanover.[33] Marlborough had to have such skills since he always commanded allied armies in which the British contingent were in a minority. At Blenheim, of the allies' sixty-five infantry battalions, and 160 cavalry squadrons, only fourteen (22 per cent) and nineteen (11 per cent) respectively were British.[34] Able to work well with other allied generals, such as Prince Eugene of Savoy, the leader of the imperial forces, who became a dear friend, Marlborough was unvanquished. As Captain Parker, who served for a decade under Marlborough, concluded, 'he never fought a battle which he did not gain, nor laid siege to a town which he did not take.'[35]

Yet this glorious career ended in failure. For one thing, Marlborough's wife fell out with the queen after accusing her of being a lesbian. A year later Anne dismissed the duke and duchess of Marlborough from all their offices both at court and in the army. For another he allowed the war to go on for too long. The terms that the allies won in 1713 at the Treaty of Utrecht could readily have been obtained three to five years earlier without the effusion of so much blood. But as Charles Davenant, one of England's first economists, recognized as early as 1696, the Glorious Revolution had greatly extended Britain's war-making capabilities, permitting the nation to carry on fighting long after it was necessary.[36]

The Post-War Army

When the war finally ended in 1714 most people were thoroughly weary of fighting, and longed desperately for peace. Abel Evans, that deservedly little known poet, expressed the public's feelings:[37]

> Thank heaven! At last our wars are o'er;
> We're very wise and very poor:
> All our campaigns at once are done:
> We've ended where we just begun,
> In perfect peace, long may it last.

As usual the transition from war to peace was difficult. Whereas 106,000 men were demobilized in 1697 at the end of the Nine Years War, 157,000 were discharged at the end of the War of the Spanish Succession. Although they comprised only 2.6 per cent of the population of the British Isles, they represented about a third of the total adult male working poor, the group least able to find steady civilian employment. Some sought salvation in matrimony. With that in view, Patrick Smith, an officer in the Royal Scots, wrote to his brother, 'I must say the smallness of our pay here, and the little expectations we have of preferment in times of peace,' requesting, 'for me pray look out for an heiress.'[38] Others turned to crime: highway robbery rose by 52 per cent, burglary by 54 per cent and horse theft by 62 per cent. The title of J.R.'s *Hanging not punishment enough for murtherers, highway-men and house breakers* (1701) suggested one popular way of dealing with criminal veterans.[39]

Ironically, those veterans who remained in the army, which by 1720 had shrunk to eighteen thousand men (the same size as Sardinia's), spent much of their time dealing with criminals, trying to stop smuggling.[40] Since soldiers received a share of what they collected from unpaid duties, anti-contraband operations could be profitable. For example, between 1713 and 1723 troops seized 192,515 gallons of brandy and over a million pounds of tobacco—those, at least, were the amounts they reported. Britain lacked a police force, so magistrates and justices of the peace welcomed the army's help. In addition, if things went wrong—as they did in Glasgow in 1725, when troops opened fire on a mob, killing eight and wounding nineteen—the civilian authorities could always blame the military.[41] In Ireland the twelve-thousand strong garrison maintained the ascendancy of Protestants over Catholics.

Between the spring of 1737 and that of 1743 a typical infantry regiment based in England spent only 1 per cent of its time dealing with riots and 20 per cent operating against smugglers. It spent 62 per cent of its time on the march, and only 16 per cent garrisoned together as a unit, profoundly affecting its character.[42] Since most Englishmen associated barracks with both slavery and with James II's attempts to use the army to restore popery, few troops were quartered in large units, there being only six thousand barrack spaces in England in 1697. Because the 1629 Petition of Right forbad the billeting of soldiers in private houses, they were lodged in public ones, with all the attendant opportunities for drunkenness and mayhem. Units tended to be dispersed. For instance, in 1726, of the thirty companies of 1st Foot Guards in London, ten were based in Southwark; nine in Holborn; two each in Clerkenwell and St Giles; and one in Spitalfields, Whitechapel, St Sepulchre, Shoreditch, Folgate, East Smithfield and St Katherine's.[43] Calvary regiments were similarly dispersed, although they tended to be stationed in the Midlands and East Anglia, where fodder for horses was more plentiful. The dispersal of soldiers lessened cohesion at the battalion and regimental level, encouraging them to identify more with their own companies and platoons, squadrons and troops, which may not have been a bad thing since most of the army's operations—policing, operating against smugglers, aiding the civil powers—were conducted by small units.

In view of their policing roles, it is surprising that attitudes towards the military improved—at least if the stage is an indication. To be sure, because many soldiers were billeted in London, and presumably would attend the theatre, it might not be wise to portray them negatively. David Garrick thought so. In *Miss in Her Teens* (1746) the heroine, alluding to both the battlefield and bedroom, declares, 'I love these men of Arms, they know their Trade.'[44] Stage names reflected a more positive attitude to military men—Captain Brazen, Colonel Bully and Corporal Toddy being replaced by Steadys, Worthies and Britons. Popular songs, such as 'The British Grenadiers', 'Britons Strike Home', 'The Roast Beef of Old England' and 'Over the Hills and Far Away', also reflected this shift. So did the rising popularity of army and navy ballads, which were increasingly aimed at middle-class tastes.[45]

Towards the end of the 1730s the nation was becoming ever more bellicose. After decades of peace and prosperity under the premiership of

Robert Walpole, the public wanted war with Spain. Some desired it because they hoped to make money by opening up Spain's American colonies for trade, others from the same sort of jingoism that led the United States into another Spanish war in 1898. Like the sinking of the U.S.S. *Maine*, Captain Robert Jenkins's tale of how some Spanish coast-guard had sliced off his ear and insulted King George as he sailed the Spanish Main outraged a public all too ready to be outraged, pushing Britain into war in 1739. Admiral Edward Vernon's attack on Porto Bello, Panama, the following year was as glorious a victory as his assault on Cartagena, Spain, in 1741 was an ignominious defeat. Between 1740 and 1744 Admiral George Anson's fleet sailed around the world, returning with £600,000 of Spanish booty. On land the War of Jenkins' Ear, which turned into the War of the Austrian Succession in 1740, went poorly. George II was worsened by the French at Dettingen. Two years later in 1745, French volley fire overwhelmed his second son, the duke of Cumberland, at Fortenoy where he led the allied forces with more courage than common sense. Fortunately for his reputation, the Scots Rising of 1745 required his services back home, enabling the duke to beat a far less formidable foe at Culloden.

The Royal Navy

In the generation after the Glorious Revolution, Britain became the world's leading naval power. The size of the fleet rose from 173 ships total-ling 101,892 tons to 247 ships weighing 167,219 tons: the average tonnage grew from 589 to 677 tons. Britain's advantage over France increased. In 1690 the British had 83 ships of the line, the French 89. Fifteen years later, in 1705, the British led the French by 122 to 105 ships. The Royal Navy continued to maintain its lead so that by 1715 it had 119 ships of the line to 62 French. After the War of the Spanish Succession the French fell out of contention, with only 27 ships to 102 British.[46] The quality of the naval officer corps also improved. Between 1702 and 1712, 43 per cent of the 695 men commissioned as lieutenants came from the merchant marine. No matter their backgrounds, however, naval officers adopted the style and manners of the gentry. These professionals were able to take full advantage of new technologies, such as the introduction of the steering wheel in the 1690s—a generation before the French. Instead of shouting orders down to below decks via a relay of men, the officer of the deck gave them directly to the helmsman standing at the steering wheel beside him, lessening confusion and ensuring commands were executed promptly.

At the start of the Nine Years War the French did surprisingly well at sea, being able to evade the Royal Navy and allow James II to land and fight in Ireland in 1689–90. They beat a combined British and Dutch fleet at the Battle of Beachy Head in June 1690, largely due to the incompetence of its commander Arthur Herbert, earl of Torrington. He was court-martialled, after parliament passed legislation removing his privilege as a peer to be tried by the House of Lords. To the surprise of many, and to the outrage of more (and of the Dutch in particular), Torrington was acquitted.

The Royal Navy atoned for its disgrace two years later in May 1692 at the Battle of Cap de la Hogue, a four-day fight that resulted in the destruction of fifteen French vessels, and ended French hopes of invading Britain. As a result they resorted to privateering, which like the German submarine campaigns of the two world wars, was the weapon of the weaker naval power. Both were effective. But unlike the U-boats operating from St Malo in the Second World War, the fifty privateers based in that port were able to make a huge profit from the two hundred prizes they captured in 1692 alone. So the British had to adopt the convoy system. Although this tied down huge numbers of their surface vessels, convoys worked: between 1706 and 1707 ship losses fell from 125 to 39.[47] Convoys were as successful as they were boring. John Baltharpe, a petty officer aboard the *St. David*, grumbled:[48]

> As we go up, so they come down,
> And so our Convoys, they go around:
> No better way was ever taken,
> Nor will be when the same's forsaken.

Nonetheless, convoys and foreign trade helped foster the development of a blue-water navy, able to project power over long distances. Using the wind, which was free, and able to carry six months' stores, a sailing ship could operate independently of land bases. Standard designs decreased the costs of shipbuilding. In the 1690s developments in the smelting of non-ferrous metals lowered the price of copper that was used to sheath the ships' hulls to thwart the growth of seaweed (which slowed the vessel), and the appetites of wood borers, which were notoriously ravenous in tropical waters.[49] Before 1688 the Royal Navy had attempted only one major blue-water expedition—to Hispaniola in 1655. Between 1688 and 1697 the navy sent five expeditions to the Caribbean. From 1701 to 1713 eleven were dispatched there, as well as a further four to North America.[50] The capture of Gibraltar in 1704 and Minorca in 1708 opened the Mediterranean to British sea power. Britain's role in the War of the Quadruple Alliance (1718–20), an attempt to thwart Spanish ambitions, was almost wholly at sea, which indicates her growing naval power. The need for shipbuilding supplies turned the Baltic into a critically strategic arena. By 1715 Plymouth had replaced Portsmouth and Chatham as the navy's main base, an indication that after making an alliance with the Dutch, the North Sea and English Channel were no longer the navy's principal areas of operations.

The navy became both popular and profitable. In 1711 Henry St John, Viscount Bolingbroke, boasted that the sea 'is our frontier'. Joseph Addison has one of his characters, 'Foxhunter,' a boneheaded Tory squire, boast in 1715, 'Our wooden walls are our security and we may bid defiance to the whole world.' In 1750 the newspaper, the *Old England*, bragged:[51]

> We have done exceedingly well without a large land army; but we never have done nor never can do well without a numerous fleet, in good conditions, plentifully supplied, and commanded by brave and experienced officers.

War and the Making of a British State

The Revolution of 1688 had two effects that have not received the attention they deserve. First, it helped consolidate a British state and then an empire. Second, it made a standing army acceptable for both civilians and officers. The two were intimately linked.

The establishment accepted the standing army because its officer corps, who had mostly bought their commissions, were members of the ruling elite. Even if—as younger sons sometimes do—they were tempted to run rogue, the Mutiny Act, which parliament had to pass each year as well as annual appropriation bills, was an effective check on any tempted to emulate Oliver Cromwell and the major generals. In each county the lord lieutenant and gentry controlled the militia, which had links with regular units, making a standing army more palatable. Regular officers such as Lieutenant General Humphrey Bland, one of the century's most distinguished commanders, accepted the army's subservience to civil authority. 'I have throughout my book taken every occasion to inculcate the necessity of Legal Military Subordination,' he wrote in the preface to *A Treatise of Military Discipline* (1727). General Bland was proud of being a member of a corps that reported to the civilian authorities, writing that 'Instead of being those servile Tools (which is so much apprehended), of bringing their country into Slavery, they [the officer corps] have behaved themselves with a Zeal for its liberty.'

War had become a gentleman's profession, not an ideological, theological or patriotic passion. Thus, men from the same nation, such as the Irish at Malplaquet, could fight on either side, firing point blank at each other with terrible effect and without recriminations. A month after the Battle of Oudenarde in 1708, John Blackadder recalled how 'The French Officers and ours, as if it had been concerted between them, went out between the two camps, and conversed with each other, and called for their acquaintances, and talked together as friends.'[52] Enemies could become professional colleagues, agreeing with General Bland's widely influential *Treatise of Military Discipline* that 'The Military Profession has, in all ages, been esteemed the most Honorable, for the dangers that attends it.'[53] General George Washington, for example, owned a first edition of the book, which he urged his officers in the Continental Army to read so as to better prepare them to beat the British.

The acceptance by soldiers and civilians alike of the standing army afforded both officers and men the hope of long-term careers, and a promotional hierarchy up which most, either through their abilities or their purses, tried to climb. Ambition became part and parcel of military culture. As Sir John Cope, a subaltern who had just joined the Royal Regiment of Dragoons, wrote to his patron, Thomas, baron Raby, in 1708, 'I hope your excellency will not think I aim at preferment too soon, for I see 'tis everybody's endeavour to rise as fast as they can.'[54] On the other hand, those whose ambitions were disappointed, complained. 'There is no man of my quality in the Island of Britain that hath served so long as Captain (which is now Fourteen years), as I have done,' wrote John Campbell in 1709. 'Men who were at school when I was a captain are now in posts superior to me.'[55]

With the development of the mess system, life as an officer—war notwithstanding—became more comfortable. As they lived and ate together, cohesion between officers of the same unit grew. In 1705 Lieutenant Colonel James Cranston wrote home asking for some more pewter to be sent out for his regimental mess, explaining that 'Officers now here, especially those of any character live much higher than they did in the last war.'[56]

While the aristocracy continued to dominate the officer corps, new military families developed, in which son followed father, often into the same regiment, being largely dependent on their pay. All of Sir James Agnew's eight sons became professional officers. Half pay, which was introduced in 1712, enabled army officers without family wealth to enjoy a career in both war and peace. Take that of William Brereton, who was commissioned in the Horse Grenadiers as an ensign in 1695. He transferred into the dragoons and then the infantry in the hope of getting a promotion, which did not come until 1710 when he was made a captain. During the War of the Austrian Succession (1740–48) he won his majority, being promoted lieutenant colonel in 1746, fifty-one years after he was first commissioned. Brereton's career illustrates the long service of the regimental officer corps. In 1740 in the infantry lieutenant colonels had an average of thirty-five years service, majors thirty and a half, captains twenty-seven and lieutenants nineteen, the figures for the cavalry being almost identical.[57] That same year the Army List was first privately published. In 1741 the Woolwich Military Academy was opened for the training of artillery and engineering officers.

Enlisted men also began to have long careers. Take Donald MacLeod, who was born on Skye in 1688. After his mother developed post-natal depression and his father left home, MacLeod went to live with his grandfather in Inverness. Hungry, he ran away, to be robbed of his last shilling by a highwayman. At the age of nineteen MacLeod enlisted in the Royal Scots. He fought at Donawart, Blenheim, Liège and Malplaquet. After the War of the Spanish Succession he served in Ireland, and was wounded in 1715 at Sheriffmuir. He transferred to the Black Watch for internal security duties in the Highlands, before being sent to Germany. He fought at the Battle of Fontenoy (1745) where he killed a French colonel, looting the corpse of 145 ducats. MacLeod missed the '45, being in Ireland at the time, but was sent to North America, being wounded at Louisburg and Quebec (where his plaid was used to carry the dying General James Wolfe in 1759). Even though he was admitted to Chelsea Hospital in 1759, he was discharged to fight on the continent the following year, being twice wounded. Donald MacLeod returned to the colours for the American Revolution to serve as a ninety-year-old drill sergeant.[58]

The Revolution of 1688 virtually completed the formation of a British state, which Linda Colley has described as 'an invention forged above all by war'. She goes on to argue that British culture has 'largely defined itself through fighting', war having played a critical role in the formation of a British nation.[59] But there was nothing inevitable about the emergence of a United Kingdom of England, Scotland, Ireland and Wales. Externally and internally they had different societies. They shared no common religion: England was Anglican and Nonconformist; Scotland and Ireland were Catholic and Presbyterian; the Welsh were Nonconformist and like the Highland Scots and Irish proudly spoke their own language. England and Scotland had different legal systems. Not until 1707 did England and Scotland share a common parliament, something England and Ireland did not enjoy (if that is the right word) until 1801. To borrow a phrase from the debate over sterling joining the euro, the three nations lacked 'convergence'. The differences were so great that the three kingdoms had to be hammered together with much military force.

For the Scots, overwhelming English power made the marriage painfully necessary. According to Christopher Whately and Derek Patrick, in an age of nation-state building the Scots 'were failing to cut it'.[60] When they tried to go it alone, as by attempting to establish a colony at Darién in Panama in 1698–1700, the results were catastrophic. Bad planning, incompetence, a terrible climate, as well as English and Spanish opposition, resulted in the colony's failure and a huge loss of money and life. 'We have,' Anthony Fletcher of Saltoun lamented to the Scots parliament in 1703, 'appeared to the rest of the world more like a conquered province than a free independent people.'[61] Four years later the same parliament passed an act uniting Scotland with England.

War played a more direct role in shaping English attitudes to union, which changed rapidly before the 1707 Act. Only seven years earlier, Sir Edward Seymour, the Tory leader, warned parliament against union, declaring that 'whoever married a beggar could only expect a louse for her portion.'[62] Once the War of the Spanish Succession broke out, Marlborough and Sidney Godolphin urged a merger to protect Scotland's security and ensure it remained a rich reservoir of recruits for the armed forces.[63] In 1706 Daniel Defoe supported union because Scotland was 'an inexhaustible treasure of men ... the best soldiers in the world'.[64]

Because the military experience of the Revolution of 1688 was extremely bloody and resulted in Protestant domination, the links between England and Ireland were far weaker than with Scotland. In Ireland the War of the Two Kings (1689–91) was fought with an all too familiar loss of life. It has been estimated that 100,000 (4.5 per cent) of its population died, about a quarter in combat and the rest from war-related diseases and starvation, while another 39,000 (1 per cent) were forced into exile.[65] At the end of the fighting in the diocese of Derry only three hundred of a stock of 250,000 cattle were left alive, and two horses (both lame) out of 460,000.[66]

After James II's defeat at the Boyne on 1 July 1690, guerrilla warfare predominated, and the fighting became especially brutal. A Williamite soldier described how the Irish insurgents would cork the barrel of their muskets, and put a quill into the touch hole, before hiding them in a stream. 'You may search till you are weary before you find one gun,' he complained, 'But yet when they have a mind to do mischief, they can all be ready in an hour's warning.'[67] William's forces reacted with accustomed ferocity. Frederick, earl of Athlone's diary for 1691 has the following entries:[68]

27 March, spy dressed as woman, hanged.
2 April, killed 32 rebels in skirmish, 9 prisoners.
6 April, ambushed rebels, 1 killed, 9 taken prisoner, of whom 7 hanged.
9 April, 'several' rebels hanged.
19 April, ambushed rebels, 20 killed, 5 prisoners, all hanged.

In a letter to Sir Robert Southwell, dated 10 August 1690, Colonel William Wolseley described how his unit had just hanged three Tories, 'the chiefest and greatest rogues', and slain eighty to a hundred more in combat. He concluded that 'an Irishman is to be taught his duty only by the rod.'[69]

For over the next century Irishmen, or at least Catholic ones, were taught their duty by a system of penal laws, as cruel as apartheid, which held them in thrall to Protestants. For instance, a Protestant could buy any horse—no matter its value—from a Catholic for no more than five pounds. If Catholics converted, they inherited the whole of their parents' estates, leaving nothing for siblings. Protestants wielded political power: Catholics were denied the right to vote, graduate from university or hold crown offices including military commissions.

No wonder many Catholics left the land of their birth, sometimes as immigrants, more often to join the armies of Britain's enemies. Between 1691 and 1791 half a million Irishmen, known as the Wild Geese, served in foreign armies, the majority in the French. They fought with great glory: Voltaire called them 'the bravest soldiers'. Jonathan Swift added that the Wild Geese were 'able to distinguish themselves in so many parts of Europe, by their valour and conduct above all other nations'.[70] While the tradition of foreign mercenary service was not new (between 1586 and 1611 twenty thousand Irish men had served in Flanders alone), after the Treaty of Limerick (1691) formalized the system, the stream of merce-naries became a flood.

In spite of the horrors of Anglo-Scots and especially Anglo-Irish warfare in the half century before 1688, in the following fifty years the English Army became the British Army. This was part of a wider process in which a growing sense of Britishness dominated the isles. Dr Johnson thought this a thoroughly good idea because 'it brings everything to a certainty'. The eighteenth was the only century in history when poets used the words 'British' and 'Britain' more often than 'England' and 'English'.[71] Military command reflected this trend. Only seven of the British regi-ments that fought at Blenheim had English commanding officers, five had Scots and four Irish. Of the twenty-five generals at Malplaquet, twelve were English, ten were Scots and three Irish. The integration of the senior-officer ranks was the culmination of the conquests of Scotland and Ireland, which came out of the British Civil Wars and the Revolution of 1688. Those events had been coercive, even brutal. Yet the transformation of the English to the British Army was surprisingly enlightened, being highly beneficial for many Irish and Scots—as Colonel Blackadder and Sergeant MacLeod would attest. For a century and a half before 1688, hundreds of thousands of Scots and Irish had fought overseas as mercenaries. Afterwards more and more of those who would in the past have served foreign monarchs joined—and thus made—the British Army. In Britain's armed forces many of them prospered. With an eighth of Britain's population, Scots constituted a quarter of the army's officers and 37 per cent of the navy's in the first half of the eighteenth century. Far from facing a glass ceiling, over time their chances of promotion increased. Sir Andrew Melville, a Scot, admitted he was made major 'because my time had come'. While in 1714 only 12 of 81 colonels (14 per cent) were Scots, over the next 49 years, of the 374 men promoted colonel, 78 (21 per cent) were from north of the border.[72] Even English attitudes to the Irish modified. In 1688 the anonymous play, *The Late Revolution: or the Happy Change of 1688*, called them 'slaves . . . like toads and serpents made to be destroyed'. Yet in 1746 Thomas Sheridan wrote a play entitled *The Brave Irishman*.[73]

CHAPTER 13

THE HURLYBURLY'S DONE:
THE AFTERMATH OF COMBAT

> First Witch: When shall we three meet again?
> In thunder, lightning, or in rain.
> Second Witch: When the hurlyburly's done
> When the battle's lost and won.
> *Macbeth*, I, i, 1–4

THIS CHAPTER WILL EXAMINE WHAT HAPPENED WHEN THE BATTLE'S lost or won. It will look at the quick and the dead, at those who survived intact or wounded in body or mind, and at those who perished to be mourned and sometimes remembered. It will investigate the joy of victory, the anguish of defeat, and see how people adjusted to both. In combat men tried to surrender, and some were successful only to experience the ordeal of being held prisoner. Those who came home from the wars had to readjust to civilian life, perhaps to rejoin old families or else start fresh ones. They had to return to old jobs or find new ones. Some lost status, others gained it. After every war demobilized servicemen created problems, yet most settled down well enough. For all veterans, war was an experience they could never forget for the rest of their lives. It was one with which they had to come to terms, and perhaps explain, even justify, to their children. The cavalier veteran, Sir John Oglander, tried to do so to his posterity. 'Thou wouldst think it strange,' he wrote that 'there was a time. . . . When thou went to bed at night, thou knewest not whether thou should be murdered afore day.'[1]

The Dead

In trying to assess the effects of war, we have a skewed sample: we cannot talk to the dead. Would they echo the words carved on the British war memorial at Kohima?

When you go home
Tell them of us, and say,
For your tomorrow
We gave our today.

Or would the dead of Kohima protest they did not *give* their lives fighting
the Japanese in 1944: their lives were taken from them? Would they
mourn what they missed: the girls they never married, the sons they never
taught to bat, the daughters they never walked up the aisle, the grandchil-
dren they never spoilt? We cannot tell. The dead cannot talk, although
they should be listened to with the care that Colonel Blackadder showed
after both Blenheim and Malplaquet. Thanking God to be numbered
among the living, he wrote 'In the evening I went down into the field of
battle, and there got a preaching from the dead.'[2]

The thing that immediately struck observers about a field after a battle was
the sight of the dead. William Patten described the aftermath of Pinkie:[3]

A Pitiful sight of the dead corpses lying dispersed abroad. Some with
their legs cut off; some but ham-strung, and left lying half dead: others
with the arms cut off; divers their necks half asunder: many their heads
cloven: of sundry the brains smashed out; some others again, their heads
quite off: with a thousand other kinds of killing.

'I have never seen the dead bodies so thick,' Captain Blackadder described
Blenheim after the battle. 'For a good way I could not go among them lest
my horse should tread on the carcasses that were lying, as it were, heaped
on one another.'[4] Many observers agreed with Blackadder's observation of
corpses being piled atop each other, as if men in their dying moments
sought comfort from the proximity of their fellows. After Malplaquet,
where thirty thousand perished, General George Douglas-Hamilton, earl
of Orkney, told a friend, 'in many places they lay as thick as ever did a
flock of sheep.' George Gascoigne used the same language to describe the
defenders he saw during the Spanish massacre at Antwerp in 1575. After
Flodden in 1513 an English poet boasted of slaughtering the Scots like
cattle. It was almost an anticipation of Wilfred Owen's eulogy for the
dead of the First World War:[5]

What passing bells for those who die as cattle . . .
And bugles calling them from sad shires.

Immediately after the fighting stopped, a battlefield must have been
like an abattoir. By the next day, after the onset of rigor mortis, and the

dead having been stripped and tossed aside, they resembled those pathet-
ically white matchstick figures seen on films of liberated concentration
camps. Soon corruption set in. According to one observer, three days after
the Battle of Worcester (1651) 'there was such a nastiness that a man
could hardly abide in the town.' Two days later the bodies were still there,
strewn 'in almost every street'. Eight days after Pinkie, William Patten
'found most part of the dead corpses lying very ruefully, with the colour of
their skins charged greenish about the place they had been smitten'.[6] It is
no wonder that Edward Cooke, a part-time soldier in the London Trained
Bands, began his *Character of Warre* (1626) with a brief poem on the
centrality of death:

> For one by one be sure to die,
> Time takes away, time will supply.
> And as He brought you to the Womb
> So back he leads you to the Tomb.

Unlike today when chaplains come to break the terrible news, there was
no systematic way of letting people know they had lost a loved one.
Towards the end of the Civil Wars, news reports of a particular battle
would publish the names of the officers who had died. Others would
spread the bad tidings by letter or word of mouth. After his commanding
officer, Colonel James Cranston, was killed by a cannonball at Malplaquet,
Major Blackadder wrote to his wife asking her to gently break 'the doleful
news' to Mrs Cranston.[7]

It is hard to compare mourning for the dead centuries ago with today.
Military cemeteries are a recent phenomenon, starting in the American
Civil War. It is no accident that the classic definition of democracy,
Lincoln's 'Gettysburg Address', was given at the dedication of a military
cemetery. Neither is it a coincidence that Sir Edwin Lutyens's moving
First World War cemeteries commemorate those who died making 'the
world safe for democracy'. Since democracy stresses the importance of the
individual, the loss of that individual becomes all the more important.[8]
But early modern Britain was not a democracy so it has no military
cemeteries, and the rare surviving tombs are for a very few aristocrats who
perished. The only Tudor pictures of common soldiers are of the sixteen
archers who accompanied Sir Thomas Assherton on the Flodden campaign,
depicted on the stained-glass window he commissioned in 1515 for
St Leonard's church, Middleton, Lancashire, which may be England's first
war memorial (see ill.1).[9] The tomb of John, Lord Semplefield, in Castle
Semple, Renfrewshire, is the only one for the four to six thousand Scots
killed at Flodden. Not even the slain Scots king, James IV, found his own

resting place. Taken to England, his corpse eventually ended up in a mass grave at St Michael's church, London. Adam Loftus, Viscount Lisburne, was luckier. His body is buried in St Patrick's Cathedral, Dublin, with the cannonball that blew off his head at the Siege of Limerick mounted above the tomb.[10]

In early modern Britain civilized men and women were socialized not to give vent to excessive expressions of personal feeling, especially mourning. The behaviour of the Irish camp followers after the Battle of Dundee, when four to five hundred soldiers perished, shocked many Scots. A correspondent reported that 'there was a desperate howling among them, and they fought desperately to recover the bodies.' Such a reaction (which surely confirmed Anglo-Scots' prejudices that the Irish were an uncivilized lot) was exceptional. While men were expected to control their emotions, that does not mean that they did not feel them. Ralph Verney described his father's death at Edgehill (1642) as the 'saddest and deepest affliction that ever befell any poor distressed man'. Ralph did not have the consolation of burying his father. In spite of strenuous efforts Sir Edmund Verney's body could not be found, having surely been tossed with all the other corpses into a mass grave.[11]

After practically every battle or skirmish the dead were buried hastily, sometimes, as Elis Gruffudd noted, in a ditch so shallow that dogs could dig them up to eat.[12] A few military manuals, such as Giles Clayton's *The Approved Order of Martial Discipline* (1591), laid down that a dead comrade be buried 'with the sound of the Drum, and as such solemnity as his service merits'. At sea the dead were tipped overboard, sewn up in their hammocks, as the captain read the prayer book service. That's if there was time: during the heat of battle they would be unceremoniously tossed into the sea to get them out of the way.

Like criminals condemned to public execution, early modern soldiers and sailors were expected to die gamely. Not to complain was a matter of manly honour: it was also a matter of belief that the state of one's mind at the moment of death was an indication of salvation or damnation. Thus, the Elizabethans held Sir Philip Sidney up as the perfect Christian knight because at the Siege of Zutphen he not only bore the agony of a smashed thigh in silence, but gave the last of his water to a dying comrade saying 'thy necessity is greater than mine.'[13]

The Wounded

The most obvious effect of being wounded was the intense pain, which, before analgesics, could usually only be relieved by alcohol. Richard Wiseman, a surgeon, operated on a soldier with a head wound sustained at the Siege of Taunton (1644–45). Seventeen days later, Wiseman recalled, the patient 'fell into a spasm, and died, howling like a dog; as most of those do who have been so wounded'.[14] Colonel Blackadder remembered one comrade who went mad from the pain of his wounds, continually blaspheming; the only way they could stop him from tearing off his bandages was to tie his hands. Wounded at Ramillies, Lieutenant James Gardiner was captured by the French, who carted him away. After two days of agonizing movement, and no medical attention, he begged them 'to kill him outright, or leave him here to die, without the torture of any further motion'. Later he ascribed his survival to the cold, which prevented him from bleeding to death. Struck by a shell at Ramillies, which fractured her skull, Christian Davies, the 'she soldier' who served in the Scots Greys, received good medical treatment, being trepanned. For ten weeks she lay in hospital, where 'I suffered great torture by this wound.' Private Matthew Bishop used the same phrase to describe his reaction to the screams and moans of the dying of Malplaquet, which could be heard four to five miles away.

Wounds produce other, more complicated physical reactions. When the body is hit the adrenal glands automatically release endorphins that act as natural pain killers, enabling men to continue fighting despite terrible damage. At the Battle of Pinkie a pike slit William, Lord Grey of Wilton's tongue piercing the roof of his mouth. Yet endorphins allowed him to continue to fight. He might well have done so until he drowned in his own blood had not John Dudley, duke of Northumberland, given him a 'firken of ale'.[15] In spite of having his dead horse fall on him, Sir Francis Vere continued to lead his regiment at Rheineberg in 1589, although, he admitted, 'in great pain with my wound'. John Taylor, the veteran of the 1595 attack on Cadiz, remembered seeing a severely wounded trooper continuing to fight, 'being warm with heat and rage', and even though his ghastly wounds were 'open like a grave, but he felt them not'. After a time the endorphins wore off, the soldier became clammy (a symptom of shock), and astounded at his own fighting madness.[16] In addition to activating the adrenal glands, wounds can produce other physical reactions. They can induce intense thirst. On being hit at Blenheim, left for dead and stripped of his shirt, Private Donald McBane of the Royal Scots eventually recovered consciousness, and was so parched that 'I drank several handfuls of the dead man's blood I lay beside: the more I drank the worse I was.' At daylight he was found and taken to the surgeons, 'who gave me a dram'.[17] Wounds may induce a more basic response. During the Siege of Kilkenny (1649) Colonel Hewson, governor of Dublin, was 'Bruised in the shoulder with a bullet, and thus beshit himself'.[18]

We do not have statistics on the nature of wounds inflicted, although we do have some for those who survived long enough to apply for a pension. Table 6 below summarizes applicants for pensions in North Wales after the Civil War, and for admission to Chelsea Hospital between 1715 and 1732.

Table 6 Wounded veterans

	N. Wales	Chelsea
Multiple	13 (44%)	283 (16%)
Head	7 (23%)	615 (38%)
Arm	3 (10%)	
Leg	6 (20%)	566 (35%)
Torso		147 (9%)
Unspecified	1 (3%)	28 (2%)
Total	30 (100%)	1,639 (100%)

In themselves the figures do not tell us as much as we might wish since they are for those who have survived their wounds, and, incapacitated, required financial assistance. It has been estimated that a casualty had a one in three chance of surviving a serious wound. Of a sample of 233 men wounded at Sedgemoor in 1685, 32 (13.7 per cent) were admitted to Chelsea Hospital.[19] The fact that ten of those who applied for pensions in North Wales had shot wounds, and only one had a cut wound (the cause of the rest not being given) supports the view that sword and pike wounds did not require long-term medical attention, being much less lethal than being hit by a musket ball, which tended to bring bits of clothing into the wound, producing gangrene. A sample of eleven soldiers who survived after being treated by George Belgrade in 1645, soon after being wounded (at what today would be called a Regimental Air Post) supports the view that shot wounds were especially lethal: one of his patients was burned, two shot and eight cut by sword or pike.[20]

Most of the wounded required medical treatment, the sooner the better. Until the end of our period there was, however, no formal system of stretcher-bearers, so if a wounded man could not walk to obtain medical attention, or did not have friends or servants to carry him, observed Hugh Mortyn, a twenty-seven-year veteran of the Irish Wars, 'He is lost.'[21] Regimental chaplains were expected to help evacuate the wounded, providing physical and spiritual comfort. The lucky ones lived long enough to make it to a field hospital. Captain Thomas Windham of Wyndham's

Regiment (Sixth Dragoon Guards) was wounded in the leg at Blenheim and evacuated twelve miles to one at Nordlingen. 'I have got all the help I can desire, and on Tuesday last was a fortnight my leg was doomed to be cut off,' he wrote to his mother, 'since which times, I thank God, there has not happened the least ill accident.' Windham recovered and fought at Ramillies and Malplaquet.[22]

Windham was operated on by a surgeon, who lacked a physician's prestige and education, being denied the title of doctor. (Today surgeons are called 'Mister' in Britain.) It has been suggested that their lack of status was due to the Catholic Church, which opposed the shedding of blood.[23] More likely poor pay was to blame. In 1513 a surgeon got 8d. a day—an archer's pay; during most of Elizabeth's reign the rate was a shilling, the same as a trumpeter's; after 1580 it rose to 1s. 10d., tuppence less than a lieutenant's. In 1540 the Surgeons Company of London amalgamated with the Barbers—who bled customers as well as cutting their hair. The Barber-Surgeons Company soon instituted exams, which seemed to have little or no effect on the quality of care. Thomas Gale, a member of the company and author of *Certaine Workes of Chirurgerie* (1586), recalled 'when I was at the wars at Montreuil [1544] there was a great rabblement that took upon them to be surgeons. Some were sow gelders, and horse gelders, with tinkers and cobblers.' Perhaps this prompted Gale to publish his text, which was the first in English on the treatment of gunshot wounds (see ill.6). It did not appear to have had much effect for three years later, during the French campaign of 1589, Gale complained that English surgeons knew so little about treating wounds that many troops died. In 1594 during the Siege of Brest an incompetent surgeon botched an operation to remove a musket ball, killing the great explorer, Sir Martin Frobisher.

Even the best of surgeons had to admit that theirs was an uncertain art. John Woodall, a naval surgeon, and Richard Wiseman, an army one, both advised that operations should be a last, desperate resort. Woodhall urged that, before an operation, the patient be allowed to make peace with his Maker, and then be placed gently on a table, with strong men behind and before him, and a well oiled, sharp saw, which he called 'this great and terrible instrument', kept out of his sight until the very last moment.[24] Patients must be reassured, wrote Thomas Gale, 'that the fear is much more than the pain'. Such advice might have come as a surprise to Private Donald McBane and Captain Peter Drake, who both likened the treatment of their wounds inflicted at Blenheim and Malplaquet respectively to being flayed alive from head to toe.[25]

Notwithstanding the pain and uncertainty of surgery, medical services did much to sustain morale. Captain William Mostyn, General George Monck and Roger Boyle, earl of Orrery, all agreed that if soldiers knew they would get decent medical care on being wounded (something most men fear more than death), they would fight harder and longer.[26] 'When a soldier is hurt the greatest comfort he can have is a good barber [surgeon],' concluded Garet Barry's *Discourse on Military Discipline* (1634). Another advantage of a good barber-surgeon, noted Thomas Digges's *Politique Discourses Concerning Militarie Discipline* (1604), was that trained soldiers did not have to drop out to help their comrades to the rear.

Women nursed the sick and wounded, usually in a rear hospital. This was especially true during the Civil Wars when fellow countrymen were fighting each other at home. Elizabeth Twysden nursed the wounded during the Siege of Scarborough Castle, as did Lucy Hutchinson, the wife of the parliamentary governor, during Nottingham's. Margaret Blague, widow of a barber-surgeon, was appointed matron of St Bartholomew's Hospital, London, in 1643, supervising twenty-nine nurses (mostly soldiers' widows) at an annual salary of £6 13s. 4d., plus the right to sell the patients beer, which was five times more profitable. Anne Murray nursed sixty royalist wounded after the Battle of Dunbar (1650), for which Charles II gave her fifty gold pieces. After the royalists shot her husband George as a spy in 1643, Elizabeth Atkin nursed roundhead prisoners held in Oxford, which gave her the opportunity to send intelligence to parliament. After the war she became a counter-intelligence officer, routing out clandestine royalists, one of whom, Edward Crouch, described her as 'a fat woman about fifty years old', who was, he had to admit, 'the most effective ferret for the government'. During the First Dutch War she organized hospitals for several hundred wounded seamen at Portsmouth and Harwich, explaining to the Admiralty that 'I cannot see them want.' A thankless government failed to pay her pension: Elizabeth died in poverty two years later.[27]

The first English military hospital was established in Porchester in 1565 to receive survivors evacuated from Le Havre.[28] It lasted for only two months. In 1600 four permanent hospitals were opened in Ireland to encourage volunteers 'more willingly to adventure their lives in Her Highness's service', as one of their founders explained.[29] None reached their projected 100 beds, and soon closed. In the Civil Wars military hospitals were opened in England, Scotland and Ireland, those in Dublin and Edinburgh each being funded at £600 a year. Parliament's Savoy Hospital in London was well financed and run: the 350 patients got clean sheets weekly, warming pans and a nourishing diet of over four thousand calories a day. Parliament even spent £1,000 sending six wagonloads of wounded to take the cure at Bath. London's hospitals seem to have done a reasonably good job: of the 1,112 patients admitted in 1644 to St Bartholomew's only 152 (or 13.6 per cent) died, as did 116 (or 15.1 per cent) of the 796 patients admitted the following year. The survival rate for St Thomas's was not quite as good: 23 per cent of the 1,063 patients admitted in 1644, and 14.7 per cent of the 825 in 1645 died.[30]

After the restoration military medical services fell apart, as budgets were slashed and the standing army was brought to its knees. On the other hand, more attention was paid to the care of elderly veterans with the establishment of the Chelsea and Greenwich Hospitals.

Following the Revolution of 1688 and the Scientific Revolution, military surgery improved greatly, helping lay the foundations for the modern profession, with its emphasis on an empirical approach to diagnostics and remedies.[31] Because soldiers required longer, and thus more expensive, training, there was an increased pressure to cure them and return them to duty as quickly as possible. Every regiment was required to have a surgeon and his assistant, with their own medical wagon. Serving as military surgeons enabled ambitious men to learn skills that were valuable in civilian practice. James Yonge left the sea to become a prosperous surgeon in Plymouth, eventually being elected to the Royal Society. In order to encourage medical men to enlist, parliament passed legislation in 1698 permitting demobilized surgeons to ply their trade without regard to guild regulations. On the other hand, the growing lethality of weapons countered improvements in medical care. The flintlock musket, and to a lesser extent, artillery, increased the proportion of more lethal gunshot wounds to cuts that were much less fatal.

Wounded veterans had to live with their injuries as best they could. After his thigh was smashed fighting for the king in 1643, William Blundell lived in 'extreme anguish [that] hath stupefied or perverted my reason', for every waking second of his remaining forty-five years.[32] Captain Robert Parker was luckier. The effects of the shoulder injury sustained during the Siege of Limerick in 1691, he wrote, 'I feel to this day on every change of weather.'[33] Even more fortunate was the Irish trooper hit by a bullet on his belt buckle: 'My belly turned black.'[34] Others overcame their disabilities. Peg-legged cooks were a tradition in the Royal Navy. In the army, after losing a leg at Almansa in 1707, Lieutenant Walter Stapleton took two years to recover before rejoining his unit, eventually becoming a brigadier. In command of a Jacobite regiment, the peg-legged veteran was mortally wounded at Culloden.[35]

Post-Traumatic Stress Disorder

In modern wars such as Iraq and Afghanistan psychological wounds, known as Post-Traumatic Stress Disorder (PTSD), are about as common as physical ones. This may be a recent development, for in the Second World War psychiatric casualties represent between 10 and 15 per cent of the whole.[36] In early modern warfare surprisingly few instances of PTSD have been found. After a bullet pierced Lieutenant Skeffington's hat at the Siege of Montreuil (1544), the gunner fell down, 'crying God be merciful unto me for I am a dead man'. Three days later he passed away without a mark on his body.[37] Following his great victories Marlborough suffered from depression, enduring migraines, which he admitted could have been psychosomatic, confessing to his wife to being 'much out of order' and suffering 'much disquietude'.[38] The most serious cases of PTSD come mainly from the Civil Wars. Sir Walter Earle, a skilled sapper and veteran of the Thirty Years War, was recalled to the colours to take part in the Siege of Corfe Castle, where a musket ball just missed him, piercing his hat. It was the last straw. Soon afterwards Earle was seen dressed in a bear's skin, walking on all fours in the hope of being mistaken for a large dog.[39] During the Siege of Cirencester in February 1643 shelling by a large mortar, as well as the subsequent sack, destroyed Lady Jordan's adult faculties. She regressed to behaving like a child, being able to find happiness only by playing with the dolls that were made specially for her.[40] After serving as a chaplain at Marston Moor, Thomas Goad, vicar of Griton, Yorkshire, 'fell ill and became distracted', languishing in this condition for at least sixteen years.[41] Another military chaplain, Richard Baxter, felt the strain of the war after he was demobilized. For three months he had a copious and unquenchable nosebleed, a sympton of intense psychological strain.[42] A maidservant who in 1644 witnessed the brutal massacre of the garrison of Hopton Castle, Shropshire, suffered mental trauma for the rest of her life.[43] Psychological wounds brought one soldier—quite literally—to the gutter. In 1659 Captain Richard Atkyns, a royalist, came across the trooper who had saved his life at the Battle of Cheriton, fifteen years before, for which he had given him ten pounds. 'I saw him begging in the streets of London, with a muffler about his face, and [he] spoke inwardly as if he had been eaten up with a foul disease.'[44] Colonel James Gardiner's reaction to being wounded at Ramillies can hardly be counted as a true case of PTSD: a notorious rake, he became a highly religious missionary.

The lack of documented psychiatric cases—those whom Wilfred Owen described as 'men whose minds the dead have ravaged'—is hard to explain. Perhaps it was because soldiers and sailors tended to be in combat for far less time than today, battles being over in a day or two. Also the syndrome was not medically recognized. The first doctor to do so was Johannes Hofer, a Swiss, who in 1678 described a state of continuous melancholy, incessant talking of home, insomnia, lack of appetite, palpitations and fever. As treatment Dr Hofer recommended sending the man home or dosing him with purgatives.[45]

Victory and Defeat

Victory was the best cure. After winning at the Boyne on 12 July 1690, Dr George Clark had a good night's sleep, while Thomas Bellingham recalled 'A glorious day,' even though 'I was almost faint with want of drink and meat.'[46] Victorious at Dunkeld (1689), the Cameronians 'gave a great shout, and threw their caps in the air, and then all joined in offering praises up to God'.[47] Joy at being alive when so many had died could be tempered both by survivor's guilt and by the apprehension that next time one might not be so lucky. 'We have acquired much glory, but it has cost us the most precious of our blood,' wrote Captain James Fitzgerald after Fontenoy (1745). A year later, after Culloden, the duke of Cumberland expressed a similar sense of survivor's guilt, asking, 'Lord, what am I, that I should be spared when so many brave men lie dead upon this spot?'[48] After writing in his diary that the English victories in the Seven Years War were due to their superior courage, honour and skill, Sergeant Millner pulled himself back, lest he be tempting fate. 'The battle not being to the strong,' he wrote, as one can almost hear him knock on wood, 'but whosoever it pleaseth God to give it unto.'[49]

Defeat is appalling. As the duke of Wellington once observed, 'Nothing except a battle lost can be half so melancholy as a battle won.' Robert Parker described defeat at Ballymore, Ireland, in June 1691:[50]

Here the miserable effects of war appeared in a very melancholy manner ... the wretches came flocking in very great number about our camp, devouring all the filth they could meet with. Our dead horses, crawling with vermin, as the sun had parched them, were delicious food to them: while their infants sucked their carcass with as much eagerness as if they were at their mothers' breasts.

Defeat is traumatic. It took six months before the chaplain, Alexander Shields, could face this experience after his regiment, the Cameronians, were routed at Steenkirk in August 1692. 'Ever since that fearful and fatal stroke at Steenkirk I have not heart to write to anybody, the dispensation being so distressing, confounding, and silencing.' In fact the only reason why he forced himself to write about the battle was that he was sending a full list of the dead back to his fellows ministers in Scotland so they could inform the next of kin.[51]

Defeat is bitter. Being beaten by the French in 1513 was 'so dolorous' that Edward Echyngham could hardly bear to write about it. After being thrashed at Prestonpans (1745), Sir John Clark 'thought Hell had broke loose, for I never heard such oaths and incriminations branding one another for Cowardice and neglect of duty'.[52] Those who could, fled the battlefield as fast and far as possible. According to the Jacobite song 'Hey Johnnie Cope', when the British General Sir John Cope heard that Princes Charles's army was about to fight his at Prestonpans,[53]

> He thought it would't be amiss
> To have a horse in readiness,
> To flee Prestonpans in the morning.

With their mounts' four feet, cavalry had a distinct advantage over two-legged infantry. So much so that after being routed at Naseby Lord John Belasyse bitterly observed that 'The horse knew well how to save themselves, though not their honour.' After the same defeat a royalist infantryman ran thirty miles to Ravenstone, Leicester, where he tried to steal a loaf of bread from a servant girl. He was so demoralized that she was able to kill him with a laundry stick.[54] After Ramillies some French infantry managed to run 108 miles to Louvain.[55] A Danish chaplain describes how on the evening of 12 July 1691 the Irish fled after the Battle of Aughrim, 'not knowing what to do. . . . Throwing away their arms.' After running for about seven miles, some tried to stop and regroup, but failed to do so because of the ensuing rabble of camp followers. Many wounded men and horses expired beside the road; some troopers begged to be put out of their misery. There was so much blood all over the place, concluded the chaplain, 'that you could hardly take a step without slipping'. Statistics give an idea of the slaughter. Seven thousand Irish died: only four hundred and fifty were taken prisoner.[56]

It took time to restore units that had broken and run. After Sir Thomas Salisbury's Denbighshire infantry did so at Edgehill, an eyewitness called them 'poor Welsh vermin, the off-scourings of the nation'. Four weeks later they redeemed their honour at the Battle of Brentford, when they drove three crack parliamentary regiments, Holles's, Hampden's and Brooke's, into the Thames.[57]

The best example of how a unit broke and had to reconstitute itself was the eight-hundred-strong regiment in French service commanded by Colonel Henry Fitzjames.[58] John Stevens, a captain in this largely Irish Catholic unit, records how they panicked at the Battle of the Boyne when their own cavalry appeared without warning on their flank. Since they had taken few, if any, casualties, Stevens felt the shame greatly; it 'so perplexed my soul that I envied the few dead'. As they retreated, the Irish looted the supply train, getting drunk on brandy. Incapable of further retreat, many fell victim to the pursuing Williamites. Stevens grew so parched that he could not quench his thirst, even though he drank from every ditch and puddle he passed. Soldiers blamed their officers: officers condemned the generals. Two days after the Boyne the survivors straggled into Dublin. Fitzjames's Regiment raised its colours, but only twenty men rallied around them. So Stevens struck off on his own in an attempt to recover the stragglers. He tried to requisition a horse from a village, but the women drove him away. Arriving at Kilkenny on 16 July, he found many of his soldiers drunk, while others had looted the castle for food. Senior officers had requisitioned rations from the town authorities, which they sold at a £300 profit as their own men starved to death.

The process of rebuilding the regiment into an effective fighting force was long and hard. By July 16 Fitzjames's Regiment had sufficient men available to storm a house in Cashel, whose owner had refused to give them food. Three days later the food supply had improved enough for the regiment to muster 150 men. Many troopers were almost naked, having lost their clothing plus their tents at the Boyne, so they started building huts. A week later the muster roll had doubled to three hundred, of whom only half were armed. The suggestion that those who had thrown away their weapons should be shot was rejected: it would have left too few alive to reconstitute the battalion as a viable unit. It was certainly not one in early August, when many were too weak, and the rest too undisciplined for duty. Stevens thought that after they had wallowed in the delights of looting and of 'being under no command', only the severest punishments would bring them back to order. Worse still, even though deserters were ordered to be shot, many, including some of the bravest troopers, ran away for a second time. Eventually the regiment was restored as a fighting unit, and a year later it fought courageously during the Siege of Limerick. Afterwards Fitzjames's Regiment was part of the Irish Brigade that served in the French Army until 1792.

Surrender

Although surrender is one of the most difficult of military transactions, training manuals—then and now—do not instruct you how to do so successfully. So troops have to work out their own codes of behaviour. Surrendering was a risky act, and even when a capitulation was accepted prisoners ran a grave risk of ill-treatment, hunger, disease and death. Wounded at Malplaquet, Peter Drake tried to surrender. A couple of enemy soldiers threatened to shoot him if he did not go away. The third did so, at the same time as Drake fired his pistol. 'I shot the upper part of his head and he tumbled forward. I saw his brains come down: his ball only grazed my shoulder.' The wadding set his coat on fire. 'It was all done in an instant,' Drake concluded.[59] During the War of the Spanish Succession, Matthew Bishop was unlucky to be captured in an ambush by partisans. 'They behaved to me in a barbarous, cruel and inhuman Manner,' stealing his clothes, watch, money and even the buckles from his shoes. When he objected they beat his head bloody. His screams attracted the notice of a corporal of regular troops, who took him to his officer, who in turn checked his wounds and gave him a meal. As he was being marched off to captivity, the drums of a large British unit were heard approaching. His captors ran to hide in some woods, while Bishop bolted to his compatriots.[60]

On being taken prisoner a soldier goes through a metamorphosis. One moment he is an enemy, determined to kill you: the next he is begging for his life. Being held prisoner was usually a most disagreeable experience, particularly for the other ranks. Eight to ten of the six hundred British prisoners incarcerated in Dinan, France, in 1703 died each day, the latrines being emptied only every fourth day. In Dunkirk seventy to eighty men, captured during the War of the Spanish Succession, were crammed into a room, in which only half could lie down at one time.[61] An anonymous dragoon recalled being captured at Brihuega, Spain, in 1710. Stripped of everything except their clothes 'that were not worth the taking', the men were force-marched twenty-one miles. Forbidden to drink from the wells they passed by, the enemy brandished burning brands of straw in their faces, 'cursing our Queen and us'. At Colmenar Viejo, nineteen miles north of Madrid, armed peasants tried to storm the house in which the English were locked, perhaps to kill, certainly to plunder them. The dragoon remained a prisoner until 1714. Throughout his captivity he was highly critical of the English officers, who got much better treatment and refused to help their men.[62] Wounded at the Siege of Denca (1707), Captain George Carleton was taken prisoner when the city surrendered. He was held, presumably on parole not to escape, at Valencia, which he thought 'the pleasantest city in Spain'. Apart from an *agent provocateur* from the Inquisition, who tried to discuss the doctrine of purgatory with him, the captain enjoyed his two years as a prisoner in Spain so much that on being liberated he travelled around the country for a couple more years as a tourist.[63] Senior officers were treated even better. Three days after the French captured Major General Sir William Cadogan near Tournai in 1706 he was paroled, and soon after exchanged.[64]

A most horrible—and most shamefully forgotten—treatment of prisoners took place after the Battle of Dunbar (1650), when Cromwell dispatched five thousand captured Scots to Newcastle with instructions for its governor, Sir Arthur Haselrig, to 'let humanity be exercised towards them'.[65] It was not. In Morpeth the captives were jam-packed into a walled garden. They were force-marched, sometimes through the night. Since many had not eaten for eight days they dug up and gobbled raw cabbages, which gave them dysentery. Most of the survivors were herded into Durham Cathedral. In one of England's loveliest buildings, now a World Heritage Site, there took place a shameful atrocity. Even though they received oatmeal, beef, more cabbages, coal for heat and straw to lie upon, the 'flux' ravaged the Scots. They 'were so unruly, sluttish and nasty', Haselrig reported, 'they acted rather like Beasts than men.' Within this holy purgetory all discipline broke down. Underneath the high Gothic ceiling and vaulted stained-glass windows, men lay dying in their own blood and excrement, their moans echoing like a ghastly plainchant amid the cathedral's superlative acoustics. Some men simply gave up. Those with money were robbed and murdered; those with warm clothes were strangled and stripped. Some of the survivors were sent to fight in Ireland, while two and a half thousand were transported to New England or to Barbados—that hellhole—as indentured servants. By the end of October 1651 the six hundred Scots remaining in Durham were dispatched to work as forced labour draining the Fens. Of the five thousand men marched south from Dunbar it would not be unreasonable to estimate that in the next couple of years at least half died as a result of their captivity—a rate twice that of British prisoners held in the Second World War by the Japanese for three and a half years.[66]

If soldiers reneged on their surrenders, custom decreed that they lost all claim to any protection. Take Du Roy's regiment, which capitulated to the Royal Scots Dragoons at Ramillies. When the Scots started to pursue other French troops who had not surrendered, Du Roy's men took up their arms again, 'for which they suffered', recalled a dragoon, what 'they deserved'.[67]

Home from the Wars

Men eagerly anticipated coming home from the wars. In 1670 with more lust than literary skill John Baltharpe, a common sailor, looked forward to doing so:[68]

We watered then and made things fit
Unto old England for to get
To think upon our English Girls
We joyful was as any Earls.

Many returning veterans' expectations were disappointed by the public's indifference. Even though they knew that Surgeon's Mate James Yonge was an exchanged prisoner who had survived over a year of hellish captivity in the hands of the Dutch, the boatmen at Deal, Kent, gouged him half a crown to be rowed ashore.[69]

Returning to England was particularly painful for those veterans who had been evacuated as sick or wounded. All too often they were abandoned at an English port, to be looked after by the local authorities. In 1590 the mayor and jurats of Rye described the wounded and sick who had been discharged from Cherbourg and dumped on them without warning:[70]

The diseased soldiers. . . . Rested upon the town's charge eight days in the most miserable sort, full of infirmities in their bodies, wonderfully sick and weak, some wounded, some their toes and feet rotting off, and lame, and the skin and flesh of their feet torn away with continual marching, all of them without money, without apparel to cover their nakedness, all of them full of vermin. . . . We constrained to wash their bodies in sweet water, to take from them all their clothes, and strip them unto new apparel. Then we appointed them several houses for their diet, and also surgeons to cure their wounds and rottenness. By this means we have saved some forty eight of them.

Such generous treatment was the exception. The sick and wounded evacuated from Ireland to Bristol and Liverpool during the Elizabethan Conquest or the Civil Wars fared far worse, as did the survivors of the Armada and the 1625 Cadiz expedition: of the latter a dozen dropped dead on a single day in the streets of Plymouth. Those, like the forty-eight from Rye fortunate enough to recover, still had to make it home.[71] Sometimes they were issued money; more often they were lucky to be given a pass requesting the local authorities to help them on their way.

After every major war large numbers of veterans were demobilized. Their treatment often depended on the nature of the war. For instance, those who fought for Richard III went home from Bosworth Field quietly, hoping to escape the notice of Henry VII who, by proclaiming that his reign began on 21 August, the day before the battle, turned them into traitors, liable to the law's hideous punishments. Henry VIII's veterans seemed to return to civilian life fairly well. At a guess twenty-five thousand Englishmen served overseas in his reign, not too large a number to present great problems. The rest of the king's troops were mercenaries who went back to their own countries. In contrast, over a quarter of a million men served overseas in the last eighteen years of Elizabeth's reign. The return of those who survived created immense problems. Charles Blount, Lord Mountjoy, recommended to the Privy Council that veterans of both sides in the Irish Wars be encouraged to serve in foreign armies: it got them out of the way, and—better still—over three-quarters of them would never return to make trouble at home.[72] In 1590 five hundred veterans discharged from the Portugal expedition threatened to loot St Bartholomew's Fair: they scared the London authorities so badly that the city mobilized two thousand of its militia.

After the Civil Wars well-off royalist veterans tended to maintain a low profile in the hope of avoiding the sequestration of their lands by parliament. Alexander Brome consoled himself with the thought that he and his comrades need no longer lock their doors—the roundheads had plundered them of everything worth stealing. The royalist poet took refuge in gallow's humour. 'Why should we not laugh and be jolly,' he asked, 'Since all the world now is grown mad?' When, in Brome's lights at least, England returned to sanity by restoring Charles II to the throne, cavalier hopes for revenge and, better still, preferment, were dashed. The poet bitterly complained:[73]

We have fought, we have paid
We've been sold and betray'd.

Nonetheless seven thousand cavaliers applied for part of the £60,000 Charles II set aside for their relief in 1663. At an average of £8 16s. 8d. per application, this bounty was far from generous. Thus, many veterans found places in the new standing army—all ranks of the Life Guards being raised from cavalier officers—or sought service overseas, where out of sight they were out of both the king's mind and pocket.

The situation for the parliamentary troops after the end of the Civil Wars was very different. For the first and only time in British history after a war the army, which had become highly radicalized, did not demobilize, remaining at an average strength of forty thousand men during the commonwealth. After the restoration, like the cavaliers a decade earlier, roundhead soldiers had to lie low, hoping not to attract the attention of the authorities. As it happened many found employment in Charles II's new standing army. At the end of both the Nine Years War and the War of the Spanish Succession large numbers of men were demobilized. Perhaps a quarter of a million men left the armed forces. Little was done for them. In 1713 only four thousand veterans were in receipt of a pension, a number that had doubled by 1750.

Adjusting to civilian life could be hard. Officers resented the loss of social and economic status. Thomas Churchyard observed that on leaving the army, captains such as he[74]

Must learn to bear a peddler's pack
And trudge to some good market town
So from a knight become a clown.

In 1719 *An Epistle from a Half Pay Officer* made a similar complaint:[75]

How whimsical our fortune! How Bizarre
This week we shine in scarlet and gold:
The next, the sword is pawned—the watch is sold.

No wonder retired officers waxed nostalgic about the past. In Thomas Otway's play *The Soldier's Fortune* (1681) an unemployed captain asks another, 'must we never see our glorious days again?' Disenchanted, his comrade sadly replies, 'Those days have been.' Disappointment could turn into anger. As the ballad, 'A Pleasant Song made by a *Souldier*' (1614), griped:[76]

I watched on the sieged walls,
In thunder, lightening, rain and snow . . .
When all my kindred took their rest,
At home in many a stately bed.

Another version of this pamphlet was printed in 1664, presumably for sale to demobilized servicemen. Claiming that 'the fruit of war is beggary', Martin Parker's ballad, 'The Maunding Souldier' (1629), requested:[77]

Good your worship, cast your eyes
Upon a soldier's miseries . . .
But like a noble friend,
Some silver lend.

Others found home hard to come home to. After an absence of eight years, which (as noted) included a very pleasant two years touring Spain, Captain George Carleton took a coach to London in 1715: 'When I arrived I thought myself transported into a country more foreign than any I had fought in.'[78] Corporal Matthew Bishop returned home to Chatham after the War of the Spanish Succession to learn that his wife had had a son by him. On being told that Matthew had been killed at the Siege of Ghent (1708), the supposed widow had remarried, and was now heavily pregnant by her second 'husband'. The misunderstanding was entirely Bishop's fault since he had not written to his wife for three or four years. Mrs Bishop—if that is her correct designation—fainted on seeing Matthew, and went into premature labour, from which she died. The two newly minted widowers had a furious row, after which Matthew returned home to Deddington, Oxfordshire.[79]

In 1566 Thomas Harman warned that if nothing was done to help returning soldiers, then they would turn—or return—to a life of mendicancy or crime.[80] Statistics show that he was right. In London before 1580 only 1.8 per cent of vagrants were ex-servicemen. Between 1620 and 1640 the proportion rose to 12 per cent. In Doncaster it peaked at 49 per cent in 1627–29. Many veterans followed Private Pistol's recommendation: 'To England will I steal, and there I'll steal.'[81] James Turner, a goldsmith's apprentice, enlisted in the London militia, rising to the rank of lieutenant colonel before being discharged. Pepys thought him 'a mad, confident, swearing fellow'. Unable to settle down to an honest job, he took up burglary, but was caught and executed in 1664.[82] Since discharged cavalry troopers were often allowed to keep their horses and pistols, a few became highwaymen. Captain James Hind, who had fought at Worcester in 1651, was hanged, drawn and quartered the following year at Oxford with two other royalist officers, Hussey and Peck, for highway robbery.[83] Even though the admittedly rudimentary statistics do not show a spike in crime following the Civil Wars, there was one after both the Nine Years War and the War of the Spanish Succession. Epping Forest east of London was reputed to be a nest of crime. In 1698 a gang of five highwaymen, all ex-servicemen, were reported plying their trade near Henley-on-Thames, while the following year Charles Sackville, earl of Dorset, was robbed between Chelsea and Fulham by ten highwaymen, all veterans.[84]

The Treatment of Veterans

There was little sense that veterans were entitled to help from the taxpayer. When asked whether ex-servicemen surely deserved benefits for having ventured their lives during the Civil Wars, Sir Thomas Wroth, a Somersetshire gentleman, curtly observed, 'they were well paid for it.'[85] For most of the early modern period civilians held soldiers in a contempt that was in part engendered by fear. Even though he was writing a *Defence of the Militarie Profession* (1597), Geoffrey Gates likened returned soldiers to vomit. They had seen and done so much evil, and plundered so widely, violating the norms of civilized society, 'that they seem to come rather from hell'.[86]

Naturally, veterans responded angrily to such treatment. Sir John Oldcastle bitterly noted (in the 1600 play of the same name) that in England 'There be more stocks to sit poor soldiers in, than there be houses to relieve them at.' Lieutenant Stumpe, the one-legged veteran in Ben Jonson's *Alarum for London*, lamented:[87]

But let a soldier that hath shed his blood
Is lamed, diseased, or anyway distressed
Appeal for succour, they look a sconce
As if you knew him not.

An early eighteenth-century ballad protested:[88]

My King and Country for to serve
I fought like a sailor so bold.
Now that the war is over
I really cannot get my gold.

Not being paid their arrears of pay angered many veterans. Ralph Bostock was particularly bitter. After spending eighteen years as an unpaid gentleman volunteer (as well as all of his £1,000 patrimony) fighting for Queen Elizabeth in Ireland, France and the Netherlands, he was discharged without a penny.[89] Being denied £70–£80 in back wages upset Lieutenant John Felton so much that in August 1628 he assassinated the duke of Buckingham, Charles I's favourite.[90]

Many veterans could not afford the luxury of anger. Because civilians did not believe that they were entitled to help from the public purse, when wounded veterans appeared before local magistrates to petition for assistance, they had to be deferential. During his three and a half years' service in the king's forces Robert Davies was wounded seventeen times, having suffered a cracked skull, lost the use of both feet and one eye—yet even after the restoration he had to grovel for a 40s.' pension.[91] Sergeant William Stoakes, of Shepton Mallet, was wounded at the Civil War's first battle, Babylon Hill; fought at Edgehill and Brentford; took part in the capture of Bristol and the Siege of Gloucester; stormed Bolton; at Marston Moor 'received many dangerous hurts'; and was taken prisoner at Naseby. In 1662 he petitioned the Somersetshire magistrates, saying how much he had suffered from 'the usurped and tyrannical power' of parliament, 'and since it had pleased God to restore his sacred majesty,' the royalist veteran begged the magistrates to grant him a pension. They did.[92] Other justices were less charitable. In 1620 Hugh Drayton was brought before the Atherstone magistrates because he 'did revile his majesty in his drink'. He apologized, explaining that his pension was £16 in arrears, and that his war wounds had addled his mind—especially after a beer or two. Nonetheless the magistrates ordered him whipped.[93]

For those who survived war, things could never be the same again. Yet many of them wanted to return to the same—to what they had done before going to the wars: to homes, jobs, having and bringing up children, to sleeping with their wives—and to doing so without nightmares. After the Elizabethan wars, Thomas Wilson noted in *The State of England* (1600) that 'gentlemen who were wont to addict themselves to wars are now grown good husbands.'[94] Nostalgically, veterans remembered comradeship, new experiences, exciting times, as they tried to suppress those things best forgotten. Remarkably many—perhaps most—managed to put the hurly-burly behind them. As a surprised Samuel Pepys wrote in his diary in 1663, 'Of all the old [i.e. New Model] army you cannot see a man begging about the street. You shall have this captain turned a shoemaker, this lieutenant a baker, that a haberdasher, this common soldier a porter, and every man in his apron and frock, etc., as if they had never done anything else.'[95]

CONCLUSION: THE HAND OF WAR

> This fortress built by nature for herself
> Against infection and the hand of war.
> *Richard II*, II, i, 45–46

IT WAS A BLEAK, TREELESS PLACE, SOME FIVE HUNDRED FEET ABOVE SEA
level. A cold east wind of sleet and rain blew into the faces of the
prince's men drawn up on the west side of the moor on 16 April 1746.
They were tired, very tired, having marched as far south as Derby, in an
impossible quest to place James II's son on the throne. Here, 130 miles
from London, they turned back north, to be harassed as they trudged the
450 miles almost to home. At Culloden, five miles east of Inverness, their
leader decided to make his stand. Facing him was the royal army,
commanded by the duke of Cumberland, George II's third son, a veteran
soldier, with a military record distinguished more for brutality than bril-
liance. After half an hour's artillery bombardment, Prince Charles ordered
his Highlanders to charge. They managed to sweep through the first line
of the king's troops, but could not break the second. 'In their rage they
could not make any impression,' Cumberland reported, 'they threw stones
at them for at least a minute or two before the total rout began.' Massed
volley fire from the king's forces broke the Highlanders into a panic fear.
Steadily the royalists advanced, bayoneting enemy wounded. 'I never saw
such dreadful slaughter as we had made,' Colonel George Stanhope told
his brother, 'and our men gave no quarter.'[1] (See ill.24.)

Cumberland's army of English and Lowland Scots killed 1,500 rebels,
and murdered half as many prisoners in cold blood. Immediately after the
battle Private Alexander Taylor, a Lowlander in the Royal Scots, wrote to
his 'loving spouse' that 'I never saw a small field thicker of dead.'[2] Of some
3,400 prisoners taken after they had fled the field, 120 were tried and
executed (40 of them as deserters from the royal army), while 1,142 were

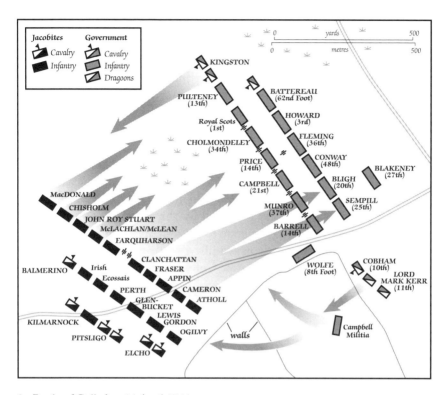

9. Battle of Culloden, 16 April 1746.

transported to the New World. In the ensuing weeks thousands of Highlanders were hunted down and butchered. After torching seven thousand crofts, the English general Henry 'Hangman' Hawley reported 'There's still so many houses to burn, and I hope still more to be put to death.'[3] The lairds who had coerced them into fighting for Prince Charles later forced many Highlanders off their lands. Many emigrated to North Carolina, and, cognizant of the cost of opposing the king, fought for George III, only to find another Culloden on 27 February 1776, at the Battle of Moore's Creek. As they shouted their battle cry 'King George and Broadswords', the patriots mowed them down.

Looking Forward

In the century after Culloden—the last of many battles between the English and the Scots or Irish, and the last battle ever on British soil—the British Isles experienced tremendous changes, such as the Industrial Revolution, defeat in the American War of Independence, victory over Napoleon, and parliamentary reform.[4] During this period a sense of

Britishness became dominant, and British culture emerged, which 'largely defined itself through fighting'. War and religion both played a critical role in the formation of a British state.[5] But there was nothing inevitable about the emergence of a United Kingdom of England, Scotland, Ireland and Wales. Indeed, in view of their past histories of incessant, even brutal conflict, there is something surprising about their ability to work together. Neither was the great success of three kingdoms (and a principality) as a world military power predestined. If the shotgun of war brought the nations of the British Isles to the marriage bed, economics made their liaisons last. Membership of a British state and British empire gave the Scots and Irish immense financial opportunities: they could make a decent living as British soldiers and sailors, as traders protected by the Royal Navy, as imperial administrators, or they could emigrate to English-speaking colonies.

These opportunities for Scots within the British state and empire became wide open immediately after Culloden. In spite of the traumatic experience of their defeat and of being cleared off their lands, Highlanders both in the old country and in North Carolina in particular displayed an amazing loyalty to the British crown. King George was only too happy to employ their broadswords. It was said that in 1794 the duchess of Gordon promised to kiss every man who enlisted in her husband's regiment, the Gordon Highlanders. Such incentives were not really necessary. Scotsmen were willing enough to accept the king's shilling without an aristocratic embrace. Ten of the eleven Scots regiments raised to fight in the Seven Years War (1756–63) were from the Highlands.[6] Between 1759 and 1793 twenty infantry regiments were raised from the Highlands, and from a population of 300,000, 74,000 men served in the British Army. In 1757, 31.5 per cent of the officers fighting in North America were Scots, as compared to 31 per cent Irish and only 24.5 per cent English.[7] The Royal Navy also provided employment for educated Scots. Tobias Smollett, the novelist who served as a surgeon in the navy after qualifying from the University of Glasgow, had his alter ego, Roderick Random, report that when he took his exams to be admitted as a surgeon's mate, the examiner told him, 'we have scarce any other countrymen to examine here: you Scotchmen have overcome us of late as the locusts did Egypt.'[8]

'The Scots,' concluded Professor Thomas Devine, 'were at the cutting edge of British global expansion.' In that expansion Highlanders did much of the dirty work, clearing, shooting and killing those who stood in the way. 'They served with fidelity,' declared Prime Minister William Pitt, 'as they fought with valour.'[9] Helped by their own military courage—and a nudge or two from Sir Walter Scott and Queen Victoria—they became the most popular figures in the British Army. The English came to perceive the Scots as a 'martial race', and in their turn the Scots came to define themselves as a military nation. Robert Burns boasted that 'our Scottish name' was 'so famed in martial story'.[10]

In many ways this was too limited a characterization, since the half century after Culloden saw the Scottish Enlightenment, graced by such thinkers as Adam Smith, David Hume, Robert Burns, James Watt and Sir Walter Scott. Much of the magnificent architecture of Glasgow and Edinburgh was built in this period. For two and a half centuries until after the Second World War, Scotland benefited greatly from membership of the British Empire.[11] Ironically, today the wheel seems to have turned full circle. It is no accident that the end of empire and the decline in the size of the British armed forces (as well as the development of the European Union) have done much to loosen the bonds between the two nations.

In the two centuries after Culloden the British armed forces and empire provided bountiful job opportunities for the Irish. As its splendid Georgian squares reveal, Dublin, at least, benefited from the British connection. By the 1770s large numbers of Catholics were being covertly recruited into the Marines and East India Company Army. At the same time Irish Protestants provided about a third of the British Army's officer corps that was to produce Wellington, Alexander and Montgomery. The Revolutionary Wars finally ended Irish mercenary service in the French Army, thus freeing tens of thousands to fight in the British. During the Napoleonic Wars, when a third of the rank and file were Irish, Lord Sidmouth, the Home Secretary, acknowledged that they 'turned the scale'.[12] By 1830 Irish-born soldiers constituted 42.2 per cent of the British Army and over half that of the East India Company. In the 1870s, 38 per cent of the Indian Medical Service were Irish, as were 65 per cent of the Palestinian Police in the mid-1920s. Seventy thousand men from the Irish Free State volunteered to fight in the British Army during the Second World War.

Looking Back

This book argues that it is the legitimate killing of our fellow creatures that makes war special and decisive. Thus, it would be logical to assume that there is a relationship between the numbers of those who died directly and indirectly as a result of war and the impact of wars upon the history of the British Isles. Table 7 estimates the number of war dead from Bosworth Field to Culloden.

These figures should be treated with the utmost caution, but they may be the best that the surviving data permit. Several conclusions may be drawn from them. Even if the figure of 1,218,587 people who died directly or indirectly as a result of war in the British Isles between 1485 and 1746 is an approximation, based on incomplete evidence and—it

Table 7 Estimates of war dead, direct and indirect, for England and the British Isles, 1485–1746[13]

	English	Scots/Irish
1485 Bosworth Field	1,100	
1487 Simnel Revolt	4,000	
1497 Warbeck Revolt	500	
1497 Cornish Rebellion	2,500	
1513 Flodden	4,000	10,000
1513 French campaign	1,000	
1520s French expeditions	1,000	
1536 Pilgrimage of Grace	300	
1540s French expedition	2,000	
1542 Solway Moss	700	300
1549 Prayer Book Rebellion	4,000	
1549 Kett's Rebellion	3,000	
1485–1560 Anglo-Scots Border	1,000	1,000
1545 Ancrum Moor	600	
1547 Pinkie	600	7,000
1558–85 Elizabeth's wars	11,000	1,000
1586–1603 Elizabeth's wars	88,285	50,000
1620s expeditions	30,000	10,000
1620–49 Mercenaries	60,000	60,000
1638–60 British Civil Wars	230,441	417,751
1660–84 Tangier/Portugal/France	5,000	1,000
1679 Dumclog and Bothwell Bridge	60	1,000
1685 Monmouth Rebellion	2,000	
1688 Glorious Revolution	150	110,000
1688–97 Nine Years War	10,000	10,000
1691–1746 Mercenaries	5,000	20,000
1701–14 War of the Spanish Succession	16,000	16,000
1715 Rebellion	200	1,000
1718–20, War of the Quadruple Alliance	1,600	1,000
1745–46 Rebellion	1,000	10,000
Total	487,036	727,051
Total British Isles		1,214,087

must be confessed—the occasional guess, the total does suggest that a very large number of people died as a result of war in early modern Britain, particularly when compared to the dead in ensuing world wars. During the American War of Independence 44,000 Britons died; the Revolutionary and Napoleonic Wars killed 311,806; while 765,339 and 418,500 Britons perished in the First and Second World Wars respectively.

More important than the raw numbers is an analysis comparing them over time, and within the British Isles. It shows that the dead are grouped into four distinct periods. The first, from Bosworth Field to 1585 (just before the Armada), was a fairly peaceful period, in which 37,300 Englishmen died (7.6 per cent of the total English dead of 487,036 from 1485 to 1746). Of those who perished in this period, 34.8 per cent did so as foreign mercenaries during the first third of Elizabeth's reign, 8.7 per cent fighting the French, 22.6 per cent the Scots and 40 per cent suppressing revolts and rebellions. The latter figure shows how much effort the Tudor regime had to use to keep itself in power. In the Anglo-Scots wars the English lost 7,200 and the Scots 18,300, which suggests that the former's dominance began in the sixteenth century, being completed in the seventeenth. In the second period, from 1586 to 1602, 88,285 English died (18.1 per cent of the English total), mainly on the continent, at sea or in Ireland. During the last third of Elizabeth's reign over half of English males saw some form of military service. The third and bloodiest period was that of the British Civil Wars. Proportionately, this was the deadliest conflict in the islands' history, in which 652,692 Britons died, 54 per cent of the deaths in our period. With their brutal conquests of Scotland and Ireland, the British Civil Wars laid the foundations for the British state. The fourth peak took place as a result of the Revolution of 1688, which committed Britain to two world wars, the Nine Years War and the War of the Spanish Succession, in total producing 189,750 dead (15.6 per cent of the total). In this period the formation of a British state was virtually completed.

These figures support two other conclusions. First, that the proportion of English to non-English dead, 487,036 to 727,051, shows that the burden of war was borne disproportionately by the Scots and Irish, who with 34.5 per cent of the population suffered 60.0 per cent of the dead.[14] Second, from the reign of Elizabeth I at least 160,000 people, the majority of them Scots and Irish, died fighting as mercenaries for foreign governments. By the end of our period many of the huge manpower surplus who had been foreign mercenaries switched to service in the British Armed Forces and Empire. Until the last half century, for half a millennium very large numbers of young British males, usually of an adventurous, even a violent disposition, left the isles for foreign service. It is interesting to speculate about the effects of the return of this cohort. Does it have any connection with the growth of hooliganism, massive public drunkenness and concerns about antisocial behaviour?

Until the Revolution of 1688 English military power was basically inwardly directed, being used to form a British state: afterwards British military mastery became directed outwards, in order to exercise world hegemony. This experience is similar to that of the United States, today's superpower, which after winning independence used its military forces internally, and did not employ them on a world stage until 1917, or even 1941. Both nations employed sophisticated technologies to exercise world power. Both had extremely bloody Civil Wars, one of which helped create a United Kingdom and an empire while the other preserved the American Union.

Preaching to the Living

After the Battles of Blenheim and Malplaquet, Colonel Blackadder wrote of the dead preaching to the living. While both these battles were important events in the macro history of the British Isles, Blackadder was thinking in micro terms, about the individuals who were slaughtered, and about their families for whom things could never again be the same. For its victims war always ends badly. For a few, such as Blackadder, it provided a full, although, as he confessed in old age, 'an odd unaccountable way of living'.[15] Looking back on half a century as a soldier, Sergeant Donald McBane of the Royal Scots vowed to 'repent for my former wickedness'.[16] Elis Gruffudd, Henry VIII's veteran Welsh captain, described himself in virtuous retirement:[17]

> Aha Sirs! Now we must listen to an old man of the king's with a red nose. Bring him a stool to sit on and a mug full of beer warmed up, and a piece of burnt toast to clear his throat so he can talk of his exploits in days gone by.

Of such a life a man could be proud! A few veterans lived to a ripe old age. Sergeant Donald MacLeod of the Royal Scots died in Inverness in 1791 aged 103.[18] Even older (so the *Derry Journal* claimed) was Terrance Gallagher, born in 1659 and who served as a sergeant at the Boyne, and lived to be 116.[19] Some veterans were lucky. Having lost a limb at the Siege of Leith in 1560, Sir Thomas Knyvett returned home to marry a rich heiress. Others were not so fortunate: after a lifetime sailing the seas, being captured, wounded and surviving many a fight and even more storms, Edward Barlow, aged sixty-six, was finally given command of a ship in 1706. Months later he was wrecked and drowned with his whole crew off Madagascar: all he left his wife and children were some silver dishes, a tankard, a pottinger, a dram cup, six tablespoons and four teaspoons.[20]

What then did all those who fought, and perhaps died, leave to us? To posterity? What do we hear the dead preach? What do those survivors, such as Barlow, Blackadder, MacLeod, Gallagher and Gruffudd, want us to learn. Some maintain that their true voices cannot be really heard, arguing like Walt Whitman, poet and American Civil War nurse, that 'The real war will never get in the books.'[21] Here I have tried my best to get it into a book by telling the story—as much as possible in their own words—of how during the early modern period war affected the people and nations of the British Isles. In doing so, I hope that I have shown how profoundly the hand of war has shaped this Seat of Mars.

NOTES

Introduction: This Seat of Mars

1. Place of publication is London, unless cited otherwise. I am grateful to Hugh Allison for information regarding the Culloden ghosts. Ghosts have been reported sighted at several US Civil War battlefields, including Bentonville, NC, Fort Macon, NC, Sailor's Creek, Antietam, Murfreesboro and Chickamauga. During the English Civil War they were reported at Cambridge, Edgehill, Tewkesbury, Woodcroft Castle, the Cotswolds and Naseby. C. H. Cooper, *Annals of Cambridge* (Cambridge, 1904), II, 303. *A Great Wonder in Heaven* (1643). *Signes from Heaven* (1646), 4, cxxxviii. E. M. Symonds, 'The Diary of John Green, 1635–37', *English Historical Review*, XLIII (1928), 39. C. Durston, 'Signs and Wonders and the English Civil War', *History Today* (October 1987), 22–27. Other sites where ghosts have been reported include Mons, Constantinople, Antioch, Sicily, Big Horn, Milvian Bridge, and the Battle of Britain. See the Discussion on H-War, May 2003. Shakespeare mentions battlefield ghosts in *Julius Caesar*, II, ii, 23–24, and Milton in *Paradise Lost*, Book II, line 553. All Shakespearean quotes from W. J. Craig, ed., *The Oxford Shakespeare* (Oxford, 1914), online edition.
2. Richard Holmes, *Acts of War: The Behaviour of Men in Battle* (New York, 1985), 7–8. P. Fussell, 'The Culture of War', in *The Costs of War: America's Pyrrhic Victories* (New Brunswick, 1997), 354. D. George, *All in a Maze: A Collection of Prose and Verse Chronologically Arranged* (1938), 154. R. Hargreaves, *This Happy Breed* (1951), 126. G. Herbert, *Jacula Prudentium*, in *The English Poems of George Herbert* (1902), 248.
3. *Essays by Lord Bacon and Clarendon* (Boston, 1820), 240–41.
4. J. Swift, *Gulliver's Travels* (New York, 1920), 252.
5. Gwynne Dyer, *War* (1986), xi.
6. Edmund Morris, *The Rise of Theodore Roosevelt* (New York, 1979), 507. J. Fletcher, *Two Noble Kinsmen*, (1883), 131.
7. S. L. A. Marshall quoted in D. Grossman, *On Killing: The Psychological Costs in Learning to Kill in War and Society* (New York, 1995), 139.
8. W. Segar, *Honour Military and Civil* (1602), A2. S. Freud, *An Outline of Psychoanalysis* (New York, 1949), 20. See also P. Paret, 'The History of War', *Daedalus* (Spring 1971), 390. C. Burke, *Aggression in Man* (New York, 1975). D. Morris, *The Naked Ape* (1967).
9. Dedicatory verse to Lt Colonel Richard Elton, *Complete Body of the art military* (1650).
10. Edward Hyde, earl of Clarendon, *History of the Rebellion and Civil Wars* (Oxford, 1826), V, 464. W. T. Divale and M. Harris, 'Population, Warfare, and the Male Supremacist Complex', *American Anthropologist*, 18 (1976), 521–33.
11. Margaret Meade, 'Alternatives to War', in M. Fried, *War* (Garden City, NJ, 1968), 215–28.

12. 'Diary of John Taylor, Clerk of Parliament', in J. Brewer, *Letters and Papers . . . Henry VIII* (1862) Vol. I, Pt 2, p. 1,624. G. Grey, *The Warriors: Reflections on Men in Battle* (New York, 1970), 28.

13. T. Becon, *Early Work of Thomas Becon* (Cambridge, 1843), 251.

14. R. Holmes, *Redcoat: The British Soldier in the Age of Horse and Musket* (2001), 144. J. McGurk, *The Elizabethan Conquest of Ireland: The 1590s Crisis* (Manchester, 1997), 193. J. Stallworthy, *The Oxford Book of War Poetry* (Oxford, 1988), 143.

15. R. Hargreaves, 'Bivouacs, Billets, and Barracks', *Army Quarterly*, 85 (1963), 235.

16. M. Howard, 'Military History and the History of War', in W. Murray and R. Sinnreich, eds, *The Past as Prologue: The Importance of History to the Military Profession* (Cambridge, 2006), 20.

17. S. L. A. Marshall, *Men against Fire* (New York, 1947), is his leading work, which while influential has recently been criticized: see Holmes, *Acts of War*, 58. Of Sir John Keegan's many works the most influential has been *The Face of Battle* (New York, 1976).

18. Dyer, *op. cit.*, 4. R. J. Lifton, *Home from the War: Vietnam Veterans: Neither Victims nor Executioners* (New York, 1973), 191.

19. Edmund Ludlow, *Memoirs* (1894), I, 45. John Ellis, *The Sharp End of War: The Fighting Man of World War II* (1982), 115.

20. M. Howard, *War and the National State* (Oxford, 1978), 4.

21. C. Barnett, *Britain and Her Army* (2000), xvii. J. Black, *War and the World* (1998), 1–2.

22. L. Stone, 'The Revival of Narrative: Reflections on a New Old History', *Past and Present* (November 1979), 10. Elton's views come from many private conversations.

23. R. H. Tawney, 'The Study of Economic History', *Economica*, XIII (February 1933), 15. F. Braudel, *The Mediterranean and the Mediterranean World in the Age of Philip II* (1973), II, 836, agrees.

24. J. F. G. Fuller, *British Light Infantry in the Eighteenth Century* (1915), 242–43. Karl von Clausewitz, *On War* (2005), I, 3.

25. Stallworthy, *op. cit.*, 167.

26. Leo Tolstoy, *War and Peace* (Harmondsworth, 1971), 921.

27. Clausewitz, *op. cit.*, III, 213.

28. 'A Royal Dragoon in the Spanish Succession War', *Journal of the Society for Army Historical Research* (1938), 57.

Chapter 1 Early Tudor Warfare, 1485–1558

1. Since the very exciting discoveries of battlefield archaeologists led by Glenn Foard, the site of the battle has been located at Crown Hill, about two miles south-east of Ambion Hill, where the visitors' centre is situated, and where for five hundred years it was considered to have been fought. *The Times*, 29 October 2009, and *www.Battlefieldstrust.com*.

2. M. Bennett, *The Battle of Bosworth Field* (1993), 110.

3. This description is by Walter Bower of a clan fight near Perth in 1440, in J. Baynes, *Soldiers of Scotland* (1988), 8.

4. *Richard III*, V, v, 16. A. R. Meyers, *English Historical Documents, 1327–1485* (1996), 340.

5. *Richard III*, V, iv, 48.

6. For more on this by two leading medievalists, see J. Huizinga, *The Waning of the Middle Ages* (1956), 197, and C. H. Haskins, *Studies in Medieval Culture* (Oxford, 1929), 104.

7. R. W. Kaeuper, *Chivalry and Violence in Medieval Europe* (Oxford, 1999), 165.

8. Sir Michael Howard, *The Lessons of History* (Oxford, 1991), 167–77.

9. G. Mattingly, 'International Diplomacy and International War', *New Cambridge Modern History* (Cambridge, 1968), III, 150.

10. Charles W. Eliot, ed., *Chronicles and Romance: Froissart, Mallory, Holinshed* (Cambridge, MA, 1905), 27.

11. J. Barnie, *War in Medieval English Society: Social Values in the Hundred Years War, 1337–99* (Ithaca, NY, 1974), 9–10.
12. H. Latimer, *Sermons* (1906), 170–71.
13. T. Esper, 'The Replacement of the Longbow by Firearms in the English Army', *Technology and Culture*, VI (1965), 382–93. M. Creveld, *Technology and War* (New York, 1988), 89. Anthony Wood, *Life and Times* (Oxford, 1891), I, 59. M. Prestwich, *Armies and Warfare in the Middle Ages: The English Experience* (New Haven, CT, 1996), 133.
14. J. A. Agnew, *Place and Politics in Modern Italy* (Chicago, 2002), 45.
15. J. Campbell, *The Anglo-Saxon State* (2000), 10. M. Bloch, *Feudal Society* (2005), II, 154.
16. R. Colls, *The Identity of England* (Oxford, 2002), 10–17. R. R. Davies, *The First English Empire and Identity in the British Isles, 1093–1343* (Oxford, 2000), 191–93. P. Corrigan and D. Sayer, *The Great Arch: English State Formation as a Cultural Revolution* (Oxford, 1985).
17. G. R. Elton, *England under the Tudors* (1955), 21–22.
18. S. Cunningham, *Henry VII* (2007), 54–57. M. Bennett, *Lambert Simnel and the Battle of Stoke* (Stroud, 1987), 90ff.
19. M. Bennett, 'Henry VII and the Northern Rising of 1487', *English Historical Review*, 105 (1990), 34–59.
20. C. J. Gilbert, *Tudor Mercenaries and Auxiliaries, 1485–1547* (Charlottesville, VA, 1980), 34–35.
21. Cunningham, *op. cit.*, 85.
22. The Rebecca, Chartist and Tonypandy Riots were too small to be counted as rebellions. A. Fletcher and D. MacCulloch, *Tudor Rebellions* (Harlow, 2008), 7.
23. T. Jones, 'A Welsh Chronicler in Tudor England', *Welsh History Review*, I (1960), 2.
24. Cunningham, *op. cit.*, 287.
25. Mick Jagger's is the best-selling postcard.
26. N. S. Tjemagel, *Henry VIII and the Lutherans* (St. Louis, MO, 1965), 19. F. A. Mumby, *The Youth of Henry VIII* (Boston, 1913), 127.
27. J. Scarisbrick, *Henry VIII* (1981), 12, 39.
28. *Ibid.*, 156.
29. S. Gunn, 'The French Wars of Henry VIII', in J. Black, ed., *The Origins of War in Early Modern Europe* (Edinburgh, 1987), 28–34.
30. E. W. Ives, *Anne Boleyn* (Oxford, 1986), 238.
31. E. Hall, *The Union of the Two Noble and Illustre Families of Lancaster and York* (1542; 1809 edn), 521.
32. *Ibid.*, 521.
33. R. Turpyn, *The Chronicle of Calais*, ed. J. G. Nichols (Camden Society, 35, 1846), 212.
34. W. and R. Chambers, *Chambers' Edinburgh Journal* (Edinburgh, 1846), VI, 165.
35. M. C. Fissel, *English Warfare, 1511–1642* (2001), 20.
36. G. R. Elton, 'War and the English in the Reign of Henry VIII', in L. Freidman et al., eds, *War Strategy in International Politics* (Oxford, 1992), 16. R. Lomis, 'The Impact of the Border Wars: The Scots and South Tweedside, c. 1290–c.1520', *Scottish Historical Review*, 75 (1996), 167.
37. J. White, *The Death of a king; being extracts from private accounts of . . . Flodden* (Edinburgh, 1970), np. N. Barr, *Flodden, 1513: The Scottish Invasion of Henry VIII's England* (Stroud, 2001), 79–95.
38. G. G. Langsam, *Martial Books and Tudor Verse* (New York, 1951), 120. G. Phillips, *The Anglo-Scots Wars, 1513–1550: A Military History* (Woodbridge, 1999), 258. R. W. Hoyle, 'Letters of the Cliffords' (Camden Society, 4th series, 44, 1992), 23–26.
39. Fletcher and MacCulloch, *op. cit.*, 33–35.
40. J. Edwards, 'The Escalation of Violence in Sixteenth-Century Ireland', in D. Edwards, P. Lenihan and C. Tait, *The Age of Atrocity: Violence and Political Conflict in Early Modern Ireland* (Dublin, 2007), 34–79.
41. This is the theme of L. B. Smith, *Henry VIII: The Mask of Royalty* (1971).

42. Ellis Gruffudd, 'Boulogne and Calais from 1545 to 1550', *Bulletin of the Faculty of Arts, Fauad University*, XII (1950), 13.
43. Quoted by J. R. Hale, *War and Society in Renaissance Europe, 1450–1620* (New York, 1985), 68.
44. Gruffudd, *op. cit.*, 71. J. Gairdner and R. H. Brodie, eds, *Letters and Papers, Foreign and Domestic, Henry VIII* (1901), XIX, part 2, 486.
45. P. Cornish, 'The English Soldier of 1544', *Military History Illustrated*, 46 (March 1992), 33.
46. G. Parker, 'The Dreadnought Revolution of Tudor England', *Mariner's Mirror*, 82, 3 (1996), 270.
47. C. M. Cipolla, *Guns and Sails in the Early Phase of European Expansion* (1965), 40. T. Dupuy, *The Evolution of Weapons and Warfare* (Fairfax, VA, 1984), 118. N. Rodger, *Safeguard of the Sea: A Naval History of Britain, 660–1649* (New York, 1997), 221. P. E. Hammer, *Elizabeth's Wars: War, Government and Society in Tudor England, 1544–1604* (2003), 79.
48. G. Parker, *Warfare* (Cambridge, 1995), 124.
49. J. Glete, *Navies and Nations: Warships, Navies, and Ship Building in Europe and America, 1500–1860* (Stockholm, 1993), I, 130–31.
50. Rodger, *op. cit.*, 221.
51. G. Modelski and W. R. Thompson, *Sea Power in Global Politics, 1494–1993* (Seattle, WA, 1988), 5.6–5.9. D. Starkey, *Henry VIII: A European Court in England* (1991), 8. J. R. Hale, 'Tudor Fortifications, 1485–1558', in J. R. Hale, *Renaissance War Studies* (1983), 63–98.
52. C. N. Robinson and John Leyland, *The British Tar in Fact and Fiction: The Poetry, Pathos, and Humour of the Sailor's Life* (New York, 1909), 54.
53. M. Rule, *The Mary Rose: The Excavation and Raising of Henry VIII's Flagship* (Annapolis, MD, 1982).
54. C. Cruickshank, *Army Royal: Henry VIII's Invasion of France, 1513* (1969), 206.
55. G. R. Elton, 'Taxation for War and Peace in Early Tudor England', in J. M. Winter, ed., *War and Economic Development* (Cambridge, 1975), 33.
56. L. Stone, *The Crisis of the Aristocracy* (1965), 266. Gilbert, *op. cit.*, 45–47. G. J. Millar, 'Mercenaries under Henry VIII, 1544–46', *History Today*, 27 (1977), 182.
57. Hammer, *op. cit.*, 26.
58. Attempts to rehabilitate Mary, such as D. M. Loades, *Mary Tudor: The Tragic History of the First Queen of England* (Kew, 2006), Anna Whitelock, *Mary Tudor* (2009), Linda Porter, *Mary Tudor* (2007), J. Richards, *Mary Tudor* (2009) and Christopher Duffy, *The Stripping of the Altars* (1992), are not convincing, at least as far as her military policies are concerned.
59. J. Loach, *Edward VI* (2002), 155.
60. *Calendar of State Papers, Scotland, 1547–1603*, 169.
61. Fletcher and MacCulloch, *op. cit.*, 54–65.
62. *Ibid.*, 70–75.
63. Richards, *op. cit.*, 213–14. H. F. M. Prescott, *Mary Tudor* (1953), 361–62.
64. Richards, *op. cit.*, 221.
65. J. G. Nichols, ed., *The Diary of Henry Machyn* (Camden Society, 1848), 162–63. C. W. Colby, *Selections from the Sources of English History* (1899), 154. J. Foxe, *Foxe's Book of Martyrs* (2007), 366.

Chapter 2 Give Me Spirit: Joining and Training

1. Sample taken from *The Norton Anthology of English Literature* (1990). A search of 'war' using the electronic database *English Poetry* produces 15,472 hits.
2. R. Trevelyan, *Sir Walter Raleigh* (2002), 11–12. My thanks to my friend and colleague M. Thomas Hester for the information on Donne.

3. B. Donagan, 'Halcyon Days and the Literature of War: England's Military Education before 1642', *Past and Present*, 147 (1995), 75. H. J. Webb, 'The Elizabethan Soldier: A Study of the Ideal and the Real', *Western Humanities Review*, 4 (1949–50), 72.

4. D. McNeil, *Grotesque Depictions of War and the Military in Eighteenth-Century English Fiction* (Newark, DL, 1990), 120. *Boswell's Life of Samuel Johnson*, ed. Anne and Irvin Ehrenpreis (New York, 1966), 307.

5. B. Rich, *A Pathwaie to Military Practice* (1587), Sig. G3. T. Barnes, *Vox Belli, or an Alarum to Warre* (1626), quoted by J. R. Hale, 'An Incitement to Violence? English Divines on the Theme of War, 1578–1631', in J. G. Rowe and W. H. Stockdale, *Florilegium Historiale: Essays Presented to Wallace K. Ferguson* (Toronto, 1971), 379.

6. D. George, *All in a Maze: A Collection of Prose and Verse Chronologically Arranged* (1938), 145. M. Bishop, *Life and Adventures of Matthew Bishop* (1744), 3.

7. The Roman military thinker Flavius Vegetius Renatus first made the point in 378CE. C. W. Freeman, *The Diplomats Dictionary* (Washington, DC, 1994), 397. P. G. Johnson, *George Gascoigne* (New York, 1972), 89.

8. Geoffrey Gates, *Defence of the Militarie Profession* (1579), 43. George Monck, Duke of Albermarle, *Observations on political and military affairs* (1671). R. B. Manning, *An Apprenticeship in Arms: The Origins of the British Army, 1585–1702* (Oxford, 2006), 119.

9. Geoffrey Gates, *The Defence of the Military Profession* (1579), 43.

10. Heywood's play was first produced in about 1600.

11. Sir James Turner, *Memoirs of his Life and Times, 1630–72* (Edinburgh, 1829), 3. S. Usherwood, 'Sir Peter Carew, 1514–1575', *History Today*, 28 (1974), 499. J. R. Hale, 'War and Society, 1300–1600', *Past and Present* (July 1982), 140. G. G. Langsam, *Martial Books and Tudor Verse* (New York, 1951), 85. John Adair, *By the Sword Divided: Eyewitness Accounts of the English Civil War* (1983), 74–84.

12. P. Young, *The Civil War: Richard Atkyns* (1967), 3.

13. Keith Thomas, *Religion and the Decline of Magic* (1973), 313. John Hodgson, *Autobiography* (1883), 21. A. J. Fletcher, *A County Community in Peace and War: Sussex, 1600–1660* (1975), 286.

14. G. H. Tupling, 'The Causes of the Civil War in Lancashire', *Lancashire and Cheshire Antiquarian Society Transactions*, 65 (1955), 1. William Maxwell, *One of King William's men: being leaves from the Diary of Colonel William Maxwell, 1685–1697*, ed. H. M. B. Reid (Edinburgh, 1898), 186.

15. J. Blackadder, *The Life and Diary of Colonel John Blackadder of the Cameronian Regiment* (1824), 173.

16. *The Works of Sir Richard Steele* (Dublin, 1759), 53.

17. D. Defoe, *The History of Colonel Jack* (Oxford, 1927), I, 124–25.

18. R. Williams, *The Actions in the Low Countries* (1618), xxxix. J. W. Stoye, 'Soldiers and Civilians', *New Cambridge Modern History* (1970), VI, 767.

19. J. W. Hayes, 'The Military Papers of Colonel Samuel Bagshawe, 1713–1762', *Bulletin of the John Rylands Library*, 39 (1957), 371n.

20. J. Smythe, *Certain Discourses Militarie* (Washington, DC, 1964), xv. C. T. Prouty, *George Gascoigne* (New York, 1947), 9, 51–71. Johnson, *op. cit.*, 16, 87–93.

21. 'George Goring', *Dictionary of National Biography* (1885–1900). P. Gordon, *Passages from the Journal of General Patrick Gordon*, ed. J. Robertson (Aberdeen, 1859), 5. S. Swartley, *The Life and Poetry of John Cutts* (Philadelphia, PA, 1917), xii.

22. S. Noyes. 'The Letters of Samuel Noyes, Chaplain of the Royal Scots, 1703–04', ed. S. H. F. Johnston, *Journal of the Society for Army Historical Research*, 37 (1959), 23–40, 67–71, 128–36, 145–52.

23. www.contemplator.com/england/far away.html has a recording of this song.

24. S. Poyntz, *The Relation of Sydenham Poyntz, 1624–36* (Camden Society, 1908), 9, 45, 125. D. Defoe, *The Military Memoirs of Captain George Carleton* (1929), 13.

25. J. Bernardi, *A Short History of the Life of Major John Bernardi* (1729), 3. S. Gledhill, *Memoirs of Lt. Colonel Samuel Gledhill* (Kendal, 1910), 3. D. Riggs, *Ben Jonson: A Life* (Cambridge, 1989), 18. R. Miles, *Ben Jonson: His Life and Work* (1986), 20–21.

26. J. Childs, 'War, Crime, and the English Army in the Late 17th Century', *War and Society*, 15/2 (October 1997), 1–19.

27. Hale, *op. cit.*, 26.

28. John Stowe, *The Annals of England* (1605), 1,281–82. W. McCaffry, *Elizabeth I: War and Politics, 1588–1603* (Princeton, NJ, 1992), 47.

29. R. B. Manning, 'Violence and Social Conduct in Mid-Tudor Rebellions', *Journal of British Studies*, 16 (1977), 37. B. Rich, *Alarme to England* (1578), 6–7r.

30. 2 March 1625, Cromwell to Carleton, National Archives: SP 84/126/3.

31. J. Stucley, *Sir Bevil Grenville and his Times* (Chichester, 1983), 25. William Beaumont, *A discourse of the war in Lancashire* (Chetham Society, 1864), 19–20.

32. C. Holmes, *Seventeenth-Century Lincolnshire* (1983), 137.

33. H. Foster, *A true and exact relation of the marching … for the relief of the City of Gloucester*, reprinted by John Washburn, *Bibliotheca Gloucestrensis* (Gloucester, 1822), I, 253.

34. C. H. Firth, 'Ballad History of the Reigns of James I and Charles I', *Transactions of the Royal Historical Society*, 3rd Series, 5 & 6 (1911–12), 20.

35. In the seventeenth century a sergeant major was not a senior non-commissioned officer but of field or general rank. 1 May 1627, Blundell to Buckingham, *Calendar of State Papers, Domestic, 1627–28*, 1.

36. D. Johnson and D. G. Vaisey, *Staffordshire in the Great Rebellion* (Stafford, 1964), 52. 28 May 1640, Conway to Countess of Devonshire, in M. H. Nicolson, ed., *The Conway Letters: The Correspondence of Anne, Viscount Conway, Henry Moor and their Friends, 1642–84* (Oxford, 1992), 18.

37. Bishop, *op. cit.*, 45. L. Von Ranke, *History of England principally in the Seventeenth Century* (Oxford, 1875), VI, 131.

38. R. Barret, *The Theorike and Practice of Modern Warres* (1598), 7. Smythe, *op. cit.*, xxxviii. R. Williams, *Works* (1972), lix.

39. E. Sanger, *Englishmen at War: A Social History in Letters, 1450–1900* (Stroud, 1993), 109.

40. J. Campbell, 'A Scottish Fusillier and Dragoon under Marlborough: Lt. General the Honourable Sir John Campbell', *Journal of the Society for Army Historical Research*, 15 (1936), 83.

41. D. Chandler, 'The Great-Captain General, 1702–1714', in *The Oxford History of the British Army* (Oxford, 1994), 75.

42. G. Farquhar, *The Recruiting Officer* (Boston, 1822), 11.

43. R. Scouller, 'Recruiting: A Familiar Problem', *Army Quarterly*, 71 (1955), 109. R. Scouller, *The Armies of Queen Anne* (Oxford, 1967), 291. N. Williams, *Redcoats and Courtesans: The Birth of the British Army, 1660–1690* (1994), 112. Blackadder, *op. cit.*, 236.

44. M. Blumeson, *The Patton Papers, 1940–1945* (Boston, 1974), 428.

45. In the twentieth century, Western soldiers have shown surprisingly little reluctance to kill, and little guilt afterwards. See J. Bourke, *An Intimate History of Killing: Face to Face Killing in Twentieth-Century Warfare* (1999), 248, and Glenn Grey, *The Warriors* (New York, 1970), 181–83.

46. John Rushworth, *Historical Collections* (London, 1680–1701), V, 43. British Library: Harleian MSS, 2,135, 72.

47. Robert Ram, *The Soldier's Catechism: composed for the Parliamentary Army* (7th edition, 1645), 1–2.

48. Quoted by Hale, *op. cit.*, 44.

49. Field Marshal Montgomery made exactly the same point when he addressed his troops before D-Day; Alun Chalfont, *Montgomery of Alamein* (1975), 228.

50. Thomas Audley, 'A Treatise on the Art of War', *Journal of the Society for Army Historical Research*, 7 (1927), 69.
51. D. Lupton, *A Warre-like Treatise of the Pike* (1642), 87.
52. R. Williams, 'A Brief Discourse on War', in idem, *Works* (1590), 14. William Barriffe, *Military Discipline for the Cavalry* (1639), 1. Richard Elton, *Compleat Body of the art military* (1650). Edward Cooke, *The Character of Warre* (1626), C3. John Raynsford, *The Yong Soldier* (1642).
53. Monck, *op. cit.*, 23.
54. W. McNeil, 'Keeping in Time Together', *Military History Quarterly*, 100 (1995), 100–9.
55. Elton, *op. cit.*, 2. J. Achesone, *The Military Garden, or instructions for all young soldiers* (Edinburgh, 1629), 1.
56. For a good description of this process, see G. Dyer, *War* (1986), 101–29.
57. Henry Reed, 'Naming of Parts', in Jon Stallworthy, *The Oxford Book of War Poetry* (Oxford, 1988), 254.
58. May 1595, Essex to Cecil, Historical Manuscripts Commission, *Calendar ... Marquis of Salisbury* (1895), IV, 164. R. N. Dore, *The Civil Wars in Cheshire* (Chester, 1966), 65.
59. J. Dryden, *John Dryden Selected Poems*, ed. S. Zwicker and D. Bywaters (2001), 508.
60. C. H. Firth, *Cromwell's Army: A History of the English Soldier during the Civil Wars, Commonwealth and Protectorate* (1962), 9. Thomas Bellingham, *Diary of Thomas Bellingham, an Officer under William III* (Preston, 1908), 136. 36.
61. R. Lawrence, *The Complete Soldier: Military Books and Military Culture in Early Stuart England, 1603–1645* (Leiden, 2009), 57. Audley, *op. cit.*, 74.
62. M. J. D. Cockle, *A Bibliography of Military Books* (1900). F. Varley, *Cambridge during the Civil War* (Cambridge, 1935), 125. Derby Museum, *Derby and the Great Civil War: Catalogue of Exhibition, 2–23 October 1971* (1971), item 59.
63. J. Childs, *The Nine Years' War and the British Army* (Manchester, 1991), 75, 79.
64. *Calendar of State Papers, Ireland, 1592–96*, 322.
65. S. Gunn, 'Tournaments and Early Tudor Chivalry', *History Today* (June 1991), 15–21. H. Watanabe-O'Kelly, 'Tournaments and their Relevance to Warfare in the Early Modern Period', *European History Quarterly*, 204 (1990), 451–63.
66. J. R. Hale, *The Civilization of Europe in the Renaissance* (New York, 1995), 428.
67. *Certain Sermons or Homilies* (1547, reprinted with introduction by R. B. Bond, Toronto, 1981), 162–67.
68. F. Tallet, *War and Society in Early Modern Europe* (1992), 123.
69. J. Scholefield, ed., *The Works of James Pilkington, BD, Lord Bishop of Durham* (Cambridge, 1843), 427. E. G. B. Warburton, ed., *Memoirs of Prince Rupert and the Cavaliers* (1849), III, 386.
70. A. H. Dodd, 'Wales and the Second Bishops' War', *Transactions of the Honourable Society of Cymmrodorion*, XII (1948), 95. Holmes, *op. cit.*, 20–21, 50–51.
71. G. Gascoigne, *George Gascoigne: the Posies* (Cambridge, 1907), 171.
72. Samuel Birch, 'Civil War Diary', Historical Manuscripts Commission, *Portland MSS*, III (1894), 173–80.
73. W. Brocklington, ed., *Monro: His Expedition with the Worthy Scots Regiment called Mac-Keys* (1999), 57.

Chapter 3 This Happy Breed of Men: Elizabethan Warfare, 1558–1603

1. The figure was about 45 per cent in the First World War.
2. G. Parker, *The Cambridge History of Warfare* (Cambridge, 2005), 111.
3. In N. Machiavelli, translated by Peter Whithorne, *Certaine Wayes for the Ordering of Souldiours* (1562).

4. There were similar foul-ups at St Valery in 1592, and at St Martin in 1627.
5. Quoted by H. Morgan, 'British Policies before the British Nation', in B. Bradshaw and J. Morrill, eds, *The British Problem, c.1534–1707: State Formation in the Atlantic Archipelago* (1996). R.H. Dewing, 'An Elizabethan Soldier in Ireland', *Army Quarterly*, 17 (1929), 88.
6. D. J. B. Trim, 'The Foundation Stone of the British Army: The Normandy Campaign of 1562', *Journal of the Society for Army Historical Research*, 77 (1999), 71–89. W. Mac-Caffrey, 'The Newhaven Expedition, 1562–1563', *Historical Journal*, 40, 1 (1997), 1–21.
7. L. Boynton, *The Elizabethan Militia* (1967), 9.
8. J. McGurk, 'The Clergy and the Militia, 1580–1610', *History*, 60 (1975), 198–210.
9. *Ibid.*, 85.
10. R. B. Manning, 'Patterns of Violence in Early Tudor Enclosure Riots', *Albion* (1974), 120–37. P. Clark, 'Popular Protest and Disturbances in Kent', *Economic History Review*, 29 (1976), 365–68. I am grateful to Wayne Lee for his thoughts on this topic.
11. *Henry VI, Part II*, IV, ii, 62–63. S. Greenblatt, 'Murdering Peasants: Status, Genre, and the Representation of Rebellion', *Representations* I, 1 (1983), 1–29.
12. A. Goodman, 'Border Ways and Border Warfare', *History Today*, 38, 9 (1988), 6–9. T. Thornton, 'The Enemy or stranger that shall invade their country: Identity and Community in the English North', in B. Taithe and T. Thornton, *War* (Stroud, 1998), 57–72.
13. A. Fletcher and D. MacCulloch, *Tudor Rebellions* (Harlow, 2008), 102–15.
14. The Essex fracas of 1601 was more an aristocratic riot than a rebellion.
15. L. Stone, *The Crisis of the Aristocracy, 1558–1641* (Oxford, 1965), 755.
16. W. MacCaffrey, 'The Armada in its Context', *Historical Journal*, 32, 3 (1989), 715.
17. J. S. Corbett, 'Papers relating to the Navy during the Spanish War, 1585–87', *Naval Records Society*, 11 (1898), 116.
18. C. A. Fury, *Tides in the Affairs of Men: The Social History of English Seamen, 1580–1603* (Westport, CN, 2002), 154.
19. J. S. Nolan, 'The Muster of 1588', *Albion*, 23 (1991), 387.
20. Thomas Deloney, *Three Ballads of the Spanish Armada* (New York, 1903), 200. G. G. Langsam, *Martial Books and Tudor Verse* (New York, 1951), 134. The wonderful and widely accepted speech in which the queen tells her soldiers, 'I know I have the body of a weak and feeble woman, but I have the heart and stomach of a king, and a king of England too,' is almost certainly a myth. It was first reported in 1623. S. Frye, 'The Myth of Elizabeth at Tilbury', *Sixteenth-Century Journal*, 23/1 (1992), 95–114.
21. T. Hobbes, *The Life of Mr. Thomas Hobbs* (1680), 2. G. Gascoigne, *The Spoil of Antwerpe* (1576), from which the anonymous play *Alarum for London* (1602), which Shakespeare's company performed, is derived. C. T. Prouty, *George Gascoigne* (New York, 1942), 236–37.
22. G. Parker, 'If the Armada had Landed', *History*, 61, 203 (1976), 358–68. A. Somerset, 'If the Armada had Landed', in A. Roberts, *What Might Have Been* (2004), 15–26. N. Younger, 'If the Armada had Landed: A Reappraisal of England's Defences before 1585', *History*, 93, 311 (2008), 328–54, is unconvincing because it does not take into account the fighting capabilities of the Spanish.
23. Deloney, *op. cit.*, 188–89.
24. D. M. Loades, *Elizabeth I* (2003), 253.
25. G. Parker, 'The Dreadnought Revolution of Tudor England', *Mariner's Mirror*, 82, 3 (1996), 269–300.
26. M. Blatcher, 'Chatham Dockyard and a Little-Known Shipwright, Matthew Baker (1530–1613),' *Archaeologia Cantiana*, 107 (1990), 165.
27. J. Glete, *Navies and Nations: Warships, Navies, and Ship Building in Europe and America, 1500–1860* (Stockholm, 1993), I, 132.
28. T. Glasgow, 'The Maturing of Naval Administration, 1556–1564', *Mariner's Mirror*, 56 (1970), 3–23.

NOTES to pp. 43-50

29. N. Rodger, *Safeguard of the Sea: A Naval History of Britain, 660–1649* (New York, 1997), 297. J. R. Hale, *War and Society in Renaissance Europe, 1450–1620* (1985), 60.
30. Quoted by Rodger, *op. cit.*, 302.
31. J. Cummins, *Francis Drake: Lives of a Hero* (1997), v.
32. Rodger, *op. cit.*, 301–10.
33. Boynton, *op. cit.* E. Sanger, *Englishmen at War: A Social History in Letters, 1450–1900* (Stroud), 34.
34. Quoted by S. C. A. Pincus, *Protestantism and Patriotism: Ideologies and the Making of English Foreign Policy, 1650–1688* (Cambridge, 1996), 256.
35. Quoted by M. Howard, *War in European History* (Oxford, 1976), 46.
36. Quoted by J. Keevel, *Medicine and the Navy* (Edinburgh, 1957), I, 80.
37. Anthony Wingfield, *A True coppie of a Discourse written by a gentleman employed in the late Voyage of Spaine and Portingale* (1589), 21–22.
38. J. R. Ruff, *Violence in Early Modern Europe, 1500–1800: New Approaches to European History* (2001), 65. R. B. Wernham, *The Expedition of Sir John Norris and Sir Francis Drake to Spain and Portugal, 1589* (1988), lxix. J. Barrow, *The Life, Voyages, and Exploits of Sir Francis Drake* (1884), 164.
39. In J. R. Hill, ed., *The Oxford Illustrated History of the Royal Navy* (Oxford, 1995), 50.
40. R. B. Wernham, *After the Armada: Elizabethan England and the Struggle for Western Europe, 1588–1595* (Oxford, 1984), 89–99. Rodger, *op. cit.*, 285–86.
41. J. Appleby, 'A Pathway out of Debt: The Privateering Activities of Sir John Hippisley during the War with Spain and France, 1625–30', *American Neptune*, 49, 4 (1989), 251–61. D. Loades, *England's Maritime Empire: Seapower, Commerce, and Policy, 1490–1690* (Harlow, 2000), 127. G. V. Scammell, 'The Sinews of War: Money and Provisioning English Fighting Ships, c. 1550–1650', *Mariner's Mirror*, 73 (1987), 354. Rodger, *op. cit.*, 253, 295–96, 361.
42. T. Churchyard, *The Mirror of Man and the Manners of Men* (1816), np. Prouty, 9, 51–71. R. C. Johnson, *George Gascoigne* (New York, 1972), 16, 87–93. T. Nun, *A Comfort against the Spaniard* (1596).
43. Thomas Morgan, *The Expedition in Holland, 1572–74*, ed. D. Caldecott-Baird (1976), 1.
44. A. Feldman, 'English Playwrights in the Netherlands War', *Notes and Queries*, 197 (1952), 530–33.
45. *Calendar of State Papers, Foreign* (1585–86), no. 154. Johnson, 90.
46. *Calendar of State Papers, Foreign* (1585–86), no. 437.
47. Sanger, *op. cit.*, 17.
48. Sir John Smythe, *Certain Discourses* (1590), 23–24.
49. M. C. Fissel, *English Warfare, 1511–1642* (2001), 154–57.
50. T. Coningsby, 'Journal of the Siege of Rouen', *Camden Miscellany*, I, 4 (1847), 39.
51. John Hooker, 'The Chronicles of Ireland', in Ralph Holinshed, *Holinshed's Chronicles of England, Scotland, and Ireland* (1808), reprinted in Charles Carlton, *Bigotry and Blood* (Chicago, 1977), 8–12.
52. C. Falls, *Elizabeth's Irish Wars* (1950), 9. J. McGurk, *The Elizabethan Conquest of Ireland: The 1590s Crisis* (Manchester, 1997), 11.
53. G. A. Hayes-McCoy, *Irish Battles: A Military History of Ireland* (Belfast, 1989), 146.
54. Tyrone's Rebellion is also known as the Nine Years War. I have not used that designation to avoid confusion with the Nine Years War of 1688–97.
55. W. MacCaffrey, *Elizabeth I: War and Politics* (Princeton, NJ, 1992), 391.
56. Hale, *op. cit.*, 64.
57. C. Hibbert, *Elizabeth I: Genius of the Golden Age* (1991), 236. J. R. Hale, 'Shakespeare and Warfare', in J. F. Andrews, ed., *William Shakespeare and his World, his Work, his Influences* (New York, 1985), I, 92.
58. Smythe, *op. cit.*, 21.

59. C. Brady, 'The Captains' Games: Army and Society in Ireland', in T. Bartlett and K. Jeffries, eds, *A Military History of Ireland* (1996), 158.

60. I. E., 'A Letter from a Souldier of a good place in Ireland', in A. Kinney, *Elizabethan Background: Historical Documents in the Age of Elizabeth* (Hamden, CT, 1975), 351. W. Farmer, 'William Farmer: Chronicler for Ireland from 1594–1613', ed. C. L. Falkiner, *English Historical Review*, 85 (1907), 125. Sean O'Faolain, *The Great O'Neill* (New York, 1942), 380ff. C. E. Maxwell, *Irish History from Contemporary Sources, 1509–1610* (1923), 196.

61. R. Bagwell, *Ireland under the Tudors* (1887), III, 249.

62. *Calendar of State Papers, Ireland* (1893), VI, 195. Hale, *op. cit.*, 114. H. Davis, 'The Military Career of Sir Thomas North', *Huntington Library Quarterly*, XII (1949), 317. Bagwell, *op. cit.*, III, 194–95.

63. *Calendar of State Papers, Ireland* (1903), IX, 417. McGurk, *op. cit.*, 222. McGurk, 'The Nine Years War in Ireland', *Journal of the Society for Army Historical Research*, 273 (1990), 23–24. P. Logan, 'Pestilence in the Irish Wars: The Earlier Phase', *Irish Sword*, 29 (1966), 284.

64. S. Hindle, *The State and Social Change in Early Modern England, 1550–1640* (2001), 54.

65. McGurk, *Elizabethan Conquest*, 30–33, 168–70.

66. N. Canny, *The Elizabethan Conquest of Ireland: A Pattern Established, 1565–1576* (1976), 124.

67. Dewing, *op. cit.*, 399.

68. Bagwell, *op. cit.*, III, 97.

69. P. E. Hammer, *Elizabeth's Wars: War, Government, and Society in Tudor England, 1544–1604* (2003), 109.

70. S. L. Cavanaugh, 'Elizabethan Views of Ireland', in B. Bradshaw, *et al.*, *Representing Ireland: Literature and the Origins of Conflict, 1534–1660* (1993), 122–23.

71. Farmer, *op. cit.*, 103–30. Bagwell, *op. cit.*, III, 41.

72. J. Gillingham, 'The English Invasion of Ireland', in Bradshaw, *op. cit.*, 24–42.

73. John Lynn, *Battle* (2003), makes some interesting points about the role racial hatred played in the Pacific Campaign.

74. Hayes-McCoy, *op. cit.*, 83.

75. Farmer, *op. cit.*, 127.

76. Bagwell, *op. cit.*, II, 244–45.

77. Farmer, *op. cit.*, 106.

78. Dewing, *op. cit.*, 390–92.

79. Hale, *op. cit.*, 184–85.

80. Churchyard, *op. cit.* 99.

81. Bagwell, *op. cit.* III, 40–41.

82. I. Heath, *The Irish Wars, 1485–1603* (1993), 34. D. Edward, 'Beyond Reform: Martial Law in Tudor Ireland', *History Ireland* (1999), 16–21.

83. Cavanaugh, *op. cit.*, 126. C. Brady, 'Spenser's Irish Crisis: Humanism and Experience in the 1590s', *Past and Present*, 111 (1986), 17–23. S. Greenblatt, *Renaissance Self-Fashioning: from Moore to Shakespeare* (Chicago, 1980). Barnaby Rich in 'A looking Glass for her Majesty Wherein to View Ireland', sent to the queen, 10 May 1599, cited McGurk, *op. cit.*, 16.

84. My thanks to Lt-Colonel Anthony Clayton (TAVR) and Lt-Colonel Joseph Caddell (USAF), both intelligence officers, for discussions about the collection of intelligence.

85. J. Sharpe, 'Social Stress and Social Dislocation', in J. Guy, ed., *The Reign of Elizabeth I* (Cambridge, 1997), 192–95.

86. MacCaffrey, *op. cit.*, 13. McGurk, *op. cit.*, 53.

87. D. Trim, *Fighting Jacob's Wars: the Employment of English and Welsh Mercenaries in the European Wars of Religion in France and the Netherlands, 1562–1610*, London, Ph.D. (2002), 340, 515. R. B. Manning, *Swordsmen: the Martial Ethos in the Three Kingdoms* (Oxford, 2003), 52.

88. C. Martin and G. Parker, *The Spanish Armada* (Manchester, 1999), 65.
89. J. S. Nolan estimates that 283,590 English and Welshmen served in the armed forces excluding the trained bands and militia: 'The Militarization of the Elizabethan State', *Journal of Modern History*, 58, 3 (1994), 405–20.
90. In fact no evidence has been found that Shakespeare ever served in the armed forces. S. Schoenbaum, *Shakespeare's Lives* (Oxford, 1991), 331.
91. Rodger, *op. cit*, 317.
92. J. Lingham, *A True Relation of all English Captains and Lieutenants that had been slain in the Low Countries* (1584). Trim, *op. cit.*, 504. H Morgan, '"Never any realm worse governed": Queen Elizabeth and Ireland', *Transactions of the Royal Historical Society*, 6th Series, 14 (2004), 308.
93. Spenser, *Works* (1805), 421.
94. Smythe, *op. cit.*, 24. Nolan, *op. cit.*, 405.
95. Logan, *op. cit.*, 185.
96. G. Henry 'The Emerging Identity of an Irish military group in the Spanish Netherlands', R. V. Commerford, *et al.*, *Religion, Conflict and Coexistence in Ireland* (Dublin, 1990), 38.
97. Rodger, *op. cit.*, 316.
98. 'World War I Casualties', 'World War II casualties', *Wikipedia*. While I recognize that *Wikipedia* must be handled with great caution, I have used these entries because they are extremely well sourced, and frequently updated.
99. Parker, *op. cit.*, 289. McGurk, *op. cit.*, 15. Hammer, *op. cit.*, 79.
100. T. Digges, *England's Defence* (1680), 12–13.
101. F. Tallet, *War and Society in Early Modern Europe* (1992), 168.
102. *Calendar of State Papers, Ireland, 1596–97*, 252.
103. Rodger. *op. cit.*, 340–41.
104. Hammer, *op. cit.*, 208.
105. Nolan, *op. cit.*, 394. Hammer, *op. cit.*, 264.
106. Professor Richard Holmes has astutely observed that by now the concept has become 'fruitless'. R. Holmes, *Battlefield: Decisive Conflicts in History* (Oxford, 2006), 62. Nolan, *op. cit.*, 394. Hammer, *op. cit.*, 264.
107. Somogyi, *op. cit.*, 55.
108. M. Calore, 'Battle Scenes in the Queen's Men's Repertoire', *Notes and Queries*, 50, 4 (2003), 394–99. N. Taunton, *1590s. Drama and Militarism: Portrayal of War in Marlowe, Chapman and Shakespeare's Henry V* (Aldershot, 2001).
109. D. R. Lawrence, *The Complete Soldier: Military Books and Military Culture in Early Stuart England, 1603–1645* (Leiden, 2009), 238. G. Langsam, *Martial Books and Tudor Verse* (New York, 1951), 49.
110. P. Jorgensen, *Shakespeare's Military Works*, (Berkeley, CA, 1959), 2.
111. Somogyi, *op. cit.*, 107.
112. Duff Cooper, *Sergeant Shakespeare* (1949), 46. T. Meron, *Henry's War and Shakespeare's Laws: Perspectives on the Law of War in the Late Middle Ages* (Oxford, 1993), 16.
113. B. Rich, *Riche: His Farewell to Militarie Profession* (1581), 64.
114. Historical Manuscripts Commission, *Buccleuch*, I, 233.
115. J. S. Adamson, 'Chivalry and Political Culture in Caroline England', in K. Sharpe and P. Lake, eds, *Culture and Politics in Stuart England* (1993), 184–85.
116. Second editions have been counted. M. J. D. Cockle, *A Bibliography of Military Books* (1900). D. Cressy, *Literacy and Social Order* (Cambridge, 1980), 162–68.
117. B. Donagan, 'Halcyon days and the literature of war: England's military education before 1642', *Past and Present*, 147 (1995), 80–81.
118. Robert Ward's *Animadversions of Warre* (1639), 10. Smythe, *op. cit.*, xv.
119. Langsam, *op. cit.*, 7.
120. F. Markham, *Five Decades of Epistles of Warre* (1622), 2. R. Barret, *The Theorike and Practice of Modern Warres* (1598), 5, agrees with Markham.

121. *Othello*, I, i, 25–31.
122. His son, Thomas, ignored his father's advice and became a distinguished soldier; Salisbury MSS, IV, 4–5. P. Jorgensen, 'Moral Guidance and Religious Encouragement for the Elizabethan Soldier', *Huntington Library Quarterly*, 13 (1950), 257. Simon Harward, *The Solace for the Souldier and Saylour* (1591), image 25. W. Garrard, *The Arte of Warre* (1591), 43.
123. Thomas Proctor agreed in *Of the Knowledge and Conducte of Warre* (1578). Langsam. *op. cit.*, 5–8.
124. C. N. Robinson and J. Leyland, *The British Tar in Fact and Fiction: The Poetry, Pathos and Humour of the Sailor's Life* (New York, 1909), 51.
125. Corbet, *op. cit.*, 134.
126. Somogyi, *op. cit.*, 16.
127. R. Barret, *op. cit.*, 3. Roger Williams, *The Works* (Oxford, 1972), xcvi.
128. *Henry V*, III, ii, 61–63.
129. P. Tsouris, *Warriors' World: a Quotation Book* (1992), 199.
130. Manning, *op. cit.*.
131. H. Barwick, *A Breef Discourse concerning the Force of all Manual Weapons* (1594), 4.
132. L. Stone, *The Crisis of the Aristocracy* (Oxford, 1965), 266. F. Markham, *Five Decades of Epistles of War* (1622), in E. Bush, ed., *Salute to the Soldier: an Anthology of Quotations, Poems and Prose* (1966), 1. A. Esler, *Aspiring Mind of the Elizabethan Younger Generation* (Durham, NC, 1966).
133. Jorgensen, *op. cit.*, 242.
134. Trim, *op. cit.*, 283. Manning, *op. cit.*, 22.
135. Barwick, *op. cit.*, 5.
136. M. James, *English Politics and the Concept of Honour* (1978), 157. Kinney, *op. cit.*, 281.
137. L. M. Marcus, J. M. Mueller, M. B. Rose, eds, *Elizabeth I: Collected Works* (Chicago, 2002), 283.
138. Jorgensen, *op. cit.*, 145.
139. Williams, *op. cit.*, xxiii.
140. W. Raleigh, *The Works of Sir Walter Raleigh* (Oxford, 1829) VIII, 246.
141. J. Fortescue, *History of the British Army* (1910), I, 157. B. Montgomery, *History of Warfare* (1968), 223. G. R. Elton, *England under the Tudors* (Cambridge, 1965), 358.
142. J. R. Hale, *War and Society in Renaissance Europe, 1450–1620* (1985), 232–36. Hammer, *op. cit.*, 254–57. B. Downing, *The Military Revolution and Policy Change* (1992), 165. Fissel, *op. cit.*, 82–180.
143. Raleigh, *Works* (1962), VIII, 325.

Chapter 4 Why Men Fought

1. T. Churchyard, *A Lamentable and Pitiful description of the woful Warres in Flaunders* (1578), 21.
2. W. Patten, 'The Expedition into Scotland', in A. F. Pollard, *Tudor Tracts* (1903), 113. Quoted by J. Keegan, *The Mask of Command* (1987), 329.
3. Roger Williams, *Works* (Oxford, 1972), 7.
4. J. R. Hale, *Renaissance War Studies* (1983), 402.
5. E. W. Harcourt, *The Harcourt Papers* (Oxford, 1880–1905), I, 116. J. Blackadder, *The Life and Diary of Colonel John Blackadder of the Cameronian Regiment* (1824), 262. Matthew Bishop, *Life and Adventures of Matthew Bishop* (1744), 17, 216. William III is supposed to have said 'every bullet has its billet', *Oxford Dictionary of Quotations* (Oxford, 1959), 570/29, anticipating the proverb about a bullet with your name on it. E. W. Harcourt, *The Harcourt Papers* (Oxford, 1880–1905), I, 116. J. Jamieson, 'Lt. Col. John Blackadder', *Transactions of the Stirling Natural History and Archaeological Society* (1925–26), 60.

6. J. Bruce, ed., *Letters and Papers of the Verney Family* (Camden Society, 1853), 276. J. P. Kenyon. *The Civil Wars of England* (New York, 1988), 47.

7. F. T. R. Edgar, *Sir Ralph Hopton: The King's Man in the West* (1968), 127.

8. Quoted by C. M. Fissel, *English Warfare, 1511–1642* (2001), 121.

9. Quoted by B. Donagan, *War in England, 1642–1649* (2008), 238.

10. John Keegan made those comments at a talk I attended in the spring of 1982 at Pembroke College, Cambridge.

11. K. Kopperman, 'The Cheapest Pay: Alcohol Abuse in the 18th-century British Army', *Journal of Military History*, 60, 3 (1966), 445–70. Richard Holmes, *Acts of War*, 245. J. A. Sharpe, *Crime in the Seventeenth Century: A County Study* (Cambridge, 1983), 131–33. C. B. Herrup, *The Common Peace: Participation and the Criminal Law in Seventeenth-Century England* (Cambridge, 1987), 26.

12. R. Kipling, *Departmental Ditties and Ballads: Barrack Room Ballads* (New York, 1899), 31.

13. D. Riggs, *Ben Jonson: A Life* (Cambridge, 1989), 18. A. Bayley. *The Great Civil War in Dorset* (Taunton, 1910), 286–88.

14. L. James, *Warrior Race: A History of the British at War* (2001), 148. H Southern and N. Nicolas, 'The Life and Times of Matthew Bishop', *Retrospective Review*, 2nd series (1828), 44–46, 53.

15. H. Herbert, 'Captain Henry Herbert's narrative of his Journey through France with his Regiment, 1671–1673', ed. J. Childs, *Camden Miscellany*, 4th Series, XXX (1990), 339.

16. J. Cruso, *Military instructions for the Cavallerie* (1632).

17. Sir James Turner, *Memoirs of his Life and Times, 1630–72* (Edinburgh, 1829), 94.

18. W. Jenkyn, *The Policy of Princes* (1656), 37.

19. R. Marbeck, 'A Brief and True Report of the Honorable Voyage unto Cadiz, 1596', A. F. Kinney, *Elizabethan Background* (Hamden, CT, 1975), 285. C. S. L. Davies, 'England and the French Wars, 1557–59', in R. Titler and J. Loach, eds, *The Mid-Tudor Polity* (1980), 165.

20. G. N. Godwin, *The Civil War in Hampshire* (1904). J. Adair, 'The Court Martial Papers of Sir William Waller's Army, 1644', *Journal of the Society for Army Historical Research*, 44 (1966), 205–26. G. Davies, 'Dundee Court Martial Record, 1651', *Miscellany of the Scottish Historical Society*, III, 2nd series, XIX (1919), 9–66.

21. These figures reflect the practices of civilian courts, where between a quarter to a half of those charged were acquitted, and about a half sentenced to die were actually executed. A. MacFarlane, *Justice and the Mare's Ale* (New York, 1981), 195. J. H. Leslie, 'A General Court Martial in 1708', *Journal of the Society for Army Historical Research*, IV, 18 (1925), 161–65.

22. A. N. Gilbert, 'Military and Civilian Justice in 18th-Century England: An Assessment', *Journal of British Studies*, 19 (1978), 59.

23. Blackadder, *op. cit.*, 316.

24. S. Crane, *The Red Badge of Courage* (2004), 27. Holmes, *op. cit.*, 58. Gwynne Dyer, *War* (1986), 120–25.

25. Karl von Clausewitz, *On War* (Harmondsworth, 1987), 139. James Touchet, earl of Castlehaven, *Memoirs* (Waterford, 1680), 130–36. *A Myrrour for English Soldiers: or an Anatomy of an Accomplished Man at Armes* (1595), np.

26. J. Keegan, *War and Our World: The Reith Lectures* (1998). Estimate made by David Van Fleet and Gary Yukl. My thanks to Stanley Carpenter of the Naval War College for this information.

27. J. Keegan, 'Towards a Theory of Combat Motivation', in P. Addison and A. Calder, eds, *Time to Kill* (1997), 3–10. C. M. Moran, *The Anatomy of Courage* (1945), 183. Robert Boyle, Earl of Orrery, *Treatise on the Art of War* (1677), 12.

28. A. Kellett, *Combat Motivation: The Behaviour of Soldiers in Battle* (Boston, 1982), 152–53.

29. Williams, *op. cit.*, xl. H. J. Webb, *Elizabethan Military Science: The Books and Practice* (Madison, WI, 1965), 36.

30. Humphrey Bland, *A Treatise of Military Discipline* (1727), 144. Bland also agreed that with good officers, soldiers 'seldom or never fail in Success'.

31. A. K. Millett, 'American Military History: Clio and Mars as "Pards"', in D. A. Charters, M. Miner, J. B. Wilson, *Military History across the Military Profession* (Westpoint, CT, 1992), 58.

32. Miss Porter, *Aphorisms of Sir Philip Sydney* (1807), 71. D. Grossman, *On Killing: The Psychological Costs in Learning to Kill in War and Society* (New York, 1995), 85. F. Vere, *The Commentaries of Sir Francis Vere* (Cambridge, 1659), 104.

33. Wellington, Supplementary Dispatches (1872), 176. G. G. Langsam, *Martial Books and Tudor Verse* (New York, 1951), 68–69. Touchet, *op. cit.* (1680).

34. B. Whitelocke, *Memorials of the English Affairs* (Oxford, 1853), I, 190–91.

35. He used the same rhetorical device with the regiments at Andover on 12 May 1649: W. C. Abbott, *The Writings and Speeches of Oliver Cromwell* (Cambridge, MA, 1937), I, 608, II, 68.

36. 6 May 1705, W. Coxe, *Memoirs of the Duke of Marlborough* (1905), I, 297.

37. D. Defoe, *The Military Memoirs of Captain George Carleton* (1929), 37. S. Baxter, *William III* (1966), 265. Historical Manuscripts Commission, *Leyborne-Popham MSS*, 273.

38. S. Noyes. 'The Letters of Samuel Noyes, Chaplain of the Royal Scots, 1703–04', ed. S. H. F. Johnston, *Journal of the Society for Army Historical Research*, 37 (1959), 131. E. G. Arni, *Hospital Care and the British Standing Army, 1660–1714* (Aldershot, 2006), 71, 80, 127.

39. E. Gruffudd, 'Suffolk's Expedition to Montdidier', *Bulletin of the Faculty of Arts, Fouad University*, 7 (1944), 60.

40. Herbert, *op. cit.*, 335.

41. R. Holmes, *Redcoat: The British Soldier in the Age of Horse and Musket* (2001), 393.

42. G. Gates, *The Defence of the Militarie Profession* (1579), 1. R. Williams, *A Brief Discourse of War* (1590), 10–12. H. J. Webb, 'The Elizabethan Soldier: A Study of the Ideal and the Real', *Western Humanities Review*, 4 (1949–50), 71.

43. 1 September 1643, T. Carlyle, ed., *Oliver Cromwell's Letters and Speeches* (1888), I, 147.

44. Langsam, *op. cit.*, 160. J. Acheson, *The Military Garden, or instructions for all young soldiers* (Edinburgh, 1629), 1.

45. A. Woolwych, 'The Cromwellian Protectorate: A Military Dictatorship?' *History*, 75 (1990), 207–31, disagrees.

46. Edward Ward, *Mars Stript of his Armour, or the Army Displayed in all its True Colour* (1709), quoted by E. Bush, ed., *Salute to the Soldier: An Anthology of Quotations, Poems, and Prose* (1966), 12.

47. Cruso, *op. cit.*, 2–12. Sir John Smythe, *Certain Discourses Military* (1590), quoted by Webb, *op. cit.*, 27–28.

48. W. Beamont, *A Discourse of the War in Lancashire* (Chetham Society, 1864), 82.

49. J. Bampfield, *Apologia* (The Hague, 1685), 4.

50. J. G. Marston, 'Gentry Honour and Royalism in Early Stuart England', *Journal of British Studies*, XIII (1973–74), 21–43.

51. Francis Markham, *The Booke of Honour* (1625), 14–19. Sir Edward Cecil, Earl of Wimbledon, 'The Duty of a Private Soldier', quoted by R. B. Manning, *Swordsmen: The Martial Ethos in the Three Kingdoms* (Oxford, 2003), 57.

52. *Othello*, III, iii, 182–85.

53. 'Mainy' may be a corruption of 'main', meaning a host. E. Arber, *The Surrey and Wyatt Anthology, 1509–47* (2009), 170.

54. *A True Copy of a Speech made by an English Colonel to his Regiment immediately before their Transportation for Flanders from Harwich* (1691), 1.

55. G. Nugent, *Some memorials of John Hampden, his party and his time* (1832), I, 308.
    J. R. Phillips, *Memoirs of the civil war in Wales and the Marches, 1642–49* (1874), I, 199.
    William Shakespeare, *Henry VI, Part II*, IV, i, 134.
56. E. Foyster, *Masculinity in Early Modern England* (1999), 147.
57. Evidence of John Thomas at Charles's trial, *Cobbett's Complete Collection of State Trials*
    (1809), IV, 1,106.
58. M. James, *English Politics and the Concept of Honour* (1978), 4–12, 73.
59. F. Bacon, *The Essays of Lord Bacon* (1889), 96.
60. F. Beaumont and J. Fletcher's *The Knight of the Burning Pestle*, V, ii, 61–62.
61. II Samuel 10:12. Quoted by B. T. Whitehead, *Brags and Boasts: Propaganda in the Year
    of the Armada* (Stroud, 1994), 91.
62. J. Hattendorf, *British Naval Documents, 1204–1906* (Naval Record Society, 131,
    1993), 290.
63. *An Exact and perfect relation of every particular of the fight at Worcester* (1651), 2.
64. P. Gordon, *Passages from the Journal of General Patrick Gordon*, ed. J. Robertson (1859), 51.
65. M. Weidhorn, *Richard Lovelace* (New York, 1970), 107–60.
66. J. Bampfield, *Apologia* (The Hague, 1685), 4.
67. Foyster, *op. cit.*, 7. V. Snow, *Essex the Rebel* (Lincoln, NB, 1970), 343.
68. L. Hutchinson, *Memoirs of the Life of Colonel John Hutchinson* (1906), I, 30. P.
    Massinger, *A new way to pay old debts* (1633), I, ii, 128–31.
69. George Monck, duke of Albermarle, *Observations on political and military affairs*
    (1671), 2.
70. *Henry IV, Part II*, II, iii, 7–12. A. P. Wavell, *Other Men's Posies: An Anthology of Poetry*
    (1985), 422. Wavell must surely be the only field marshal to edit such an anthology.
71. Edward Chisenhale, *A Brief Journal of the Siege of Latham Hall, 1644* (1823), 9.
72. S. Murdock, 'John Brown: A Black Female Soldier in the Royal Africa Company',
    World History Connected: The Online Journal of World History, II (2004), note 7: I am
    grateful to Dr Murdock for bringing this site to my attention.
73. British Library: Harleian MSS, 164, 233.
74. A. Fraser, *The Weaker Vessel* (1985), 221. Anne Lawrence, 'Women's Work and the
    English Civil War', *History Today*, 42/6 (1992), 21.
75. Murdock, *op. cit.*, 2.
76. In the *Dictionary of National Biography* (1885–1900) she is listed under Christian
    Davies. E. Sanger, *Englishmen at War: A Social History in Letters, 1450–1900* (Stroud,
    1993), 109. T. McGuffie, *Rank and File: The Common Soldier in Peace and War, 1642–
    1914* (1964), 4.
77. S. D. Safford, *Quaint Epitaphs* (1902), 53. C. J. M. Martin, 'Ancrum Moor: a Day of
    Reckoning', *Scots Magazine*, 83 (May 1965), 149.
78. D. Dugaw, 'Ballad's Female Warriors: Women, Warfare and Disguise in the Eighteenth
    Century', *Eighteenth Century*, IX (1985), 2.
79. Richard Baxter, *Reliquiae Baxterianae* (1696), 53.
80. Johnston, *op. cit.*, 37.
81. G. F. Nuttal, *Richard Baxter* (1965), 38–39.
82. 'Butty' comes from coal mining, and is a phrase used by Welsh soldiers. While the
    Oxford English Dictionary says it comes from a group of men who work together for a
    set sum ('buddy' has the same etymology), in the Welch Regiment soldiers told me the
    term came from working to fill the same butt, or small rail car with coal.
83. See Introduction.
84. S. L. A. Marshall, *Men against Fire* (New York, 1947), 42. Holmes, *Acts of War*, 293.
    Grossman, *op. cit.*, 152–53. Dyer, *op. cit.*, 140.
85. J. P. Collier, W. C. and C. E. Trevelyan, *Trevelyan Papers* (Camden Society, 1872), I,
    80–84.
86. W. Brocklington, ed., *Monro: His Expedition with the Worthy Scots Regiment Called
    Mac-Keys* (1999), x, 203.

87. John Adair, *By the Sword Divided: Eyewitness Accounts of the English Civil War* (1983), 159. J. Stevens, *The Journal of Captain John Stevens* (Oxford, 1912), 188. M. McManners, *The Scars of War* (1983), 331.
88. Historical Manuscripts Commission, *Heathcote Manuscripts* (1899), 44.
89. 'Neptune's Raging Fury', in C. H. Firth, *Naval Songs and Ballads* (1908), 46.

Chapter 5 Those Were Golden Days: Early Stuart Warfare, 1603–1639

1. Lou Potter, *Secret Rites and Secret Writing: Royalist Literature, 1641–1660* (Cambridge, 1991), 26.
2. This section is based on C. Carlton, *Charles I: The Personal Monarch* (orig. 1983, 2rd edn, 1995). Since the first publication of my book, several new studies have appeared, including fine biographies by J. Reeve, *Charles I and the Road to Personal Rule* (2003), M. Young, *Charles I* (1997), Richard Cust, *Charles I: A Political Biography* (2007), and K. Sharpe, *The Personal Rule of Charles I* (1996). More recently, M. Kishlansky has tried to restore the king's reputation in 'Charles I: A Case of Mistaken Identity', *Past and Present*, 189 (2005), 41–81. The debate on his article, *ibid.*, 205 (2009), 212–37, suggests that Professor Kishlansky's interpretation has not been universally accepted, and that the latest scholarship may not necessarily be the most convincing.
3. F. Bamford, *A Royalist's Notebook: The Commonplace Book of Sir John Oglander* (1936), 193.
4. D. H. Willson, *James VI and I* (New York, 1967), 102. James VI and I, *Works* (New York, 1971), 165–66. *Henry V*, V, Chorus, 48. S. Murdoch, *Scotland and the Thirty Years War* (Leiden, 2001), 5–18. My thanks to Steve Murdoch for bringing these points to my attention.
5. Raymond Gillespie, 'An Army sent by God: Scots at War in Ireland, 1642–49', in N. MacDougall, *Scotland and War* (Savage, MD, 1991), 114.
6. N.A.M. Rodger, *Safeguard of the Sea: A Naval History of Britain, 660–1649* (New York, 1997), 376.
7. S. R. Gardiner, *History of England, 1603–42* (1883–84), I, 341.
8. Rodger, *op. cit.*, 366.
9. T. Digges, *Four Paradoxes* (1604), 107.
10. R. Lockyer, *Buckingham* (1981), 251.
11. N. de Somogyi, *Shakespeare's Theatre of War* (Aldershot, 1998), 124.
12. B. Rich, *The Fruites of Long Experience* (1604), dedication.
13. F. Bacon, *The Major Works* (Oxford, 2002), 402. F. Drake, *Works* (1829), III, 519–20.
14. J. Corbet, *A True and impartial History of the Millitarie Government of the Citie of Gloucester* (1647), 11. For a discussion of James's sexuality, see Carlton, *op. cit.*, 18–19.
15. Charles was married by proxy on 1 May, his wedding night being 13 June. Carlton, *op. cit.*, 29, 63.
16. *Ibid.*, 41–45.
17. T. Cogswell, 'Foreign Policy and Parliament: The Case of La Rochelle, 1625–27', *English Historical Review*, 99, 391 (April 1984), 241–67.
18. 13 October 1627, Charles to Holland, *Calendar of State Papers, Domestic, 1627–28*, 385.
19. 13 July 1625, Pesaro to Doge, *Calendar of State Papers, Venetian, 1625–26*, 245.
20. J. Nichols, ed., *The Progresses, processions and magnificent festivities of King James the First* (1828), 971.
21. 2 March 1625, Cromwell to Carleton, National Archives: State Papers 84/126/3.
22. Anthony Weldon, *The Court of King Charles* (1811), II, 27.
23. John Glanville, *The Voyage to Cadiz*, ed. Alexander Grant (Camden Society, 1883), 59–60.
24. 8 November 1625, Wimbledon to Buckingham, National Archives: SP/6/9/30.

25. J. Rous, *The Diary of John Rous* (1856), 1. British Library: Stowe MSS, 176, 268.
26. *A Journal of all the Proceedings of the Duke of Buckingham* (1627). *A Continued Journal of all the Proceedings of the Duke of Buckingham* (1627), and *A true Report of all the Special passages of note lately happened in the Island of Re* (1627).
27. F. Tallet, *War and Society in Early Modern Europe, 1496–1715* (1992), 82.
28. Sir Edward Conway to his father, the Secretary of State, National Archives: State Papers 16/78/71.
29. John Ashburnham, *A narrative . . . Of his attendance on King Charles* (1830), 363.
30. B. Ingram, *Three Sea Journals of Stuart Times* (1936).
31. T. Barnes, *Vox Belli: an Alarum to Warre* (1626), 40. F. Markham, *Five Decades of Epistles of War* (1622), 31. V. Slater, 'The Lord Lieutenancy on the Eve of the Civil Wars: The Impressment of George Plowright', *Historical Journal*, 29, 2 (1980), 284. T. Cogswell, *The Blessed Revolution: English Politics and the Coming of the War, 1621–1624* (Cambridge, 1989).
32. Sir John Oglander, *The Oglander Memoirs* (1888), 37.
33. R. Bean, 'War and the Birth of the Nation State', *Journal of Economic History*, 32 (1973), 214.
34. R. A. Anselment, 'Clarendon and the Caroline Myth of Peace', *Journal of British Studies*, 23, 2 (1984), 37–55. T. Carew, *The Poems of Thomas Carew* (1899), 107.
35. W. Schumaker, 'Vox Polpuli: The Thirty Years Wars in English Pamphlets and Newspapers', Princeton Ph.D. (1975), 248. Barbara Donagan, 'Codes and Conduct in the English Civil War', *Past and Present*, 118 (1988), 68–69.
36. Sydenham Poyntz, *The Relations of Sydenham Poyntz, 1624–36* (Camden Society, 1908), 60.
37. Folger Library MSS, V. A. 436, fol. 26v.
38. Oliver Millar, *Rubens and the Whitehall Ceiling* (1958), 18.
39. P. Bjurstrom, 'Rubens's "St. George and the Dragon"', *Art Quarterly* (Spring, 1955), 27–42.
40. Abraham Cowley, *Poems* (2002), 22.
41. T. Carew, *The Poems and Masque of Thomas Carew*, ed. J. W. Ebsworth (1893), 115.
42. W. D'Avenant, *The Dramatic Works* (1872), 312.
43. G. Hammond, *Fleeting Things: English Poets and Poetry 1616–1660* (1990), 31.
44. Joyce Malcolm, *Caesar's Due: Loyalty and King Charles, 1642–1646* (1983), 234–35.
45. Corbet, *op. cit.*, 11. Thomas Palmer, *Bristol's Military Garden* (1635), quoted by R. B. Manning, *An Apprenticeship in Arms: The Origins of the British Army, 1585–1702* (Oxford, 2006), 141.
46. W. Barriffe, *Military Discipline for the Young Artilleryman* (1643), Chapter 1.
47. A. Clark, 'The Essex Territorial Force, 1625–38', *Essex Review*, 18 (1909), 68.
48. H. Oakes–Jones, 'The Old March of the English Army', *Journal of the Society for Army Historical Research*, 6 (1927), 5–8. M. C. Fissel, 'Tradition and Invention in the Early Stuart Art of War', *Journal of the Society for Army Historical Research*, 65 (1987), 133–47.
49. A. Fletcher, *A Country Community in Peace and War: Sussex, 1600–1660* (1975), 187.
50. G. Markham, 'The Muster Master', ed. C. L. Hamilton, *Camden Miscellany*, 4th series, 14 (1975), 49–75. T. G. Barnes, *Somerset, 1625–1642* (1961), 264.
51. D. P. Carter, 'The Exact Militia in Lancashire, 1625–1649', *Northern History*, 11 (1975), 87–108.
52. L. Boynton, *The Elizabethan Militia* (1967), 269.
53. P. Haythornthwaite, *The English Civil War* (Poole, 1984), 17. J. Roberts, *Great Yarmouth Exercises in a very Complete and martial manner performed by the Artillery Men* (1638), 4.
54. B. Jonson, *Works*, ed. F. Cunningham (1875), VIII, 410.
55. T. S. Scanlon, 'Citizen Soldiers: The Role of the London Trained Bands in the Puritan Revolution', Harvard Ph.D. (1974). Boynton, *op. cit.*, 262.
56. J. R. Hale, *Renaissance War Studies* (1983), 501.

57. P. M. Wilson, *The Thirty Years War: Europe's Tragedy* (Cambridge, MA, 2009), 322. Manning, *op. cit.*, 65, 70–71, estimates that between fifty and eighty-five thousand Britons fought overseas in the Thirty Years War, including twenty-five thousand Scots. In addition, as many as a hundred thousand Scots emigrated.

58. E. A. Beller, 'The Military Expedition of Sir Charles Morgan to Germany, 1627–29', *English Historical Review*, 43 (1928), 530–37. F. Prinzing, *Epidemics Resulting from War* (Oxford, 1916), 1–18.

59. T. A. Devine, *Scotland's Empire, 1600–1815* (2003), 13.

60. V. G. Kiernam, 'Foreign Mercenaries and Absolute Monarchy', *Past and Present*, 11 (1959), 69. G. S. Simpson, *The Scottish Soldier Abroad* (Edinburgh, 1992), ix. W. Brocklington, ed., *Monro: His Expedition with the Worthy Scots Regiment Called Mac-Keys* (1999), xxxviii. K. M. Brown, 'From Scottish Lords to British Officers: State Building, Elite Integration, and the Army in the Seventeenth Century'. N. MacDougall, *Scotland and War* (Savage, MD, 1991), 141, says the Privy Council authorized the levying of 47,110 troops. R. D. Fitzsimon, 'Irish Swordsmen in the Imperial Service in the Thirty Years War', *Irish Sword*, IX (1969), 22–31. J. Ohlmeyer, 'The Wars of Religion, 1603–66', 19–21. E. M. Furgol, 'Scotland Turned Sweden: The Scots Covenanters and the Military Revolution, 1638–1651', 5–6. I am most grateful to Dr Ohlmeyer and to Dr Furgol for sending me a copy of their unpublished papers.

61. A. Grosjean, *An Unofficial Alliance: Scotland and Sweden, 1569–1654* (Lieden, 2004). Murdock, *op. cit.*, 18–21. G. Parker, *Warfare* (Cambridge, 1995), 149. G. Parker, *The Military Revolution: Military Innovation and the Rise of the West, 1500–1800* (Cambridge, 1988), 49.

62. G. Henry, 'Ulster Exiles in Europe, 1605–41', in B. McCurtuart, *Ulster, 1641* (Belfast, 1993), 43. G. Henry, 'The Emerging Identity of Irish Military Groups in the Spanish Netherlands', ed. R. V. Cornford *et al.*, *Conflict and Coexistence in Ireland* (Dublin, 1990), 64. Nicholas Canny, 'What Really Happened in Ireland in 1641', in J. Ohlmeyer, *Ireland from Independence to Occupation* (Cambridge, 1995), 42, argues that from 1603 to 1641 a hundred thousand young men left Ireland. Wilson, *op. cit.*, 322.

63. Sir James Turner, *Memoirs of his Life and Times, 1630–72* (Edinburgh, 1829), 6–7.

64. J. Beveridge, 'The Scottish Expedition in Norway in 1612', *Proceedings of the Antiquarian Society of Scotland*, 6th series, 7 (1932–33), 209–23.

65. D. Hebb, *Piracy and the English Government, 1616–42* (Aldershot, 1994).

66. *Calendar of State Papers, Domestic, 1625–26*, 274, 288. *Calendar of State Papers, Domestic, 1627–28*, 84–85, 151. *Calendar of State Papers, Domestic, 1635–36*, 15. National Archives: SP16/295/44, II.

67. Rodger, *op. cit.*, 382–83. Gardiner, *op. cit.*, IX, 64–69.

68. G. Thorn-Drury, *The Poems of Edmund Waller* (1893), I, 15.

69. W. Lilly, *The Life and Death of Charles I* (1774), 190.

70. C. H. Firth, *Naval Songs and Ballads* (1908), 40.

71. D. Brunton and D. H. Pennington, *Members of the Long Parliament* (1954). M. F. Keeler, *The Long Parliament, 1640–41* (1954).

72. Turner, *op. cit.*, 13–14.

73. D. Stevenson, *The Scottish Revolution, 1637–44* (Newton Abbot, 1973), 131. Edward Hyde, earl of Clarendon, *History of the Rebellion and Civil Wars* (Oxford, 1826), IV, 75–76.

74. *Calendar of State Papers, Domestic, 1640–41*, 212.

Chapter 6 Low-Intensity Combat: Campaigning

1. Millner does not give complete figures for 1702 and 1712. J. Millner, *A Compendious Journal of all the Marches* (1737). W. Churchill, *Marlborough: His Life and Times* (1933), I, 489.

2. Q. Wright, *A Study of War* (Chicago, 1965), 223–24.

3. G. Parker, *The Military Revolution* (Cambridge, 1988), 40.
4. Richard Kane, *Campaigns of King William and Queen Anne from 1689 to 1712* (1745), 291, 302. P. Drake, *Amiable Renegade: The Memoirs of Captain Peter Drake* (Stanford, CA, 1960), 236.
5. R. A. Houston, 'The Military and Edinburgh Society, 1660–1760', *War and Society*, II, 2 (1993), 48.
6. J. Bernardi, *A Short History of the Life of Major John Bernardi* (1729), 28.
7. Sir James Turner, *Memoirs of his Life and Times, 1630–72* (Edinburgh, 1829), 6.
8. Quoted by B. Whelan, 'Women and Warfare, 1641–91', in P. Lenihan, ed., *Conquest and Resistance, War in Seventeenth-Century Ireland* (Lieden, 2001), 331.
9. E. Gruffudd, 'Suffolk's Expedition to Montdidier', *Bulletin of the Faculty of Arts, Fouad University*, 7 (1944), 40–41.
10. A. Kingston, *East Anglia in the Great Civil War* (1897), 147.
11. Turner, *op. cit.*, 22.
12. P. Logan, 'Medical Services in the Armies of the Confederate Wars', *Irish Sword*, IV (1960), 221. Kane, *op. cit.*, 2.
13. J. McGurk, *The Elizabethan Conquest of Ireland: The 1590s Crisis* (Manchester, 1997), 234.
14. S. Noyes, 'The Letters of Samuel Noyes, Chaplain of the Royal Scots, 1703–04', ed. S. H. F. Johnston, *Journal of the Society for Army Historical Research*, 37 (1959), 132.
15. D. Stewart, 'Sickness and Mortality Rates in the English Army until the Twentieth Century,' *Journal of the Royal Army Medical Corps*, 91 (1948), 23–35. R. Harding, *Amphibious Warfare in the Eighteenth Century: The British Expedition to the West Indies, 1740–1742* (Woodbridge, 1991), 3.
16. J. Blackadder, *The Life and Diary of Colonel John Blackadder of the Cameronian Regiment* (1824), 173. M. Bishop, *Life and Adventures of Matthew Bishop* (1744), 119. 15 May 1702, W. Coxe and J. Wade, eds, *Memoirs of the Duke of Marlborough* (1905), 83.
17. *Five Newes Letters* (1678), np.
18. C. N. Robinson and J. Leyland, *The British Tar in Fact and Fiction: The Poetry, Pathos, and Humour of the Sailor's Life* (New York, 1909), 5.
19. E. Sanger, *Englishmen at War: A Social History in Letters, 1450–1900* (Stroud, 1993), 102. The royalist newspaper *Mercurius Aulicus* printed Susan's letter: John Adair, *By the Sword Divided: Eyewitness Accounts of the English Civil War* (London, 1983), 118. For evidence that Rodway most likely died, see C. Carlton, *Going to the Wars: The Experience of the British Civil Wars, 1638–51* (1992), 129, note 120.
20. T. M. Devine, *Scotland's Empire, 1600–1815* (2003), 5.
21. S. R. Gardiner, *History of the Great Civil War* (1987), III, 207. F. P. and M. M. Verney, *Memoirs of the Verney Family during the Civil War and Commonwealth* (1892–99), II, 200.
22. C. Carlton. 'The Widow's Tale: Male Myths and Female Reality in Sixteenth- and Seventeenth-Century England', *Albion*, X, 2 (Summer, 1978), 95–103.
23. Blackadder, *op. cit.*, 173.
24. Two years later he lost eighteen horses crossing the Channel. Historical Manuscripts Commission, *Cowper*, II, 456.
25. E. Gruffudd, 'The Enterprise of Paris and Boulogne', *Bulletin of the Faculty of Arts, Fouad University*, II (1949), 40–41. J. Deane, *A Journal of the Campaign in Flanders* (Camden Society, 1846), 6.
26. T. Raymond, C. and J. Guise, *Autobiography of Thomas Raymond and Memoirs of the Family of Guise* (2007), 43. B. Riche, *Riche: His Farewell to the Militarie Profession* (1581, 1959 edn), 4.
27. In the foreword to William Garrard, *The Art of War* (1591).
28. J. P. Collier, W. C. and C. E. Trevelyan, *Trevelyan Papers: Part II* (Camden Society, 1872–73), I, 180.
29. D. Lupton, *A Warre-like Treatise of the Pike* (1642), quoted by W. Emberton, *Skippon's Brave Boys: The Origins, Development, and Civil War Service of London's Trained*

Bands (Buckingham, 1984), 34. Turner, *op. cit.*, 23. G. Carleton, *The Military Memoirs of Captain George Carleton* (1929), 67.

30. Historical Manuscripts Commission, *Cowper*, III, 26. Blackadder, *op. cit.*, 199, 213, 219, 220, 238, 241, 246, 272, 376.
31. Turner, *op. cit.*, 22.
32. Stewart, *op. cit.*, 40. 'A Royal Dragoon in the Spanish Succession War', *Journal of the Society for Army Historical Research* (1938), 11.
33. Noyes, *op. cit.*, 40.
34. McGurk, *op. cit.*, 225.
35. Quoted by D. Grossman, *On Killing: The Psychological Cost of Learning to Kill in War and Society* (New York, 1995), 67.
36. Blackadder, *op. cit.*, 363.
37. Raymond, *op. cit.*, 42.
38. R. Alexander, 'A Journal of a Soldier in the Earl of Ellington's Troop of Horse', *Glasgow Archaeological Society* (1859–68), 38–50.
39. P. Hardacre, 'The English Contingent in Portugal, 1662–1668', *Journal of the Society for Army Historical Research*, 38 (1960), 112–25.
40. T. Churchyard, 'An Eyewitness Account of the Siege of Guienne', in A. F. Pollard, *Tudor Tracts* (1903), 326. R. Atkyns, *Vindication of Richard Atkyns* (1968), 22.
41. Historical Manuscripts Commission, *Leyborn-Popham MSS*, 273.
42. British Library, Harleian MSS, 986, 6.
43. J. Stevens, *The Journal of Captain John Stevens* (Oxford, 1912), 153.
44. R. Brereton, *The British Soldier: A Social History from 1661 to the Present Day* (1986), 10.
45. R. Coe, *An Exact Diarie* (1644), 4.
46. B. Fergusson, *The Wild Green Earth* (1946), 194. Justin Wintle, *Dictionary of War Quotations* (1969), 52.
47. C. Jones, 'New Military History for Old? War and Society in Early Modern Europe', *European Studies Review*, 13 (1982), 31.
48. H. W. Gillman, 'The Siege of Rathbury Castle, 1642', *Journal of the Cork Historical Society*, I (1895), 12.
49. D. Trim and M. Fissel, eds, *Amphibious Warfare, 1000–1700* (Boston, 2006).
50. Quoted by P. Jorgensen, 'Moral Guidance and Religious Encouragement for the Elizabethan Soldier', *Huntington Library Quarterly*, 13 (1949), 243.
51. Raymond, *op. cit.*, 40. Bishop, *op. cit.*, 162.
52. E. Sanger, *Englishmen at War: A Social History in Letters, 1450–1900* (Stroud, 1993), 17.
53. J. Keegan and J. Durracott, *The Nature of War* (1981), 206.
54. T. Dekker, *The Plague Pamphlets of Thomas Dekker* (1977), 109.
55. *Calendar of State Papers, Ireland, Elizabeth* (1903), IX, xxviii.
56. McGurk, *op. cit.*, 225. H. A. L. Howard, 'Army Surgeons and the Care of Sick and Wounded in the British Campaigns during the Tudor and Stuart Periods', *Journal of the Royal Army Medical Corps*, 2 (1904), 733. C. T. Atkinson, 'Gleanings from the Cathcart MSS', *Journal of the Society for Army Historical Research*, 30 (1952), 97.
57. V. J. Harlow, *Christopher Codrington, 1668–1710* (Oxford, 1928), 144, 171.
58. Quoted by J. R. Hale, *War and Society in Renaissance Europe, 1450–1620* (New York, 1985), 178.
59. Raymond, *op. cit.*, 38.
60. J. Aston, 'The Diary of John Aston', in J. C. Hodgson, *North Country Diaries* (Surtees Society, 118, 1890), 5–7.
61. R. Symonds, *Diary of the Marches of the Royal Army during the Great Civil War* (Camden Society, 1859).
62. C. Croke, *Fortune's Uncertainty, or Youth's Inconstancy* (Oxford, 1959), 55–65.
63. H. Herbert, 'Captain Henry Herbert's Narrative of his Journey through France with his Regiment, 1671–1673', ed. J. Child, *Camden Miscellany*, 4th Series, XXX (1990), 281–82.

64. *A Journal of the Late Motions and Actions of the Confederate Forces . . . by an English Officer who was there* (1690), np.
65. J. Hodgson, *Memoirs* (1883), 37.
66. E. M. Hinton, *Ireland through Tudor Eyes* (Philadelphia, PA, 1935), 65–66.
67. Raymond, *op. cit.*, 39.
68. B. C. Hacker, 'Women and Military Institutions in Early Modern Europe: A Reconnaissance', *Signs: Journal of Women in Culture and Society*, 6 (1980–81), 654.
69. Herbert, *op. cit.*, 321. Noyes, *op. cit.*, 146.
70. *Calendar of State Papers, Scotland, 1547–1603*, 169.
71. W. C. Strickland, 'Irish Soldiers in the Service of Henry VIII', *Journal of the Royal Society of Antiquaries of Ireland* (1923), 94–97. D. G. White, 'Henry VIII's Irish Kern in France and Scotland, 1544–45', *Irish Sword*, 3, 13 (1958), 220.
72. White, *op. cit.*, 220.
73. T. Coningsby, 'Journal of the Siege of Rouen', *Camden Miscellany*, I, 4 (1847), 184. J. Sprigge, *Anglia Rediva* (1854), 80.
74. Carleton, *op. cit.*, 39. Noyes, *op. cit.*, 146.
75. R. Parker, *Memoirs of the Most Remarkable Military Transactions* (1741), 121.
76. P. Young, *Marston Moor* (London, 1970), 6.
77. M. Stoyle, 'Memories of the Maimed: The Testimonies of Charles I's Former Soldiers, 1660–1732', *History*, 88, 290 (2003), 212–13.
78. Historical Association, *English History in Contemporary Poetry* (1970), 29.
79. Richard Gough, *The History of Myddle* (Harmondsworth, 1981), 73–74.
80. 'Memories of Captain John Creighton, from his own material', Jonathan Swift, *Works*, ed. Sir Walter Scott (1824), XI, 159–65.
81. M. C. Fissel, *English Warfare, 1511–1642* (2001), 19. Carleton, *op. cit.* (1809), 21–22.
82. H. Foster, *A True and Exact Relation of the Marchings . . . for the relief of Gloucester* (1643), reprinted in J. Washbourne, *Bibliotheca Gloucestrensis* (Gloucester, 1828), I, 253–71.
83. www.woodenswords.com/WMA/reviews_galicswordmanship.htm.

Chapter 7 All Diseas'd: Civil Wars and Commonwealth: Events, 1638–1660

1. D. McCullough, *John Adams* (2001), 359.
2. A. J. Slavin, *The Precarious Balance* (New York, 1973). John Morrill, 'The Religious Context of the Civil War', *Transactions of the Royal Historical Society*, 5th series, XXXIV (1984), 155–78. M. Kishlansky, 'Saye What?', *Historical Journal*, 38 (1990), 917–37. J. S. A. Adamson, 'Politics and the Nobility in Pre-Civil War England', *Historical Journal*, 39 (1991), 231–55, and *The Noble Revolt: The Overthrow of Charles I* (2007). Historiographical surveys can be found in P. A. M. Taylor, *The Origins of the English Civil War* (Boston, 1960) and R. C. Richardson, *The Debate on the English Revolution* (1967).
3. *The Widowes Lamentation for the Absence of their dear children and suitors and for divers of their deaths in these fatal civil wars* (1643).
4. C. Russell, 'Corporate Monarchies in Early Modern Europe: The British and Irish Examples', in A. Grant and K. Stringer, *Uniting the Kingdom? The Making of British History* (1995), 133.
5. L. Hutchinson. *Memoirs of the Life of Colonel John Hutchinson* (1906), 116.
6. Richard Ward, *Anatomy of Warre* (1642), 1.
7. L. Winstock, *Songs and Music of the Redcoats: A History of War Music of the British Army, 1642–1900* (Harrisburg, PA, 1975), 15. J. Taylor, *Works* (Manchester, 1877), 5.
8. S. Butler, *Hudibras*, ed. T. R. Nash (1835), I, 3.
9. W. A. Day, *Pythouse Papers* (1879), xvii.

10. B. Schofield, ed., *The Knyvett Letters (1620–44)* (1949), 50, 101–3. R. W. Ketton-Cremer, *Norfolk in the Civil War: A Portrait of a Society in Conflict* (Hamden, CT, 1970), 180–89.
11. M. Bennett, *The Civil Wars in Britain and Ireland* (Oxford, 1997), 27.
12. J. O. Halliwell, ed., *Letters of the Kings of England* (1846), II, 290–303.
13. David Stevenson, *The Scottish Revolution, 1637–44* (Newton Abbot, 1973), 140–45. M. C. Fissel, 'Bellum Episcopale: The Bishops' Wars and the End of the Personal Rule in England, 1638–1640', California at Berkeley Ph.D. (1983), 61, 85–87.
14. E. Furgol, 'Beating the Odds: Alexander Lesley's Campaign in England', in S. Murdock and A. MacKillop, *Fighting for Identity: Scottish Military Experience, 1350–1900* (Leiden, 2002), 41.
15. John Aston, 'The Journal of John Aston', in J. C. Hodgson, ed., *North Country Diaries* (Surtees Society, CXVIII, 1890), 5.
16. C. H. Firth, 'The Reign of King Charles I', *Transactions of the Royal Historical Society*, 3rd series, VI (1921), 41.
17. J. L. Malcolm, *Caesar's Due: Loyalty and King Charles, 1642–1646* (1983), 12–13. C. Holmes, *Seventeenth-Century Lincolnshire* (1983), 137. W. Knowles, ed., *The Earl of Strafford's Letters and Dispatches* (1739), II, 371.
18. Edward Hyde, earl of Clarendon, *History of the Rebellion and Civil Wars* (Oxford, 1849), I, 161.
19. Earl of Hardwicke, *Miscellaneous State Papers, 1501–1726* (1778), II, 119.
20. National Archives: SP16/423/29.
21. Historical Manuscripts Commission, *Twelfth Report*, appendix, part IV, 552. Fissel, *op. cit.*, 63. J. Bruce, ed., *Letters and Papers of the Verney Family* (Camden Society, 1853), 228. National Archives: SP16/455/no. 38. *Calendar of State Papers, Domestic, 1640*, 241.
22. Bodleian Library: Rawlinson MSS, B210, 36.
23. O. Ogle, W. H. Bliss and W. D. MacGray, eds, *Calendar of Clarendon State Papers* (Oxford, 1867–76), II, 101.
24. G. Wrottesley, 'The Stafford Muster of AD 1640', *Collections for a History of Staffordshire*, XV (1894), 201–10.
25. M. C. Fissel, *The Bishops' Wars: Charles I's Campaigns against Scotland, 1638–1640* (Cambridge, 1994), 279–85.
26. *Calendar of State Papers, Domestic, 1640*, 477, 523. *Calendar of State Papers, Domestic, 1639*, 59.
27. W. Knowler, *The Earl of Strafford's Letters and Dispatches* (1739), I, 351.
28. 12 December 1641, *Calendar of State Papers, Ireland, 1633–47*, 344, 354.
29. Thomas Fitzpatrick, *The Bloody Bridge and Other Papers Relating to the Insurrections of 1641* (Dublin, 1903, reprinted Port Washington, NY, 1970), 76.
30. A. Macfarlane, *The Justice and the Mare's Ale* (Cambridge, 1981), 191. Fitzpatrick, *op. cit.*, 22, 75–77. *A Bloody Battell, or the Rebell's overthrow* (1641), np.
31. *The Autobiography of the Rev. Devereux Spratt*, ed. T. Spratt (1886), 10. R. Baxter, *Reliquiae Baxterianae* (1696), 40. Hutchinson, *op. cit.*, I, 173. J. Temple, *The Irish Rebellion* (1646), A. Woolrych, *Britain in Revolution, 1625–1660* (Oxford, 2004), 197. R. Clifton, '"An Indiscriminate Blackness?" Massacre, Counter Massacre and Ethnic Cleansing in Ireland, 1640–1660', in M. Levene and P. Roberts, eds, *The Massacre in History* (New York, 2000), 107–25, 160. P. Lenihan, 'War and Population, 1649–52', *Irish Economic and Social History*, 24 (1997), 19.
32. K. Lindley, 'The Impact of the 1641 Rebellion upon England and Wales, 1641–45', *Irish Historical Studies*, XVIII (1972), 143–76. B. Donagan, 'Codes and Conduct in the English Civil War', *Past and Present*, 118 (1988), 71.
33. Malcolm, *op. cit.*, 16, note 40.
34. J. Lister, *Autobiography*, ed. T. White (London, 1842), 6. Baxter, *op. cit.*, 40.
35. M. Walzer, *Just and Unjust Wars* (New York, 1977), 104–5.
36. *The King's Cabinet Opened* (1645), 26.

37. Clarendon, *op. cit.*, I, 589.
38. *The King's Cabinet Opened* (1645), 26–27.
39. Norman Tucker, 'Denbigh's Loyal Governors', *Denbighshire Historical Society Transactions*, V (1956), 12.
40. R. Spaulding, *The Improbable Puritan: A Life of Bulstrode Whitelocke* (1975), 95. W. A. Day, *Pythouse Papers* (1879), xvii.
41. D. Kennedy, 'The Crown and the Common Seamen in Early Stuart England', *Historical Studies*, II (April 1965), 170–77.
42. Clarendon, *op. cit.*, I, 272.
43. Karl von Clausewitz, 'Key Points', in L. Freedman, ed., *War* (Oxford, 1994), 210–12.
44. J. Ohlmeyer, 'Irish Privateering during the Civil War, 1642–50', *Mariner's Mirror* (1990), 130.
45. Figures from P. Young, *Edgehill* (Kineton, 1967), 105.
46. J. S. Clarke, *The Life of James the Second* (1816), I, 12.
47. Clarendon, *op. cit.*, I, 632.
48. Clarke, *op. cit.*, 12.
49. *Parliamentary History*, XII, 38. Clarendon, *op. cit.*, II, 316.
50. The king's order 'If York be lost, I shall esteem my crown a little less' is in *The Letters, speeches and proclamations of King Charles I*, ed. C. Petrie (1935), 144–45. This description of Marston Moor is mainly based on P. Young, *Marston Moor* (Kineton, 1977), A. Woolrych, *Battles of the English Civil War* (1961), 66–80, and W. Seymour, *Battles in Britain* (1979), II, 83–103.
51. Lion Watson, *A more exact relation of the late battell fought neer York* (1644), 6.
52. C. H. Firth, *The Letters and Speeches of Oliver Cromwell* (1904), 1, 176.
53. A. Miller, *Sir Richard Grenville of the Civil War* (1979), 89.
54. 25 February 1645. Charles to Henrietta Maria, *Reliquiae Sacrae Carolinae* (The Hague, 1649), 262–63.
55. P. Young, *Naseby, 1645: The Campaign and the Battle* (1985), 4.
56. Panic caused by confused orders is fairly common in battle. For instance, they caused the Royal Welsh Fusiliers to run at Alma in the Crimea in 1854; R. Holmes, *Acts of War* (New York, 1985), 225.
57. R. E. Maddison, 'The King's Cabinet Opened: A Case Study in Pamphlet History', *Notes and Queries* (1966), 13, 2–9.
58. Clarendon, *op. cit.*, V, 179.
59. W. Coster, 'Massacres and Codes of Conduct in the English Civil War', in M. Levene and P. Roberts, eds, *The Massacre in History* (1999), 92.
60. M. Stoyle, 'The Road to Farndon Field: Explaining the Massacre of Royalist Women at Naseby', *English Historical Review*, 208, 503 (2008), 895–923.
61. E. Drake, 'Civil War Diary', in A. R. Bayley, *The Great Civil War in Dorset* (Taunton, 1910), 188.
62. J. E. Auden, 'The Anglo-Irish troops in Shropshire', *Transactions of the Shropshire Archaeological Society*, 50 (1939–40), 59–60. R. Gough, *History of Myddle* (1981), 75. E. G. B. Warburton, *Memoirs of Prince Rupert and the Cavaliers* (1849), III, 73, 391.
63. J. T. Gilbert, *A Contemporary History of the Affairs of Ireland from 1641 to 1652* (Dublin, 1879–80), IV, vii.
64. R. B. Manning, *Swordsmen: The Martial Ethos in the Three Kingdoms* (Oxford, 2003), 182, 188–89.
65. John Spalding, *Memorials of the Troubles in Scotland* (Aberdeen, 1835), II, 452.
66. D. Stevenson, *Alasdair MacColla and the Highland Problem in the Seventeenth Century* (Edinburgh, 1980), 128–35, 156–57, 188, 218–19.
67. *Ibid.*
68. James M. Hill, *The Celtic Way of Warfare* (Edinburgh, 1980), 1–3, 45–48, 58–59.
69. E. M. Furgol, *A Regimental History of the Covenanting Armies, 1639–1651* (Edinburgh, 1988), 196. P. Gaunt, *A Cromwellian Gazetteer* (1987), 209.

70. Woolrych, *Britain in Revolution*, 230–31.
71. Deposition of Grany ny Mullen of 25/5/53 in M. Dickson, *Ireland in the Seventeenth Century* (1884), I, 152.
72. F. Warner, *The History of the Rebellion in Ireland* (1768), 162.
73. T. Carte, *Life of James, Duke of Ormonde* (1851), II, 186, 277. 4 June 1642, Conway to Crawford, II, 138. Gilbert, *op. cit.*, II, 138.
74. *True Relation of the . . . Relieving of Tredagh* (1642), 1. *A True Relation of Diverse Great Defeats given to the Rebels of Ireland* (1642), 12.
75. C. R. Browning, *Ordinary Men: Reserve Police Battalion 101 and the Final Solution* (1999). Gilbert, *op. cit.*, I, xxxii, 35–39. For another example of similar brutality, see *A Full Relation, not of our Good Successe* (1642).
76. W. Damon, *Welcome Newes From Ireland* (1642).
77. *A Perfect Narrative of the Battle of Knocknones by an officer in the Parliament's army present and Acting at the Fight* (1648), 9–10.
78. Gilbert, *op. cit.*, xxxiv. R. Boyle, earl of Orrery, *A letter from Lord Broghill . . . concerning . . . defeating the Rebels in Ireland* (1651), 5.
79. C. I., *A New Remonstrance from Ireland* (1642), 2, 13. J. Turner, *Memoirs of his life and times, 1630–70* (Edinburgh, 1829), 14–20. Clanricarde made the warning in at least two letters in May 1642 to the Lord Justices, and to Ormonde: T. Carte, *Ormonde Letters* (1739), III, 74, 98.
80. J. Spraggon, *Puritan Iconoclasm during the English Civil War* (Woodbridge, 2003), 250.
81. 10 June 1646, Historical Manuscripts Commission, 4th Report, 522.
82. 10 June 1646, Charles to Henrietta Maria, in J. Bruce, *Charles I in 1646* (Camden Society, 1856), 45.
83. Sir John Berkeley, 'Memoirs', in John Ashburnham, *A narrative . . . Of his attendance on King Charles* (1830), cliv.
84. C. MacKay, *The Cavalier songs and ballads of England from 1642 to 1684* (1863), 2. When the British surrendered at Yorktown in 1781, a band played 'The World turned upside down' using the same tune to which Parker's lyrics had been set. Colonial Williamsburg Foundation, *Jamestown, Williamsburg, Yorktown: The Official Guide* (2007), 78.
85. *Oxford Dictionary of National Biography* (Oxford, 2004–9). A. Kingston, *East Anglia in the Great Civil War* (1897), 264. R. W. Ketton-Cremer, *Norfolk in the Civil War* (1970), 325.
86. Descriptions of the Siege of Colchester from *A Diary or Account of the Siege . . . of Colchester*, in D. Defoe, *A Tour . . . of Great Britain* (1927), 18–31. 'Diary of the Siege of Colchester', in Historical Manuscripts Commission, Twelve Report, appendix part 9, pages 24–29. *Diary of the Siege of Colchester by the Forces under the command of General Fairfax* (1650). Matthew Carter, *A most true and exact relation of the . . . unfortunate expedition of Kent, Essex, and Colchester* (1650), 136–37, 166. D. C. Woodward and C. Cockerill, *The Siege of Colchester, 1648: A History and a Bibliography* (Chelmsford, 1979), 7–21. *The Siege of Colchester, 1648* (Colchester, n.d.), 9–18. B. Donagan, *War in England, 1642–49* (Oxford, 2008), 312–88.
87. B. P. Lyndon, 'Parliament's Army in Essex, 1648', *Journal of the Society for Army Historical Research*, LIX (1981), 152.
88. *The Earl of Norwich, Lord Capel, and Sir Charles Lucas, their peremptory Answer on refusing to surrender Colchester* (1648), 7.
89. T. S., *A True and exact relation of the taking of Colchester sent in a letter from an officer in the Army who was present during the Siege* (1648), 1–2.
90. J. Rushworth, *A letter . . . before Colchester* (1648), 6. *Another Fight at Colchester and the Storming of the Town by the Parliamentary Forces* (1648), 2–3.
91. R. Markham, *A Life of the Great Lord Fairfax* (1870), 327.
92. A. Brady, 'Dying with Honour: Literary Propaganda and the Second English Civil War', *Journal of Military History* 70, 1 (2006), 9–30. G. K. Fortescue, *Catalogue of the*

Pamphlets . . . Collected by George Thomason (1908), I, 168. 20 September 1648, Edmund Verney to Ralph Verney, F. P. and M. Verney, *Memoirs of the Verney Family during the Civil War and Commonwealth* (1892–99), II, 340.

93. W. C. Abbott, *The Writings and Speeches of Oliver Cromwell* (New York, 1937), I, 641. J. Hodgson, Memoirs (Bradford, 1902), 120.

94. Sir James Turner, *Memoirs of His Life and Times* (Edinburgh, 1829), 66–70.

95. 20 August 1648, Cromwell to Lenthall, T. Carlyle, ed., *Oliver Cromwell's Letters and Speeches* (1904), II, 32.

96. I. Roots, *The Speeches of Oliver Cromwell* (1989), 5. Abbott, *op. cit.*, II, 107, 326–27. A. Fraser, *Cromwell: Our Chief of Men* (1973), 5.

97. Abbott, *op. cit.*, II, 120–25. J. G. Simms, 'Cromwell at Drogheda', *Irish Sword*, 11 (1973–74), 217–20. Fraser, *op. cit.*, 332–34. I. Gentles, *The English Revolution and the Wars in the Three Kingdoms, 1638–1652* (2007), 392–7. J. Morrill, 'The Droghda Massacre in Cromwellian Context', in D. Edwards, P. Lenihan and C. Tait, *The Age of Atrocity: Violence and Political Conflict in Early Modern Ireland* (Dublin, 2007), 252–82.

98. 17 September 1649 Carlyle, *op. cit.*, II, 148. True casualty figures: about 2,000 defenders and 150 roundheads.

99. S. R. Gardiner, *History of the Commonwealth and Protectorate, 1649–1656* (1903), I, 13. Abbott, *op. cit.*, II, 139. Fraser, *op. cit.*, 344–46.

100. T. Reilly, *Cromwell: An Honorable Enemy* (1999).

101. Cromwell to Lenthall, 25/11/91. Abbott, *op. cit.*, II, 173.

102. Carlyle, *op. cit.* (1901), 552.

103. Abbott, *op. cit.*, II, 172, 214, 222, 223, 234.

104. J. Hewitt, ed., *Eye-Witness accounts to Ireland in Revolt* (Reading, 1974), 28. E. I. Hogan, ed., *The History of the War in Ireland from 1641 to 1653 by a British Officer in Sir James Clotworthy's Regiment* (Dublin, 1873), 107.

105. H. Slingsby, W. Scott and J. Hodgson *Memoirs . . . Henry Slingsby . . . John Hodgson* (Edinburgh, 1806), 130.

106. 3 September 1650, Rushworth to Speaker Lenthall, *Parliamentary History of England* (1752–61), XIV, 341–42. O. Cromwell, *A True Relation of the Routing of the Scots near Dunbar* (1650), 4–5. C. H. Firth, 'The Battle of Dunbar', *Transactions of the Royal Historical Society*, 2nd series, XIV (1900), 19–52. Slingsby, *op. cit.*, 278.

107. B. Whitelocke, *Memoirs* (1860), 507.

108. Woolrych, *op. cit.*, 494. *An Exact and perfect relation of every particular of the fight at Worcester* (1651), 1–2. 3 September, Stapleton to Lenthall, in J. W. Willis Bund, *The Civil War in Worcestershire* (1905), 249. 8 September 1651, Cromwell to Lenthall, in Abbott, *op. cit.*, II, 467.

Chapter 8 Talk You of Killing: Civil Wars and Commonwealth: Impact, 1638–1660

1. There is a huge debate about English/British history, which is well summarized in Jane Ohlmeyer, 'The "Old British Histories?"', *Historical Journal*, 50/2 (2007), 499–512. Daniel's poem is in Samuel Daniel, *The Complete Poetical Works* (1718), 123.

2. P. Wenham, *The Great and Close Siege of York* (Kineton, 1970), 57–74, leans towards the higher end of the range.

3. In the early nineteenth century the annual death rate for British troops in Jamaica was 14.3 per cent compared to 1.7 per cent at home. R. N. Buckley, *The British Army in the West Indies: Society and the Military in the Revolutionary Age* (Gainesville, FL, 1998), 299.

4. This is based on C. Carlton, *Going to the Wars: The Experience of the British Civil Wars, 1638–51* (1992), 201–14. Since working on these figures I have found some more incidents, such as the Battle of Olney Bridge, 4 November 1643.

5. G. Parker, *The Military Revolution* (Cambridge, 1988). D. Stewart, 'Sickness and Mortality Rates in the English Army until the Twentieth Century', *Journal of the Royal Army Medical Corps*, 91 (1948), 23–35. P. Slack, *The Impact of Plague in Tudor and Stuart England* (1985), 151, 180ff. I. Roy, 'The English Civil War and English Society', *War and Society*, I (1977), 31.
6. The bloody flux and spotted fever were typhus. The symptoms include bloody stools and red spots on the chest and abdomen. My thanks to John Riddle for this point. J. Bampfield, *Colonel Joseph's Apology*, ed. J. Loftis and P. H. Hardacre (1993), 43.
7. K. Manchester, 'Paleopathology of a Royalist Garrison', *OSSA: the Journal of the Osteological Research Laboratory, University of Solna, Sweden* (1979), 25–33.
8. Most of the accidents involved aircraft. Two of those who died from disease did so as Japanese POWs. NCSU archives, UA 050.001 (box 29).
9. www.civilwarhome.com/casualties.htm
10. A. Gunkel and J. S. Handler, 'A German indentured servant in Barbados in 1652', *Journal of the Barbados Museum and Historical Society*, 33 (1977), 91–96. C. Bridenbaugh, *No Peace beyond the Line: The English in the Caribbean, 1624–1690* (New York, 1973), 110–11. V. T. Harlow, *A History of the Barbados, 1625–85* (Oxford, 1926), 302. H. Beckles, *White Servitude and Black Slavery in Barbados, 1627–1715* (Knoxville, TN, 1989), 53.
11. M. Stoyle, 'Memories of the Maimed: The Testimonies of Charles I's Former Soldiers', *History*, 88 (2003), 223–24. A. C. Dow, *Cromwellian Scotland* (Edinburgh, 1979), 20. Historical Manuscripts Commission, 12th Report, appendix part 7, page 35.
12. N. Lockyer, *England Faithfully Watched* (1649), quoted by S. Baskerville, 'Blood Guilt in the English Revolution', *Seventeenth Century*, VIII (1993), 4. G. F. Nuttal, *The Manuscripts of the Reliquiae Baxterianae* (1954), 39. W. C. Abbott, *The Writings and Speeches of Oliver Cromwell* (New York, 1937), III, 438–39.
13. H. Peters, *God's Doings and Man's Duty* (1646). T. Hobbes, *Behemoth* (1969), 95.
14. These figures may be on the low side since Dr Furgol, the pre-eminent historian of the covenanting army, gives their losses as follows:

Year	Killed	Prisoners
1644	3,000	800
1645	7,200	
1646	2,000	
1648	1,000	4,600
1650	4,000	10,000
1651	4,800	10,000
Total	22,000	25,400

Letter to author of 1/3/90. Furgol's total of 22,000 is 35 per cent higher than mine. Covenanters have been counted as parliamentarians.
15. P. Ellis, *Hell or Connaught: The Cromwellian Colonization of Ireland, 1652–1660* (1975), 82. R. B. Manning, *An Apprenticeship in Arms: The Origins of the British Army, 1585–1702* (Oxford, 2006), 88.
16. P. Lenihan, 'War and Population, 1649–52', *Irish Economic and Social History*, 24 (1997), 1–21. I am most grateful to Dr Lenihan for answering my queries by email.
17. J. Ohlmeyer, 'The Wars of Religion, 1603–1660', in I. Bartle and H. K. Jeffrey, *A Military History of Ireland* (Cambridge, 1993), 171–83. R. Bagwell, *Ireland under the Stuarts* (1906–16), II, 301.
18. J. G. Simms, *The Williamite Confiscation of Ireland, 1690–1703* (1956), 14, 22, 59, 195.
19. Father Peter Walsh, *A Continuation of the brief narrative and suffering of the Irish under Cromwell* (1660), quoted by J. Prendergast, *The Cromwellian Settlement in Ireland* (1865), 164n.

20. J. Morrill, 'The Cromwellian Massacre in Cromwellian Context', in D. Edwards, P. Lenihan and C. Tait, *The Age of Atrocity: Violence and Political Conflict in Early Modern Ireland* (Dublin, 2007), 263.

21. P. J. Cornish, 'The Rising of 1641', and 'The Cromwellian Regime', in T. X. Moody *et al., A New History of Ireland* (Oxford, 1974), III, 292, 357.

22. J. S. Wheeler, *Cromwell in Ireland* (New York, 1999), 226. D. Scott, *Politics and War in the Three Kingdoms* (2004), 198. R. Clifton, '"An Indiscriminate Blackness?" Massacre, Counter-Massacre, and Ethnic Cleansing in Ireland, 1640–1660', in M. Levene and R. Roberts, eds, *The Massacre in History* (New York, 2000), 108.

23. Lenihan, *op. cit.*, 1–22.

24. Michael Bennet confirms this view in an email to the author. M. Clodfelter, *Warfare and Armed Conflicts: A Statistical Reference to Casualty and Other Figures, 1500–2000* (2002), 52, says that there were 105,000 casualties in the Wars of the Roses. M. Hicks, *The Wars of the Roses, 1455–1485* (2003), 88, writes 'No satisfactory estimates of total casualties can be attempted.' P. M. Wilson, *The Thirty Years' War: Europe's Tragedy* (Cambridge, MA, 2009), 787. C. V. Wedgwood, *The Thirty Years' War* (New York, 1961), 493. G. Parker, *The Thirty Years' War* (1984), 211.

25. I am grateful to my colleague Bill Harris for the figures on the US Civil War.

26. J. Ellis, *The Sharp End of War* (1980), 198.

27. They do not connect to either Battle of Newbury. For more details, see C. Carlton, *Going to the Wars: The Experience of the British Civil Wars, 1638–51* (1992), 207.

28. Slack, *op. cit.*, 72–73. R. and T. Kelly, *A City at War: Oxford, 1642–46* (Cheltenham, 1987), 25–26.

29. F. Tallet, *War and Society in Early Modern Europe* (1992), 107. F. Prinzing, *Epidemics Resulting from War* (Oxford, 1916), 1–18.

30. Slack, *op. it.*, 151, 180ff. S. Porter, 'Property Damage in the English Civil War', London Ph.D. (1984), 198. R. H. Morris, *The Siege of Chester* (1923), 210.

31. A. Wood, *Life and Times of Anthony Wood* (Oxford, 1891), I, 62.

32. R. W. Cotton, *Barnstaple and the Northern Part of Devonshire during the Great Civil War* (1889), 105–6.

33. G. Nugent, *Some memorials of John Hampden, his party and his time* (1832), II, 441.

34. E. Furgol, *A Regimental History of the Covenanting Armies, 1639–1651* (Edinburgh, 1988), 54.

35. J. Rushworth, *Historical Collections of the Private Passages of State* (1680), V, 288.

36. E. Burghall, 'The Diary of Edward Burghall', in T. W. Barlow, *Cheshire: its Historical and Literary Associations* (Manchester, 1855), 166.

37. Edward Hyde, earl of Clarendon, *History of the Rebellion and Civil Wars* (Oxford, 1843), IV, 485.

38. M. Stoyle, '"Whole Streets Converted to Ashes": Property Destruction in Exeter in the English Civil War', in R. C. Richardson, *The English Civil Wars: Local Aspects* (Stroud, 1997), 141. S. Porter, *Property Damage in the English Civil Wars* (Stroud, 1994), 6ff.

39. http://www.firstworldwar.com/audio/howyagonna.htm.

40. J. Turner, *Memoirs* (Edinburgh, 1829), 76.

41. W. Haller, *Liberty and Reformation in the Puritan Revolution* (New York, 1955), 209. Hugh Peters, *Mr. Peters' last report on the English Wars* (1646).

42. J. R. Phillips, *Memoirs of the Civil War in Wales and the Marches, 1642–1649* (1874), II, 127.

43. C. V. Wedgwood, *The King's War, 1641–1647* (1966), 425. J. A. Atkinson, *Tracts Relating . . . to the civil war in Cheshire, 1641–59* (Chetham Society, 1909), 109. Abbott, *op. cit.*, I, 360. P. Young, *Naseby* (1985), 339.

44. Quoted by Hill, *op. cit.*, 86.

45. E. Reynolds, *Orders from the Lord of Hosts* (1646), 8–9.

46. T. Edwards, *Gangraena* (1646), I, 111.

47. R. J. Lifton, *Home from the War: Vietnam Veterans: Neither Victims nor Executioners* (New York, 1973), 126–30, describes this process with Vietnam veterans, while Christopher Hill, in *A Tinker and a Poor Man: John Bunyan and His Church* (New York, 1989), discusses it with regard to a soldier who almost certainly never saw action. O. G. Body, 'The New Model Army Under Sir Thomas Fairfax,' *Journal of the Royal Artillery*, 65 (1938), 215. *The Watchman's Warning Piece, Or, Parliament Soldiers Prediction* (1646), 1.

48. R. Ashton, *The English Civil War: Conservatism and Reaction, 1603–49* (1989), 312.

49. J. P. Wogaman and D. M. Strong, *Readings in Christian Ethics* (1996), 164.

50. As the captain of his aircraft carrier ordered, 'Stone, you're an Oxford man so you better teach the sailors.' Private conversation with Professor Stone. J. A. Crang, 'Politics on Parade: Army Education and the 1945 General Election', *History*, 81 (1997), 215–27.

51. September 1643, Carlyle, *op. cit.*, I, 147. R. Baxter, *The Practical Works of Richard Baxter*, ed. W. Orme (1830), VI, 123.

52. C. Carlton, 'Sieges during the British Civil Wars', in *Cities under Siege*, ed. Lucia Carle and Antoinette Fauve-Chamoux (Florence, 2002), 241–49.

53. R. Holmes, *The Siege of Pontefract Castle, 1644–48* (Pontefract, 1887), 210.

54. S. R. Gardiner, *Constitutional Documents of the Puritan Revolution* (1968), 373–5.

55. Abraham Cowley, *Poems* (Cambridge, 1905), 425. R. Herrick, *Poems*, ed. J. Masefield (Oxford, 1906), 190.

56. H. M. Reece, 'The Military Presence in England, 1649–1660', Oxford University D.Phil. (1981), 50–52, 286. J. Brewer, *Sinews of Power: War, Money, and the English State, 1688–1783* (New York, 1989), 11. G. Parker, *The Military Revolution* (Cambridge, 1988), 62 and 81.

57. Quoted by L. B. Smith, *This Realm of England, 1399–1688* (Boston, 1996), 298.

58. M. J. Braddick, *Parliamentary Taxation in Seventeenth-Century Europe* (Woodbridge, 1994).

59. Most of the Royal Navy were in the West Indies at the time.

60. A. Woolrych, *Britain in Revolution, 1625–1660* (Oxford, 2004), 626.

61. Lucy Hutchinson, *Memoirs of the Life of Colonel John Hutchinson* (1885), II, 203. C. Durston, *Cromwell's Major Generals: Godly Government during the English Revolution* (Manchester, 2001), 46.

62. 'The Men behind the Wire', in C. Carlton, *Bigotry and Blood: Documents on the Ulster Troubles* (Chicago, 1976), 111.

63. R. Blair, *The Life of Mr. Robert Blair* (1848), 291–2.

64. B. Capp, *Cromwell's Navy: The Fleet and the English Revolution, 1648–1660* (Oxford, 1989), 7, 397.

65. D. Baugh, 'Great Britain's "Blue Water" Policy, 1689–1815', *International History Review*, 10 (1988), 35–39. J. D. Davis, *Gentlemen and Tarpaulins: The Officers and Men of the Restoration Navy* (Oxford, 1991), 79. M. A. Palmer, 'The Sails' Right Hand: Command and Control in the Age of Fighting Sail, 1652–1827', *Journal of Modern History*, 64, 4 (October 1997), 679–81.

66. Historical Manuscripts Commission, *Various*, VIII, 78.

67. G. Modelski and W. R. Thompson, *Sea Power in Global Politics, 1494–1993* (1988), 206.

68. E. Waller, *The Poems of Edmund Waller*, ed. G. Drury (1893), 138.

69. *ibid.*, 152.

70. J. H. Elliott, 'World of Corporate States', *Past and Present*, 137 (1992), 48–72. C. Russell, 'Composite Monarchy in Early Modern Europe: The British and Irish examples', in A. Grant and K. Stringer, eds, *Uniting the Kingdom? The Making of British History* (1995), 133.

71. C. Tilly, *The Formation of the Nation State in Western Europe* (1975), 42. R. A. Brown, *The Origins of Modern Europe* (1972), 93. J. Lynn, 'Clio in Arms: The Role of the Military Variable in Shaping History', *Journal of Modern History*, 55 (1991), 84.

J. Lynn, *Tools of War* (Chicago, 1990), 1–21. J. Black, *A Military Revolution? Military Change and European Society, 1550–1800* (Basingstoke, 1991), 7.

72. 10 March 1643, Carlyle, *op. cit.*, I, 161.
73. J. S. Wheeler, 'Sense of Identity in the Army of the English Republic, 1645–51', in A. MacInnes and J. Ohlmeyer, *The Stuart Kingdoms in the Seventeenth Century: Awkward Neighbours* (Dublin, 2002), 151–68.
74. J. Morrill, 'Three Kingdoms and One Commonwealth: The Enigma of Mid-Seventeenth-Century Britain and Ireland', in Grant and Stringer, 170.
75. N. Rodger, *The Command of the Ocean: A Naval History of Britain, 1649–1815* (2004), 2–3.

Chapter 9 High-Intensity Combat: Battles and Sieges

1. A. Kellett, *Combat Motivation: The Behavior of Soldiers in Battle* (Boston, 1982), 246.
2. J. Hattendorf, *British Naval Documents, 1204–1906* (Naval Record Society, 13, 1993), 290.
3. J. Blackadder, *The Life and Diary of Colonel John Blackadder of the Cameronian Regiment* (1824), 277.
4. Quoted by G. Dyer, *War* (1986), 103.
5. Hugo Grotius, *De Jure Belli* (1625), quoted by J. R. Hale, *Renaissance War Studies* (1983), 341. J. Prebble, *Culloden* (1961), 102.
6. Quoted by S. R. Gardiner, *History of the Great Civil War* (1987), I, 44.
7. S. L. A. Marshall, *Men against Fire* (Norman, OK, 2000), 27.
8. Dyer, *op. cit.*, 13.
9. G. Monck, duke of Albermarle, *Observations on political and military affairs* (1671), 23.
10. B. L. Montgomery, *Memoirs* (1958), 82. Karl von Clausewitz, *On War* (Harmondsworth, 1968), 227. R. Boyle, earl of Orrery, *Treatise on the Art of War* (1677), 499, np. J. Cruso, *Treatise on Modern War* (1640), 123.
11. Brian Manning, 'Neutrals and Neutralism in the English Civil War, 1642–46', Oxford D.Phil., 1957, 214–15.
12. James Touchet, earl of Castlehaven, *Memoir . . . of his engagement and carriage in the war of Ireland* (1680), 62. C. T. Atkinson, 'Gleanings from the Cathcart MSS', *Journal of the Society for Army Historical Research*, 29, 117 (1951), 101.
13. M. Blumenson, *Patton* (New York, 1985), 128. J. Campbell, 'A Scottish Fusillier and Dragoon under Marlborough: Lt. General the Honourable Sir John Campbell', *Journal of the Society for Army Historical Research*, 15 (1936), 52.
14. Quoted by J. Keegan, *The Face of Battle* (New York, 1976), 117.
15. Quoted by J. Black, *Culloden and the '45* (Stroud, 1990), 165. W. Patten, 'The Expedition into Scotland', in A. F. Pollard, *Tudor Tracts* (1903), 113.
16. J. Stevens, *The Journal of Captain John Stevens* (Oxford, 1912), 123.
17. R. Bulstrode, *Memorials of the English Affairs* (1712), 84.
18. P. Paret, *Understanding War: Essays on Clausewitz* (Princeton, NJ, 1992), 85. I am most grateful to Professor Paret for elaborating on this incident via email.
19. Patten, *op. cit.*, 112.
20. Campbell, *op. cit.*, 88.
21. J. Jordan, 'The Battle of Aughrim: Two Danish Sources', *Transactions of the Galway Archaeological and Historical Society*, 26 (1954–55), 6–7. G. M. Trevelyan, 'Narrative and Diary of Colonel John Richards', *Cambridge Historical Journal*, 3 (1931), 258.
22. P. Delaney, *British Autobiography in the Seventeenth Century* (New York, 1969), 1, 16–17. Roger Williams, *The Works* (Oxford, 1972), 58.
23. 'The Siege and Capture of Boulogne', ed. J. H. Lesley, *Journal of the Society for Army Historical Research* (1920), 188–200, is typical.
24. J. Millner, *A Compendious Journal of all the Marches* (1737), 55–56.

25. Kellett, *op. cit.*, 219–20.
26. G. Hamilton, 'The Letters of the First Earl of Orkney during Marlborough's Campaigns', *English Historical Review*, 19 (1904), 318. Millner, *op. cit.*, 170–71, 273.
27. Blackadder, *op. cit.*, 350.
28. J. MacPherson, *Original Papers containing the Secret History of Great Britain* (1775), I, 37.
29. *Exact and True relation of a bloody Fight* (1642), 6. C. Duffy, *The '45* (2003), 512. E. Archer, *A True Relation of the Red trained-bands* (1643), 7. Blackadder, *op. cit.*, 340.
30. General Sir William Napier, in P. Tsouris, *Warriors' World: A Quotation Book* (1992), 247.
31. Touchet, *op. cit.*, 61, 67–68.
32. Thomas Carte, *Ormonde Papers* (1739), I, 55.
33. James Audley, earl of Castlehaven, *Memoirs* (Waterford, 1680), 136. J. G. Fyfe, *Scottish Diaries and Memoirs, 1550–1746* (Stirling, 1928), 308. S. H. F. Johnston, 'The Cameronians at Steenkirk, 1692', *Scottish Historical Review*, 27 (1948), 73–75. S. H. F. Johnston, 'A Scots Chaplain in Flanders', *Journal of the Society for Army Historical Research*, 27 (1949), 8.
34. The battles are Bosworth Field, Flodden, Marston Moor, Naseby, Auldean, Dunbar, Sedgemoor, Boyne, Blenheim and Culloden.
35. N. Barr, *Flodden, 1513: the Scottish Invasion of Henry VIII's England* (Stroud, 2001), 286.
36. P. Drake, *Amiable Renegade: The Memoirs of Captain Peter Drake* (Stanford, CA, 1960), 79.
37. Patten, *op. cit.*, 124–25. G. Bonnivert, 'Some Extracts Relating to Ireland from the Journals of Gideon Bonnivert, 1690', *Louth Archaeological Journals*, VIII (1933), 21. Millner, *op. cit.* (1737), 217.
38. W. Patten, 'The Expedition into Scotland', *Fragments in Scottish History*, ed. J. G. Dalyell (Edinburgh, 1798), 67–68, 71. C. Oman, 'The Battle of Pinkie, September 10, 1547', *Archaeological Journal*, 90 (1932), 1–25.
39. T. Coningsby, 'Journal of the Siege of Rouen', *Camden Miscellany*, I, 4 (1847), 53.
40. 'Continuation of the Siege of Ostend, from 25 July and as far as 7 Mar 1602', in C. H. Firth, ed., *Stuart Tracts* (1964), 177. T. Gilby, ed., *Britain at Arms: A Scrapbook from Queen Anne to the Present Day* (1953), 190.
41. G. Walker, *Journal of the Siege of Derry* (1689).
42. Fynes Moryson, *An Itinerary containing his two years travel* (Glasgow, 1907), II, 115. J. M. Hill, *Celtic Warfare* (Edinburgh, 1986), 73.
43. P. Elliot-Wright, 'The Birth of the Thin Red Line: English Firing Tactics, 1660–1708', *Military History Illustrated*, 80 (June 1995), 20–25. D. Nosworthy, *The Anatomy of Victory: Battle Tactics, 1689–1763* (New York, 1990), 40. A. Clayton, *The British Officer* (2005).
44. It became known as the Brown Bess in the later part of the eighteenth century. R. O'Connell, *Of Arms and Men: A History of War, Weapons, and Aggression* (Oxford, 1990), 158.
45. Millner, *op. cit.*, ix, 274.
46. Blackadder, *op. cit.*, 320.
47. F. Tallet, *War and Society in Early Modern Europe* (1992), 45. Quoted by C. Barnett, *Marlborough* (1974), 169.
48. Stevens, *op. cit.*, 122.
49. J. Deane, *A Journal of the Campaign in Flanders* (Camden Society, 1846), 12–14.
50. Elliot-Wright, *op. cit.*, 20–25. Nosworthy, *op. cit.*, 40. Clayton, *op. cit.*
51. Dyer, *op. cit.*, 15.
52. Clausewitz, *op. cit.*, 359. *Macbeth*, V, v, 2–4.
53. Monck, *op. cit.*, 119.
54. Charles I pardoned him at the last moment. *The Earle of Essex His Letter to Master Speaker, July 9, 1643* (1643), 6.
55. F. Vere, *The Commentaries of Sir Francis Vere* (Cambridge, 1659), 14.
56. Roger Boyle, *Treatise on the Art of War* (1677), 15.

57. C. T. Atkinson, 'Marlborough's Sieges', *Journal of the Society for Army Historical Research*, 13 (1934), 195–205.

58. M. Cervantes, *Don Quixote* (1925), I, 403. B. Jonson, *Works* (1875), VIII, 409. Quoted by Hale, *op. cit.*, 395–96. Royal Commission on Historical Monuments, *Newark on Trent: The Civil War Siegeworks* (1964), 19.

59. *Henry V*, III, iii, 37–42.

60. W. J. Blake, 'The Rebellion in Cornwall and Devon in 1549', *Journal of the Royal Institute of Cornwall*, 18 (1910), 808.

61. L. Hutchinson, *Memoirs of the Life of Colonel John Hutchinson*, ed. H. Child (1904), 164.

62. H. Hexham, *A Journal of the Taking of Venlo* (1633), 19–27.

63. D. Defoe, *The Military Memoirs of Captain George Carleton* (1929), 33–37.

64. Vere, *op. cit.*, 39–40.

65. Blackadder, *op. cit.*, 327–29.

66. In fact, the sack of Magdeburg went on for three days, its population fell from 30,000 to 5,000. Justin Wintle, *Dictionary of War Quotations* (1969), 230.

67. 'A Diary of the Siege of Athlone', *Irish Sword*, 4 (1959–60), 88–92.

68. John Shawe, 'The Life of Master John Shawe', *Yorkshire Diaries*, ed. Charles Jackson (Surtees Society, 1877), 136. G. Chinnery, M. Bateson and H. Stocks, eds, *Records of the Borough of Leicester, 1603–88* (Leicester, 1923), 359.

69. R. Symonds, *Diary* (Camden Society, 1859), 180–81.

70. D. Stewart, 'Sickness and Mortality Rates in the English Army in the Sixteenth Century', *Journal of the Royal Army Medical Corps*, 91 (1948), 23–35. Coningsby, *op. cit.*, 61.

71. E. M. Thompson, *Correspondence of the Family of Haddock* (Camden Society, 1881), 50–51. Atkinson, *op. cit.*, 66.

72. E. Gruffudd, 'The Enterprise of Paris and Boulogne', *Bulletin of the Faculty of Arts, Fouad University*, II (1949), 57.

73. Stevens, *op. cit.*, 186–87.

74. E. G. B. Warburton, ed., *Memoirs of Prince Rupert and the Cavaliers* (1849), II, 261. G. S., *A true relation of the sad passages of the two armies* (1644), 6–11. B. Donagan, 'Codes and Conduct in the English Civil War', *Past and Present* (1988), 89–91.

75. *A Full and True Account of the besieging of Carrickfergus* (1689). *Great News from the Duke of Schomberge's Army* (1689).

Chapter 10 Restoration to Glorious Revolution, 1660–1688

1. J. Evelyn, *Diary and Correspondence of John Evelyn* (1889), I, 355.

2. *Ibid.*, I, 355.

3. T. Carlyle, ed., *Oliver Cromwell's Letters and Speeches* (1888), III, 461.

4. A. Woolrych, *Britain in Revolution, 1625–1660* (Oxford, 2004), 769.

5. C. H. Firth, 'A New Ballad', *Journal of the Society for Army Historical Research*, IV, 18 (1925), 80.

6. P. Muskett, 'Military Operations against Smugglers in Kent and Sussex, 1698–1750', *Journal of the Society for Army Historical Research*, 52 (1974), 89–110.

7. *Calendar of State Papers, Domestic, 1678*, 183–84.

8. J. Childs, 'The English Brigade in Portugal, 1662–68', *Journal of the Society for Army Historical Research*, 53 (1975), 125–37. J. Childs, 'The British Brigade in France, 1672–1698', *History*, 69 (1984), 384–97.

9. E. Sanger, *Englishmen at War: A Social History in Letters, 1450–1900* (Stroud, 1993), 108. M. Belloff, *Public Order and Popular Disturbances* (1938), 107.

10. T. B. Macaulay, *Selections from the Writing of Lord Macaulay*, ed. G. M. Trevelyan (1903), 31.

11. L. Schwoerer, *No Standing Armies!* (Baltimore, MD, 1973). J. Addison, *Works* (1889), V 356. D. Defoe, *An Argument Shewing that a standing army is inconsistent with a free government and absolutely destructive to the constitution of the English Monarchy* (1697). Edmund Burke, *Collected Works* (1803), V, 17. J. Madison *et al.*, *The Federalist Papers* (1987), 174.
12. D. Allen, 'The Role of the London Trained Bands in the Exclusion Crisis, 1678–81', *English Historical Review*, 87 (1972), 303.
13. M. Braddick, *State Formation in Early Modern England* (Cambridge, 2001), 227.
14. A. P. C. Bruce, *The Purchase System in the British Army, 1660–1871* (1980), 14.
15. Henry Hyde, *The Correspondence of Henry Hyde, the Earl of Clarendon* (1828), II, 113.
16. C. Hill, *The Century of Revolution* (1961). W. B. Wilcox, *The Age of Aristocracy* (New York, 2001). See also J. Cannon, *Aristocratic Century: The Peerage in 18th-Century England* (Cambridge, 1989).
17. In contrast, those who fought in the American Civil War did think of it in terms of slavery: Chandra Manning, *What This Cruel War is Over* (New York, 2007). For *Going to the Wars: The Experience of the British Civil Wars, 1638–51* (1992), I read hundreds of soldiers' letters and memoirs, and cannot recall one that talked about a 'Baronial Revolt'. For this theory, see J. S. A. Adamson, *The Noble Revolt: The Overthrow of Charles I* (2007).
18. R. B. Manning, *An Apprenticeship in Arms: The Origins of the British Army, 1585–1702* (Oxford, 2006), 270. G. Dyer, *War* (1986), 63. S. Clark, *State and Status: The Rise of the State and Aristocratic Power in Western Europe* (Montreal, 1995), 285. P. Drake, *Amiable Renegade: The Memoirs of Captain Peter Drake* (Stanford, CA, 1960), 245.
19. Carlton, *op. cit.*, 185. R. O'Connell, *Of Arms and Men: A History of War, Weapons, and Aggression* (Oxford, 1990), 155.
20. P. Hardacre, 'Patronage and Purchase in the Irish Standing Army under Thomas Wentworth, Earl of Strafford, 1632–40', *Journal of the Society for Army Historical Research*, 67 (1989), 40–45, 94–104.
21. Edward Hyde, earl of Clarendon, *The History of the Great Rebellion and Civil Wars in England* (Oxford, 1888), I, 589.
22. A. Clayton, *The British Officer* (2005).
23. K. Brown, 'Gentlemen and Thugs in Seventeenth-Century Britain', *History Today*, 40 (1990), 29. Cannon, *op. cit.*, 118–20.
24. S. Huntingdon, *The Soldier and the State* (1957), xviii. J. Connell, *Wavell: Scholar and Soldier* (1964), 74.
25. R. K. Merton, 'Science and Military Techniques', *Scientific Monthly*, 41 (December 1935), 542–45.
26. J. Childs, *The Nine Years' War and the British Army* (Manchester, 1991), 75, 79.
27. Clayton, *op. cit.*, 23–25.
28. H. Oakes-Jones, 'The Evolution of the Gorget', *Journal of the Society for Army Historical Research*, 1 (1925), 247–55.
29. J. Laver, 'The Meaning of Military Uniforms', *Journal of the Royal United Services Institution*, 96 (1951), 425–53. B. Lyndon, 'Military Dress and Uniformity', *Journal of the Society for Army Historical Research*, 54 (1997), 109–20.
30. N. Rodger, 'The New Atlantic: Naval Warfare in the 16th Century', in J. B. Hattendorf and R. Unger, *War at Sea* (Woodbridge, 2002), 236–38.
31. J. Glete, *Navies and Nations: Warships, Navies, and Ship Building in Europe and America, 1500–1800* (Stockholm, 1993), I, 179, 195.
32. N. Rodger, *The Command of the Ocean: A Naval History of Britain, 1649–1815* (2004), 113.
33. N. Bard, ed., 'The Earl of Warwick's Voyage of 1627', *Naval Miscellany: Naval Records Society*, 125 (1985), 17.
34. N. Elias, 'Studies in the Genesis of the Naval Profession', *British Journal of Sociology* (1950), 291–300. Shovell was in fact the son of a yeoman farmer from Norfolk. S. Harris, *Cloudesley Shovell: A Stuart Admiral* (Staplehurst, 2000).

35. This is based on a sample from *Dictionary of National Biography*, Clark, *op. cit.*, 285.
36. Manning, *op. cit.*, 268.
37. R. G. Glass, 'The Image of the Sea Officer in English Literature, 1660–1710', *Albion*, 26 (1994), 583–99.
38. S. Pepys, *Diary* (New York, 1887), VII, 55.
39. C. S. Knighton, 'A Century on: Pepys and the Elizabethan Navy', *Transactions of the Royal Historical Society*, 6th series, 14 (2004), 141–56.
40. P. Godwin, 'The Influence of Iron in Ship Construction, 1660–1830', *Mariner's Mirror*, 84 (1998), 26–27. 29 July 1667, Pepys, *op. cit.*, VII, 269.
41. M. Ashley, *James II*, 76.
42. J. Haswell, *James II: Soldier and Sailor* (1972), 146.
43. Rodger, *op. cit.*, 106.
44. *Ibid.*, 7. M. S. Anderson, *War and Society in the Old Regime, 1618–1789* (1988), 104.
45. Quoted by G. Holmes, *Augustan England: Professions, State, and Society, 1680–1730* (1982), 277.
46. J. Davies, *Gentlemen and Tarpaulins: The Officers and Men of the Restoration Navy* (Oxford, 1991), 26–38. N. Rodger, *The Wooden World: An Anatomy of the Georgian Navy* (1986), 253.
47. J. R. Jones, *The Anglo-Dutch Wars of the Seventeenth Century* (1996), 9–11. S. Pincus, *Protestantism and Patriotism: Ideologies and the Making of Foreign Policy, 1650–1668* (Cambridge, 1996). Pepys, *op. cit.*, IV, 82.
48. Firth, *op. cit.*, 54.
49. *Ibid.*, 66–67.
50. Pepys, *op. cit.*, ed. H. Wheatley (1905), VII, 28.
51. E. S. de Beer, *The Diary of John Evelyn* (1959), 516.
52. Sanger, *op. cit.*, 91.
53. A. Wheeler, *Military Diary, June–July 1685* (Camden Society Miscellany, XII, 1910), 157–63. T. McGuffie, 'The Last Battle on English Soil', *History Today*, 5 (1955), 59–60.
54. Pincus, *op. cit.*, 183.
55. J. McGuire, 'James II and Ireland', in W. A. Maguire, *Kings in Conflict: Ireland in the 1690s* (1990), 52. J. C. Becket, 'The Irish Armed Forces, 1660–1685', in J. Bossy and P. Jupp, *Essays Presented to Michael Roberts* (Belfast, 1976), 41–45. H. McDonnell, 'Irishmen in the Stuart Navy, 1660–1690', *Irish Sword*, 16, 63 (1985), 87–104. C. Dalton, *The Scots Army, 1661–1688* (1909), 405.
56. McDonnell, *op. cit.*, 87–104. Tim Harris, *Revolution: The Great Crisis of the British Monarchy, 1685–1720* (2006), 115–16, 192. J. Miller, 'Catholic Officers in the Late Stuart Army', *English Historical Review*, 88 (1973), 43. S. Pincus, *1688: The First Modern Revolution* (2009), 148.
57. 12 July 1667, Pepys, *op. cit.*, 240. H. Strachan, *The Politics of the British Army* (Oxford, 1997), 20–23. J. Malcolm, *To Keep and Bear Arms: The Origins of an Anglo-American Right* (Cambridge, 1994), 106.
58. Malcolm, *op. cit.*, 107. D. Defoe, *The Advantages of the Present Settlement* (1689), 13.
59. Harris, *op. cit.*, 189.
60. G. Davies, 'Letters of the Administration of James II's Army', *Journal of the Society for Army Historical Research*, 29 (1951), 81–82.
61. Quoted by Haswell, *op. cit.*, 171.
62. Harris, *op. cit.*, 260–61.
63. Quoted by *Harris*, *op. cit.*, 271.
64. Sanger, *op. cit.*, 95.
65. www.exclassics.com/ballards/lilli/
66. G. Burnet, *Bishop Burnet's History of his own time* (1823), III, 139. Harris, *op. cit.*, 284. After a generation 'Lillibullero' was forgotten, to be revived as the BBC World Service's signature tune.
67. Burnet, *op. cit.*, (1883), III, 1.

68. Quoted by Ashley, *op. cit.*, 49. J. Callow, *The Making of King James II* (2000), does not accept this view.
69. C. Carlton, *Royal Warriors: A Military History of the British Monarchy* (2004), Chapter IV. Quoted by Haswell, *op. cit.*, 24.
70. Harris, *op. cit.*, 341, 361.
71. Pincus, *op. cit.*, 63, 93.
72. Ashley, *op. cit.*, 275, Harris, *op. cit.*, 474.
73. Harris, *op. cit.*, 304.

Chapter 11 The Peril of the Waters: War at Sea

1. Quoted by N. A. M. Rodger, *Safeguard of the Sea: A Naval History of Britain, 660–1649* (New York, 1997), 311.
2. S. Harris, *Cloudesley Shovell: A Stuart Admiral* (Staplehurst, 2000).
3. J. Smith, *Work, 1608–1631*, ed. E. Arber (1895), II, 803.
4. J. Yonge, *The Journal of J. Yonge, 1647–1712, Plymouth Surgeon* (1963), 37. Richard Allyn, *A Narrative of the Victory obtained by the English and Dutch Fleet* (1744), 10.
5. G. Barnett, *Illustrated British Ballads* (1881), 5.
6. S. Brown, *Scurvy: How a Surgeon, Mariner, and Gentleman Solved the Greatest Medical Mystery in the Age of Sail* (2003), 24.
7. P. Kemp, *The British Sailor: A Social History of the Lower Deck* (1970), 7. N. Rodger, *The Command of the Ocean: A Naval History of Britain, 1649–1815* (2004), 307. Rodger, *Wooden World*, 100–1.
8. W. Raleigh, *Works* (1829), 254.
9. J. D. Alsop, 'Sickness in the British Mediterranean Fleet, the *Tiger* Journal of 1706', *War and Society* 11, 2 (October 1993), 61. J. J. Keevil, *Medicine and the Navy* (1957), I, 246, 276. Yonge, *op. cit.*, 162.
10. E. Barlow, *Barlow's Journal* (1934), I, 119, 162, 213–14, 226; II, 60. *Oxford Dictionary of National Biography* (1885–1900).
11. H. Teonge, *The Diary of Henry Teonge, Chaplain aboard HMS Assistance, Bristol and Royal Oak,* ed. G. Manwaring (1927), 83. Rodger, *Command*, 124. J. D. Davies, *Gentlemen and Tarpaulins: The Officers and Men of the Restoration Navy* (Oxford, 1991), 106.
12. K. B. Andrews, 'The Elizabethan Seaman', *Mariner's Mirror* (1982), 246.
13. Robartes to Committee of Both Kingdoms, J. R. Powell and E. K. Timings, *Documents Relating to the Civil War* (Naval Records Society, 1963), 172.
14. A. Spont, *Letters and Papers relating to the War with France, 1512–13* (Naval Records Society, X, 1897), xxxiii.
15. Pepys, *Diary*, ed. R. Latham and W. Matthews (2001), X, 289.
16. W. Rogers, *A Cruising Voyage around the World* (1928), xiii. C. N. Robinson and J. Leyland, *The British Tar in Fact and Fiction: The Poetry, Pathos, and Humour of the Sailor's Life* (New York, 1909), 107.
17. Rodger, *Safeguard*, 235–38.
18. Rodger, *Command*, 54.
19. Alsop, *op. cit.*, 57–76.
20. T. Allin, *Journals* (Naval Records Society, 1939), 304.
21. W. G. Perrin, *Boteler's Dialogues* (Naval Record Society, 1927). Kemp, *op. cit.*, 48.
22. D. Howarth, *The Voyage of the Armada* (New York, 1981), 243. G. Mattingly, *The Armada* (Boston, 1959), 374.
23. J. Black, *A Military Revolution? Military Change and European Society, 1550–1800* (1991), 38. H. Bowen, *War and British Society, 1688–1815* (Cambridge, 1998), 12. L. James, *Warrior Race* (2001), 354.

24. Barnaby Slush, *Naval Royal: or a Sea Cook turn'd projector* (1709), 2–3.
25. E. Sanger, *Englishmen at War: A Social History in Letters, 1450–1900* (Stroud, 1993), 88–89.
26. J. Smith, *Sea-Grammar* (1868), 58.
27. B. S. Ingram, *Three Sea Journals of Stuart Times* (1936), 33.
28. A. N. Gilbert, 'Crime as Disorder. Criminality and the Symbolic. The Universe of the Eighteenth-Century British Officer', in R. W. Leve, *Changing Interpretations and New Sources in Naval History* (New York), 115–18.
29. Rodger, *Safeguard*, 302.
30. Rodger, *Command*, 59.
31. Davies, *op. cit.*, 79, 96.
32. *Oxford Dictionary of National Biography* (Oxford, 2004–9).
33. A skipkennel was a lackey or someone who jumped over kennels or gutters.
34. H. Southern and N. Nicolas, 'The Life and Times of Matthew Bishop', *Retrospective Review*, 2nd series (1828), 49.
35. R. R. Holmes, *Redcoat: The British Soldier in the Age of Horse and Musket* (2001), 144.
36. 'A Relation of a Short Survey of the Western Counties made by a Lieutenant of the Military Company of Norwich in 1635', ed. L. G. Legg, *Camden Miscellany*, XVI (1936), xviii, 90. Rodger, *Safeguard*, 315.
37. S. Pepys, *Diary*, 1 July 1666. Keevil, *op. cit.*, I, 114–15.
38. R. Harding, *The Evolution of the Sail Navy* (1995), 49.
39. 13 May 1694, Arthur Todd to Lord Irwin, Historical Manuscripts Commission, *Various*, VIII, 75–76.
40. E. Coxere, *Adventures by Sea of Edward Coxere* (Oxford, 1946), xi, 23–24.
41. Quoted by P. Padfield, *Maritime Supremacy and the Opening up of the Western Mind* (2000), 185.
42. D. French, *The British Way of Warfare, 1688–2000* (1990), 7.
43. J. Boswell, *The Life of Dr. Johnson* (1900), 212.
44. Barlow, *op. cit.*, II, 60.
45. R. Marbeck, 'A Brief and True Report of the Honorable Voyage unto Cadiz, 1596', in A. F. Kinney, *Elizabethan Background* (Hamden, CT, 1975), 290.
46. J. Weale, *The Journal of John Weale, 1654–56* (Naval Records Society, 92, 1952), 89.
47. Southern and Nicolas, *op. cit.*, 46.
48. Rodger, *Command*, 382.
49. Ingram, *op. cit.*, 28.
50. C. H. Firth, *Naval Songs and Ballads* (1908), 41.
51. L. James, *Warrior Race: A History of the British at War* (2001), 148. Rodger, *Safeguard*, 127–28, 321–22. Rodger, *Command*, 54, 196, 210.
52. E. M. Thompson, *Correspondence of the Family of Haddock* (Camden Society, 1883), 52–53.
53. Teonge, *op. cit.*, 29. S. J. Stark, *Female Tars: Women Aboard Ship in the Age of Sail* (1996), 50.
54. For a virtual tour, go to *www.historicdockyard.co.uk*
55. D. C. Coleman, 'Naval Dockyards under the Stuarts', *Economic History Review*, 6 (1953), 139. D. Defoe, *A Tour thro' the whole Island of Great Britain* (1726), 21.
56. J. Keegan, *The Price of Admiralty* (1988), 47.
57. C. Barnett, *Marlborough* (1974), 40.
58. Allin, *op. cit.*, 279.
59. Firth, *op. cit.* (1908), xvi.
60. *Ibid.*, 161.
61. Quoted by C. M. Fissel, *English Warfare, 1511–1642* (2001), 36.
62. Southern and Nicolas, *op. cit.*, 46.
63. *Account of the Late Great Victory* (1692), 22.
64. Ingram, *op. cit.*, 49–51.

65. *Ibid.*, xxii. 19 July 1645, Inchiquin to Lords, in Charles McNeil, ed., *The Tanner Letters: Documents on Irish Affairs in the Sixteenth and Seventeenth Centuries Extracted from the Tanner Collection* (Dublin, 1943), 191.
66. M. Lewis, *Life and Letters of Tobias Smollett* (Fort Washington, 1996), 46.
67. 'A True Narrative of the Life of Mr. George Elliot, who was taken and sold as a slave, with his Travails, Captivity and Escape from Salle', in A. Elliot, *A modest Vindication of Titus Oates* (1682), 15–16. Coxere, *op. cit.*, 54.
68. Barlow, *op. cit.*, I, 228.
69. Yonge, *op. cit.*, 92–100.

Chapter 12 Let Slip the Dogs of War: After the Glorious Revolution, 1688–1746

1. J. Brewer, *The Sinews of Power: War, Money, and the English State, 1688–1783* (1989). L. Stone, *An Imperial State at War: Britain from 1689 to 1815* (1994), 20. D. French, *The British Way of Warfare, 1688–2000* (1990), xi.
2. Quoted by J. Miller, *The Life and Times of William and Mary* (London, 1974), 199.
3. J. Millner, *A Compendious Journal of All the Marches* (1733), x. French, *op. cit.*, 3–4. J. Addison, *Works* (1889), VI, 541.
4. J. Braddick, *Parliamentary Taxation in Seventeenth-Century Europe* (Woodbridge, 1994), 69. M. Braddick, 'The Rise of the Fiscal State', in B. Coward, *A Companion to Stuart Britain* (Oxford, 2003), 84.
5. B. McCarthy, 'Warrior Values: A Socio-Historical Survey', in J. Archer, ed., *Male Violence* (1994), 113. C. Carlton, *Royal Warriors: A Military History of the British Monarchy* (2004), Chapter 5.
6. J. H. Plumb, *The Growth of Political Stability in England, 1675–1725* (1967). J. Cannon, *Aristocratic Century: The Peerage in 18th-Century England* (Cambridge, 1989), 106–7. Braddick, *op. cit.*, 84.
7. Quoted by G. Curtis, *Life and Times of Queen Anne* (London, 1972), 133.
8. J. Childs, *The Nine Years' War and the British Army* (Manchester, 1991), 47–48. Brewer, *op. cit.*, 40–41. C. T. Atkinson, 'The Cost of Queen Anne's Wars', *Journal of the Society for Army Historical Research*, 136 (1955), 183.
9. S. Pincus, *1688: The First Modern Revolution* (New Haven, CT, 2009), 83.
10. Ian Roy, 'The English Civil War and English Society', *War and Society* (1975), 29.
11. F. Tallet, *War and Society in Early Modern Europe* (1992), 212. P. Padfield, *Maritime Supremacy and the Opening up of the Western Mind* (2000), 153. P. G. M. Dickson and J. Sperlin, 'War Finance, 1689–1714', *New Cambridge Modern History* (1970), VII, 284–90.
12. Quoted by Brewer, *op cit.*, 146.
13. J. R. Jones, 'Limitations of British Sea Power in the French Wars, 1689–1815', in J. Black and P. Woodfine, eds, *The British Navy and the Use of Sea Power in the 18th Century* (Leicester, 1980), 40. N. Rodger, *The Command of the Ocean: A Naval History of Britain, 1649–1815* (2004), 201, 578.
14. Quoted by D. G. Chandler, *Marlborough as Military Commander* (Staplehurst, 2003), 61.
15. C. Hibbert, *The Marlboroughs* (2002), 105.
16. J. Falkner, *Marlborough's Battlefields* (Barnsley, 2008).
17. C. Spencer, *Blenheim: Battle for Europe* (2004), 243–84.
18. 14 August 1704, Francis Hare to George Naylor, Historical Manuscripts Commission, *Hare*, 200. S. Noyes. 'The Letters of Samuel Noyes, Chaplain of the Royal Scots, 1703–04', ed. S. H. F. Johnston, *Journal of the Society for Army Historical Research*, 37 (1959), 149.
19. R. Holmes, *Marlborough: England's Fragile Genius* (2008), 64, 151–52. Chandler, *op. cit.*, 28.

20. J. C. K. Fuller, 'Marlborough', in B. Parker, *Famous British Generals* (1951), 52. Chandler, *op. cit.*, 331. J. Fortescue, *Six British Soldiers* (1928), 105.
21. R. Parker, *Memoirs of the Most Remarkable Military Transactions* (1741), 107–9.
22. M. Bishop, *Life and Adventures of Matthew Bishop* (1744), 267.
23. B. L. Montgomery, *The Memoirs of Field-Marshal the Viscount Montgomery* (1958), 85.
24. Parker, *op. cit.*, 31.
25. M. Clodfelder, *Warfare and Armed Conflicts: A Statistical Reference to Casualty and Other Figures* (Jefferson, NC, 2001), 3. J. K. Mahon, 'Anglo-American Methods of Indian Warfare, 1676–1794', *Mississippi Valley Historical Review* (1958), XLV, 254–60.
26. B. Nosworthy, *The Anatomy of Victory: Battle Tactics, 1689–1763* (New York, 1990), 61.
27. J. Blackadder, *The Life and Diary of Colonel John Blackadder of the Cameronian Regiment* (1824), 197: he makes the same point on pages 221 and 312.
28. Parker, *op. cit.*, 88–89. P. Wilson, 'Warfare in the Old Regime, 1648–1789', in J. Black, ed., *European Warfare, 1453–1815* (Basingstoke, 1999), 91.
29. Parker, *op. cit.*, 88–89.
30. C. Barnet, *Marlborough* (1974), 116.
31. H. R. Southern and N. Nicolas, 'The Life and Adventures of Matthew Bishop', *Retrospective Review*, 2nd series (1828), 53.
32. D. Defoe, *The Complete English Tradesman* (1738; 2007 edn), I, 247.
33. Barnet, *op. cit.*, 128.
34. M. Barthorp and A. McBride, *Marlborough's Army, 1700–11* (Botley, 1980), 5.
35. D. Chandler, *Military Memoirs of Malborough's Campaigns* (1998), 125.
36. C. Davenant, 'Ways and Means', *Works* (Edinburgh, 1872), I, 15.
37. Abel Evans, *Vertumnus* (1713), quoted by D. George, *All in a Maze: A Collection of Prose and Verse Chronologically Arranged* (1938), 181.
38. Parker, *op. cit.*, 129. G. S. Thomson, 'A Scots Officer in the Low Countries, 1714', *Scottish Historical Review*, 27 (1948), 68.
39. F. McLynn, *Crime and Punishment in Eighteenth-Century England* (1991), 321–27.
40. French, *op. cit.*, 37.
41. McLynn, *op. cit.*, 321. S. H. Palmer, 'Calling out the Troops: The Military, the Law and Public Order in England, 1650–1850', *Journal of the Society for Army Historical Research*, 56 (1978), 198–224.
42. Figures are an amalgam for the 17th and 23rd Regiments from J. A. Houlding, *Fit for Service: The Training of the British Army, 1715–1795* (Oxford, 1981), 1–2.
43. R. Holmes, *Redcoat: The British Soldier in the Age of Horse and Musket* (2001), 267.
44. D. Garrick, *Miss in Her Teens* (1824), 32.
45. C. H. Firth, *Naval Songs and Ballads* (1908), lx–lxviii. T. M. Freeman, *Dramatic Representations of British Soldiers and Sailors on the London Stage, 1660–1880* (1995), 3–7, 74, 110–12, 191.
46. J. Ehrman, *The Navy in the Wars of William III, 1689–1697* (1953), xv–xx. J. Glete, *Navies and Nations: Warships, Navies, and Ship Building in Europe and America, 1500–1800* (Stockholm, 1993), I, 220–21.
47. R. Crowhurst, *The Defence of British Trade, 1689–1815* (Folkstone, 1977), 15–19.
48. J. Baltharpe, *The Straights Voyage or St. David's Poem* (1959), 56.
49. C. Jones, 'New Military History for Old? War and Society in Early Modern Europe', *European Studies Review*, 13 (1982), 329–44.
50. R. Harding, *Seapower and Naval Warfare, 1650–1850* (1999), 118–19.
51. J. S. Bromley and A. N. Ryan, 'Armies and Navies', *New Cambridge Modern History*, VI (1970), 797. G. Holmes, *Augustan England: Profession, State, and Society, 1680–1730* (1982), 274. J. Black and P. L. Woodfine, eds, *The Royal Navy and the Use of Naval Power in the Eighteenth Century* (Leicester, 1988), 2–3.
52. Blackadder, *op. cit.*, 349.
53. H. Bland, *A Treatise of Military Disciplines* (1727), 114.

54. Quoted by I. F. Burton and A. N. Newman, 'Sir John Cope: Promotion in the 18th-Century Army', *English Historical Review*, 78 (1963), 659.
55. W. L. Burn, 'A Scots Fusillier and Dragoon under Peterborough: Lt. General Sir John Campbell', *Journal of the Society for Army Historical Research*, 15 (1936), 93.
56. Historical Manuscripts Commission, *Portland*, Fifteenth Report, Appendix, IV, 309.
57. Houlding, *op. cit.*, 109.
58. D. MacLeod, *Memoirs of the Life and Gallant Exploits of the Old Highland Sergeant Donald MacLeod*, ed. J. G. Fyfe (1933). S. Brumwell, *Redcoats: The British Soldier and War in the Americas, 1755–63* (Cambridge, 2002), 303–5, says MacLeod was ten years younger than he claimed.
59. L. Colley, *Britons: Forging the Nation* (1992), 5, 8, 367–68.
60. C. Whately and D. Patrick, *The Scots and the Union* (Edinburgh, 2006), 5–6.
61. K. M. Brown, 'Scottish Identity in the Seventeenth Century', in B. Bradshaw and P. Roberts, *British Consciousness and Identity: The Making of Britain, 1533–1707* (Cambridge, 1998), 238.
62. T. M. Devine, *Scotland's Empire, 1600–1815* (2003), 50.
63. B. Levack, *The Formation of the British State: England, Scotland, and the Act of Union* (Oxford, 1987), 225.
64. D. Defoe, *An Essay at Removing National Prejudices against Scotland* (1706), 28.
65. Manning, *op. cit.*, 397–98.
66. Pincus, *op. cit.*, 273. R. B. Manning, *An Apprenticeship in Arms: The Origins of the British Army, 1585–1702* (Oxford, 2006), 397–98.
67. G. Story, *A True and Impartial History of Ireland during the last two years* (1691), 10.
68. Earl of Athlone, *An Exact Journal of the Victorious Progress of their Majesties Forces* (1691), 5–7.
69. J. T. Gilbert, ed., *A Jacobite Narrative of the War in Ireland, 1688–91* (Dublin, 1892), 258–59.
70. G. A. Hayes-McCoy, *The Irish at War* (Cork, 1965), 99. J. Swift, *Works* (Chicago, 1912), 489. J. McGurk, 'The Wild Geese: Irish in European Armies', in P. O. Sullivan, ed., *Patterns of Migration: I* (Leicester, 1992), 36, 41.
71. J. Boswell, *Boswell's Life of Johnson* (Oxford 1953), 122. Based on a search of the electronic data base *English Poetry*.
72. A. Melville, *Memoirs of Sir Andrew Melville and the Wars of the Seventeenth Century* (2003), 215. J. Hayes, 'Scottish Officers in the British Army, 1714–63', *Scottish Historical Review*, 38 (1958), 25–27. S. Allen and A. Carwell, *The Thin Red Line: War, Empire, and Visions of Scotland* (Edinburgh, 2004), 91. H. Streets, 'Identity in the Highland Regiments in the 19th Century: Soldiers, Region, Nation', in S. Murdock and A. MacKillop, *Fighting for Identity: Scottish Military Experience c. 1550–1900* (Leiden, 2002), 213–19.
73. T. Newark, 'Why Are the Irish Good at Fighting?' *Military History Illustrated*, 89 (September 1995), 19. Alan Guy, 'The Irish Military Establishment, 1660–1776', in T. Bartlett and K. Jeffries, *A Military History of Ireland* (1996), 217–19. K. Kenny, 'The Irish and the Empire', in Kenny, ed., *Ireland and the British Empire* (Oxford, 2006), 104–12. Alvin Jackson, 'Ireland, the Union, and the Empire, 1800–1960', in Kenny, *op. cit.*, 138–45.

Chapter 13 The Hurlyburly's Done: The Aftermath of Combat

1. F. Bamford, *A Royalist's Notebook: The Commonplace Book of Sir John Oglander* (1936), 99.
2. He used the same phrase 'preaching from the dead' twice in his description of Malplaquet, and once to describe the aftermath of Blenheim. J. Blackadder, *The Life and Diary of Colonel John Blackadder of the Cameronian Regiment* (1824), 99, 163–64, 219, 351–52.

3. W. Patten, 'The Expedition into Scotland', A. F. Pollard, *Tudor Tracts* (1903), 125.
4. Blackadder, *op cit.*
5. G. M. Trevelyan, *England under Queen Anne* (1946) III, 18. N. Barr, *Flodden, 1513: The Scottish Invasion of Henry VIII's England* (Stroud, 2001), 286. C. T. Prouty, *George Gascoigne* (New York, 1942), 236–37. J. Stallworthy, *The Oxford Book of War Poetry* (Oxford, 1988), 188.
6. J. W. Willis Bund, *The Civil War in Worcester* (1905), 251. Patten, *op. cit.*, 141.
7. Blackadder, *op. cit.*, 353.
8. D. G. Faust, *This Republic of Suffering: Death and the American Civil War* (New York, 2008). A visit to Gettysburg or Vicksburg makes the same point.
9. J. R. Hale, *The Art of War and Renaissance England* (1961), 263.
10. Barr, *op. cit.*, 120. J. T. Gilbert, ed., *A Jacobite Narrative of the War in Ireland, 1688–91* (Dublin, 1892), 159. Historical Manuscripts Commission, *Ormonde*, X, v, 161.
11. J. T. Rosenthal, 'Other Victims: Peeresses as War Widows, 1450–1500', *History*, 72 (1987), 227. Charles McNeil, ed., *The Tanner Letters: Documents of Irish Affairs in the Sixteenth and Seventeenth Centuries Extracted from the Tanner Collection* (Dublin, 1943), 186. F. P. and M. Verney, *Memoirs of the Verney Family during the Civil War and Commonwealth* (1892–99), II, 120.
12. E. Gruffudd, 'Suffolk's Expedition to Montdidier', *Bulletin of the Faculty of Arts, Fouad University* (1944), 80.
13. P. Aries, *The Hour of our Death* (Ann Arbor, MI, 1981). F. Greville, *Life of Sir Philip Sidney, etc. First Published 1652* (Oxford, 1897), 130.
14. R. Wanderles and G. Broce, 'The Final Moments before Death in Early Modern England', *Sixteenth-Century Journal*, XX, 21 (1989), 260. Sir T. Longmore, *Richard Wiseman: Surgeon General to Charles II* (1891), 45.
15. P. Egerton, *Commentary on the Service and Charge of William, Lord Grey of Wilton* (Camden Society, 1847), 15.
16. F. Vere, *The Commentaries of Sir Francis Vere* (Cambridge, 1659), 7–9. E. G. B. Warburton, *Memoirs of Prince Rupert and the Cavaliers* (1849), III, 22.
17. Blackadder, *op. cit.*, 332. WWW.theroyalscots.co.uk/histmacbane. J. Doddridge, *The Life of Colonel James Gardiner who was slain at Prestonpans* (1747), 24. T. M. McGuffie, *Rank and File: The Common Soldier in Peace and War* (1961), 367–78. M. Bishop, *Life and Adventures of Matthew Bishop* (1744), 215.
18. *Journal of the Royal Society of Ireland* (1893), 46.
19. E. G. Von Arni, *Hospital Care and the British Standing Army, 1660–1714* (2006), 42.
20. Known in US Army as a Battalion Aid Station. C. H. Firth, *Cromwell's Army* (1962), 256. N. Tucker, *North Wales in the Civil War* (Denbigh, 1958), 171–73. E. G. Von Arni, *Justice to the Maimed Soldier: Nursing, Medical Care, and Welfare for Sick and Wounded Soldiers and their Families during the English Civil War and Interregnum, 1642–1660* (Burlington, VT, 2001), 209.
21. Quoted by J. McGurk, *The Elizabethan Conquest of Ireland: The 1590s Crisis* (Manchester, 1997), 242.
22. G. E. Gask, 'A Contribution to the History of the care of the Sick and Wounded ... Blenheim', in *Essays in the History of Medicine* (1950), 114. *Journal of the Royal Army Medical Corps*, 38 (1922), 287.
23. D. Stewart, 'The English Army Surgeon in the Sixteenth Century', *Journal of the Royal Army Medical Corps*, I (1903), 111–24. G. E. Gask, 'A Contribution to the History of the Care of Sick and Wounded during Marlborough's March to the Danube in 1704, and at the Battle of Blenheim', *ibid*, 88 (1947), 231–47. H. A. L. Howell, 'The Army Surgeon and the Care of the Sick and Wounded in the Tudor and Early Stuart Period', *ibid*, II (1904), 606–15.
24. J. Woodhall, *The Surgeon's Mate* (1614), 5, 156. W. B. Richards, 'Richard Wiseman and the Surgery of the Commonwealth', *Asclepiad*, II (1986), 231–55.

25. I. Morrison, 'Survival Skills: An Enterprising Highlander in the Low Countries with Marlborough', in G. S. Simpson, *The Scottish Soldier Abroad* (Edinburgh, 1992), 95. P. Drake, *Amiable Renegade: The Memoirs of Captain Peter Drake* (Stanford, CA, 1960), 170.

26. Mostyn to Cecil, *Calendar of State Papers, Ireland, 1598–99*, 385–86. George Monck, duke of Albermarle, *Observations on political and military affairs* (1671), 78. Roger Boyle, *Treatise on the Art of War* (1677), 53.

27. G. Robinson, 'Wounded Sailors and Soldiers in London during the First Dutch War, 1652–1654', *History Today*, 16 (1966), 38–44. Von Arni, *op. cit.*, 198–204.

28. D. Stewart, 'Some Early Military Hospitals', *Journal of the Society for Army Historical Research*, 25 (1950), 174–79.

29. Quoted by F. Tallet, *War and Society in Early Modern Europe* (1997), 111.

30. *A true Report of the great cost and charge of four Hospitals in this City of London* (1646). G. Robinson, 'Wounded Soldiers in London during the First Dutch War', *History Today*, XVI, 1 (1966), 38–45. Von Arni, *Hospital Care*, 181, 192.

31. H. J. Cook, 'Practical Medicine and the British Armed Forces after the "Glorious Revolution"', *Medical History*, 34 (1990), 1–26. Von Arni, *Hospital Care*, 86, 181–87.

32. William Blundell, *Crosby Record: A Cavalier's Note Book* (1880), 93.

33. Robert Parker, *Memoirs of the Most Remarkable Military Transactions* (1741), 6.

34. M. K. Walsh, 'Letters from Fontenoy', *Irish Sword* 19, 78 (1995), 244.

35. *Ibid.*, 246–47.

36. J. Ellis, *The Sharp End of War: The Fighting Man in the Second World War* (1982), 240.

37. Gruffudd, *op. cit.*, 70.

38. C. Barnett, *Marlborough* (1974), 124, 239. C. Hibbert, *The Marlboroughs* (2002), 143.

39. C. Duffy, *Siege Warfare: The Fortress in the Early Modern World* (1979), 146.

40. J. Aubrey, *Brief Lives* (Harmondsworth, 1982), 19.

41. *Calendar of State Papers, Domestic, 1660–61*, 205.

42. Richard Baxter, *Reliquiae Baxterianae* (1696), 59.

43. John Shawe, 'The Life of Master John Shawe', *Yorkshire Diaries*, ed. Charles Jackson (Surtees Society, 1877), 136.

44. R. Atkyns, *Vindication of Richard Atkins* (1968), 16.

45. W. Owen, *Collected Poems*, ed. E. Blunden (1965), 69. A. Babbington, *Shell-Shock: A History of Changing Attitudes to War Neurosis* (1997), 8.

46. Historical Manuscripts Commission, *Leyborne-Popham MSS*, 273. Thomas Bellingham, *Diary of Thomas Bellingham, an Officer under William III* (Preston, 1908), 136.

47. J. Jamieson, 'Lt Col John Blackadder', *Transactions of the Stirling Natural History and Archaeological Society* (1925–26), 53.

48. J. Nichols, *The Gentleman's Magazine* (1746), XVI, 235.

49. J. Millner, *A Compendious Journal of all the Marches* (1737), XII. Walsh, *op. cit.*, 244.

50. C. Hibbert, *Wellington: A Personal History* (1999), 185. Parker, *op. cit.*, 25–26.

51. S. H. F. Johnston, 'A Scots Chaplain in Flanders', *Journal of the Society for Army Historical Research*, 27 (1949), 7.

52. 5 May 1513, Echyngham to Wolsey, *Publications of the Naval Records Society: the War with France, 1512–1513* (1887), x, 145.

53. F. J. Child, ed., *English and Scots Ballads* (1859), VII, 274.

54. P. Young, *Naseby, 1645: The Campaign and the Battle* (1985), 270. E. Sherwood, *Civil Strife in the Midlands, 1642–51* (1974), 201.

55. Millner, *op. cit.*, 174.

56. D. and H. Murtagh, 'The Irish Jacobite Army, 1689–91', *Irish Sword* 18, 70 (1990), 87–98.

57. G. Nugent, *Some memorials of John Hampden, his party and his time* (1832), I, 308.

58. J. Stevens, *The Journal of Captain John Stevens* (Oxford, 1912), 127–61. *Oxford Dictionary of National Biography* (Oxford, 2004–9).

59. Drake, *op. cit.*, 167.

60. Bishop, *op. cit.*, 151.
61. R. Scouller, *The Armies of Queen Anne* (Oxford, 1967), 379.
62. McGuffie, *op. cit.*, 275–76.
63. D. Defoe, *The Military Memoirs of Captain George Carleton* (1929), 289.
64. *Oxford Dictionary of National Biography*. Parker, *op. cit.*, 109.
65. T. Carlyle, *The Letters and Speeches of Oliver Cromwell* (1904), III, 261.
66. Sir Arthur Haselrig, *A Letter from Sir Arthur Haselrig to the . . . Council of State* (1650), 1–3. *Calendar of State Papers, Domestic, 1649–50*, 105, 334, 397, 402, 419. W. C. Abbott, *The Writings and Speeches of Oliver Cromwell* (New York, 1937), I, 321.
67. Millner, *op. cit.*, 174.
68. J. S. Bromley, *Straits' Voyage* (1671, 1959), 5.
69. J. Yonge, *The Journal of J. Yonge, 1647–1712, Plymouth Surgeon* (1963), 92–100.
70. Quoted by D. Stewart, 'Disposal of the Sick and Wounded in the English Army during the Sixteenth Century', *Journal of the Royal Army Medical Corps*, 92 (1949), 133.
71. *Calendar of State Papers, Domestic, 1625–26*, 164, 214, 216, 227.
72. T. D. Hardy and J. S. Brewer, *Report of the Carte and Carew Manuscripts, 1601–03*, IV, 50–51.
73. A. Brome, *A Collection of Loyal Songs written against the Rump Parliament between the years 1639–1661* (1731), I, 199–200. A. Brome, *Poems* (Toronto, 1982), I, 111.
74. G. G. Langsam, *Martial Books and Tudor Verse* (New York, 1951), 147.
75. R. Lonsdale, *The New Oxford Book of Eighteenth-Century Verse* (Oxford, 1984), 111.
76. W. Chappel, *Roxburghe Ballads* (1874) VI, 285.
77. *Ibid.*, III, 111.
78. Defoe, *op. cit.*, 289.
79. Bishop, *op. cit.*, 268–71.
80. H. J. Webb, *Elizabethan Military Science: The Books and Practice* (Madison, WI, 1965), 172.
81. A. L. Beier, *Masterless Men: The Vagrancy Problem in England, 1560–1640* (1985), 93–95. *Henry V*, V, i, 40.
82. *Oxford Dictionary of National Biography*.
83. J. Mather, 'The Moral Code of the English Civil War and Interregnum', *Historian*, 44 (1982), 223. J. A. Shape, *Crime in Seventeenth-Century England: A County Study* (Cambridge, 1983), 106, 206–9. W. A. Speck, *Reluctant Revolutionaries: Englishmen and the Revolution of 1688* (1988), 197. C. V. Wedgwood, 'Captain Hinde, the Highwayman', *Truth and Opinion* (1961), 249–51.
84. J. Childs, 'War, Crime Waves and the English Army in the late Seventeenth Century', *War and Society* 15/2 (1997), 8. R. B. Manning, *An Apprenticeship in Arms: The Origins of the British Army, 1585–1702* (Oxford, 2006), 426.
85. J. T. Rutt, ed., *Diary of Thomas Burton* (1828), I, 17.
86. G. Gates, *The Defence of the Militarie Profession* (1597), 43.
87. Some have suggested Oldcastle as a model for Falstaff. Langsam, *op. cit.*, 111. Webb, *op. cit.*, 173. N. de Somogyi, *Shakespeare's Theatre of War* (Aldershot, 1998), 37.
88. C. N. Robinson and J. Leyland, *The British Tar in Fact and Fiction: The Poetry, Pathos, and Humour of the Sailor's Life* (New York, 1909), 383.
89. R. Bagwell, *Ireland under the Tudors* (1887), III, 250.
90. J. Rushworth, *Historical Collections of the Private Passages of State* (1680), I, 638.
91. P. Young, *Naseby, 1645: The Campaign and the Battle* (1985), 157, and *Edgehill, 1642: The Campaign and the Battle* (Kineton, 1967), 229.
92. P. Young and W. Emberton, *The Cavalier Army: Its Organization and Everyday Life* (1974), 22–21.
93. M. Mann, *The Veterans* (Norwich, 1997), 16.
94. J. R. Hale, *War and Society in Renaissance Europe, 1450–1620* (New York, 1985), 91.
95. 9 November 1663, S. Pepys, *Diary* (New York, 1887), IV, 12.

Conclusion: The Hand of War

1. Quoted by J. Black, *Culloden and the '45* (Stroud, 2000), 166
2. 'The Battle of Culloden, 16 April 1746, as described in a letter from a soldier of the Royal Army to his wife', *Journal of the Society for Army Historical Research*, 1 (1921), 21–24.
3. W. Speck, *The Butcher: The Duke of Cumberland and the Suppression of the '45* (Oxford, 1981), 161.
4. The Battle of Britain was fought *above* British soil.
5. L. Colley, *Britons: Forging the Nation* (1992), 9, 367–68.
6. J. Sadler, *Scotland's Battles* (Edinburgh, 1996), 224.
7. S. Carpenter, 'The British Army', in H. T. Dickinson, *Longman's Guide to Eighteenth-Century Britain* (Oxford, 2002), 476. T. M. Devine, *Scotland's Empire, 1600–1815* (2003), 294–96.
8. T. Smollett, *The Adventures of Roderick Random*, ed. P. Bouché (2002), 86.
9. Devine, *op. cit.*, 167, 360. William Pitt, *Correspondence of William Pitt* (1838), II, 365.
10. D. Allen, *Scotland in the Eighteenth Century* (2002), 38–39. J. Burke, ed., *Poems and Songs of Robert Burns* (1983), 557.
11. Email from Professor T. H. Devine to author, 23 September 2010.
12. C. J. Wheatley, ' "I hear the Irish are naturally brave": Dramatic Portrayals of the Irish Soldier in the 17th and 18th Centuries', *Irish Sword*, 77 (1995), 187–96. T. Denman, 'Hibernia officina militum: Irish Recruitment to the British Regular Army, 1660–1815', *Irish Sword*, 78 (1996), 148–67.
13. These figures are taken from material in this book, and from websites including the Battlefields Trust. Welsh figures included with English.
14. Population figures for the middle of the seventeenth century.
15. J. Blackadder, *The Life and Diary of Colonel John Blackadder of the Cameronian Regiment* (1824), 219, 247, 351 and 354. J. Jamieson, 'Lt. Col. John Blackadder', *Transactions of the Stirling Natural History and Archaeological Society* (1925–26), 53–68.
16. www.aboutscotland.com/theroyalscots/histmcbane.html/.
17. T. Jones, 'A Welsh Chronicler in Tudor England', *Welsh History Review*, I (1960), 15.
18. D. MacLeod, *Memoirs of the Life and Gallant Exploits of the Old Highland Sergeant Donald MacLeod*, ed. J. G. Fyfe (1933).
19. 'A Williamite Veteran', *Irish Sword*, 2 (1956), 331.
20. *Oxford Dictionary of National Biography* (Oxford, 2004–9).
21. W. Whitman, *The Complete Writings of Walt Whitman* (1902), IV, 140.

INDEX

Note: Page references in bold refer to Tables and Maps